YOU WILL NEV[...] TO WORRY ABOUT CHOOSING A GREAT VIDEO AGAIN!

If you're in the mood for...

>"one of the classiest of Hollywood ghost stories" or
>
>"a landmark achievement in documentary journalism" or
>
>"the funniest of the nine Tracy-Hepburn movies" or
>
>"an epic thriller about Nazis on the run in Canada" (yes, Canada) or
>
>"Jean Renoir's classic of pacifism" or
>
>"Lee Marvin as a Communist short-order cook" or
>
>"the single finest drama of the silent years" or
>
>"the best travel-adventure series ever made"

...you'll find all of them listed in this guide—along with many more—so that you can choose the movie you *really* want to see. Here are 1,000 reviews selected by the editors of ENTERTAINMENT WEEKLY, covering 100 of the top films in 10 different categories, from dramas and comedies to musicals and documentaries. From *Batman* to *My Life as a Dog*...from *Gun Crazy* to *Girl Crazy*...from *Mildred Pierce* to *Mother Teresa*, you'll find a movie that's truly terrific no matter what you're into.

And that includes *The Conqueror Worm* (see entry No. 76 under Sci-Fi & More)!

The movies referred to above, in the order quoted: *The Uninvited* (1944), *Harlan County, USA* (1977), *Adam's Rib* (1949), *49th Parallel* (1941), *La Grande Illusion* (1937), *Shack Out on 101* (1955), *The Wind* (1927), *Ring of Fire* (1988).

THE
Entertainment WEEKLY

GUIDE TO THE
GREATEST
MOVIES
EVER MADE

WARNER BOOKS

A Time Warner Company

Warner Books, Inc., 1271 Avenue of the Americas, New York, New York 10020

⦿ A Time Warner Company

Printed in the United States of America
First Printing: December 1994
10 9 8 7 6 5 4 3 2 1

Library of Congress Cataloging-in-Publication Data
The Entertainment Weekly guide to the greatest movies ever made/the editors of Entertainment Weekly.
        p.   cm.
Includes index.

    1. Motion pictures—Catalogs. 2. Video recordings—Catalogs.
I. Entertainment Weekly.
PN1998.E62   1994   016.791437'5—dc20   94-20785

ISBN 0-446-67028-6

COVER Clockwise from top left: Henry Thomas in *E.T.*: Foto Fantasies; Janet Leigh in *Psycho*: Kobal Collection; Nick Nolte and Eddie Murphy in *48 HRS.*: Kobal Collection; Orson Welles in *Citizen Kane*: Photofest; Ann-Margret and Elvis Presley in *Viva Las Vegas*: Photofest.

THE ENTERTAINMENT WEEKLY GUIDE TO
THE GREATEST MOVIES EVER MADE

ACKNOWLEDGMENTS

ADAPTED AND EXPANDED from the pages of ENTERTAINMENT WEEKLY, this book owes a great debt to the editors, writers, designers, reporters, and others who have contributed to the magazine's unique popular-arts criticism and journalism.

For their special contributions to *The Entertainment Weekly Guide to the Greatest Movies Ever Made*, thanks to

◆ EW assistant managing editors Donald Morrison and Peter Bonventre, who oversaw the project;

◆ EW senior editor David Hajdu, who served as the book's principal editor and who, as editor of our regular Movies, Video, Kids, and Multimedia sections, has played a key role in developing the EW style of criticism;

◆ EW senior associate editor Ellen Cannon and associate editor Caren Weiner, who juggled the myriad tasks essential to making this book a reality;

◆ Alexander Isley Design, which developed the book's format; EW designers Arlene Lappen, George Karabotsos, Bobby B. Lawhorn Jr., and Stacie Harrison; picture editor Doris Brautigan and picture researchers Lynn Bernstein, Olga Liriano, and L. Michelle Perreault;

◆ Reporter/researchers James Bufalino and Louis Vogel (who received invaluable help from fellow reporters Tim Purtell and Laura C. Smith, and editorial intern Andrea Foshee), copy chief Mary Makarushka, copy editor Matthew Weingarden, and proofreaders Jaimie Epstein and S. Kirk Walsh;

◆ Technical-support staffers Steven Moonitz and Michael T. Rose;

◆ And, of course, those who wrote the text: Ty Burr (EW's principal video critic, who contributed this book's main introduction and chapter introductions, as well as more reviews than any other writer), Rebecca Ascher-Walsh, Doug Brod, Pat H. Broeske, Jess Cagle, Bob Cannon, Ellen Cannon, Terry Catchpole, Kenneth M. Chanko, Susan Chumsky, Steve Daly, Chip Deffaa, David Everitt, Jim Farber, Bruce Forer, Bruce Fretts, Juliann Garey, Ron Givens, Owen Gleiberman, Nisid Hajari, Roy Hemming, Elayne J. Kahn, Dotti Keagy, Heather Keets, Glenn Kenny, Taehee Kim, Peter Kobel, Allan Kozinn, Hilton Kramer, Frank Lovece, Mary Makarushka, George Mannes, Douglas A. Mendini, Kate Meyers, Linda Movish, David Nagler, Chris Nashawaty, Lawrence O'Toole, Melissa Pierson, Tim Purtell, Jill Rachlin, Ira Robbins, Michael Sauter, Steve Simels, Tom Soter, Jeff Unger, and Dave Van Ronk.

James W. Seymore Jr.
Managing Editor, ENTERTAINMENT WEEKLY

C O N T E N T S

INTRODUCTION

As soon as they hear what we do for a living, people love to ask us ENTERTAINMENT WEEKLY film critics two questions: 1. "What's your favorite movie?" and 2. "What do you think I should rent this weekend?"

This book holds the answers to both questions (and others). It covers more great movies than we could ever wedge into a single conversation at the food court, and it saves us the embarrassment of having our minds go completely blank about every film we've ever seen except for *Citizen Kane* (see No. 1 in the Drama chapter) or *Mommie Dearest* (see a different book). In response to all those questions from movie fans, we decided to put together a cover story called "The 100 Best Movies on Video" in August 1990— and the response was phenomenal. Some readers wrote to grouse that we had left off a favorite film, but most everyone was thrilled to have a list that could actually *be taken to the video store*, the better to ward off the brain fog that sets in after you crane your neck to read 10 tape spines in a row.

We followed up that issue with "The 100 Best Movies You've Never Heard Of" (July 1991) and "The 100 Funniest Movies on Video" (October 1992), both retrofitted for inclusion here as the Sleepers and Comedy chapters, respectively. Those issues also went over pretty well, except among rabid fans of *It's a Mad, Mad, Mad, Mad World* (it's *still* not in the Comedy chapter, folks, but it is on the Laserdisc list). At which point, given the genres we had yet to cover and wanting to get it over with before 2003, we decided to pack it all into a format that would last longer than your average weekly magazine.

We should warn you right off: The *EW Guide to the Greatest Movies Ever Made* does not contain a précis of every film available on tape in alphabetical order. Other video guides do that and do it well. What this book does contain are suggestions, appreciations, provocations, and a mess of lists, principally arranged by genre.

Why genre? First of all, genre seems to be the way many of us choose what to rent. Think about it: You don't say to yourself, "I'm in the mood for a Columbia TriStar flick tonight." You say, "I need a laugh." It also jibes with the way most video stores are set up, regardless of whether the stockperson actually puts the dramas in the Drama section or slots *Children Shouldn't Play With Dead Things* on the Family Fun shelf. Besides, since we're ranking movies against each other, it makes sense to compare apples with apples (or cheesy erotic thrillers with cheesy erotic thrillers).

All that is only part of what sets this video guide apart from other guides. More important is that we address the *video experience*. The 15-year revolution in home viewing has meant that you can proactively collect all the great movie experiences instead of waiting for them to show up on cable or at the nearest college film festival. It doesn't matter whether you rent movies from the corner store, tape them off TV, or purchase them prerecorded; you're still collecting them in your head, and you want to know *which* ones to collect. Most guides throw as many movies at you as they can—their covers boast 13,000 titles, 19,000 titles, 22,000 titles. That's fine: We all need dictionaries. But a dictionary won't help you find just the word you need, and those mongo movie guides won't help you decide what to watch tonight, or what might be considered an essential video library.

You may be surprised, as you read on, by what we consider "essential." In deciding which movies made it in and which got left out, we held ourselves to one underlying rule: How does it play on TV? Because the small screen favors smaller movies, video stores are loaded with goodies that died in theaters only to find their audience on tape (*The Terminator*— No. 15 on our Sci-Fi list—is one such success story). Conversely, if you can't watch a wide-screen epic on a wide screen, why should you rent it? One reason you won't find *Apocalypse Now* in any section other than Laserdisc is that the disc version is letterboxed—so you get to see *all* of director Francis Coppola's meticulous visuals. In fact, because laserdiscs represent the best of what home video *can* be—with their superior image quality and the extras that are often packaged along—we've included a whole chapter on the 100 best discs available (*Apocalypse Now* is No. 6).

3

So: There may be only a thousand reviews presented at length here, but we guarantee they're reviews of the movies that matter: movies that wrote the rules or that broke them; movies that are perfectly of their time, ahead of their time, or timeless. And in case you get bored with lists, we've included a treasure trove of the short pieces that have made EW's video coverage the most readable, reliable, and thorough around. There are interviews with stars and directors, tests on movie trivia, and a lot of stuff designed solely to make you laugh out loud. In short, we hope this book will give you ideas, so that the movies we recommend can give you *their* ideas— or classic laughs, or cheap thrills, or whatever it is that they set out to do.

DRAMA

DRAMAS GET A BUM RAP at the video store, and you know why, don't you? Here's how it works: You're on your way home from a wicked day at work; you want to unwind; somehow *Sophie'sChoice* doesn't leap off the shelf into your hand. But if comedies and rock-'em, sock-'em action films are the tasty junk food of our rental diets, dramas don't have to be the bran muffins. They can be laced with the epic entertainment of a great read (see *Gone With the Wind* at No. 2), rich with the magic of a daydream (see *Field of Dreams* at No. 33), breathless with pulpy excitement (see *The Manchurian Candidate* at No. 8), or punchy with romance (see *The Year of Living Dangerously* at No. 97). Not to mention those irresistible old standbys, sex (see *Last Tango in Paris* at No. 57) and violence (see *Straw Dogs* at No. 63). Above all, the 100 titles on this list pull you into other, fictional lives—some just like yours or mine, some radically different—and make them matter through the artistry of storytelling. They show us human beings at their best, at their worst, and navigating all the shoals between those extremes. They *dramat*ize us.

1 **CITIZEN KANE** *(1941, Turner, B&W, not rated)* The life and death of Charles Foster Kane, as told by a 25-year-old kid who would come to live out his own version of the story. If you've never seen *Kane*, you may wonder why the hoopla: Many of Orson Welles' technical and narrative breakthroughs became movie clichés, and you probably know what "Rosebud" is through cultural osmosis. But the energy here is still beautiful, and *Kane* rewards endless viewings by peeling away layers of biography to reveal a moving, thoroughly American tale of regret. Video alert: See the 1988 cassette, *not* the ballyhooed-but-blurry "remastered" edition. Better yet, watch it on laserdisc.

2 **GONE WITH THE WIND** *(1939, MGM/UA, not rated)* Two hundred and twenty minutes of wonderful corn, and the most celebrated collaboration between moviemakers and the viewing public in Hollywood history. By mass fiat, it was unthinkable for anyone but Clark Gable to play novelist Margaret Mitchell's dashing Rhett Butler; likewise, producer David O. Selznick made his search for the perfect Scarlett O'Hara into a 2½-year cliffhanger before finally settling on Vivien Leigh. That the movie turned out to be such eye-popping entertainment was icing on the cake. Yeah, it reduces the Civil War to an epic women's flick. If that bothers you a lot, maybe you're in the wrong book.

6

EVERETT COLLECTION

THE GODFATHER TRILOGY: AL PACINO

3 THE GODFATHER TRILOGY 1901–1980 *(1992, Paramount, R)* At a time when Hollywood sorely needed a return to old-fashioned filmmaking values (not to mention family values), Coppola's *Godfather* was reassurance that a movie in the grand style—epic, moral, entertaining—could still be made. The second film deepens and broadens the rot, moving it away from gangster-movie tradition toward modern alienation. And the latter-day third? It's baroque, playful, more personal, and in many ways riskier. Taken together (in the reworked director's cut available only on video), they trace the sweep of a director's ambition, the growth of an actor named Pacino, and the slow, bloody unraveling of one of America's greatest products—its criminal enterprise.

4 REBEL WITHOUT A CAUSE *(1955, Warner, not rated)* James Dean's best film, it's also supremely emblematic of director Nicholas Ray, a romantic misfit in Hollywood's company town. Gathering his adoring cast around him—Natalie Wood, Nick Adams, Dennis Hopper—Ray worked with Dean to map out the anguished terrain of adolescence, giving the star rare latitude in dialogue and even camera placement. The result is an impressionistic cry of teen pain, with a stunning visual beauty best appreciated in its wide-screen glory (i.e., watch it in the letterboxed laserdisc edition, if at all possible).

5 CASABLANCA *(1942, MGM/UA, B&W, not rated)* Michael Curtiz directed as pages of the script came in, and when it was time to shoot

7

CAN YOU REMEMBER THIS?

Everyone knows Bogie never said, "Play it again, Sam." But did you realize he almost didn't get to say that famous beginning-of-a-beautiful-friendship line? Or that a TV actor played Rick in an '80s series? Put on your thinking fez and find out how much you know about *Casablanca*. —*Tim Purtell*

1. *Casablanca* material is among the most-sought-after movie memorabilia. What prop sold at a 1988 Sotheby's auction?
A. Bogie's trench coat for $156,000
B. The box Bogie stood on in the airport scene for $85,000
C. The piano from the Paris flashback scene for $154,000

2. Who tried to fill Bogart's raincoat as Rick Blaine in the short-lived 1983 *Casablanca* TV series?
A. Robert Urich
B. David Soul
C. Stephen Bogart (Humphrey's son)

3. Though Dooley Wilson (who didn't play the piano) melts hearts with his rendition of "As Time Goes By," he was not the first choice for the part. Who else was considered?
A. Hoagy Carmichael
B. Andy Williams
C. Lena Horne

4. Match the following characters with their headwear:
A. Rick   B. Ferrari   C. Victor   D. Renault

3. TOUPEE

1. FEZ

2. KEPI

4. PANAMA

5. Match the following lines with their characters.
A. "Is that cannon fire or is my heart pounding?"
B. "The Germans wore gray, you wore blue."
C. "My impression was he was just another blundering American."
D. "As leader of all illegal activities in Casablanca, I'm an influential and respected man."
E. "I'm only a poor, corrupt official."

1. Strasser
2. Ilsa
3. Renault
4. Rick
5. Ferrari

8

6. Match the actors with the films they made together before and after *Casablanca*.

A. Bogart, Lorre
B. Greenstreet, Henreid, Lorre
C. Bogart, Greenstreet, Lorre, Rains
D. Bogart, Greenstreet, Lorre
E. Greenstreet, Lorre
F. Bogart, Greenstreet

1. *Passage to Marseilles*
2. *The Maltese Falcon*
3. *The Mask of Dimitrios*
4. *The Conspirators*
5. *Across the Pacific*
6. *Beat the Devil*

---

7. It was Hal Wallis, the producer of *Casablanca*, who selected the film's final line, which later became one of the most frequently quoted lines in all of movie history: "Louis, I think this is the beginning of a beautiful friendship." What was one of the original scripted lines that Wallis got to choose from?

A. "Louis, I might have known you'd mix your patriotism with a little larceny."
B. "Louis, our predicament is as thick as this damn fog."
C. "Louis, how can we ask for the moon when we can't even find it in this damn fog?"

8. Which of the following actresses were considered for the role of Ilsa?

A. Ann Sheridan
B. Hedy Lamarr
C. Rita Hayworth
D. Tamara Toumanova

9. Ingrid Bergman once said: "I kissed Humphrey Bogart, but I never knew him." Why was Bogie so cool to his co-star on the *Casablanca* set?

A. Because his wife at the time, Mayo Methot, was insanely jealous
B. Because Bergman had bad breath
C. Because Lauren Bacall was watching from the wings

10. Turner Entertainment, which owns the license to the film, says there's no sequel in the works at this time. But insatiable fans can turn to author David Thomson's 1985 novel, *Suspects*, which imagines what happens to Rick and Renault after the fade-out.

A. They head south to adopt a lioness named Ilsa.
B. They head south to live as a gay couple in Marrakech.
C. They are tragically killed when Ilsa and Victor's plane lands on them after getting lost in that fog.

11. Composer Herman Hupfeld's "As Time Goes By" had already been a modest hit for Rudy Vallee in 1931. Which song was written expressly for *Casablanca*?

A. "Sweet Georgia Brown"
B. "Knock on Wood"
C. "It Had to Be You"

12. What mid-'70s disco mogul named his record label Casablanca and modeled its Los Angeles corporate offices after Rick's Café Américain, complete with Moroccan rugs, ceiling fans, palm trees, and a life-size stuffed camel?

9

the close-up of Bogart nodding at the house band to play "La Marseillaise," the actor didn't even know what he was supposed to be nodding *at*. No matter. This is Exhibit A in defense of the Hollywood factory system: proof that you can end up with a timeless classic even when the people making it aren't sure what the hell they're doing.

6 NASHVILLE *(1975, Paramount, R)* Robert Altman's teeming mosaic follows 24 characters as their paths crisscross during a long weekend. Though set in the country-music industry, this is really the finest political film of its time, capturing with deceptive ease the hope, confusion, and errant violence of the post-'60s years. Rarely forcing the connection, Altman turns little tragedies into metaphors for national unease, and he's helped by a cast that includes Lily Tomlin, Keith Carradine, Lauren Hutton, Shelley Duvall, Barbara Harris, and Ned Beatty.

***NASHVILLE*: KAREN BLACK**

7 MEAN STREETS *(1973, Warner, R)* Martin Scorsese's street-level look at a group of Little Italy punks established the director's career, put stars Harvey Keitel and Robert De Niro on the map, and founded a genre that hundreds of film-school tyros have honored. What remains extraordinary 20-some years later is the rocketing *force* of the thing: delirious colors, mad bursts of violence, startling moments of tenderness, a howling rock & roll soundtrack, and, in the middle of it all, De Niro snapping like a Method-trained pit bull.

8 THE MANCHURIAN CANDIDATE *(1962, MGM/UA, B&W, not rated)* Just about the wackiest political thriller ever made, and truly farseeing in its dark comic paranoia. War hero Raymond Shaw (cold, cold Laurence Harvey) has been brainwashed by Chinese Commies in league with his own dragon-mother (Angela Lansbury) into an assassination machine. Scripted by George Axelrod and directed by John Frankenheimer, this was said to be one of John F. Kennedy's favorite films—and rarely surfaced for viewing after his death made it seem both glib and prescient.

9 SUNSET BOULEVARD *(1950, Paramount, B&W, not rated)* Director Billy Wilder's blackest joke is cast like a cruel fun-house mirror: Aging silent-film star Gloria Swanson plays the aging silent-film star Norma Desmond, who enlists a hack writer (William Holden) as lover and coconspirator in a demented comeback bid. With such nightmarish set pieces as a funeral for a chimp, *Boulevard* peers

DO THE RIGHT THING: RICHARD EDSON, SPIKE LEE

behind Hollywood's sunny facade to find a mansion full of bugs.

10 **DO THE RIGHT THING** *(1989, MCA/Universal, R)* Too early to judge whether this is one of the greats? Then name another film that shows the deep cracks in our society during the Reagan years. Spike Lee's teeming, funny, clear-eyed street scene pulls no punches and dares to take sides—and that's the real source of its controversy. This is one of the few '80s movies that even *tries* to matter, and Lee's style spins with heart, rage, and imagination. Ten main characters, and not a bum performance in the bunch.

11 **ONE FLEW OVER THE CUCKOO'S NEST** *(1975, Facets, R)* Who else but Jack Nicholson could take Randle Patrick McMurphy—institutionalized but defiantly sane—and make him a metaphor for man's rebel spirit while keeping him so grungily *specific*? *Nest* boosted Nicholson to the superstar level and became the first movie since *It Happened One Night* to sweep the Oscars. Ken Kesey didn't like what they did to his novel. He seems to have been the only one.

12 **SWEET SMELL OF SUCCESS** *(1957, MGM/UA, B&W, not rated)* A fiendishly

DRAMA

BLUE VELVET: DENNIS HOPPER, ISABELLA ROSSELLINI

watchable, astoundingly cynical tale set in the harsh light of Manhattan nightlife, this features Tony Curtis' best performance by far, as Sidney Falco, small-time press agent, big-time hustler, and a man with the "scruples of a guinea pig." Grinning to hide the sweat, Sidney sucks up to powerful columnist J.J. Hunsecker, played by Burt Lancaster as a soulless dynamo with an unhealthy interest in his own sister. Under Alexander Mackendrick's direction, it's like a Weegee photo in real time.

13 **BLUE VELVET** *(1986, Warner, R)* Andy Hardy meets Salvador Dalí. David Lynch's finest two hours is a fever dream of small-town Americana: *Twin Peaks* compressed into a black hole of nightmare power. Wholesome teen Kyle MacLachlan is torn between goody-goody Laura Dern and sad, soul-bruised Isabella Rossellini; meanwhile, Dean Stockwell sings a Roy Orbison song, and Dennis Hopper portrays a most evil man. With all that, it's the frills ("You know the chicken walk?") that haunt you well past rewind.

14 **CHINATOWN** *(1974, Paramount, R)* Jack Nicholson investigates political corruption and Faye Dunaway in 1930s Los Angeles. On the surface, it's another of those trendy hard-boiled-detective revamps that everybody made in the '70s. Director Roman Polanski took the genre so far into the dark, though, that Hollywood has been backing away from its wormy truths ever since. Robert Towne's script (reworked by Polanski) is one of the all-time champs, and Nicholson, Dunaway, and John Huston turn in career-defining performances.

15 THE PHILADELPHIA STORY *(1940, MGM/UA, B&W, not rated)* Tracy Lord, Macaulay Connor, C.K. Dexter Haven: Even the *names* are graceful in George Cukor's tale of upper-class love and honor. The original play was written by Philip Barry as a paean to Katharine Hepburn, but the movie ended up garnering James Stewart an Oscar for his role as the reporter dazzled by melting ice maiden Tracy. As her once and future husband, Cary Grant gets to spout lines like "No mean Machiavelli is smiling, cynical Sidney Kidd." My, it's yar.

16 THE MAGNIFICENT AMBERSONS *(1942, Turner, B&W, not rated)* Orson Welles' next film after *Citizen Kane* turned him from Boy Genius into Misunderstood Genius. Welles adapted Booth Tarkington's saga of a family's decline into a subtle, sympathetic emotional epic, but the studio shortened it (by 43 minutes) into something more prosaic. Compromised it may be, but Welles' vision of the small-town changes wrought by the industrial revolution is still human and moving. With Tim Holt, Joseph Cotten, and—heartrendingly intense as the family spinster—Agnes Moorehead.

13

THE PHILADELPHIA STORY:

JOHN HOWARD, CARY GRANT, KATHARINE HEPBURN, JAMES STEWART

THE LAST PICTURE SHOW: CYBILL SHEPHERD

17 **THE LAST PICTURE SHOW** *(1971, Columbia TriStar, B&W, R)* Peter Bogdanovich's breakthrough film adapts Larry McMurtry's novel into a tragic farewell to many things: the corner Bijou, teen innocence, black-and-white cinematography, the idea of Texas as unspoiled territory, uncomplicated great men like Ben Johnson's Sam the Lion. It has indelible performances from Timothy Bottoms, Jeff Bridges, Ellen Burstyn, Cybill Shepherd, and Cloris Leachman —and Hank Williams songs that mock the characters from beyond the grave.

18 **THE BIRTH OF A NATION** *(1915, Republic, B&W, not rated)* Along with Leni Riefenstahl's *Triumph of the Will*, this is the rare film that is as artistically essential as it is morally abhorrent. With *Birth*, the movies grew up as a narrative medium: D.W. Griffith follows the Stoneman and Cameron families through the Civil War and its aftermath with an eye toward epic battle scenes, blood-and-thunder characters, and a messed-up historicism that celebrates the KKK as the saviors of the Reconstruction South. Pointing back to 19th-century stage melodramas and forward to the Hollywood dream machine, *Birth* reflects this country with a much darker accuracy than Griffith intended.

19 **THE THIRD MAN** *(1949, Facets, B&W, not rated)* The glimmering black and white of Robert Krasker's camera work hides rich complexities in Carol Reed's gripping postwar thriller. Joseph Cotten is an out-of-his-depth American in Vienna, looking to claim the body of pal Harry Lime. But Harry may not be dead—and maybe he should be, given what he's been up to. Graham Greene wrote the arch script, while costar Orson Welles chipped in the devastating Ferris-wheel monologue. Plus, a zither score you'll remember for the rest of your life.

20 **FIVE EASY PIECES** *(1970, Columbia TriStar, R)* When we first meet Bobby Dupea (Jack Nicholson), he's a raffish oil-rig grunt; it turns out he's from a family of upper-class musicians and has been running from all they represent until he doesn't know how to do anything else. In director Bob Rafelson's hands, it's a series of snapshots of a charming, helpless American rat, played by Nicholson with a barroom bonhomie that turns sour in the morning's bleak light.

21 **DOUBLE INDEMNITY** *(1944, MCA/Universal, B&W, not rated)* Grade-A sleaze from two grade-A cynics, novelist James M. Cain and director Billy Wilder. Fred MacMurray has the role of his life as the small-time insurance salesman, and Barbara Stanwyck is all brass and cheap perfume as the bored tootsie who persuades him to kill her husband. It's not the murder that's the meat here; it's the way these two so willingly jump at the chance for moral degradation. A million movies have ripped off the plot, but none of them—not even 1981's *Body Heat*—has captured the original's seamy erotic thrill.

22 **RAGING BULL** *(1980, MGM/UA, B&W, R)* So effectively does Martin Scorsese pull apart the myths sustaining boxer Jake La Motta (Robert De Niro)—myths of macho sex appeal, of physical prowess, of athletic honor—that this movie would be difficult to watch even without the grueling fight sequences. De Niro transforms himself astoundingly, but equal praise is due Joe Pesci (as La Motta's brother), Cathy Moriarty (as the girl he marries and ruins), and cinematographer Michael Chapman.

23 **TOUCH OF EVIL** *(1958, MCA/Universal, B&W, not rated)* In the late '50s, when no one was looking, Orson Welles made an artistic (if not commercial) comeback with this gorgeously sleazy crime drama. Set in a Mexican border town, *Touch* pits upright federal agent Charlton Heston against bloated and corrupt police chief Welles. The casting

15

TOUCH OF EVIL:
JANET LEIGH, CHARLTON HESTON

WHEN ACTORS YELL 'ACTION'

Jack Nicholson (*The Two Jakes*) and Kevin Costner (*Dances With Wolves*) are just two examples of movie stars becoming movie directors. Here are the major one-shot efforts of actor-auteurs on video:

THE NIGHT OF THE HUNTER *(1955)* Charles Laughton didn't appear in the only film he directed, but his personality—a strange mixture of the effete and the physically foreboding—comes through strongly. A unique, dreamlike parable of two children menaced by a bogus preacher (Robert Mitchum, in what is easily his best performance), *The Night of the Hunter* is close to folk art in its naive power.

THE KENTUCKIAN *(1955)* This frontier adventure remains Burt Lancaster's sole stint behind the camera, and, like Lancaster, the film is both rugged and spry. What starts out as an uninspired action saga takes a philosophical turn when Lancaster's character falls for a schoolmarm and the movie debates the values of civilization versus frontier spirit. The wide-screen photography has been poorly cropped on video, but any movie that features Walter Matthau (in his film debut) as a whip-wielding bad guy is worth renting.

ONE-EYED JACKS *(1961)* After having Stanley Kubrick fired from the project, star Marlon Brando decided he could be a directorial contender. The result? An overstuffed Method Western that features a mumbling Brando as vengeful bandit Kid Rio. The movie's a fanny-warmer at almost 2½ hours, but by trying to refashion the horse opera into existential myth, Brando came close to inventing the spaghetti Western three years before Sergio Leone's *A Fistful of Dollars*.

JO JO DANCER, YOUR LIFE IS CALLING *(1986)* Director-cowriter-star Richard Pryor used his own flaming brush with death as the jumping-off point for examining the life of a famous comedian; but because he fictionalizes his story, we're never sure what to take as real (and therefore meaningful). While one hopes *Jo Jo* gave its maker some needed therapy, the finished film is a creepy exercise in heartfelt voyeurism.

TV Listings Alert: Some additional directing projects by well-known actors that aren't yet available on cassette: *Short Cut to Hell* (James Cagney, 1957), *Scalawag* (Kirk Douglas, 1973), *Charlie Bubbles* (Albert Finney, 1968), and *Gangster Story* (Walter Matthau, 1960). *—Ty Burr*

16

throughout is *muy* kinky: Dennis Weaver as a Peeping Tom, Mercedes McCambridge as a street tough, unbilled Marlene Dietrich as a seen-it-all fortune teller. A justly celebrated opening shot kicks it all off.

24 A STREETCAR NAMED DESIRE
(1951, Facets, B&W, not rated) When Stanley Kowalski (Marlon Brando) howled "Stella!" to the tenement skies, a new age in movie acting was born. Tennessee Williams' play about a Southern belle (Vivien Leigh) who cracks when the real world pushes in on her was gutted by Hollywood censors—and Jessica Tandy was denied the chance to re-create her Broadway interpretation of Blanche. But Brando carries all of the play's incendiary meanings within him—and gets them across with a walk, a snarl, a corroded look.

25 THE NIGHT OF THE HUNTER
(1955, MGM/UA, B&W, not rated) The only movie directed by actor Charles Laughton, this plays like the dream of a gifted child. Two kids (Billy Chapin and Sally Jane Bruce) flee their wicked stepfather (Robert Mitchum), a psychotic preacher who's after a stash of cash hidden in the girl's doll. They find sanctuary with deceptively fragile Lillian Gish, and the battle between Good and Evil is on. The photography by Stanley Cortez shimmers, and Mitchum comes on like the Devil himself.

26 LAWRENCE OF ARABIA *(1962, Columbia TriStar, not rated)* How very perverse:
a sweeping 3½-hour extravaganza at the center of which lies...a puzzle. Director David Lean created an epic for the Age of Anxiety, an idea that made sense in the early '60s and that still holds water today. Old-fashioned filmgoers can find grand entertainment, while jaded youth will see an antihero for all seasons in blue-eyed Peter O'Toole. It's tough to appreciate the film's visual glory on TV; at the very least, make sure to rent the restored 216-minute version.

27 IT'S A WONDERFUL LIFE
(1946, Republic, B&W, not rated) Bet you're sick to death of it by now, even if both director Frank Capra and star Jimmy Stewart called it their favorite. The tale of a small-town hero who realizes how *necessary* he is only through angelic interference is mighty syrupy— but it's grounded by a frank knowledge of all the disasters that can lie in our paths. Stewart walks the edge of that darkness in his rawest performance.

28 GLORY *(1989, Columbia TriStar, R)* One of the finest of war films, if only
because it's so clear why these particular Union soldiers were willing to die: They were *black* recruits, embodying the very idea that was tearing the country apart. Incisive performances from Morgan Freeman, Denzel Washington, Andre Braugher, and Matthew Broderick (muted and thoughtful as the white officer who commanded them), but *Glory*'s strong suit is the aching realism of its battle scenes.

17

29

AMERICAN GRAFFITI *(1973, MCA/Universal, PG)* This is the movie that made co-writer-director George Lucas' name—and launched the careers of Richard Dreyfuss, Ron Howard (his grown-up career, anyway), Cindy Williams, Suzanne Somers, Harrison Ford, Mackenzie Phillips, Kathleen Quinlan, Paul Le Mat....Oh, yeah, it's also the source for TV's *Happy Days.* In fact, it just may be the movie that invented contemporary nostalgia. Not bad for a flick about a bunch of teenagers doin' nothing on a summer night.

30

DODSWORTH *(1936, Facets, B&W, not rated)* This adaptation of the Sinclair Lewis novel is one of Hollywood's classiest acts. Walter Huston is a can-do industrialist who takes early retirement, takes his wife (Ruth Chatterton) to Europe—and gets taken for a ride when she runs off with a gigolo. He wakes up to life, though, after meeting divorcée Mary Astor. Huston perfectly balances heart, brain, and soul, while Chatterton—far from making her character a fool—shows the all-too-human fear under Fran Dodsworth's vanity.

31

DANGEROUS LIAISONS *(1988, Warner, R)* In 18th-century France, the Vicomte de Valmont (John Malkovich) and the Marquise de Merteuil (Glenn Close) take their leisure by vying to see who's the more decadent. Valmont pledges to seduce the uptight Madame de Tourvel (Michelle Pfeiffer), but makes the cataclysmic mistake of falling in love. Fringe benefits include opulent sets, stunner costumes, young lovelies Uma Thurman and Keanu Reeves—but Malkovich and Close are viciously front and center. A mesmerizing display of civilized carnivores at their most ravenous.

32

THE GRAPES OF WRATH *(1940, FoxVideo, B&W, not rated)* Producer Darryl Zanuck turned John Steinbeck's novel of the dust-bowl diaspora into a populist drama of almost unbearable power. Henry Fonda finally reached stardom as Tom Joad, the terse leader of an Okie family bound for California and finding more poverty and oppression. While Zanuck and director John Ford traded in Steinbeck's politics for sentiment, they still had to watch their backs: Hostility from banks and agricultural interests forced the production to work under the title *Highway 66*—and to post armed guards at the soundstage doors.

33

FIELD OF DREAMS *(1989, MCA/Universal, PG)* With *Bull Durham* and *No Way*

DODSWORTH:
RUTH CHATTERTON, WALTER HUSTON

DRAMA

THE NAME BEFORE THE TITLE

Here's your chance to play studio honcho: See if you can match up each film in the left column with its original title on the right. —*Tim Purtell*

1.	**MARKED FOR DEATH**	A.	*Screwface*
2.	**MY GIRL**	B.	*Valkenvania*
3.	**COMPANY BUSINESS**	C.	*Returning Napoleon*
4.	**NOTHING BUT TROUBLE**	D.	*Last to Surrender*
5.	**OUT FOR JUSTICE**	E.	*The Rest of Daniel*
6.	**ONCE UPON A CRIME**	F.	*Born Jaundiced*
7.	**THE MIGHTY DUCKS**	G.	*Hero Worship*
8.	**UNDER SIEGE**	H.	*Bombay*
9.	**KUFFS**	I.	*The Last Days of Eden*
10.	**BRAIN DONORS**	J.	*Lame Ducks*
11.	**FOREVER YOUNG**	K.	*Dinosaurs*
12.	**MEDICINE MAN**	L.	*The Price of Our Blood*

Answers: 1-A, 2-F, 3-K, 4-B, 5-L, 6-C, 7-H, 8-D, 9-G, 10-J, 11-E, 12-I.

Out, one of Kevin Costner's best films. Here he's an Iowa Everyman who hears a mysterious voice telling him that if he builds a baseball diamond in his cornfield, "he will come." Hewing closer to its source (W.P. Kinsella's magical novel *Shoeless Joe*) than most movies dare, Phil Alden Robinson's film is about forgiveness, and it holds everything from the 1919 Chicago White Sox to the family upheavals of the '60s in its healing embrace.

34 **MR. SMITH GOES TO WASH-INGTON** *(1939, Columbia TriStar, B&W, not rated)* When politicians talk of "family values," what they mean are the virtues found in Frank Capra movies: idealism, respect for kin, and, above all, *faith* in democracy and by extension in one's fellow man. *Mr. Smith* (no accident his first name is Jefferson) is Capra's finest moment, a supremely entertaining, ultimately urgent tale of a hick (James Stewart) being sobered by—but not giving in to—political shades of gray. With Claude Rains, Jean Arthur, and Thomas Mitchell all caving in under the weight of Stewart's goodness.

35 **TAXI DRIVER** *(1976, Facets, R)* Though *Raging Bull* is often considered director Martin Scorsese's finest two hours, this earlier film speaks to its volatile times like no other. Robert De Niro's doomed, despairing Travis Bickle drives his cab down through the circles of a color-saturated New York hell—and at the bottom finds damnation and gory redemption. A pitying look into the mind of a politician's would-be assassin, this turned out to be one of those rare films that ripple into the future as well as the past.

36 **THE WIND** *(1927, MGM/UA, B&W, silent, not rated)* An amazing film that might be considered the single finest drama of the silent years. In a psychologically perceptive, emotionally tough performance, Lillian Gish plays a naive bride who journeys to the Great Plains, marries a creep, shoots a rapist, and battles

19

FROM HERE TO ETERNITY:

DEBORAH KERR, BURT LANCASTER

the elements in a climactic sandstorm of almost erotic visual power. Directed by Victor Sjöström decades before he starred in Ingmar Bergman's *Wild Strawberries*.

37 **FROM HERE TO ETERNITY** *(1953, Columbia TriStar, B&W, not rated)* James Jones' antimilitary novel was diluted on film into a hugely entertaining World War II soap opera. Unforgettable pop imagery abounds throughout: the good-guy sergeant (Burt Lancaster) rolling in the surf with his commander's wife (Deborah Kerr); tormented Private Prewitt (Montgomery Clift), torn between the bugle and the boxing ring; Frank Sinatra resurrecting his career as Maggio, standing up to Ernest Borgnine's sadistic Fatso. With all this, it's easy to forgive the miscasting of Donna Reed as a hooker.

38 **HENRY V** *(1944, Paramount, not rated)* In his directorial debut, Laurence Olivier dusted off Shakespeare's charismatic hero king and created a beacon of hope for an England swamped in the darkness of war. Technically adroit—it starts in the Globe Theatre circa 1600, then bursts into Technicolor you-are-there realism—*Henry* is savvy about the carnage of battle yet idealistic in matters of national destiny. And Olivier's a swain of a monarch, leading his army, his audience, and his country once more into the breach.

39 **ON THE WATERFRONT** *(1954, Columbia TriStar, B&W, not rated)* Elia Kazan's stark tale of a lone palooka fighting a crooked dockworkers' union was seen by many as self-defense by the director for his naming of names during the blacklist era. Whatever the motive, Marlon Brando brings tremendous dignity and pathos to the part of Terry Malloy, especially in the famous "I coulda been a contender" speech to brother Charlie (Rod Steiger) in the back of a taxicab.

40 **GOODFELLAS** *(1990, Warner, R)* Based on crime reporter Nicholas Pileggi's nonfiction best-seller *Wiseguy*, Martin Scorsese's *GoodFellas* is a "my life as a mobster" saga told from the viewpoint of midlevel goon Henry Hill (Ray Liotta). Despite the strong personalities on this project—actors Liotta, Robert De Niro, and Oscar winner Joe Pesci—this is the director's film all the way. From the opening sequence in which a supposed corpse

EVERETT COLLECTION

is kicking in the car trunk, Scorsese daringly treats this as the blackest of comedies, a symphony of hilarious, pungent verbal riffs that can escalate into violence in seconds. There are scenes that are so well made you may find yourself playing them over and over, marveling at their wit and texture.

41 **ALL ABOUT EVE** *(1950, Fox-Video, B&W, not rated)* This Broadway-backstager is the shining example of the role that language can play in a predominantly visual medium. Writer-director Joseph L. Mankiewicz was a past master of wordplay, and strings of his fine irony cascade from characters who are as brilliant and hard as diamonds. Bette Davis hit a bitch-goddess peak as Margo Channing, a stage star who'll put

up with any neurosis as long as she isn't bored.

42 **HANNAH AND HER SISTERS** *(1986, Facets, PG)* The least self-conscious (and thus the most dramatically successful) of Woody Allen's more serious efforts, *Hannah* starts with three Manhattan sisters (Barbara Hershey, Mia Farrow, Dianne Wiest) and radiates out to examine their friends and family with troubled grace. With Michael Caine as a hapless adulterer, the Woodman providing not-really-necessary comic relief, and a breathtaking camera dance around a sisterly dinner at a restaurant.

43 **MILDRED PIERCE** *(1945, MGM/UA, B&W, not rated)* Based on a novel by James M. Cain, this is the masochistic

EVERETT COLLECTION

HANNAH AND HER SISTERS: **MIA FARROW, DIANNE WIEST**

REPEAT WHEN UNNECESSARY

Call it a video identity crisis: In many cases, two tapes have titles in common and nothing else, leading to frustration when you go to the store to rent *Fatal Attraction*, expecting Glenn Close as a sexy psycho and ending up with Sally Kellerman as a sex fantasist. Or looking for Arnold Schwarzenegger in *Red Heat* and finding Linda Blair instead. Beware of these other video doppelgängers. —*Steve Simel*

THE ONE YOU WANT	THE ONE YOU MIGHT GET
THE ACCUSED *(1988)* Jodie Foster, Kelly McGillis. Gang-raped blue-collar woman is defended by idealistic assistant DA.	**THE ACCUSED** *(1949)* Loretta Young, Robert Cummings. Student-killing lady professor is defended by victim's guardian.
ALWAYS *(1989)* Richard Dreyfuss, Holly Hunter. Dead pilot returns as guardian angel of novice flyboy; Steven Spielberg directs.	**ALWAYS** *(1986)* Henry Jaglom, Patrice Townsend. Ex-wife returns to reconcile with self-absorbed filmmaker; Jaglom directs.
BETRAYED *(1988)* Tom Berenger, Debra Winger. FBI agent infiltrates fascist group by romancing handsome farmer/murderer.	**BETRAYED** *(1954)* Clark Gable, Lana Turner. Suspected traitor infiltrates Nazi high command by going undercover as chanteuse.
BLUE STEEL *(1990)* Jamie Lee Curtis, Ron Silver. Wall Street psycho finds gun, goes on killing spree.	**BLUE STEEL** *(1934)* John Wayne, Gabby Hayes. The Duke finds gold mine; town goes on buying spree.
THE FRESHMAN *(1990)* Marlon Brando, Matthew Broderick. College boy scams crooked feds in big sting, gets komodo dragon.	**THE FRESHMAN** *(1925)* Harold Lloyd, Jobyna Ralston. College boy scores winning touchdown in big game, gets girl.
GLORY *(1989)* Matthew Broderick, Denzel Washington. Black soldiers enlist to fight in Civil War.	**GLORY** *(1956)* Margaret O'Brien, Walter Brennan. White horsewoman enters filly in Kentucky Derby.

DRAMA

height of the Hollywood women's picture (with more than a little film noir angst thrown in). Mildred (Joan Crawford, who picked up an Oscar for this performance) suffers through a failed first marriage, a caddish second husband, and—worst of all—a feral, ungrateful devil-daughter (Ann Blyth). The movie totters on the edge of camp, but Crawford plays it with such shoulder-padded stoicism that *Mildred* becomes a slice of neurotic American apple pie.

44 SUNRISE (1927, Facets, B&W, silent, not rated)

F.W. Murnau's silent classic is as transparent and as delicate as a butterfly wing, following a married couple (George O'Brien and Janet Gaynor, who won an Oscar for her performance) as they break up, drift toward violence, and finally return to each other. That simple plotline is graced with one of the most subtle and beautiful visual sensibilities the movies have seen; Murnau could have shot a stop sign with enough emotion to make you cry.

45 THE TREASURE OF THE SIERRA MADRE (1948, MGM/UA, B&W, not rated)

"Can you stake a fellow American to a meal?" asks Bogart's Fred C. Dobbs, before proving that luck—good, bad, and lousy—is what you make it. Heading into the Mexican mountains to dig for gold with Tim Holt and old-timer Walter Huston, Bogart slowly lets greed erode what's left of his soul. With young Robert Blake selling lottery tickets, director John Huston in a cameo, and Alfonso Bedoya as the bandito who don' need no steenkin' badges.

THE DIFFERENCE

Foster's role led to a new career as a mature actress; Young's, to a career as a TV hostess.

Director Spielberg is a legend; director Jaglom is a legend in his own mind.

Winger's character, unlike Turner's, wears sensible shoes.

Silver's beard is black; Hayes' is white.

Lloyd in football cleats versus Brando on ice skates.

The horse gets more respect.

46 **THE PLAYER** (*1992, Columbia TriStar, R*) This pitiless look at the modern Hollywood anthill would seem to be a comedy, if a sardonic one. Underneath the hollow laughter, though, is an appalled conscience. Tim Robbins is the "player" of the title, a studio executive so confidently detached from reality that his murder of a screenwriter seems like just another story arc. Gazillions of well-known actors pop up in cameos, but this is clearly Robert Altman's baby: It has his hallmark bemused rage, and it's made with a fluid skill that can take one's breath away.

47 **WRITTEN ON THE WIND** (*1957, MCA/Universal, not rated*) Douglas Sirk made Trojan-horse melodramas: glossy Technicolor sob stories with nasty little social critiques squirreled away inside. Here he watches as the fortunes of a Texas oil family dwindle away in booze, impotence, and lost lust. It's campy, all right—who can forget Dorothy Malone doing the mambo while Dad Robert Keith has a heart attack on the stairs?—but *Written* is remarkably tender toward its nominal losers (Malone and sour-eyed Robert Stack) and pitilessly cool to its so-called heroes (Lauren Bacall and Rock Hudson).

48 **THEY LIVE BY NIGHT** (*1948, Facets, B&W, not rated*) Nicholas Ray's keening romantic fatalism was already in flower in his first film. Farley Granger and Cathy O'Donnell star as Bowie and Keechie, two hicks in love and in hiding from the law, their bank-robbing accomplices—the whole world, in fact. Ray's sense of young love as equally privileged and doomed casts an unbearably moving spell, and the now-forgotten O'Donnell seems lit from within.

49 **REBECCA** (*1940, FoxVideo, B&W, not rated*) After making his name with a series of deft British thrillers, Alfred Hitchcock chose to adapt Daphne du Maurier's psychological gothic for his Hollywood debut. It's an almost clinical examination of feminine insecurity, as mousy Joan Fontaine marries brooding Laurence Olivier and tries to exorcise the spirit of his venal first wife from his heart and hearth. With Judith Anderson dodging the censor's bullets as an all-too-devoted keeper of dead Rebecca's dark flame.

50 **THE ASPHALT JUNGLE** (*1950, MGM/UA, B&W, not rated*) Another cynical character smorgasbord courtesy of director John Huston. Here he uses the planning, execution, and botching of a robbery as an excuse to pin desperate characters to racks of their own making. The performances are sourly unforgettable: Sterling Hayden as a bummed-out tough guy; Louis Calhern as a morally damned Mr. Big; young Marilyn Monroe as a blank-faced Kewpie doll; and, the oddest of an odd bunch, Sam Jaffe as a poindexter crime genius with a nagging itch for bobby-soxers.

51 **THE BRIDGE ON THE RIVER KWAI** (*1957, Columbia TriStar, not rated*) You've whistled the tune, now see the movie. In a tragically dead-on depiction of

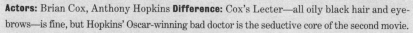

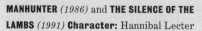

CASTING A SHADOW

What happens when two actors tackle the same film role (like Alec Baldwin and Harrison Ford, who play Jack Ryan in *The Hunt for Red October* and *Patriot Games*, respectively)? Some revealing cases from moviedom's Oddities file:

BRIGHTON BEACH MEMOIRS *(1986)* and **BILOXI BLUES** *(1988)* **Character:** Eugene Jerome **Actors:** Jonathan Silverman, Matthew Broderick **Difference:** His performance may be stagestruck, but Silverman's younger Eugene exudes more chutzpah than Broderick's supposedly older one.

MANHUNTER *(1986)* and **THE SILENCE OF THE LAMBS** *(1991)* **Character:** Hannibal Lecter **Actors:** Brian Cox, Anthony Hopkins **Difference:** Cox's Lecter—all oily black hair and eyebrows—is fine, but Hopkins' Oscar-winning bad doctor is the seductive core of the second movie.

THE PINK PANTHER *(1964)* and **INSPECTOR CLOUSEAU** *(1968)* **Character:** Inspector Clouseau **Actors:** Peter Sellers, Alan Arkin **Difference:** Arkin's one-time outing as the bumbling detective is wryly charming, but no match for slap-shtickster extraordinaire Sellers.

THE STING *(1973)* and **THE STING II** *(1983)* **Characters:** Henry Gondorff and Johnny Hooker, Fargo Gondorff and Jake Hooker **Actors:** Paul Newman and Robert Redford, Jackie Gleason and Mac Davis **Difference:** Glamorous buddies Newman and Redford morph into porcine Gleason and putty-faced Davis, the characters inexplicably separated by a generation.

SUPERFLY *(1972)* and **THE RETURN OF SUPERFLY** *(1990)* **Character:** Priest **Actors:** Ron O'Neal, Nathan Purdee **Difference:** Purdee's cleaned-up, processed Priest makes one pine for O'Neal's ultrasexy sideburns, malevolent mustache, and long hair. —*Tim Purtell*

25

stiff-upper-lipness, Alec Guinness plays a British commander in a World War II Japanese prison camp who's too blind to see that the bridge his men are building will help the enemy. Fellow POW William Holden plots to destroy it, while David Lean's directorial eye hovers above the fray with vast, ironic reserve.

52 **DELIVERANCE** *(1972, Warner, R)* This film marked the death of unexamined macho in the movies; after this, things got pretty self-conscious. John Boorman's film based on James Dickey's novel sends four businessman pals (Jon Voight, Burt Reynolds, Ned Beatty, and Ronny Cox) down an Appalachian river into a terrifying rendezvous with natural and human savagery. It's probably the best role of Reynolds' career (his daunted he-man is genuinely complex), but you'll come away feeling sorrier for Voight and Beatty—and unable to shake that leering banjo music from your head.

53 GREED *(1924, MGM/UA, B&W, silent, not rated)* Erich von Stroheim's classic silent film is as simple and corrosive as its title. Two friends (Gibson Gowland and Jean Hersholt) are slowly reduced to their basest instincts when Gowland's lady love (ZaSu Pitts) wins the lottery. The original *10-hour* cut was destroyed by studio head Irving Thalberg, but even butchered to 133 minutes, this is detailed, powerful stuff. If you've seen Pitts only in her flustery old-lady roles, her money-crazed Trina—a tin-pot Lady Macbeth—will come as a shock.

54 IN A LONELY PLACE *(1950, Columbia TriStar, B&W, not rated)* The sourest and most deeply romantic of the inside-Hollywood movies. As a paranoid screenwriter, Humphrey Bogart shows his tough-guy mask cracking open to reveal a bitter neurotic. And what went through Nicholas Ray's head as he directed scenes of Bogie breaking up with Gloria Grahame, while in real life Ray's own marriage to Grahame was on the rocks?

55 THE VERDICT *(1982, Fox-Video, R)* Twenty-five years after he made *Twelve Angry Men*, Sidney Lumet directed a far darker courtroom drama—but the glittering light of idealism is still there. Paul Newman gives a performance of great, gnawing doubt as an alcoholic lawyer who—through some slipup of destiny—gets one final case worth fighting for. David Mamet's script is a pungent earful, but this is Lumet's triumph: His storytelling here has an honesty that holds firm all the way to the final, brilliantly open-ended shot.

56 TO KILL A MOCKINGBIRD *(1962, MCA/Universal, B&W, not rated)* A sentimental favorite of baby boomers, who instantly related to Scout Finch (Mary Badham), 9 years old and trying to make sense of a baffling grown-up world. Oscar winner Gregory Peck is an icon of sensible righteousness as her lawyer father, defending a black man (Brock Peters) falsely accused of rape and saving his small Alabama town from all kinds of rabid dogs. With a spectral debut performance by Robert Duvall as Boo Radley.

57 LAST TANGO IN PARIS *(1972, MGM/UA, R or X)* Banned in its director's native Italy, the subject of outraged mail when *Time* magazine ran nude stills, Bernardo Bertolucci's film was quite the scandal in '73. Now that the controversy has died down, this simply looks like Marlon Brando's last great performance, as a dazed widower trying to erase sorrow and self through anonymous sex with Maria Schneider. It's an unblinking dissection of the male ego, and it's not a pretty picture.

58 **EL NORTE** *(1984, Facets, subtitled, R)* Gregory Nava's wrenching drama about illegal immigrants is one of the great lost '80s movies. Brother and sister Enrique (David Villalpando) and Rosa (Zaide Silvia Gutierrez) flee a military massacre in Guatemala, survive a hideous border crossing in Mexico, and wind up doing laundry and busing dishes in Los Angeles, gawking at the American dream even as it shuts them out. Although it sounds like the deck is stacked, the compassion in the playing will reduce you to tears.

59 **BLACK NARCISSUS** *(1947, Facets, not rated)* Deborah Kerr heads a group of British nuns whose isolated Himalayan convent inflames their imaginations in ways not at all in keeping with vows of chastity. With Jean Simmons as an erotically inclined Indian girl, David Farrar as a local colonial who should know better than to go around in shorts, and Kathleen Byron as the sister who goes nuts from all that *sex* hanging in the thin air. A stunningly sensual psychology lesson from British director Michael Powell.

60 **ATLANTIC CITY** *(1981, Paramount, R)* Beautiful losers Burt Lancaster and Susan Sarandon bet it all on one last shot in Louis Malle's haunting tale of redemption. The title city, caught like a fly in amber in the transformation from sleepy resort to high roller's mecca, is the perfect metaphor for a world in

ATLANTIC CITY: **SUSAN SARANDON**

which love and luck suddenly appear and are just as suddenly gone.

61 **I KNOW WHERE I'M GOING** *(1945, Facets, B&W, not rated)* This rapturously sly love story is a lot of people's secret favorite film. Headstrong English girl Wendy Hiller is on her way to an island off the Scottish coast to marry its owner for money and security. But a storm and a gentle laird (Roger Livesey) keep her mainland-bound, and as the countryside works its craggy magic, her cynicism begins to crumble. Directed by Michael Powell, it's a forebear to the more comic *Local Hero.*

62 **TWELVE ANGRY MEN** *(1957, MGM/UA, B&W, not rated)* A New York City jury room on a sweltering summer day, 11 cranky guys who just want to get home to a cold beer—and Henry Fonda quietly, stubbornly insisting that they don't have what it takes to prove a kid

27

DRAMA

killed his father. Quite the opposite, in fact. One by one, the other men—ranging from businessmen to bigots—cave in to the inexorable democracy of his logic. Even if the camera rarely leaves the room, director Sidney Lumet packs the screen with action.

63

STRAW DOGS (*1971, Fox-Video, R*) Sam Peckinpah's claustrophobic essay on the dangers of thwarted machismo still provokes arguments more than two decades after its release. Dustin Hoffman is a milk-and-water mathematician watching nervously as horny Cornish locals drool over his frustrated wife (Susan George). The suspense builds unbearably, then snaps in a paroxysm of violence. Does the wife provoke it, "earning" what she gets? Is the husband protecting "property" or

DRAMA

just avenging his own humiliation? Peckinpah asks brutal questions and leaves the answers up to us.

64 **RAIN MAN** *(1988, MGM/UA, R)* Dustin Hoffman won his second Oscar for reminding us of the joys of craftsmanship. His autistic savant Raymond Babbitt, accompanying callow little brother Charlie (Tom Cruise) on a cross-country soul search, is an unsettlingly cool portrait of a gentle man lost in the windstorms of misfiring neurons. While Barry Levinson's film trades in sentiment, Hoffman doesn't make the mistake of "explaining" Raymond for us. He simply *inhabits*.

65 **BADLANDS** *(1973, Warner, PG)* Lovers on the lam were nothing new in the movies, but Terrence Malick's fictional telling of a real-life Midwest murder spree was the first to pull the rug out from under the characters' own dreams of glory. Martin Sheen (as a punk killer patterned after Charles Starkweather) and Sissy Spacek (as his teen girlfriend, based on Caril Fugate) are empty vessels of all-American wrath, moving across vast Western landscapes like locusts feeding on fan magazines.

66 **HOWARDS END** *(1992, Sony Classics, PG)* Out of all those tweedy Merchant Ivory movies, this is the one that can actually *move* you. Adapting E.M. Forster's most symbolic novel (the title cottage could stand for England, if you wish, and the characters for all the different classes who stand to inherit her), the good-taste boys deliver the goods, with effortlessly moving performances from, among others, Oscar winner Emma Thompson (as a woman who radiates sense *and* sensibility) and Anthony Hopkins (as a wealthy man who loves his own power too much). Nice wallpaper, too, as usual.

67 **THE CROWD** *(1928, MGM/UA, B&W, silent, not rated)* The first American film to examine the toll that modern cities take on the people who live in them, King Vidor's drama follows a couple (James Murray and Eleanor Boardman) as they meet, marry, have children, and slowly revise the ideals that brought them to New York in the first place. Sounds depressing, but Vidor's rich compassion embraces his audience as well as his characters, and Manhattan has never been caught with such visual poetry.

68 **DOG DAY AFTERNOON** *(1975, Warner, R)* On a broiling day in Brooklyn, Sonny (Al Pacino) and his pal Sal (John Cazale) try to rip off a bank; they end up holding hostages while staring down the barrel of the entire New York City police force. Based on a true incident, this is a robbery movie for its times: raucous, bravura, a little political ("Attica!"), and a little kinky (you'll never believe what Sonny wants the money for). Sidney Lumet directs quietly while Pacino explodes in every imaginable direction.

69 **PATHS OF GLORY** *(1957, MGM/UA, B&W, not rated)* Stanley Kubrick hit the big time with this scathing in-

SEX, LIES, AND VIDEOTAPE: PETER GALLAGHER, LAURA SAN GIACOMO

dictment of the military mind-set; it's the angry flip side to *Dr. Strangelove*'s farce. After a French attack during World War I goes wrong, the general who ordered it chooses three enlisted fall guys to stand trial and face execution. As their defender, Kirk Douglas is the bristling voice of reason, not that anyone in the army brass wants to hear it. Kubrick hit a nerve: This movie was banned in France for two decades.

70 **REVERSAL OF FORTUNE** *(1990, Warner, R)* Did Claus von Bülow (Jeremy Irons) try to murder his socialite wife, Sunny (Glenn Close)? Director Barbet Schroeder plays out the possibilities with sardonic invention; it takes a certain nerve to have Sunny narrate from a coma. Ron Silver plays von Bülow's attorney, Alan Dershowitz, as a brilliant puppy, nibbling at the edges of the court appeal and barking perceptively at his stu-

dents. But it's Oscar winner Irons who takes the breath away as a man daintily bemused by his own empty soul.

71 **SALVADOR** *(1986, LIVE, R)* Made before Oliver Stone became Saint Ollie on the Mount, this scabrous drama has all of his urgency, skill, and acumen and none of the pretension. Well, almost none. James Woods, at his most charismatically scuzzy, plays battle photographer Richard Boyle, who drives to El Salvador with a drinking buddy (Jim Belushi) to check out the civil war. There he finds that it's hard to stay cynical when your country is playing the bad guy.

72 **THE SUGARLAND EXPRESS** *(1974, MCA/Universal, PG)* Until *Schindler's List*, this was the only Steven Spielberg film that dealt with grown-up themes and didn't sugarcoat them. Goldie Hawn is downright ferocious as a trashy Texas mom who breaks her old man (William Atherton) out of jail, takes a cop (Michael Sacks) hostage, and leads the law and the media on a merry chase to get her baby back from the adoptive parents. It's as smart as anything Spielberg's ever done, and twice as honest.

73 **STAGE DOOR** *(1937, Turner, B&W, not rated)* Here's where Katharine Hepburn says, "The calla lilies are in bloom again," droning her lines as a raw-boned actress in her first play. Despite her star billing, Gregory La Cava's sparkling backstage drama is an ensemble act: Ginger Rogers shares the nominal spotlight with Hepburn, while Eve Arden, Lucille Ball, and Ann Miller meow and scratch in the background, and spooky Andrea Leeds climbs the back stairs to Broadway martyrdom.

74 **CHOOSE ME** *(1984, Facets, R)* This intoxicating roundelay of love stories is the ultimate litmus test for separating cynics from romantics. Five yearning oddballs (including Keith Carradine, Lesley Ann Warren, Geneviève Bujold, and Rae Dawn Chong) collide like charged ions in the moody L.A. twilight. A deep, abiding sleeper from cult director Alan Rudolph, with a score sung by Teddy Pendergrass that defines the phrase *make-out music.*

75 **THE LETTER** *(1940, MGM/ UA, B&W, not rated)* The opening has few rivals for sheer in-medias-res chutzpah: Bette Davis, playing the wife of a rubber-plantation owner, advances down her front steps and coolly pumps her lover's body full of bullets. The rest of the film, directed by William Wyler from a Somerset Maugham play, can't help but be a bit of a letdown, but Davis never once draws back, painting Leslie Crosbie as a vibrant, amoral heroine greedily embracing her own damnation.

76 **SEX, LIES, AND VIDEOTAPE** *(1989, Columbia TriStar, R)* Despite the title, most everyone keeps his or her clothes on; despite everyone keeping their clothes on, the movie's erotic as hell. Steven Soderbergh's debut probes the no-man's-land between desire and deed, guilt and pleasure, watching and acting. The four leads stake out varied turf: yuppie self-absorption (Peter Gallagher), risky sensuality (Laura San Giacomo), delicate repression (Andie MacDowell), aesthetic perversion (James Spader). Watch it on video with someone you love.

77 **49TH PARALLEL** *(1941, Facets, B&W, not rated)* An epic thriller about Nazis on the run in Canada, of all places. When a U-boat is sunk in Hudson Bay, the German crew (led by Eric Portman) crisscrosses the continent, trying to sneak over the border to an America that at that point hadn't entered the war. Michael Powell intended it as emotional propaganda, and he enlisted the likes of Laurence Olivier, Leslie Howard, and Raymond Massey for nifty guest shots.

31

THELMA & LOUISE: SUSAN SARANDON, GEENA DAVIS

78 ORDINARY PEOPLE *(1980, Paramount, R)* Hampered by being just a little *too* sane, Robert Redford's directorial debut is still daring for the way it plunges elbow-deep into the neuroses of wealthy suburbia. It's an actor's movie all the way: Tim Hutton is a teenage wraith reeling from his brother's accidental death, while Donald Sutherland is quietly courageous as his father and Mary Tyler Moore shockingly subverts Our Mary into a rigid control freak.

79 THE STUNT MAN *(1980, Fox-Video, R)* A dazzling, multilayered entertainment about filmmaking, forgiveness, God, and ice cream. Vietnam vet Steve Railsback is already having these little reality/fantasy problems, but when he's hired by movie director Peter O'Toole to replace the stuntman he accidentally killed—maybe—the mind games begin in earnest. Richard Rush directs with engaging eccentricity, Barbara Hershey resurrects her acting career by playing an actress, and O'Toole swoops through the proceedings like Louis XVI deigning to peer through a viewfinder.

80 THE CLOCK *(1945, MGM/UA, B&W, not rated)* A soldier (Robert Walker) on leave in New York City spends 48 hours in the company of a sweet-faced clerk (Judy Garland) he has just met. Both slowly realize—to their astonishment, delight, and terror—that they have met the person with whom they are going to spend the rest of their lives. Directed by Vincente Minnelli (who married Garland shortly after the film wrapped), *The Clock* is a charming

DRAMA

LINES YOU ONLY THOUGHT YOU HEARD

MYTH: "Play it again, Sam." —Humphrey Bogart in *Casablanca* (1942)
REALITY: Ingrid Bergman says, "Play it, Sam. Play 'As Time Goes By.'" Later, Bogie says, "You played it for her, you can play it for me."

MYTH: "Come weeth me to zee Casbah." —Charles Boyer in *Algiers* (1938)
REALITY: Boyer often pointed out, crankily, that he never said this line in this or any other movie. He held a press agent responsible for coining it.

MYTH: "Ooh, you dirty rat." —James Cagney in *The Public Enemy* (1931)
REALITY: Cagney says, "Why, that dirty, no-good, yellow-bellied stool."

MYTH: "On the whole, I'd rather be in Philadelphia." —W.C. Fields
REALITY: Fields is supposed to have said this on film, and it's also supposed to be the epitaph on his vault. But Fields' marker actually says, "W.C. Fields, 1880–1946." The Philadelphia quote, composed by a magazine writer in the 1920s, was attributed to Fields after he died.

MYTH: "Judy, Judy, Judy." —Cary Grant
REALITY: Grant never said this except when imitating his imitators. Actor-impersonator Larry Storch (TV's *F Troop*) put the words in Grant's mouth in the mid-1930s, because "you always imagined him talking to a woman," says Storch, "and the name Judy has a lot of spark." The device stuck after he coached Tony Curtis and Sammy Davis Jr. in the art of imitating Grant in the 1940s. —*Jess Cagle and Steve Daly*

33

wisp of a thing whose very simplicity makes it endure.

81 **FURY** *(1936, MGM/UA, B&W, not rated)* German film director Fritz Lang (*The Big Heat*) brought his abiding obsession with fate to his first Hollywood picture: Spencer Tracy plays an average schmo who is traveling through a small town, gets mistaken for a kidnapper, and is attacked by a mob that sets fire to the jail he's in. He survives, only to be warped by desire for revenge. Tough stuff, especially the scene in which Tracy's character appears at his brother's apartment and says, "I could smell myself burn."

82 **THELMA & LOUISE** *(1991, MGM/UA, R)* The absurd controversy over whether this glorifies criminality (how come Butch and Sundance never faced these charges?) obscures what a finely crafted, gloriously acted piece of work it is. When tough-gal waitress Susan Sarandon and dim wifey Geena Davis hit the road after shooting a would-be rapist, they run a gauntlet of vivid

DÉJÀ VIEW

Unbeknownst to most renters, some of those unfamiliar films on video-store shelves are productions previously shown on broadcast and cable TV, retitled to sound like theatrical releases. Here's the truth about nine TV movies whose names have been changed to exploit the innocent:

For TV: *Doing Life* (1986, NBC) **For Video:** *Truth or Die* **Why the Change?** This docudrama starring Tony Danza as a convicted killer–turned–prison attorney received a spicy new title that video renters could easily mistake for 1991's acclaimed musical documentary about a blonder, bustier, only slightly less muscular Italian-American.

For TV: *Arthur the King* (1985, CBS) **For Video:** *Merlin and the Sword* **Why the Change?** The Sword in the Stone cachet conjured up by the retitling would seem to place this fantasy in Disney territory. But instead of cartoony medieval

fare, we get flesh-and-blood Malcolm McDowell and Dyan Cannon in a silly retelling of the Camelot legend.

For TV: *Chernobyl: The Final Warning* (1990, TNT) **For Video:** *Final Warning* **Why the Change?** Retaining only the subtitle, Turner trashed the historical element from this drama about the 1986 Soviet nuclear disaster. Now no one

will mistake it for a documentary; it sounds just like one of those urban butt-kickers with Michael Paré.

For TV: *Clinton and Nadine* (1988, HBO) **For Video:** *Blood Money: The Story of Clinton and Nadine* **Why the Change?** The added prefix gives this sexy thriller, with Andy Garcia and Ellen Barkin, a vehicle more suitable for their gun-running exploits. No longer does the title suggest a heartwarming, Midwestern domestic drama, which this never was.

For TV: *Where the Hell's That Gold?!!?* (1988, CBS) **For Video:** *Dynamite and Gold* **Why the Change?** The bawdy, excessively punctuated original title of this Western comedy screams, "Make no mistake—this is a cable-style

movie made for network TV!" The decaffeinated new name politely whispers, "Mid-'70s, good-ol'-boy trucker flick."

For TV: *Margaret Bourke-White* (1989, TNT) **For Video:** *Double Exposure: The Story of Margaret Bourke-White* **Why the Change?** The suggestive retitling manages to inject some tease into this biopic about the late *Life* magazine photographer. It also cleverly introduces the photo angle for video renters unfamiliar with Bourke-White's work or name.

For TV: *A Gathering of Old Men* (1987, CBS) **For Video:** *Murder on the Bayou* **Why the Change?** Out went the feeling of geriatric camaraderie, and in came the image of conspiracy in a dark and exotic locale. Actually, this acclaimed drama is about neither: It's a serious fictional account of the killing of a white racist by a frustrated black man.

For TV: *Sweet Revenge* (1984, CBS) **For Video:** *Code of Honor* **Why the Change?** The rechristening of this military drama avoids confusion with two other videos titled *Sweet Revenge*, but now invites confusion with many similarly titled Steven Seagal flicks. Also, the box art and reshuffled credits play up the presence of supporting player Alec Baldwin.

For TV: *Vendetta: Secrets of a Mafia Bride* (1991, syndicated) **For Video:** *A Family Matter* **Why the Change?** The "new" name, actually this Mafia drama's original title, leaves a tonier impression, but makes all this violent business sound less like a feature film and more like an *Afterschool Special* on teen pregnancy. —*Doug Brod*

male types (more varied than critics claimed) and inhale the sudden freedom of the road. A boy's own adventure turned inside out, and much, much richer for it.

83 **THE RIGHT STUFF** *(1983, Warner, PG)* The early history of space flight presented as a humane 16-year farce: No wonder it crash-landed in theaters. Philip Kaufman directs smartly from Tom Wolfe's smart book, but it's the hydra-headed cast that makes this so playful to watch. Ed Harris' John Glenn is a complex Boy Scout, Fred Ward's Gus Grissom may or may not be a coward, and Sam Shepard's Chuck Yeager —the man who broke the sound barrier—is a laconic touchstone for future heroes.

84 **DAVID COPPERFIELD** *(1935, MGM/UA, B&W, not rated)* Hollywood always did right by Dickens—the writer's mix of sharp caricature, pell-mell narrative, and soggy sentiment fit the town like a pearl-buttoned glove. But it took a showman like producer David O. Selznick and a humanist like director George Cukor to make the most of the match. The secret's in the cast: toffee-voiced Freddie Bartholomew as the adventurous David, sneering Basil Rathbone as Mr. Murdstone (even the names sound alike), and above all W.C. Fields as Mr. Micawber, vainly and happily hoping for a better day.

85 **BLOW OUT** *(1981, Warner, R)* Brian De Palma never gets any respect. But this one—in which John Travolta plays a

RIVER'S EDGE: KEANU REEVES (FAR LEFT), CRISPIN GLOVER (SECOND FROM LEFT)

movie sound recordist who catches an assassination on tape and lives to regret it—has a *moral* dimension that for once brings the director within shouting distance of Hitchcock. More than any other De Palma film, *Blow Out* is about the dark price we pay for being voyeurs.

86 **HIGH TIDE** *(1987, Facets, PG-13)* The title is perfect for this modern-day weepie from Australia: An irresponsible rambler (the great Judy Davis) gets stranded like a piece of post-'60s driftwood in the coastal town that holds the daughter she abandoned more than a decade before. Under the direction of Gillian Armstrong (*My Brilliant Career*), it's a devastating portrait of a woman with nowhere to grow but up.

87 **PRETTY POISON** *(1968, In-gram, not rated)* A sick little winner that finds the essence of evil in a smiling teenage drum majorette. Tuesday Weld has her finest role as Sue Ann Stepanek, latching on to a local misfit (Anthony Per-kins) and leading him down a primrose path that ends in the murder of her mother. Perkins is a marvelous mess of statutory fidgets and tics, while Weld exudes winsome sex as a very bad girl in good girl's clothing.

88 **RIVER'S EDGE** *(1987, Facets, R)* Based on a true inci-dent, Tim Hunter's film is the end of a journey that started with *Rebel Without a Cause*. Instead of Jim Stark's angst, the teens who stare at the murdered body of one of their own have only hip numbness going for them. It would all be a little glib if not for the performances: Keanu Reeves as a kid fanning the embers of his con-science, Joshua Miller as a feral little loser, Crispin Glover as the group's leader in stoner paranoia.

89 **CAUGHT** *(1949, Republic, B&W, not rated)* Max Ophüls, the high priest of continental melodrama, made this down-and-dirty sob story during his brief Hollywood stay. Barbara Bel Geddes marries a slick millionaire (Robert Ryan) who mutates into a bul-lying monster; she finds salvation with a kindhearted doctor (James Mason). As always with Ophüls, that True Romance plot is cut with the harsh essence of love and death. As a bonus, Ryan offers a cruelly precise Howard Hughes impersonation.

90 **SAY ANYTHING...** *(1989, Fox-Video, PG-13)* Cameron Crowe's wonderful teen romance about a lovable kickboxer courting the class valedictorian shows how one song can symbolize every-

DRAMA

thing two people could possibly feel for each other. While making love for the first time—in the backseat of his car, no less—Lloyd (John Cusack) and Diane (Ione Skye) hear Peter Gabriel's haunting "In Your Eyes" on the radio. Many scenes later, after Diane has dumped him, Lloyd parks near her house, hoists a boom box over his head, and lets Gabriel blow. It's all he needs to say; it's all she needs to know.

91

DETOUR (1946, Facets, B&W, not rated) Meet the all-time chump of movie history. Trying to get across the country to meet his fiancée, a musician (Tom Neal) has the bad fortune to give a lift to a sexually predatory shrew (the aptly named Ann Savage), who jumps his bones and drags him into a life of crime before the poor sap can draw a breath. Hard to say what's more outrageous in Edgar Ulmer's sweaty little B classic: Savage's performance or that truly gonzo wrap-up.

92

NORTH DALLAS FORTY (1979, Paramount, R) This was a double whammy when it originally came out: No one expected a football movie to be this smart, and no one expected Nick Nolte (as an aging gridiron star staring at his own mortality) to be this good. A rowdy, incisive look at professional athletes, this adaptation of a novel by former Dallas Cowboy Peter Gent remains (along with *Bull Durham*, in the Comedy chapter) one of the best sports movies ever. Hell, even Mac Davis is impressive, as Nolte's much shallower teammate.

93

MANHUNTER (1986, Warner, R) *The Silence of the Lambs* has its mass audience and its Oscars, but this earlier movie featuring the character of Hannibal Lecter—adapted by Michael Mann from Thomas Harris' novel *Red Dragon*—has a creepier, less articulate sense of dread. William Petersen plays a fed who tracks serial killers by learning to think like them—not a good strategy for his mental health. Brian Cox is no Anthony Hopkins as Lecter, but Tom Noonan is unforgettably insane as Petersen's prime quarry.

94

TWO FOR THE ROAD (1967, FoxVideo, not rated) The swinging-'60s visual tricks and costumes have dated (did anyone wear sunglasses like Audrey Hepburn's?), but Stanley Donen's movie remains a bittersweet, full-bodied look at modern marriage (okay, *wealthy* modern marriage). Flashing back and forth within the 12 years that Hepburn and Albert Finney have been together, Donen gives us a perspective his characters don't have: We see their foibles, their quarrels, and the grace that saves them—their lasting faith in romance.

95

NO WAY OUT (1987, HBO, R) A breathlessly convoluted thriller that transplants 1948's *The Big Clock* to Washington's corridors of power. Kevin Costner is a naval officer assigned by his boss, the secretary of defense (Gene Hackman), to find the killer of party girl Sean Young. The catch is that Hackman did it and Costner knows it—but he can't stop the finger of guilt from pointing back at himself.

37

WHEN AUTEURS ARE ACTORS

FRANÇOIS TRUFFAUT

When director Orson Welles needed money to finish a movie, actor Orson Welles took over, helping to raise it by appearing in other filmmakers' pictures. When director-actor Woody Allen sought novelty, he starred in Paul Mazursky's *Scenes From a Mall* as a non-nebbish. In fact, directors have often traded in their directorial hats for character costumes, sometimes with remarkable results.

Orson Welles in *The Third Man* (dir. Carol Reed, 1949): Welles appears for only about 20 minutes all told, but his presence as the charming, ruthless Harry Lime dominates the style of this classic, which uses the kind of cinematic devices more associated with Welles (*Citizen Kane*) than with Carol Reed (*Oliver!*)—askew camera angles, deep focus, and shadowy figures.

Erich von Stroheim in *Sunset Boulevard* (dir. Billy Wilder, 1950): Creepy and amusing, Wilder's piercing parable on the cult of celebrity is full of insight into the destructiveness of self-delusion. Von Stroheim plays the butler, Max, a former director whose silent stares and cryptic comments paint an unnerving picture of a man destroyed by an all-consuming love.

John Huston in *Chinatown* (dir. Roman Polanski, 1974): Huston, whose presence links this '70s film noir to his own thrillers of the '40s (*The Maltese Falcon*), is exquisitely cast as the personification of evil. His folksy manner veils a juggernaut of immorality that will stop at nothing to prevail.

Woody Allen in *The Front* (dir. Martin Ritt, 1976): Allen plays the character he created for himself in his own early films—a neurotic geek—only this time he's a geek who fronts scripts for blacklisted writers during the McCarthy era. Movingly, he finds his conscience.

François Truffaut in *Close Encounters of the Third Kind* (dir. Steven Spielberg, 1977): As in his other noteworthy performance (as a filmmaker plagued with problems in his own *Day for Night*, 1973), Truffaut brings a probing gaze, curiosity, and a director's authority to Claude Lacombe, a UFO scientist methodically searching for extraterrestrial life.

Martin Scorsese in *Akira Kurosawa's Dreams* (dir. Akira Kurosawa, 1990): Scorsese may seem a bizarre choice for Vincent van Gogh, one of many characters in this collection of short, gloomy tales. But the gritty director of *GoodFellas* is the personification of Kurosawa's notion of the artist as obsessive perfectionist. Neurotically intense, fast-talking, and self-absorbed, he is driven by a powerful inner vision. —*Tom Soter*

Some people hated the lollapalooza twist ending; to us it pushes the movie to risky greatness.

96 THE BAD AND THE BEAUTIFUL *(1952, MGM/UA, B&W, not rated)* Hollywood periodically likes to take the lash to itself, but Vincente Minnelli's Tinseltown melodrama sidesteps bitterness in favor of a good, trashy wallow. Kirk Douglas plays bad-boy producer Jonathan Shields, who uses and abuses starlets (such as Lana Turner), directors (such as Barry Sullivan), and screenwriters (such as Dick Powell, in a daft cartoon of William Faulkner). Shot like a creamy nightmare, this is a Hollywood hell made by people who loved the place.

97 THE YEAR OF LIVING DANGEROUSLY *(1983, MGM/ UA, PG)* Peter Weir's thriller teeters on the edge of overwrought romanticism—it's that nervy. Mel Gibson plays an Australian reporter in mid-'60s Indonesia—when the political shit was hitting the civilian fan—whose affair with a British attaché (Sigourney Weaver, exuding brainy sex) endangers their careers and then their lives. Linda Hunt nabbed an Oscar for her hair-raising, cross-dressing performance as Billy Kwan, Gibson's protector, idolizer, and conscience.

98 THE PIANO *(1993, LIVE, R)* As Ada, a mute Victorian Scotswoman who journeys with her daughter (Oscar winner Anna Paquin) to the New Zealand bush for an arranged marriage, Oscar winner Holly Hunter has an austere, mythical presence. Written and directed by Jane Campion, *The Piano* is a romantic melodrama of almost classical grandeur, with Ada caught between her stunted husband (Sam Neill) and the illiterate settler (Harvey Keitel) who seduces and saves her. By the end, Campion views all her characters with a compassion bordering on grace.

99 GUN CRAZY *(1949, Fox-Video, B&W, not rated)* John Dall is a sad sack with a yen for guns and no love in his life. Then he meets avaricious carnival sharpshooter Peggy Cummins, a honeyed dream in buckskin clothing. Directed by B-movie auteur Joseph H. Lewis, this is a feverishly sexy, really *mean* look at the all-American intersection of sex and firearms. Bonuses include a bank robbery filmed entirely from the backseat of the getaway car, and young Russ Tamblyn playing Dall as a kid.

100 PUMP UP THE VOLUME *(1990, Columbia TriStar, R)* Shy high school kid Christian Slater gains messy celebrity as a pirate-radio operator. Critics sniffed and audiences ignored it—just another dumb teen drama aimed at the mall-monkey set. Except that this overlooked gem from writer-director Allan Moyle burrows under the essence of late-20th-century adolescence: the masks, the sex, the self-pity, the despair—the sense that each new day is the only one that matters. Some of the physical details are muffed, but the emotional reality is dead-on.

All reviews written by Ty Burr.

COMEDY

IT USED TO BE that movie comedy was one thing and one thing only: a pie flying toward someone's eminently deserving kisser. But the years have sliced that pie into a thousand different pieces—there's high comedy, low comedy, and black comedy; there's screwball, slapstick, and satire. In short, to quote Zero Mostel in *A Funny Thing Happened on the Way to the Forum* (see No. 35), there's "something for everyone—comedy tonight!" So, which comedy should *you* rent tonight? Trying to answer that question—and needing a good laugh ourselves—we came up with the following 100 Greatest Comedies of All Time. Our selections may not be among the greatest *films* ever made, and some good but only mildly funny ones didn't make the list. Instead, we picked movies that, quite simply, provide the most yuks for the bucks. There are classic knee-slappers like *Duck Soup* (see No. 7) and *Adam's Rib* (see No. 44) and modern-day favorites (see *City Slickers* at No. 92). There are also lesser-known gems we're positive will have you roaring. Take our list with you the next time you go to the video store—we guarantee you'll exit laughing.

1 **AIRPLANE!** *(1980, Paramount, PG)* By packing this one with more laughs per minute than any other movie in history, writer-directors Jerry Zucker, Jim Abrahams, and David Zucker (the ZAZ team) set the flight pattern for film comedy to come. This takeoff on '70s disaster movies bombards you with a barrage of sight and sound gags—from Otto the pilot to "Don't call me Shirley"—that leaves you grabbing for an oxygen mask. And unlike most comedies, this one *requires* repeat viewings on video to pick up the swarm of jokes in every piece of background action.

2 **SOME LIKE IT HOT** *(1959, MGM/ UA, B&W, not rated)* Tony Curtis and Jack Lemmon learn to walk the walk (in heels) and talk the talk (up a few octaves) as they flee mobsters and join an all-girl band in Billy Wilder's fall-down-funny gender-confusion farce. Happy endings all around: Boy gets girl (Curtis gets Marilyn Monroe), and boy gets boy (Lemmon accepts a proposal of marriage from Joe E. Brown). "Nobody's perfect," but few comedies come as close as this.

3 **THIS IS SPINAL TAP** *(1984, Columbia TriStar, R)* First-time director Rob Reiner's knowing mockumentary of a band of English heavy-metal bozos gets everything right—even tiny details like the contents of a backstage deli tray. That the songs, including the deathless "Tonight I'm Gonna Rock You Tonight," are this clever and genuine bespeaks the creators' grasp of the essential ingredient for classic satire: a deep affection for the subject of ridicule.

THIS IS SPINAL TAP:
HARRY SHEARER, GLORIA GIFFORD

4 **ANNIE HALL** *(1977, MGM/UA, PG)* Is this the end of Funny Woody? Or is it the start of Serious Woody, with seeds of future insights and pretensions? Maybe it's just best to watch this cross-cultural, bicoastal romance as if it were the only movie the Woodman ever made: Few comedies have this much wit *and* heart *and* soul.

5 **BRINGING UP BABY** *(1938, Turner, B&W, not rated)* Sublime silliness, directed by Howard Hawks in his best rat-a-chat-chat style, with Katharine Hepburn as a dizzy heiress whose pet leopard, Baby, leads paleontologist Cary Grant on a merry chase from Manhattan to Connecticut. Bonus: Grant wears a woman's robe and grouses, "I just went gay all of a sudden!"

6 **THE PRODUCERS** *(1968, Columbia TriStar, not rated)* Mel Brooks' first, and arguably best, film has Zero Mostel and Gene Wilder ripping off their backers by staging the worst musical on Broadway, a trifle called *Springtime for Hitler.* That's what he wanted to call the movie, too, but producer Joe Levine wouldn't let him.

7 **DUCK SOUP** *(1933, MCA/Universal, B&W, not rated)* The Marx Brothers, let loose in the mythical land of Freedonia, will not let anything—or anyone—sane stay that way for long. In one of their finest films, Harpo, Groucho, Chico, and Zeppo take insult humor to a place it has never been before or since. "I'll teach you to kick me," a man threatens Chico. "You don't have to—I know how," says Chico, kicking him.

8 **TOOTSIE** *(1982, Columbia TriStar, PG)* It was a legendary battle: Dustin Hoffman and director Sydney Pollack fought over the motivations of Michael Dorsey, the actor who poses as a woman to land a much-needed job on a soap. Jessica Lange was in no mood for comedy after *Frances*. And it took forever to get Hoffman's breasts right. The moral? Even when it seems as if no one knows what he's doing, things can still turn out fine.

A CLOWNING ACHIEVEMENT FOR THE ZAZ TRIO

THE KINGS OF COMEDY

Not every movie buff may rank *Airplane!* as the funniest movie of all time, but there's no doubt that David Zucker, Jerry Zucker, and Jim Abrahams (left to right) have brought film

comedy into the ZAZ age. Together or separately, they're responsible for four of the 100 comedies listed in this book: *Airplane!* (No. 1), *The Naked Gun* (No. 75), *Kentucky Fried Movie* (No. 89), and *Top Secret!* (No. 93).

Why, in their view, has *Airplane!*, the top-ranking flight farce, endured? Jim has the answer. "It's just bad moviemaking," he says. "In one shot in the airport you can see the grip putting cable down." The all-time funniest? "Probably *Midway*," deadpans David. "Or *Airport 1975*, or the Concorde one," Jerry adds.

As writers and directors of three of the top 100 comedies (John Landis directed *Kentucky Fried Movie*), the ZAZsters may be considered true auteurs, but are there any little people they'd like to thank? "The ones who are in the credits," David says, "but who didn't really do anything."

And is being named the creators of the funniest movie on video indeed the pinnacle of their ZAZ careers? "Well," David says playfully, "we already have that giant vibrating dildo mounted on a plaque." *—Doug Brod*

43

PHOTOFEST

***DR. STRANGELOVE*: GEORGE C. SCOTT, PETER BULL, PETER SELLERS**

9 **THE GENERAL** *(1926, Video Yesteryear, B&W, silent, not rated)* Buster Keaton imbues silent slapstick with historical grandeur in this Civil War comedy, an epic of elaborately unfolding gags. Inexplicably, it's one of the few Keaton classics you can find on tape—even the peerless *Sherlock Jr.*, which would also make the top 10 all-time great comic films, isn't available. A sad loss for comedy lovers.

10 **UNFAITHFULLY YOURS** *(1948, FoxVideo, B&W, not rated)* For all the charm of Preston Sturges' beloved early farces, it's the comparatively little-known *Unfaithfully Yours* that can make you simply insane with laughter. Rex Harrison is sublime as a conductor dreaming up ways to deal with a possibly cheating wife while conducting Rossini, Wagner, and Tchaikovsky. When he tries to enact his plots outside his head, reality refuses to play ball.

11 **DR. STRANGELOVE: OR HOW I LEARNED TO STOP WORRYING AND LOVE THE BOMB** *(1964, Columbia TriStar, B&W, not rated)* Stanley Kubrick's uproarious and grim satire was the first film to prescribe laughter as the antidote to what was then mankind's foremost fear: imminent destruction when the Big One dropped. Peter Sellers plays the fascistic professor Strangelove—whose prosthetic arm has a mind of its own—plus two other roles.

12 **THE LADYKILLERS** *(1955, Facets, not rated)* A gang of hoods led by Alec Guinness is no match for its oblivious old dearie of a landlady. This was Peter Sellers' first major film, and as you

watch Guinness you'll see where the younger man picked up his bag of tricks.

13 THE MIRACLE OF MORGAN'S CREEK *(1943, Paramount, B&W, not rated)* Trudy Kockenlocker (Betty Hutton) gets drunk with—and pregnant by—a soldier whose name she vaguely remembers as Ratskiwatski. In Preston Sturges' wicked satire on the Virgin Birth, Eddie Bracken, as a stuttering Joseph, wants to do the right thing by Trudy. How this all got past the Production Code remains as big a mystery as the Holy Trinity.

14 A FISH CALLED WANDA *(1988, Facets, R)* British comedy of embarrassment meets American farce. There's no way to reconcile the outrageousness of Kevin Kline with the mournful sexiness of John Cleese with Jamie Lee Curtis' sneaky grin with Michael Palin's agonized stutter, but the movie, thankfully, doesn't give you a chance to try.

15 CADDYSHACK *(1980, Warner, R)* Not since the Little Rascals has anyone made golf as funny as the amazing assemblage of Chevy Chase, Rodney Dangerfield, Ted Knight, and Bill Murray. This lowbrow hoot cheekily indulges in the hoary slob-versus-snob conceit much imitated since but never matched.

16 HIS GIRL FRIDAY *(1940, Facets, B&W, not rated)* Howard Hawks had a bright idea: Turn Broadway's *The Front Page* on its head by making one of its newspapermen a woman. The result is probably

Hawks' purest view of romance as mutually delighted verbal slugfest—and Cary Grant's performance is nimble enough to leave you gasping.

17 SPLASH *(1984, Touchstone, PG)* Finally, a fish-out-of-water comedy about a fish out of water. Tom Hanks is a lonely Everyguy, and Daryl Hannah is a mermaid who grows legs for love: Together

CADDYSHACK: **BILL MURRAY**

they create a cross-species romance so infectious it makes Manhattan feel like a small town.

18 IT HAPPENED ONE NIGHT *(1934, Columbia TriStar, B&W, not rated)* The opening salvo in the screwball-comedy war of the sexes—and the classes—with the rich always crazier than the rest of us. Reporter Clark Gable and heiress Claudette Colbert are a perfect mis-

45

match, and Frank Capra gives their strange coupling emotional pull—something that few imitators have achieved.

19 **THE GRADUATE** *(1967, Columbia TriStar, PG)* The movie that reinvented comedy for the '60s generation, *The Graduate* crystallized the bemused contempt with which the under-30s regarded the over-30s. Dustin Hoffman's debut film is satiric, surreal, and a little self-absorbed—in other words, a perfect reflection of its audience.

20 **TO BE OR NOT TO BE** *(1942, Warner, B&W, not rated)* Hammy Jack Benny and gloriously scattered Carole Lombard head a group of Polish actors trying to outwit the Nazis in Ernst Lubitsch's unlikely, feathery comedy. "I hope you'll forgive me if I acted clumsy, but this is the first time I ever met an

TO BE OR NOT TO BE: JACK BENNY

actress," gushes infatuated flyboy Robert Stack. "Lieutenant," replies Lombard, "this is the first time I met a man who could drop three tons of dynamite in two minutes. Bye."

21 **BANANAS** *(1971, MGM/UA, PG)* Here's the Woody Allen that yuk buffs miss—a rude prankster with a mind on fast-forward and no time for Art. He's Fielding Mellish (the name could have been a gift from Groucho or Fields), a product tester who ends up president of a Communist banana republic.

22 **SULLIVAN'S TRAVELS** *(1941, MCA/Universal, B&W, not rated)* Joel McCrea plays a successful Hollywood comedy director who wants to make a serious movie about suffering and despair. The problem is, he's never suffered, so he dresses like a hobo and sets out to *find* suffering. One of writer-director Preston Sturges' best films, this seriocomedy shows that laughter itself is a great treasure.

23 **ABBOTT AND COSTELLO MEET FRANKENSTEIN** *(1948, MCA/Universal, B&W, not rated)* Plus Dracula and the Wolf Man in this surprisingly atmospheric vehicle for the screen's most consistent comic duo. As the vampire who tries to put Lou's scattered brain into Frankenstein's monster, Bela Lugosi deftly parodies the role that made him infamous.

24 **VICTOR/VICTORIA** *(1982, MGM/UA, PG)* Blake Edwards' finest moment and certainly the most fun Julie Andrews has had on screen. James Garner is fine

HAPPY ACCIDENTS

"It has been a long journey, Helen. Welcome to the moon," says a cat woman to Marie Windsor, navigator of a spaceship to the moon, which is populated by women who "have no use for men." Fascinating in the way that truly peculiar people are, *Cat Women of the Moon* (1953) is a "found" comedy—one that doesn't mean to be hilarious and is all the funnier for it.

The '50s were especially rich in found comedy, much of it in the cheesy sci-fi flicks churned out for teens—from the boozed-up housewife who wrecks everything in sight in *Attack of the 50-Foot Woman* (1958) to the evil ex-Nazi who disfigures buxom island girls in the delectable *She Demons* (1958). But sci-fi doesn't have the franchise on idiocy; it can be found in *Reefer Madness* (1936), a cautionary tale of how marijuana leads, with alarming speed, directly to lunacy. Bare-chests-and-big-breasts biblical epics such as *Samson and Delilah* (1949), with lines like "Your tongue will dig your grave," leave viewers helpless with mirth.

Modern times, too, have contributed to the unintentionally funny fund. In *The Island* (1980), the only fertile woman left among a race of near-extinct pirates trapped in a time warp tells reporter Michael Caine he is needed for his "thrust." And in 1984, Bo Derek, the cornrows having clearly pressed too tightly into her brain, went looking for "thrust" as a 1920s heiress trying to lose her maidenhead in *Bolero*, which has laughable pretensions to reality. Every time Bo opens her mouth, another of her thoughts drops its laundry to reveal only the barest of essentials.

Deliciously dumb and blissfully unaware, these found comedies may have come to theaters, but they rarely visited earth.

—*Lawrence O'Toole*

47

as a gangster drawn to Andrews while remaining befuddled as to exactly which *sex* she is, but it's Robert Preston, as the lady's camp follower, who steals this dizzy show.

25 **THE GOLD RUSH** *(1925, Facets, B&W, silent, not rated)* Charlie Chaplin caught at the moment when he teetered—like that shack on the cliff—

***THE GOLD RUSH**: CHARLIE CHAPLIN*

between pratfall élan and future bathos. It's the actor-director's confident peak, with hilarious set pieces like that fillet-of-boot-sole dinner, as well as an epic feel for the Alaskan frontier.

26 **THE LONGEST YARD** *(1974, Paramount, R)* In this rambunctious bruiser of a comedy, Burt Reynolds, a former college player himself, plays a pro quarterback turned convict who gets to organize a team of prisoners for a game against the hated guards. A cast of wacko characters and Reynolds' wiseguy expertise deliver a lot of laughs, and the big-game climax is one of the most rousing finishes in a sports movie.

27 **BLAZING SADDLES** *(1974, Warner, R)* Bringing the Catskills to Black Rock, Mel Brooks' raunchy Western about a black sheriff's efforts to tame a town overflows with surreal gags and groaners and contains something to offend absolutely everyone. Shameless in its political incorrectness, this is a picture Hollywood wouldn't dare remake.

28 **LOCAL HERO** *(1983, Warner, PG)* In Bill Forsyth's droll, enchanting movie, a Texas oil executive (Peter Riegert) hies to a sleepy Scottish village, where he encounters a single pay phone, the aurora borealis, and a population for whom the word *eccentric* is tame. It'll leave a smile on your face for days.

29 **IT'S A GIFT** *(1934, Facets, B&W, not rated)* Masterful mumbler W.C. Fields, who turned foul moods and a hatred for children into genius, is at his drawliest and nastiest as a store owner and family man ("Don't let the posy fool ya") whose crosses include a customer requesting kumquats, a careless blind man in his shop, and Baby LeRoy, who makes a persuasive case for infanticide.

30 **RAISING ARIZONA** *(1987, FoxVideo, PG-13)* Before they got serious (*Miller's*

RAISING ARIZONA: T.J. KUHN

Crossing) and seriously weird (*Barton Fink*), the brothers Coen spun this cartoony tale of an infertile couple who decide to steal a baby. Nicolas Cage and Holly Hunter shine as the loony duo, but John Goodman and William Forsythe are unforgettable as a pair of chicken-fried, coop-flying jailbirds.

31 **A NIGHT AT THE OPERA** *(1935, MGM/UA, B&W, not rated)* "A thousand dollars a night! Just for singing? Why, you can get a phonograph record at Minnie the Moocher's for 75 cents. For a buck and a quarter you can get Minnie," remarks Groucho, who, along with Chico and Harpo, tears into *Il Trovatore* and scourges pearl-strung Margaret Dumont, who's not having much luck getting into society *or* ships' staterooms.

32 **REPO MAN** *(1984, MCA/ Universal, R)* As the prototypical suburban punk, Emilio Estevez deadpans his way through a surreal landscape of repo—philosophers, fascist scientists, infantile rockers, and aliens in the trunk. Alex Cox's fantasy brilliantly captures subdivision anomie in *the* epigram for the blasé-and-proud generation: "Let's go get sushi…and not pay!"

33 **NATIONAL LAMPOON'S ANIMAL HOUSE** *(1978, MCA/ Universal, R)* The halls of academe were forever defaced by this lewd and crude frat-house farce, which captures John Belushi (as bloated future senator Bluto Blutarsky) in all his disgusto glory. Irony alert: Despite siring countless pretenders to the throne, this royal treatment of truly gross jokers never begat a sequel.

34 **M*A*S*H** *(1970, FoxVideo, PG)* Robert Altman's innovative, free-for-all Korean War comedy (really about the Vietnam War) was the first time an audience was invited to laugh at the absurdity of violence while geysers of blood sprayed all over makeshift operating rooms and a medical unit attempted to carry on with life as if nothing unusual were happening.

YOUNG FRANKENSTEIN: **MARTY FELDMAN**

35 **A FUNNY THING HAPPENED ON THE WAY TO THE FORUM** *(1966, Facets, not rated)* It's the borscht belt on the Tiber, with songs by Sondheim and a siblings-mixed-up-at-birth plot out of Plautus, the Neil Simon of 200 B.C. Zero Mostel, Phil Silvers, and Jack Gilford provide the rim shots in the *original* toga party.

36 **ROXANNE** *(1987, Columbia TriStar, PG)* The movie with a nose for pure pleasure. Steve Martin plays C.D. Bales, an inspired derivative of Cyrano de Bergerac, with an outlandish proboscis and a poetic soul. The highlight is Bales thinking up 20 big-nose insults, such as, "It must be wonderful to wake up and smell the coffee…in Brazil!"

37 **YOUNG FRANKENSTEIN** *(1974, FoxVideo, B&W, PG)* Mel Brooks' spoof of the Universal monster movies is his most stylish and subtle film. The cast is a corker:

49

coscreenwriter Gene Wilder as young Doc Frank; Madeline Kahn, in an Elsa Lanchester hairdo, as his fiancée; klutzy monster Peter Boyle; and Marty Feldman as Igor, the humpback valet in total denial about his hump.

38 **A HARD DAY'S NIGHT** *(1964, MPI, B&W, not rated)* Richard Lester's zippy, raw backstage take on Beatlemania was actually meticulously scripted. So what? It worked in '64 and it still does—only now it seems a lovely remnant of our lost innocence. And it's slyly funny: To paraphrase Ringo, *Night*'s a mocker.

39 **KIND HEARTS AND CORONETS** *(1949, Facets, B&W, not rated)* Alec Guinness plays all of the snooty relatives (even the female ones) that greedy Dennis Price has to knock off before the family fortune is his. Elegant and dark, *Coronets* points a manicured finger toward Pythonesque black comedy to come.

40 **GROUNDHOG DAY** *(1993, Columbia TriStar, PG)* Bill Murray plays a cynical TV weatherman who doesn't like anybody, and nobody, including his cameraman (Chris Elliott) and his producer (Andie MacDowell), likes him. When the team gets sent to a rural town to cover the Groundhog Day festivities, the cosmos throws him a curveball: He must endlessly relive the day. Every scene has a belly laugh stemming from either the situation or Murray's playing of it.

41 **DINER** *(1982, MGM/UA, R)* Writer-director Barry Levinson's affectionate

reminiscence of being a young male coming of age in 1950s Baltimore serves up food for thought in addition to memorably delirious comic vignettes, including Steve Guttenberg's sports quiz and Mickey Rourke's movie-theater bet.

42 **HAIL THE CONQUERING HERO** *(1944, MCA/Universal, B&W, not rated)* Hero worship, mother love, and the U.S. Marines all take their lumps when geeky Eddie Bracken gets passed off as a WWII war hero to his hometown. Along with *The Miracle of Morgan's Creek*, it's Preston Sturges' most demented assault on mid-'40s American sacred cows.

43 **THE MAN WITH TWO BRAINS** *(1983, Warner, R)* In this anything-goes spoof of

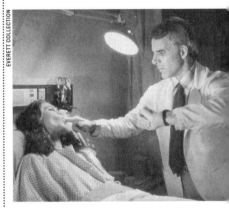

THE MAN WITH TWO BRAINS:
STEVE MARTIN, KATHLEEN TURNER

mad-doctor movies, in which cats get kicked across rooms and poodles roll over and die, Steve Martin plays the sex-starved brain surgeon Dr. Hfuhruhurr, who falls in love with a jar of brains he names Anne. To watch him place a pair of rubber lips on Anne's jar and plant a kiss is a wild and crazy joy.

44 ADAM'S RIB *(1949, MGM/UA, B&W, not rated)* The funniest of the nine Tracy-Hepburn movies, with the scratchy relationship of married but opposing lawyers Adam and Amanda embodying the essence of this starch-and-stubble pair. Even if real life didn't comply, on screen Kate and Spence seemed a snug, smart domestic unit. As a bonus, you also get Judy Holliday playing a spurned wife with a good heart and bad aim.

45 DINNER AT EIGHT *(1933, MGM/UA, B&W, not rated)* A great, serious comedy about death. The delicious cast trying to make it to the table includes Wallace Beery, Jean Harlow, Lionel and John Barrymore, and Marie Dressler, carrying a pack of dead animals on her person. George Cukor directs with unerring timing, wit, and a beautiful sense of balance.

46 THE NUTTY PROFESSOR *(1963, Paramount, not rated)* The Jerry Lewis movie that proves the French may actually be right: *Professor* is one discomfiting comedy. A nerd's potion turns him into contemptuous hepcat swinger Buddy Love—Lewis' possible revenge on fickle ex-partner Dean Martin. Mining neuroses for Day-Glo fool's gold, the movie provides belly laughs punctuated by empathic winces.

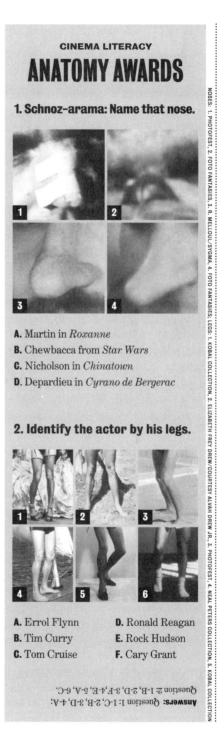

CINEMA LITERACY

ANATOMY AWARDS

1. Schnoz-arama: Name that nose.

A. Martin in *Roxanne*
B. Chewbacca from *Star Wars*
C. Nicholson in *Chinatown*
D. Depardieu in *Cyrano de Bergerac*

2. Identify the actor by his legs.

A. Errol Flynn
B. Tim Curry
C. Tom Cruise
D. Ronald Reagan
E. Rock Hudson
F. Cary Grant

Answers: Question 1: 1-C, 2-B, 3-D, 4-A;
Question 2: 1-B, 2-D, 3-F, 4-E, 5-A, 6-C.

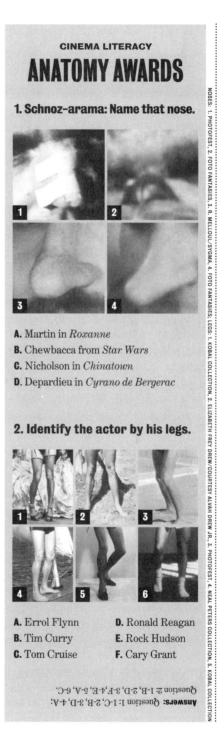

51

47 GHOSTBUSTERS *(1984, Columbia TriStar, PG)* "Big budget" and "funny" don't often go together, but *Ghostbusters* is the exception. The ectoplasmic FX may make us gasp, but when Bill Murray and Dan Aykroyd unshackle the old *Saturday Night Live* party ethos, *'Busters* clicks. That, and the Stay Puft Marshmallow Man.

48 THE GREAT DICTATOR *(1940, FoxVideo, B&W, G)* A daring slap at a time when it was thought Hitler could still be pacified. The funniest moments come when Charlie Chaplin's Adenoid Hynkel meets Jack Oakie's Il Duce–esque Napaloni; their scenes together critique Fascist ideals more convincingly than any political speech.

49 TAKE THE MONEY AND RUN *(1969, FoxVideo, PG)* Director-cowriter-star Woody Allen's first triple-threat treat is also one of his most consistently amusing. The faux documentary of an inveterate hood's inept pursuits (including an illegible stickup note and a pistol carved from soap), it's all the more relevant in these true-crime-obsessed times.

50 SHE'S GOTTA HAVE IT *(1986, Facets, B&W, R)* "Please-baby-*please*-baby-*please*-baby-baby-baby" is Spike Lee's constant refrain. As the funniest of Tracy Camila Johns' three suitors, director-star Lee gives his comic wooings the same urgency he would soon bring to graver matters. Made before he became the big, famous Spike Lee, it's his loosest and lightest work.

51 HOUSE PARTY*(1990, Columbia TriStar, R)* Rappers Kid 'N Play (Christopher Reid, Christopher Martin) are high school buddies planning a big blowout while dodging parents, bullies, and assorted

SHE'S GOTTA HAVE IT:
TRACY CAMILA JOHNS, SPIKE LEE

party crashers. Director Reginald Hudlin's debut, the movie features dance numbers with amazing snap and infectiously silly humor.

52 LOVER COME BACK *(1961, Facets, not rated)* We'll take the second Doris Day–Rock Hudson comedy over *Pillow Talk* any day. For one thing, the Madison Avenue satire remains fresh. For another, Tony Randall is a riot as Hudson's neurotic boss. For a third, Doris wears the damnedest hats you've ever seen.

53 THE SHOP AROUND THE CORNER *(1940, MGM/UA, B&W, not rated)* By day, department-store clerks James

Stewart and Margaret Sullavan hate each other's guts; at closing time, they go home and write anonymous mash notes to each other. Romantic illusions have never crumbled more deliciously than in Ernst Lubitsch's charming tussle between heart and mind.

54

BIG *(1988, FoxVideo, PG-13)* A gentle text for baby boomers staring at the stark fact of adulthood as Tom Hanks plays a carefree kid suddenly transformed into an adult. (Admit it: Most of us feel like kids in grown-up skin.) If not for Hanks' grace, *Big* would seem to be a gimmick; if not for his comic gifts, it would drown in schmaltz.

THE SHOP AROUND THE CORNER:
MARGARET SULLAVAN, JAMES STEWART

GIFT SETS WE'D LIKE TO SEE

WACKY PACKAGES

53

Boxed sets would be much more fun if they weren't such conceptual yawns. A *Die Hard* box? An Astaire and Rogers set? Bo-o-ring. These things are supposed to be conversation pieces, right? We're sure the following sets would be:

THE GOOD-ENOUGH-TO-EAT COLLECTION *Hot Dog...The Movie, Meatballs, Heroes, Bananas, Animal Crackers, Wild Strawberries, Nuts.*

THE ONOMATOPOEIA GIFT SET *Huk, Phffft!, Hawmps!, Boin-n-g!, Eegah!*

THE VICTOR FRANKENSTEIN HOMAGE BODY-PARTS BOX *The Hand, Head, Claire's Knee, Cold Feet, The Belly of an Architect.*

THE DESIGNER COLLECTION *Andy Warhol's Bad, Sidney Sheldon's Bloodline, Paul McCartney's Get Back, Akira Kurosawa's Dreams, Fellini's Roma.*

THE FILMS OF THE WIVES OF CARY GRANT *City Lights* (Virginia Cherrill), *Clarence The Cross-Eyed Lion* (Betsy Drake), *Bob & Carol & Ted & Alice* (Dyan Cannon). —*Ty Burr*

55
MR. HULOT'S HOLIDAY *(1953, Facets, B&W, subtitled, G)* French comic Jacques Tati brought slapstick into the postwar world. The plot's an extended sketch in which the amiable dunce battles deck chairs, fishing gear, and bratty kids during a seaside vacation, but for all *Holiday*'s summer-rental looseness, you'll rarely see better timing.

56
PEE-WEE'S BIG ADVENTURE *(1985, Warner, PG)* You've got to hand it to Paul Reubens: Blessed with a playfully smirky alter ego and a visionary director (upstart Tim Burton in his feature-film debut), he pulled off a sweet and singular feat, making the world a better place for imbecilic nerds everywhere.

**PEE-WEE'S BIG ADVENTURE:
PAUL REUBENS**

FILMS ON COMEDY TAKE A SAD TURN

BUT SERIOUSLY, FOLKS

Comedy is a dramatic subject, too. And all the serious films about comedians and their craft seem to say, "Putting on a happy face for a living can be hell."

The bulk of comedy-themed dramas are biographies, and they are hardly happy affairs. Indeed, the chronicles of real-life comics' careers are slaphappy with self-destruction, ranging from alcoholism (Frank Sinatra as Joe E. Lewis in *The Joker Is Wild*, 1957) to drug addiction (Dustin Hoffman as Lenny Bruce in *Lenny*, 1974). Yet fiction is no less felicitous: Take Charlie Chaplin's broken-down music-hall clown in *Limelight* (1952) or Laurence Olivier's overpoweringly self-loathing vaudevillian Archie Rice in *The Entertainer* (1960).

In recent years, films about the comedy craft have uncovered an even darker, more disturbing dimension, whether it's Robert De Niro's creepy aspiring comic Rupert Pupkin in Martin Scorsese's *The King of Comedy* (1983) or Eric Bogosian's deejay, whose acerbic, provocative wit courts danger and, ultimately, death in *Talk Radio* (1988). The lesson: Where there's comedy, crisis is often the punch line. *—Lawrence O'Toole*

57 BORN YESTERDAY *(1950, Columbia TriStar, B&W, not rated)* Judy Holliday is Billie Dawn, the gum-chewing tycoon's tootsie (and gin-rummy whiz) with a voice that could peel paint off toenails. She asks Washington reporter William Holden to help her "learn how to talk good." Culturally, she gets "couth"; romantically, he gets wise. Washington has never been so much fun.

58 STRIPES *(1981, Columbia TriStar, R)* Bill Murray's first smash hit also offers the most genuine belly laughs of any of his star vehicles. Here he's totally in command as a lovable layabout who joins the Army and ends up whipping a squadron of misfits (including riotous John Candy) into fighting shape.

59 BEETLEJUICE *(1988, Warner, PG)* Before *Batman*, Tim Burton directed this uproarious parade of afterlife oddities, body transformations, and calypso poltergeists, with Michael Keaton in the title role and Alec Baldwin and Geena Davis as newlyweds negotiating their way through the afterlife.

60 RIFF RAFF *(1993, Columbia TriStar, not rated)* The English dialects are so thick in this terrific Ken Loach film about construction workers that the film has subtitles. The humor around the site is sharp but natural, and the working-class stiffs, played by actors who seem like people picked off the street, keep you smiling from beginning to end. But beneath the merriment, there's a grim and angry picture of life in contemporary Britain—a portrait of dreams smashed as soon as they're formed.

61 THE COURT JESTER *(1956, Paramount, not rated)* In this swashbuckling comedy, Danny Kaye goes undercover as a court jester to dethrone an evil king. Kaye's specialty was double-talking patter, and *Jester* has some of the best. Is the pellet with the poison in the vessel with the pestle? Does the chalice from the palace have the brew that is true? Just try saying it when you're laughing.

EVERETT COLLECTION

UP IN SMOKE: TOMMY CHONG
(RIGHT) AND FRIENDS IN WEED

62 UP IN SMOKE *(1978, Paramount, R)* With several successful comedy albums to their name, Cheech and Chong took their one-note act to the big screen. The peak of their brief glory, *Smoke* is a bunch of inspired bong gags in search of coherence. Present-day proof that our culture has lost its sense of humor: If this movie were released today, there would be "Just Say No" protesters around the block.

PLAY IT AGAIN, ROBIN

Like many actors, Robin Williams brings his own personal style to his movie characterizations. The thing is, Williams' style is such an idiosyncratic splatter of improv shtick that it's often hard to tell exactly whom he's supposed to be playing. See if you can, by matching the Williams material in the left column with the characters in the right. —*Nisid Hajari, Tim Purtell*

1. "Thank you, Judge Wapner." Later: "Hi-ho, Silver!"

2. Impressions of Billie Burke, Munchkins, the Wicked Witch, and two references to ruby slippers. Later: "We're not in Kansas."

3. Adaptation of lyrics to Groucho Marx song "Lydia, the Tattooed Lady": "When her muscles start relaxin'/Up the hill comes Michael Jackson."

4. Impressions of John Wayne and Marlon Brando.

5. With an aristocratic accent: "So long, constable. ...You won't have [me] to kick around anymore."

6. "Are you related to Mighty Mouse?" Later: "What is this, some sort of *Lord of the Flies* preschool?"

A. Army disc jockey in *Good Morning, Vietnam*

B. Homeless ex-professor in *The Fisher King*

C. English teacher at boys prep school in *Dead Poets Society*

D. Used-car salesman in *Cadillac Man*

E. Adult Peter Pan in *Hook*

F. Ex-fireman turned island club owner in *Club Paradise*

Answers: 1-D, 2-A, 3-B, 4-C, 5-F, 6-E.

63 **THE HEARTBREAK KID** *(1972, Media, PG)* Not only did Elaine May direct this ode to romantic chutzpah—in which honeymooning Charles Grodin meets Cybill Shepherd and promptly dumps his new wife—she also cast daughter Jeannie Berlin as the dumpee. Good thing she lobbed *Kid* past tastelessness into inspired, hard hilarity.

64 **THE LAVENDER HILL MOB** *(1951, Facets, B&W, not rated)* More droll, dark

English mirth from the Ealing Studios, with Alec Guinness as a drab little bank clerk who concocts a plan to steal gold bullion and melt it into miniature replicas of the Eiffel Tower. Don't miss the young Audrey Hepburn's (brief) appearance.

65 WAY OUT WEST *(1937, Facets, B&W, not rated)* Few Laurel and Hardy feature films sustain the whimsy of their short films: This and *Sons of the Desert* are the exceptions. *Way Out West* takes Stan and Ollie out to sagebrush country, where Stan gets assaulted by a feather-wielding villainess.

66 BULL DURHAM *(1988, Orion, R)* Writer-director Ron Shelton's rascal's-eye view of baseball's minor leagues offers pleasures athletic, carnal, and literary. Kevin Costner has his edgiest role as the burned-out catcher, and Susan Sarandon is the ultimate thinking-sports-fan's sex fantasy.

67 LOST IN AMERICA *(1985, Warner, R)* Harried L.A. yuppies Albert Brooks and Julie Hagerty decide to get away from it all and see America in an RV, but much to their horror, especially in Las Vegas, they discover that they can't escape themselves. Brooks turns whining into a high form of comic art.

68 THE BELLBOY *(1960, International Video Entertainment, B&W, not rated)* Looking for a project to jam out before *The Ladies' Man*, Jerry Lewis brought a crew to Miami's Fountainbleau hotel

HOLLYWOOD SHUFFLE:
**LUDIE WASHINGTON, ROBERT
TOWNSEND, KEENEN IVORY WAYANS**

and filmed skits pegged to a mute, bumbling luggage jockey. The result is this daft one-shot, with an encounter between the bellboy and a star named Jerry Lewis that boosts the film into the nearly experimental.

69 HOLLYWOOD SHUFFLE *(1987, Facets, R)* One of the first in the oft-cited "new wave" of African-American films, Robert Townsend's bittersweet ensemble parody turns a send-up of blaxploitation flicks into an indictment of the limited roles for black actors. Yet the message always defers to the inventive, outrageous caricatures that tickle both your funny bone and your conscience.

70 A CHRISTMAS STORY (1983, MGM/UA, PG) Based on Jean Shepherd's tales of rust-belt childhood, *Story* is a lovely piece of anti-nostalgia that dismantles family holidays with sass. It's all here: the monstrous department-store Santa, the pink bunny pajamas from Grandma, the little brother hiding under the sink.

71 WHAT'S UP, DOC? (1972, Warner, G) Peter Bogdanovich's valentine to *Bringing Up Baby* shows an irresistible love for High Screwball. And if you think Barbra Streisand isn't sexy, here's your wake-up call: She works up real steam as a free spirit who loosens Ryan O'Neal's emotional necktie.

72 HEATHERS (1989, Facets, R) A wry Winona Ryder and a devilishly unhinged Christian Slater indulge in teen angst, racking up an impressive body count among Westerburg High's cool and vapid along the way. The duo's hysterical blend of homicide and puppy love ensures that the perversity of high school will never be forgotten.

73 ARTHUR (1981, Warner, PG) This is just a genial screwball-comedy throwback, but Dudley Moore seems so delighted as the pickled millionaire of the title and Sir John Gielgud mouths his naughty lines with such Oscar-winning condescension that as *Arthur* unreels, it reminds you that the best comedies are often the simplest.

74 MY FAVORITE BRUNETTE (1947, Facets, B&W, not rated) The *Road* films are fine in their hellzapoppin fashion, but Bob Hope always seemed more inspired when he went Bing-less. Not that he's wanting for inspired support here: Dorothy Lamour, Peter Lorre, Alan Ladd—and Crosby for a one-shot gag.

75 THE NAKED GUN: FROM THE FILES OF POLICE SQUAD! (1988, Paramount, PG-13) The ZAZ men gave their failed TV series, *Police Squad!*, the featurelength *Airplane!* overhaul and emerged with this cockeyed cop picture, which has spawned numerous sequels. As the clueless Lieut. Frank Drebin, Leslie Nielsen proves he possesses the deadliest deadpan in the business.

LIBELED LADY: SPENCER TRACY

58

STAND UP AND BE DELIVERED

A funny thing happens to some comedians on the way from their stand-up comedy beginnings to motion-picture stardom: They lose a bit of the personal spark, the sense of surprise, that caught our attention in the first place. Sometimes, as in the case of Martin Short, they're just not as funny anymore—or don't try to be. To see them stand out, you have to see them doing what they did best: stand-up.

RICHARD PRYOR: LIVE IN CONCERT *(1979)* finds the controversial Pryor at his uproarious best: profane, insightful, and angry. Nothing, from racism to reenacting his own heart attack, is off-limits. Fifteen years later, no one has approached the level of hard-won hilarity Pryor reaches here.

After Pryor's soul-baring performance, **BILL COSBY, HIMSELF** *(1982)* comes off as a tad tame, but don't let that throw you. This show is a vivid reminder that Cos was the best G-rated storyteller on the scene before TV made his act too familiar.

GEORGE CARLIN: AT CARNEGIE HALL *(1983)* captures the eccentric veteran in top form. His fascination with language ("Seven Words You Can Never Say on Television") and skewed news flashes ("A man attempting to walk around the world...drowned today") are perfectly silly, and totally necessary.

AN EVENING WITH ROBIN WILLIAMS *(1983)* has the comic's trademarks: uncanny impersonations, off-the-wall parodies (Jack Nicholson doing Hamlet), and Elmer Fudd singing Bruce Springsteen, all delivered at such a breathtaking pace that you'd swear he had a half hour left to live and an hour's worth of material. Keep those fingers near the pause and rewind buttons.

Just as brainy is **LIVE FROM WASHINGTON IT'S DENNIS MILLER** *(1988)*, which showcases the acerbic talk-show casualty during his *Saturday Night Live* heyday. Miller's material here is largely topical—though far from timeworn—and consistently sharp. —*Bob Cannon*

59

76 **WHERE'S POPPA?** *(1970, MGM/UA, R)* George Segal is a New York lawyer buckling under senile mama Ruth Gordon in this cult comedy directed by Carl Reiner. The "tush" scene was notorious back then, but it's when Trish van Devere tells Segal about a honeymoon faux pas that the bad-taste envelope gets pushed to uproarious extremes.

77 **LIBELED LADY** *(1936, MGM/UA, B&W, not rated)* Tabloid editor Spencer Tracy is engaged to brassy Jean Harlow, see, but he marries her off to William Powell so Harlow can play the outraged wife when Powell romances snooty heiress Myrna Loy so Spence can get a scoop, but then...oh, never mind. Just rent it and laugh your butt off.

BEDAZZLED: DUDLEY MOORE (CENTER) AND PETER COOK (RIGHT)

JERRY OHLINGER'S

78 **ALL OF ME** *(1984, Facets, PG)* Serious lawyer Steve Martin is invaded by the spirit of the rich, crabby, and deceased Lily Tomlin in a sidesplitting metaphysical share-a-ride. Martin's physical comedy revives the glory days of Keaton, Lloyd, and Chaplin, offering a priceless example of having the feeling you want to go but also want to stay.

79 **THE BIG PICTURE** *(1989, Columbia TriStar, PG-13)* *Spinal Tap* vet Christopher Guest's film directorial debut offers a snide, if sentimental, insider's look at Hollywood—a town that corrupts talent and murders art in pursuit of the lowest common denominator. Guest's jabs at overbaked student films and reptilian producers have real sting.

80 **THE IN-LAWS** *(1979, Warner, PG)* Before he made it big with *Honeymoon in Vegas*, Andrew Bergman wrote this cult favorite. CIA spook Peter Falk spins his usual line of seedy, paranoid BS to New York dentist and future in-law Alan Arkin. The gag is that it's all true. A loosey-goosey affair, as rumpled as Falk's face.

81 **SMILE** *(1975, MGM/UA, PG)* Michael Ritchie's witty satire of beauty contests manages to be incisive *and* humane—no wonder it stiffed at the box office. It holds up terrifically, though, with sharp performances by Barbara Feldon as the pageant's mother hen and Annette O'Toole and Melanie Griffith as contestants.

82 **BEVERLY HILLS COP** *(1984, Paramount, R)* Forget about the crummy sequel—this first film of the Eddie Murphy franchise jerks the action comedy into the '80s with superior smart-ass repartee and breathless movement; it even has a good banana gag. At the movie's center: an obvious fish-out-of-water tale. At its edges: the infectious, turbocharged charm of its star.

83 **BEDAZZLED** *(1967, Facets, PG)* The Faust legend told through a cheeky British blender. Satan (Peter Cook) sells Dudley Moore seven chances for love—one of which ends up with Moore in an order of trampolining nuns. Freeze-frame alert: Watch for Raquel Welch's appearance as "Lilian Lust, the babe with the bust."

84 **SLACKER** *(1991, Facets, R)* A deliciously deadpan, independent comedy that only pretends to be about the lives of semi-employed loafers hanging around the sunbaked college town of Austin, Tex. Sure, it's about these slackers—but it's also a slyly metaphysical portrait of the post-counterculture era, an era in which, more and more, people are living inside their own heads.

85 **SILVER STREAK** *(1976, Fox Video, PG)* Someone had the genius to put Richard Pryor and Gene Wilder in a train-station bathroom, with Pryor trying desperately to teach Wilder the gestalt of "walking black." That scene sparks *Streak* to another level—one that the two actors have sought in vain since.

86 **DESPERATELY SEEKING SUSAN** *(1985, Facets, PG-13)* Rosanna Arquette is an amnesiac sprite mistaken for downtown girl Madonna in director Susan Seidelman's funky Manhattan farce. A film that earns many of its laughs from its whacked-out characters—including Mark Blum's uptight hubby and Steven Wright's frizzy dentist—it also gave the Blond One her best role to date.

87 **SHE DONE HIM WRONG** *(1933, MCA/Universal, B&W, not rated)* Mae West specialized not in laugh-out-loud comedy but in the bawdy, hidden smile of subversive sex. Here she seduces missionary Cary Grant, sings "I Wonder Where My Easy Rider's Gone," and, as in everything she did, ends up on top.

88 **THE WAR OF THE ROSES** *(1989, FoxVideo, R)* Some nasty notions here: Marriage can turn on a dime into corrosive loathing; the best way to hurt people is to destroy what they *own*. Director Danny DeVito's playful camera work and stars Kathleen Turner and Michael Douglas are all that keep it from being a horror flick.

89 **KENTUCKY FRIED MOVIE** *(1977, Facets, R)* The best of the '70s spate of spoofy anthologies, this delirious omnibus, written by the ZAZ team (and directed by *Animal House*'s John Landis), has as its centerpiece a brilliant send-up of the chopsocky classic *Enter the Dragon*. Superior sexy and stoopid faux commercials, coming attractions, and court-room dramas complete this gumbo.

61

WAS WHO REALLY ON FIRST?

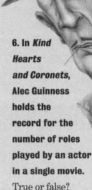

1. Who is taller: Danny DeVito or Dudley Moore?

A. Danny DeVito, by 3 inches

B. Dudley Moore, by 2 inches

C. Danny DeVito, by 5 inches

D. They're the same height

2. What was the first feature-length comedy?

A. The Russian-made *Volga, Volga,*
   with Lubov Orlova

B. *The Freshman,* with Harold Lloyd

C. *Tillie's Punctured Romance,*
   with Charlie Chaplin

D. *The Saphead,* with Buster Keaton

3. Although he dropped out of the act before the Marx Brothers went to Hollywood and never appeared in one of their movies, Gummo Marx made his mark in what film comedy?

A. *Get to Know Your Rabbit*

B. *Stardust Memories*

C. *Hardly Working*

D. *Weekend at Bernie's*

4. Match the classic comedy with its some-what inferior musical remake:

A. *The Philadelphia Story*	1. *Let's Do It Again*
B. *Ball of Fire*	2. *Silk Stockings*
C. *Bachelor Mother*	3. *A Song Is Born*
D. *The Awful Truth*	4. *Bundle of Joy*
E. *Ninotchka*	5. *High Society*
F. *The Shop Around the Corner*	6. *In the Good Old Summertime*

5. Who was the first to film a pie fight?

A. Charlie Chaplin   C. Buster Keaton

B. Mack Sennett   D. Harold Lloyd

6. In *Kind Hearts and Coronets,* Alec Guinness holds the record for the number of roles played by an actor in a single movie. True or false?

7. Woody Allen's *The Purple Rose of Cairo* was influenced by what film?

A. Ingmar Bergman's *The Seventh Seal*

B. Buster Keaton's *Sherlock Jr.*

C. Jean Cocteau's *Orpheus*

D. Luis Buñuel's *The Exterminating Angel*

8. Match the Marx Brothers' stage names with their real ones:

A. Chico	1. Adolph
B. Groucho	2. Leonard
C. Harpo	3. Julius
D. Zeppo	4. Herbert

9. What comic actor was the model for the Buster Brown shoe boy?

A. Jackie Coogan

B. Jackie Cooper

C. Milton Berle

D. Leo Gorcey

10. Match the member of a famous comedy team with the previous or future partner who is now nearly forgotten.

A. Bud Abbott	1. Connie Stevens
B. Lou Costello	2. Larry Semon
C. George Burns	3. George Byrne
D. Oliver Hardy	4. Joe Lyons
E. Bob Hope	5. Betty Smith

11. What was the first movie to include Abbott and Costello performing a complete version of their "Who's on First?" routine?

A. *The Naughty Nineties*
B. *Who Done It?*
C. *Here Come the Co-eds*
D. *One Night in the Tropics*

12. What actress supplied the voice of the brain—Steve Martin's love interest—in *The Man With Two Brains*?

A. Kathleen Turner
B. Meryl Streep
C. Sissy Spacek
D. Gilda Radner

13. What movie funnyman said, "A lot of people were hostile because I was a multifaceted, talented, wealthy, internationally famous genius"?

A. Jerry Lewis
B. Charlie Chaplin
C. Chevy Chase
D. Cantinflas

14. Match the comic actor and animal who have a close encounter:

A. Buster Keaton in *Go West*	1. A gorilla
B. Gene Wilder in *Everything You Always Wanted to Know About Sex*	2. A fish
	3. A cow
	4. A goat
C. Lily Tomlin in *The Incredible Shrinking Woman*	5. A lion
	6. A sheep

D. Don Knotts in *The Incredible Mr. Limpet*
E. W.C. Fields in *My Little Chickadee*
F. Danny Kaye in *Merry Andrew*

15. It's hard to imagine that neither Jack Lemmon nor Tony Curtis was among director Billy Wilder's first choices for the roles of Jerry and Joe (aka Daphne and Josephine) in *Some Like It Hot*. Which one of the following actors almost got to wear lipstick and heels?

A. Peter Lawford
B. Dean Martin
C. Frank Sinatra
D. Sammy Davis Jr.

16. Match the *Saturday Night Live* and Second City TV alums with the comedies they appeared in, sometimes together:

A. *Ghostbusters*
B. *Little Shop of Horrors*
C. *Caddyshack*
D. *It Came From Hollywood*
E. *National Lampoon's Vacation*
F. *Stripes*

1. Dan Aykroyd, John Candy, Gilda Radner
2. Chevy Chase, Bill Murray
3. John Candy, Bill Murray, Harold Ramis
4. John Candy, Chevy Chase, Eugene Levy
5. Dan Aykroyd, Rick Moranis, Bill Murray, Harold Ramis
6. Jim Belushi, John Candy, Rick Moranis

—*Tim Purtell*

Answers: 1. B 2. C (1914) 3. B 4. A-5, B-3, C-4, D-1, E-2, F-6 5. B 6. False (Rolf Leslie played 27 roles in 1913's *Sixty Years a Queen*) 7. B (Both feature a character entering a movie within the movie) 8. A-2, B-3, C-1, D-4 9. C 10. A-5, B-4, C-1, D-2, E-3 11. A 12. C 13. A 14. A-3, B-6, C-1, D-2, E-4, F-5 15. C 16. A-5, B-6, C-2, D-1, E-4, F-3.

63

90 MOONSTRUCK *(1987, MGM/ UA, PG)* A perfect cast meets an enormously entertaining, even profound, script by John Patrick Shanley in this sweet romantic comedy about a Brooklyn woman who falls for her suitor's younger brother. Star Cher has rarely been sexier, and as the older beau, Danny Aiello gives a performance that's a marvel of sympathetic comic bluster.

91 STRANGER THAN PARADISE *(1984, Facets, B&W, R)* Jim Jarmusch's road movie, in which two dudheads from New York's East Village (John Lurie and Richard Edson) and a Hungarian cousin (Eszter Balint) head for Cleveland and Florida, is so deadpan it seems barely alive in an endearing, kicky kind of way. With its long takes and blackouts between scenes, it's like a movie on drugs.

92 CITY SLICKERS *(1991, New Line, PG-13)* Some people dumped on this dude-ranch lark for its soggy center, in which three buddies nearing middle age finally grow up. But Billy Crystal, Bruno Kirby, and Daniel Stern have a natural comic chemistry that comes only from real-life friendship. Besides, Kirby gets to tell the screen's funniest VCR joke.

93 TOP SECRET! *(1984, Paramount, PG)* The ZAZ boys apply their magic touch to the spy flick, posting an ersatz Elvis (Val Kilmer) in Germany, where he gets mixed up with Nazis. In perfectly cast supporting roles, old Britons Peter Cushing and Michael Gough

appear to be having a great time sending up their usual character parts.

94 HOME ALONE *(1990, Fox- Video, PG)* John Hughes churns this stuff out like Pringles, and even he probably didn't expect it to become the biggest-grossing comedy in history. The plot's in the title, so what's the secret of its success? Simple: a 10-year-old star with a sleepy-duck face, acting like the kid he is.

95 MONTY PYTHON AND THE HOLY GRAIL *(1975, Columbia TriStar, PG)* The Python crew's second feature takes an irreverent knife to one of the most cherished myths of its native England: King Arthur and his Round Table. Creating a land populated by killer rabbits, shrubbery-seeking warriors, holy hand grenades, and vulgar Frenchmen, Cleese & Co.'s manic reworking of Shakespeare's sceptered isle raises silliness to high art.

96 BEYOND THE VALLEY OF THE DOLLS *(1970, FoxVideo, NC-17)* Critic Roger Ebert (and shameless schlockster Russ Meyer) wrote this three-thumbs-up parody of Jacqueline Susann's pill-popping soap opera about an all-woman rock band, all of the women Amazonian and with, as comedian David Steinberg used to say, "breasts as big as Ethiopia."

97 ROGER & ME *(1989, Warner, R)* As a documentary, the film, with its juggled chronology, may be a little spurious, but Michael Moore's record of his attempts to talk to General Motors chairman

PUTNEY SWOPE: ADVERTISING EXECUTIVES BEFORE THEIR AGENCY'S MAKEOVER

Roger Smith makes for one of the funniest nonfiction movies ever. Peopled with characters too strange to be real—but they *are*—and imbued with a deep sadness for the plight of GM-forsaken Flint, Mich., this is social commentary at its most wittily enlightening.

98 ARSENIC AND OLD LACE *(1944, MGM/UA, B&W, not rated)* Suck on *these* family values: Two sweet spinsters invite lonely men to tea, poison them, and stuff the bodies in the window seat. Their brother thinks he's Teddy Roosevelt and the stairs are San Juan Hill. Their nephew—Cary Grant at his most whinnyingly perplexed—just wants to get married. In Frank Capra's hands, it's as dainty as a barbed-wire doily.

99 PUTNEY SWOPE *(1969, Facets, B&W, R)* The parody commercials created by

African-American Putney Swope when he takes over an ad agency don't seem so outrageous after *Saturday Night Live*—but it's hard not to give credit to a movie that envisions the President of the United States as a midget pothead.

100 BOUDU SAVED FROM DROWNING *(1932, Facets, B&W, not rated)* and **DOWN AND OUT IN BEVERLY HILLS** *(1986, Touchstone, R)* The French classic and its Hollywood remake. In Jean Renoir's anarchic original, a shopkeeper takes home, and gets taken in by, scuzzy bum Michel Simon. Paul Mazursky's update has Nick Nolte, Richard Dreyfuss, and Bette Midler, but it wants to leave you feeling good, where *Boudu* wants you to feel. It's the difference between a great comedy and a great film.

Reviews written by Ty Burr, Doug Brod, Nisid Hajari, Lawrence O'Toole, and David Everitt.

COMEDY

ACTION & MORE

OF ALL THE GENRES that lure us into movie theaters, the
action movie may suffer most on video. All those giant explosions
and strapping heroes; such an itsy-bitsy screen. Ironically, action-
adventures are among the most rented movies on tape. Perhaps
the noisier they are, the more we feel as though we've actually
shelled out $7.50 for the full Bijou experience. Perhaps we just like
our movies to *move*.

Whatever sociological theory you choose, the video revolution
has definitely resulted in a glut of titles, the majority of which seem
to fall into the action-adventure and mystery-suspense categories
(and subcategories—the "erotic thriller" genre is a not-so-pure by-
product of the VHS age). In the process of separating what's often
theatrically released wheat from straight-to-tape chaff, we've
ranked the 40 finest action films, the 30 greatest mystery-suspense
films, and—oh, yes—the 30 best Westerns, a genre currently enjoying one of its cyclical booms. You say you disagree? Fine: We'll meet
you outside town at midnight, and settle this thing like politically
incorrect, fully armed, strong and silent...people.

two sequels) revived the action flick after half a century's slump.

2 **THE ADVENTURES OF ROBIN HOOD** *(1938, FoxVideo, not rated)* All pretenders can stay out of the forest: Errol Flynn's Robin Hood still reigns. Impossibly hale and hearty, he starts out by crashing a royal banquet with a slain deer across his shoulders, then leads his merry men in revolt against corrupt Prince John. Filmed in Technicolor (Will Scarlet's scarlet outfit may be too much for cheaper VCRs), this swashbuckler set a bold new standard for its genre.

1 **RAIDERS OF THE LOST ARK** *(1981, Paramount, PG)* With his snap-brim hat and whip, Harrison Ford's Indiana Jones is the most heroic archaeologist ever to dig up a magical thingy. He leaps from certain-death situations with such tongue-in-cheek cool that you'd laugh out loud if you weren't out of breath. Sure, the priceless artifacts and nefarious Nazis are straight out of a 1930s Saturday matinee. But old serials didn't have the kinetic camera of Steven Spielberg, who with this debut Indy picture (not to mention its

3 **THE ROAD WARRIOR** *(1981, Warner, R)* Mel Gibson's early star vehicle is a nonstop demolition derby. Although it is set in a postapocalyptic desert where survivors wage war over precious gasoline, the future-shock message takes a backseat to the perpetual motion on screen. Gibson wears his battle scars well as the avenger Mad Max; careering around in souped-up cars, he does deadly battle with biker marauders sporting medieval weapons and Mohawk haircuts. It's debatable which is more brilliant: the breakneck stunts or the whip-crack editing. Call it a dead heat.

THE ADVENTURES OF ROBIN HOOD:
HERBERT MUNDIN, ERROL FLYNN

4 **GOLDFINGER** *(1964, MGM/UA, PG)* Could the Cold War have been more fun? Not likely. This is the best of the archetypal Sean Connery Bond movies, for several fab reasons: Bond's Aston Martin arsenal-on-wheels, inscrutable Oddjob (Harold Sakata) and his killer bowler hat, and beautiful Shirley Eaton in her coat of toxic gold paint. All that, plus a climax that finds

TARZAN, THE APE MAN: MAUREEN O'SULLIVAN, JOHNNY WEISSMULLER

with twice the speed and style—and half the blood and bluster. Paul Muni is overpowering as the two-bit thug who shoots his way to the top. Surrounded by characters *almost* as tough—including Boris Karloff as his British counterpart—Scarface prevails by being the most ambitious, the most relentless, *and* the most ruthless. Muni easily dominates every scene he's in—except those that get stolen by Ann Dvorak as his sassy little flirt of a sister.

Bond fighting Oddjob in the bowels of Fort Knox while handcuffed to an atomic time bomb.

5 TARZAN, THE APE MAN *(1932, MGM/UA, B&W, not rated)* or **TARZAN AND HIS MATE** *(1934, MGM/UA, B&W, not rated)* The moment they met on screen, Johnny Weissmuller and Maureen O'Sullivan became the definitive Tarzan and Jane, and they were never more naturally charismatic than in their first two films. The former is essential for bringing the couple together, while the latter finds them comfortably settled in their winning formula: He fights rhinos and crocodiles; she does treetop swan dives into his arms and joins him for sensuous swims (her pre–Production Code loincloth would make Madonna blush). For plot, as always, there are greedy white hunters who incur Tarzan's wrath. This guy was saving the rain forest long before it was fashionable.

6 SCARFACE *(1932, MCA/Universal, B&W, not rated)* Forget the De Palma remake: Howard Hawks' original charts a gangster's rise and fall

7 BATMAN *(1989, Warner, PG-13)* Casting a grim shadow on the stark Gotham City skyline, Tim Burton's version of Batman (Michael Keaton) seems to have emerged from a German Expressionist film. His crime-fighting style, however, is classically comic-book. So is Jack Nicholson as the evil Joker, who steals everything in sight, including the movie. In this duel between the Dark Knight and his doppelgänger, the action keeps spiraling further over the top. That's exactly where it belongs.

8 THE BLACK PIRATE *(1926, Facets, not rated, silent)* As the first action hero, Douglas Fairbanks Sr. doesn't need dialogue. He lets his swashbuckling speak for itself. In this prototypical adventure, our hero swears revenge on pirates who have killed his father. Then he goes out and gets it. The spectacle of Fairbanks plunging his knife into a ship's sail, then slashing his way onto the deck below, is what movies were invented for.

9 INDIANA JONES AND THE TEMPLE OF DOOM *(1984, Paramount, PG)* Indy's second adventure starts

69

out fast with a nightclub free-for-all, slows down just enough to take in a tortuous temple, then speeds up again for a fantastic finish: a high-speed mining-car chase through the innards of a mountain. Zigzagging along on rickety rails, it's the ultimate screen roller-coaster ride.

10 THE FUGITIVE *(1993, Warner, PG-13)* Adapted from the popular 1960s TV series, this movie couldn't match the scope of David Janssen's four-year odyssey. So it did something better: It jam-packed the adventures of fugitive Dr. Richard Kimble (Harrison Ford) into two breathless hours. Attempting to clear his name by finding the man who killed his wife, Kimble leads the cops on a hide-and-seek chase that sprawls across Chicago. Beginning with the best train wreck in movie history, director Andrew Davis keeps the cliffhangers coming. As for Ford, all he does is confirm his standing as *the* action star of his generation.

11 THE LAST OF THE MOHICANS *(1992, FoxVideo, R)* Director Michael Mann takes some welcome liberties with James Fenimore Cooper's musty old frontier tale. Daniel Day-Lewis is surprisingly sleek and sinewy as Hawkeye—and so ruggedly romantic that he commands a love interest (Madeleine Stowe) the novelist never gave him. As the camera glides through the forest on cat feet, Mann stirs up some startlingly vivid battles. You can almost feel the toma-hawks whizzing past your ears. Rarely has a costume adventure seemed so potently primal.

12 INDIANA JONES AND THE LAST CRUSADE *(1989, Paramount, PG-13)* In his third adventure, Indy Jones doesn't do much that he hasn't done before. But this time he does it with Dad, played all gruff and tweedy by the Harrison Ford of the '60s, Sean Connery. As these two tumble in and out of tough scrapes, they bring a new camaraderie to the Indy series—even if they do spend most of the time bitching at each other. Nothing like an honest difference of opinion to ease the tension of being trapped together in a burning château or a nose-diving plane.

13 48 HRS. *(1982, Paramount, R)* Nick Nolte and Eddie Murphy are an improbably perfect pair as a slob cop and a slick con who are forced to work together to track down vicious killers. It's the vola-tility of this star chemistry that makes it work so well. In each other's faces

48 HRS.: **EDDIE MURPHY**

whenever their lives aren't in immediate danger, these two find the comic possibilities in genuine animosity. Lively proof that "buddies" can hate each other and still get the job done.

14 **THE UNTOUCHABLES** *(1987, Paramount, R)* Coming on like gangbusters, Eliot Ness (played Boy Scout straight by Kevin Costner) and street-smart copper Jimmy Malone (Sean Connery, complete with full Irish brogue) lead their intrepid Untouchables against Al Capone (Robert De Niro). Brian De Palma directs the mayhem with tommy-gun explosiveness, building to a train-station shoot-out inspired by Eisenstein's famous Odessa-steps sequence in *Potemkin.* As all hell breaks loose on a marble staircase, the movie shifts into slo-mo, the better to savor De Palma's dazzling dynamics.

15 **LETHAL WEAPON** *(1987, Warner, R)* By the time this movie came along, black-white buddy cops were a screen cliché. But wild man Mel Gibson and family man Danny Glover are a breed apart, playing off their differences like a great comedy team. Of course, it also helps that their pursuit of big-time heroin smugglers hurls them from one astonishing action sequence into another. Rent this with the almost-as-good *Lethal Weapon 2*—but skip *LW 3.*

16 **FROM RUSSIA WITH LOVE** *(1963, MGM/UA, PG)* James Bond's second-best adventure—mainly because it shows him at his most resourceful (and the scriptwriters at theirs). While escorting

LETHAL WEAPON:

MEL GIBSON, DANNY GLOVER

a beautiful defector out of Eastern Europe, Bond (Sean Connery) doesn't rely on too much gadgetry, nor does he have to confront the usual ultravillain out to conquer the world. He does, however, have to contend with an icy assassin (Robert Shaw) and Lotte Lenya's Rosa Klebb, who possesses the movie's most memorable gadget—a poison switchblade in the tip of her sensible shoe.

17 **DIRTY HARRY** *(1971, Warner, R)* Controversial in its time—and still not exactly politically correct—Clint Eastwood's first case as Harry Callahan established him as the enforcer who shoots first and reads rights later. His pursuit of a rooftop serial sniper is low-key by *Lethal Weapon* standards—but that doesn't stop him from gunning down a gang of bank robbers while finishing his lunchtime hot dog. The tough cop by which all the others shall forever be measured.

18 **DIE HARD** *(1988, FoxVideo, R)* Bruce Willis earned his action-star stripes in this high-rise thriller. But the real stars are director John McTiernan and his stunt coordinators. While Willis' off-duty

71

ASSAULT ON PRECINCT 13:
AUSTIN STOKER

detective plays cat and mouse with an office building full of hostage-holding terrorists, the action escalates right through the roof.

19 **ON HER MAJESTY'S SECRET SERVICE** *(1969, MGM/UA, PG)* If Sean Connery had played James Bond on this mission, it might have been the series' best. As it happens, George Lazenby had just inherited the role, which means the movie must get by on its multitiered plot, its exhilarating action (including a climactic battle aboard a runaway bobsled), and leading lady Diana Rigg, the best "Bond girl" of all. Part Emma Peel, part Audrey Hepburn, she was the only one with the right stuff to become Mrs. 007. Too bad Connery wasn't there to make the most of the moment.

20 **THE WARRIORS** *(1979, Paramount, R)* In Walter Hill's vision of urban tribal war, the street gangs wear vividly stylized "colors" (one gang sports New York Yankees–type uniforms and wields baseball bats). You always know exactly who's fighting whom—and that's good, because the fighting almost never stops. A 90-minute chase on and off the subway system, the film barrels along at express-train speed as one gang tries to get from the Bronx to Coney Island while the other gangs try to stop them. A darkly dazzling comic book come to life.

21 **ASSAULT ON PRECINCT 13** *(1976, Facets, R)* In John Carpenter's low-budget classic, the skeleton crew of a ghetto police station fights off a horde of street creeps who are seeking revenge against a locked-up prisoner. It's a *Rio Bravo* for our lawless modern age; once the siege starts, the screen appears to explode in bullets and flying glass. The action is so raw it doesn't seem choreographed, so fast it doesn't seem implausible, and so intense you never ask what it's all about—you just hang on.

22 **SOUTHERN COMFORT** *(1981, Facets, R)* A squad of National Guardsmen goes out on bayou maneuvers. One clown shoots blanks at angry Cajuns, and suddenly these weekend warriors have a real war on their hands. Stalked through the swamp by unseen adversaries, the soldiers drop one by one until only Keith Carradine and Powers Boothe are left to stagger into a backwater village, where you can't tell the hostiles from the friendlies. Director Walter Hill probably meant this as a Vietnam allegory. However you take it, it's harrowing.

23 THE MOST DANGEROUS GAME

(1932, Sinister, B&W, not rated) The people who brought you *King Kong* also cooked up this much-imitated classic. Joel McCrea plays a big-game hunter who finds the tables turned when a shipwreck dumps him on the private island of demented Count Zaroff (Leslie Banks). Something

of a hunter himself, Zaroff sets his guest loose in a primordial jungle, then tracks him down with his huge, hungry hounds. A still-striking depiction of "civilized" man at his most savage.

24 SAHARA

(1943, Facets, B&W, not rated) Stuck behind enemy lines with a broken-down tank and a handful of soldiers, Allied commander Humphrey Bogart has to hold off hundreds of thirsty Germans trying to get at the desert well they're guarding. Bogie

CALCULATED CHAOS

THEY SHOOT, WE KEEP SCORE

Choose your *Weapon*: the first Mel Gibson–Danny Glover action flick (for its nostalgic focus on the detective buddies' old Vietnam days), *Lethal Weapon 2* (for its emphasis on automobile destruction), or *LW3* (for its lively debates on who gets to drive the car). There are even more differences among the films, enumerated below.
—*Bruce Fretts, Kate Meyers*

73

	LETHAL	LETHAL 2	LETHAL 3
Number of cars wrecked	7	14	5
Number of people killed	24	29	16
Number of explosions	3	7	4*
Number of times Mel contemplates suicide	2	0	0
Number of times Mel and Danny remember their days in Vietnam	9	0	0
Number of times Danny says "I'm getting too old for this"	3	1	2
Number of times Joe Pesci says "Okay"	N/A	108	77**
Number of Three Stooges gags	1	5	4
Number of arguments about who is going to drive	3	2	4
Number of times Mel runs after a speeding car	1	2	3
Number of times Mel gets wet	4	2	1

*But the first one's a whopper. **Estimated figure owing to Pesci's machine-gun delivery, okay?

leads the usual ethnic mix, played by an unusually strong supporting cast. Dan Duryea and Lloyd Bridges are among the enlisted heroes who go out in a blaze of glory.

25 KING SOLOMON'S MINES *(1950, Sinister, not rated)* The second filming of the H. Rider Haggard classic—and one of those rare remakes that outdo the original. Stewart Granger is impressively stalwart as adventurer Allan Quartermain, who guides Deborah Kerr through untamed Africa in search of her missing husband. Somewhere at the end of the journey lie the legendary lost diamond mines of the title. Getting there is more than half the fun. Vibrant location footage, in glorious Technicolor, brings the African fauna right into your lap.

26 THE GUNS OF NAVARONE *(1961, Columbia TriStar, not rated)* They don't make these dinosaurs anymore, but when they did, this was the *T. rex.* Gregory Peck, David Niven, and Anthony Quinn head a heavy-artillery cast, as Allied commandos assemble to sabotage huge German guns on an Aegean island. It's one of those top secret missions that take forever to get into gear. But once it does, it thunders along like an armed battalion.

27 ENTER THE DRAGON *(1973, Warner, R)* In his final film, Bruce Lee was poised on the brink of mainstream stardom. Sticking to a plot of sorts, he enters a kung fu tournament on an opium czar's island compound and, in his spare time,

ENTER THE DRAGON: **BRUCE LEE**

spies for British intelligence. Action veteran John Saxon and future martial-arts star Jim Kelly (*Black Samurai*) back Bruce up, ensuring that there's hardly a moment when someone isn't kicking his way through a screenful of acrobatic stuntmen.

28 LA FEMME NIKITA *(1991, Facets, R)* Playing a vicious street punk trained to be a chic assassin, Anne Parillaud shows how lethal a lady in a little black dress can be. Frenchman Luc Besson directs with such Hollywoodized high style that he outguns most recent American films at their own action game. Don't believe it? Rent this alongside *Point of No Return*, the 1993 Bridget Fonda remake.

29 UNDER SIEGE *(1992, Warner, R)* Steven Seagal crosses over from chopsocky in this hijack thriller, which, among other things, shows that he knows the value of self-mocking humor. Wearing a silly chef's hat, he's slaving away in a battleship galley when Tom-

THE MAN WHO WOULD BE ARNOLD

The day is leaning toward 10 p.m. and the cast and crew of Jean-Claude Van Damme's movie *Double Impact* are getting cranky. "Okay," shouts Van Damme, who suddenly decides to entertain the troops during the dinner break, "all the ladies naked now!" He sets aside his Chinese food and saunters through a bunch of production assistants. "Do you know what's great about being a big star?" he asks in his fetching Belgian accent. "I can walk into a movie studio and say, 'You guys want my movie?' And I go [he mimics the sound of flatulence]. And they stay and say, 'Yeah, yeah, we want it!'"

A curious negotiating style, perhaps, but for Van Damme it seems to work. After kick-boxing his way through eight independent films in the last six years, the 30-year-old action mogul signed a three-picture deal with Columbia Pictures that commenced with the release of *Double Impact*. Though Van Damme became a bona fide superstar on video relatively early in his career, he hopes that the support of a major studio will make him a full-fledged box office attraction in the mold of Arnold Schwarzenegger (his idol and favorite topic) and Steven Seagal, both of whom found their original audience in the action-adventure section of the video store. "Right now [producers] want me as an action star because they don't know better," says Van Damme. "Nobody wanted Arnold to do *Twins*. They say, 'It's going to flop.'"

In *Twins* (1988), Schwarzenegger proved he had a warm, fuzzy side. With *Double Impact*, Van Damme hopes to do the same by playing, not coincidentally, twins—one tough, one soft...well, softer. It's his chance to flex his acting skills along with his biceps. "I love karate," he says. "It's like a bible to me, but deep inside I'm so..." He gropes for the English equivalent of the French word. He pounds his chest. "I mean, I'm so sensitive. I can do those movies with a romantic part or a dramatic part. No problem."

Van Damme grew up in Belgium, going to the movies "all the time." In the early '80s, he sold his health club in Brussels and moved to Los Angeles, "naked," he says, except for a black belt and a burning desire to become a star (a sort of Eve Harrington to Arnold's Margo Channing). He learned English on the street, cleaned carpets, and stole food—until he impressed Cannon Pictures chairman Menahem Golan by doing a high kick over the producer's head outside a restaurant. Golan cast him as the lead in the 1988 quickie *Bloodsport*. The movie sold a respectable 2,831,000 tickets, but the video has been rented nearly 20 million times. Naturally, more followed, including *Cyborg* (1989), *Kickboxer* (1989), and *Death Warrant* (1990).

Whether Van Damme can join the ranks of his idol remains to be seen. But his dreams are even mightier than his scissors kick, and that gives him energy to spare. Back on the set, an 18-hour day is coming to an end. Still, Van Damme is strutting around doing what he does best—and loudest: "Do you know who farts most?" he asks an actor before boarding his black Mercedes. "Arnold." —*Jess Cagle*

75

ACTION & MORE

KNOWLEDGE ON THE SLY

On screen, Sylvester Stallone is a man of few words. So when he's not rappelling off a cliff or punching a speed bag, his lines are usually loaded with his special brand of wisdom. Try matching these Sly quotes with their sources. —*Chris Nashawaty*

1. "The world meets nobody halfway. You know what that means—you gotta take it."

2. "I don't want to use my biscuit to sop up some gravy. I got other plans for my biscuit, and they involve butter."

3. "I learn a new word every day. You should expand your vocabulary."

4. "D.T.A.—Don't Trust Anybody. Words to survive by."

5. "I always believed the mind is the best weapon."

6. "My friend let me in one day, and I hit the beef and I kinda liked it."

7. "I don't deal with psychos. I put 'em away."

8. "The more maps you read, the more you know about where you want to go."

9. "I don't want to get promoted. I don't want to get married. I like my life."

10. "At times, I've been accused of being too aggressive in taking criminals off of the streets. If that's a crime, then I'm guilty."

76

Answers: 1. H-*Over the Top*; **2.** D-*Rhinestone*; **3.** A-*Oscar*; **4.** I-*Lock Up*; **5.** E-*Rambo: First Blood Part II*; **6.** C-*Rocky*; **7.** B-*Cobra*; **8.** G-*The Lords of Flatbush*; **9.** F-*Stop! Or My Mom Will Shoot*; **10.** J-*Tango & Cash*.

my Lee Jones and his terrorists storm aboard to seize the warheads. Little do they know that the kitchen help is an ex–Navy SEAL. Seagal supplies the hard-ass heroics, while Jones sails away with the movie as a memorably mad modern pirate.

30 THE THREE MUSKETEERS *(1973, Columbia TriStar, PG)* Richard Lester's version of the oft-told tale is still the one to rent. Spicing his high adventure with ribald wit and throwaway slapstick, the director keeps the pace so rollicking that you almost don't notice there's nothing more at stake than the queen's royal reputation. But of course this only renders the Musketeers' heroics all the more *gallant*. Michael York and Oliver Reed lead a cast that makes Charlie Sheen and his cutups in the 1993 remake look like callow clods.

31 THE SPY WHO LOVED ME *(1977, MGM/UA, PG)* If he's lucky, Roger Moore will be remembered as the second-best Bond. And it will be largely because of this elaborate entry, which makes up in splash and spectacle what it lacks in style and wit. Among its assets: Richard Kiel's first appearance as Jaws, Barbara Bach's delicious turn as Soviet agent XXX, and a first-rate pre-credit sequence in which Moore's stunt double outdoes himself on a breakneck ski slope.

32 MIDNIGHT RUN *(1988, MCA/ Universal, R)* Robert De Niro is loose and funny as a beleaguered bounty hunter, but Charles Grodin nearly pilfers the movie as his booby prize: a former Mob accountant wanted by both the Mob and the FBI. While De Niro tries to get him from New York to L.A. alive, Grodin whines, waxes philosophic, and offers unwanted advice. Not even the shoot-outs can shut him up. Together, this utterly incompatible twosome pulls off the perfect marriage of comedy and action.

33 THE KILLER *(1989, Fox Lorber, not rated)* Hong Kong director John Woo rigs this movie like a fireworks display: One eye-popping gunfight explodes on top of another. Not surprisingly, Woo needs two heroes to maintain the momentum. One (Chow Yun-Fat) is a hit man doing his last job; the other (Danny Lee) is his longtime police nemesis. Together, they seem to mow down the entire criminal element of the eastern hemisphere. By the time they find themselves blowing away zillions of extras, you've come to expect nothing less.

34 THE CRIMSON PIRATE *(1952, Warner, not rated)* In his bright red pants and widescreen smile, Burt Lancaster is brimming with such brio that he surely seems intended as a pirate spoof. Yet his Caribbean exploits are so splashily plotted that they also work as an ebullient boy's adventure. A former acrobat, Lancaster is uniquely suited to the swashbuckling stunts. Whether leaping between windows or skiing down sails, he's nothing short of spectacular.

35 THE MARK OF ZORRO *(1940, FoxVideo, B&W, not rated)* Tyrone Power cuts a dashing figure as Zorro, the masked aven-

THE BASEBALL MOVIE HALL OF FAME

Baseball may be a team sport, but the spotlight usually shines on individual heroics. The same is true of baseball movies, most of which focus on star players in their moments of glory. Accordingly, we've chosen the most memorable screen players for our Baseball Movie Hall of Fame.

FIRST BASE: Gary Cooper, *The Pride of the Yankees* (1942). Cooper's Lou Gehrig matches the Iron Horse of Yankee lore: He's strong, soft-spoken, decent. As American archetypes, the movie star and the ballplayer were virtually interchangeable in 1942. Of course, if Gehrig had been cursed with Cooper's stiff batting stroke, he'd never have hit 493 home runs. On the other hand, if he was really anything like the man Coop makes him out to be, he deserves to be a legend anyway. In black and white.

SECOND BASE, SHORTSTOP: Frank Sinatra and Gene Kelly, *Take Me Out to the Ball Game* (1949). Sinatra is Ryan, the second baseman, Kelly is O'Brien, the shortstop, and they spend more time singing and dancing than they do fielding grounders. This lesser Busby Berkeley film (directed by Stanley Donen and Kelly) is so corny it's almost camp, although Sinatra and Kelly make a great double-play combination.

THIRD BASE, LEFT FIELD: John Cusack and D.B. Sweeney, *Eight Men Out* (1988). As George "Buck" Weaver and "Shoeless" Joe Jackson—the only Chicago "Black Sox" stars who, according to the film, weren't trying to throw the 1919 World Series—Cusack and Sweeney bring a dose of reality to baseball-movie tradition. While most big-screen ballplayers go from underdogs to champions, Cusack and Sweeney sympathetically portray two guys who went the opposite way.

CENTER FIELD: Anthony Perkins, *Fear Strikes Out* (1957). Perkins plays Jimmy Piersall, who overcame mental illness to become a star of the Boston Red Sox between 1952 and 1958. As a player, Perkins runs well, fields okay, hits lousy. Yet he captures Piersall's inner torments, reminding us that sports heroes are human too—an almost subversive message in 1957.

RIGHT FIELD: Robert Redford, *The Natural* (1984). In this adaptation of the 1952 Bernard Malamud novel, Redford is suitably iconic as "middle-aged rookie" Roy Hobbs, a man with a mysterious past and a mythical talent: When he hits the ball, he literally knocks the cover off. If Redford weren't such a natural himself, he'd never have pulled off this role. But the guy's got such a sweet swing that you never doubt the myth for a minute.

CATCHER: Kevin Costner, *Bull Durham* (1988). As journeyman slugger Crash Davis, Costner adds brains and sex appeal to the standard ballplayer profile. Okay, so he's a lifelong minor leaguer. But how many major leaguers could hold their own with Susan Sarandon?

PITCHER: Tatum O'Neal, *The Bad News Bears* (1976). Coach Walter Matthau's star pitcher is spunky and practically unhittable—important qualities when you're the only girl on a misfit Little League team. In her swan song as a tomboy, Tatum supplies the star power to an otherwise motley crew.
—*Michael Sauter*

ger of old Spanish California. But he's just as much fun when he takes off his disguise and becomes Don Diego, the aristocratic fop whose hankie-sniffing act keeps everyone from guessing his secret identity. In what amounts to a dual role, Power is at his peak as a romantic hero.

36 **THE DIRTY DOZEN** *(1967, MGM/UA, PG)* Major Lee Marvin's mission is simple: Take 12 hardened convicts, train them as assassins, then dump them behind enemy lines to kill a houseful of Nazi officers. An extended boot camp is necessary to sort out all the antisocial personalities, but by the time they go into battle, these murderers and rapists are just a grungier version of your basic GI melting pot. An ensemble that includes Charles Bronson, Jim Brown, and John Cassavetes makes it impossible not to root for these bad guys.

37 **NEW JACK CITY** *(1991, Warner, R)* Wesley Snipes plays Nino Brown, the Donald Trump of drug lords: smart, smooth, and filthy rich. Compared with him, the street cops on the case (rapper Ice-T in his starring debut and cartoonishly seedy Judd Nelson) look like small potatoes. But they do carry big guns. Seductive street rhythms pump up this "Just Say No" message movie, directed with a sharp, serrated edge by Mario Van Peebles.

38 **GLORIA** *(1980, Columbia TriStar, PG)* Gena Rowlands is too classy to be running around New York shooting it out with mobsters. That's why watch-

79

ing her do it is such a kick. She's a former Mob moll protecting a little boy whose parents have been rubbed out—and she doesn't even like kids! Director John Cassavetes (Rowlands' husband) tightens up his usual improvisational style but gives free rein to his offbeat sense of humor. The brilliant Mrs. Cassavetes does the rest.

39 JACKIE CHAN'S POLICE STORY
(1985, Facets, not rated) Hong Kong auteur Jackie Chan is a one-man cinematic army: He directs, stars, and does his own stunning stunts. In this charming potboiler, he plays a maverick cop who takes on a powerful drug ring single-handedly (how else?). But ignore the plot mechanics; concentrate instead on the outrageous action sequences—including a downhill car chase that totals an entire peasant village. Elsewhere in the world, Chan is box office dynamite. This movie shows why.

40 CLEOPATRA JONES *(1973, Warner, PG)* Shaft and Superfly have nothing on Cleopatra (Tamara Dobson), the most colorful title character who ever graced a blaxploitation flick. At 6'2" (not counting her Afro or platform shoes), this Amazonian narc makes her presence felt when she comes home to the Los Angeles area of Watts to clean up the neighborhood. Shelley Winters is equally larger than life as the local pusher queen—an orange-haired harridan surrounded by lovely handmaidens. Her final slugfest with Cleo is quite a sight to behold.

GLORIA: GENA ROWLANDS, JOHN ADAMES

1 **THE SEARCHERS** *(1956, Warner, not rated)* The finest film by Hollywood minimalist director John Ford features the finest performance of his acting counterpart, John Wayne. Simmering with grief, rage, and racial hatred, the Duke's Ethan Edwards leads a five-year search for his niece (Natalie Wood) and her Comanche kidnappers. Unfolding across the magnificent Monument Valley in Utah and Arizona, the odyssey alone would have made a great Western. Its depiction of a man at war with his demons makes it a great movie, period.

2 **RED RIVER** *(1948, MGM/UA, B&W, not rated)* This sweeping cattle-drive epic is a *Mutiny on the Bounty* for the open trail. The fact that the antagonists are hard-bitten rancher John Wayne and rebellious adopted son Montgomery Clift makes the conflict even more compelling—and explosive. Director Howard Hawks rustles up plenty of action set pieces but offsets them with campfire scenes full of classical Hawksian touches.

3 **HIGH NOON** *(1952, Facets, B&W, not rated)* Gary Cooper stands tall—and alone—in the ultimate showdown Western. While waiting for four killers to arrive on the noontime train, Coop's middle-aged marshal seeks support from the cowardly townsfolk. As the minutes tick away on various clock faces, it becomes increasingly clear that only his bride (Grace Kelly) will be standing by her man. When it was released, Stanley Kramer's classic production was widely interpreted as a McCarthy-era allegory. More than 40 years later, it's easier to see how timeless its themes really are.

EVERETT COLLECTION

THE SEARCHERS: **JOHN WAYNE**

4 **SHANE** *(1953, Paramount, not rated)* Ex-gunslinger Shane (Alan Ladd) rides down from the hills, helps out some struggling homesteaders (Van Heflin, Jean Arthur), and inevitably must strap on his gun to battle a ruthless rancher. Director George Stevens has mounted it on a conspicuously mythic scale—Shane's blond buckskins look like something Buffalo Bill should have worn—but his cast keeps the movie rooted in solid ground. Jack Palance, as a hired killer, gives a career-defining performance.

5 **STAGECOACH** *(1939, Warner, B&W, not rated)* John Ford's first talkie Western made the genre respectable. Not so coincidentally, it also marked the A-movie breakthrough of its star, John Wayne. As the outlaw Ringo Kid, Wayne rides shot-

81

gun on a horse-drawn *Grand Hotel.* Among his fellow passengers: Claire Trevor as a golden-hearted whore, John Carradine as a silky gambler, and Thomas Mitchell as a drunken doctor who sobers up when it counts. Building this ensemble piece around a masterful Indian chase, Ford showed Hollywood how big a Western could be.

6 LONESOME DOVE *(1989, Cabin Fever, not rated)* It took a TV miniseries to cover all the ground of Larry McMurtry's Pulitzer Prize–winning novel. At eight hours, this cattle-drive saga is epically stuffed with shoot-outs, stampedes, natural disasters—and more memorable characters than your average Shakespeare play. Especially unforgettable are Robert Duvall and Tommy Lee Jones as two old Texas Rangers who decide to blaze one more trail. Deglamorizing the cowboy's life, but reaffirming its romantic lure, *Lonesome Dove* is a neoclassic for an enlightened age.

7 RIDE THE HIGH COUNTRY *(1962, MGM/UA, not rated)* Randolph Scott and Joel McCrea climbed back in the saddle for this Peckinpah masterpiece, set against autumnal mountain backdrops. The two stars play ex-lawmen who ruefully recall their pasts while guarding a wagonload of gold. The last shot of a dying McCrea looking over his shoulder at the frontier he will leave behind is one of the most stirring in Western cinema.

8 UNFORGIVEN *(1992, Warner, R)* Clint Eastwood put a new burnish on his old persona, playing a retired gunman who takes on one more

UNFORGIVEN: CLINT EASTWOOD

job. This wintry morality tale won him his first Oscar, for directing. He probably should have won for his acting, too. Whittling his complex killer down to his bare essentials—so that we can see how conflicted he really is—Eastwood gives a rawhide-tough performance that just may stand as his finest.

9 THE WILD BUNCH *(1969, Warner, R)* Through Sam Peckinpah's lens, the slow-motion eruption of violence became a bloody ballet. It was abstract, poetic, entrancing—and never more profound than in this story of outlaws on the run. William Holden leads his band of robbers south of the border, pursued by the posse of old comrade Robert Ryan. At the end of the line is a Mexican general whose atrocities force the wild bunch to take a moral stand they didn't know they had in them. Video has restored key flashbacks never seen theatrically. They bring out extra facets in an already brilliant film.

10 MY DARLING CLEMENTINE *(1946, FoxVideo, B&W, not rated)* The best OK Corral movie, bar none. Henry Fonda is (un)retired marshal Wyatt Earp, with a never-better Victor Mature as Doc Holliday. Forging their legendary, if unlikely, alliance, they tame the town of Tombstone, sending several Clantons to their graves. Taking place largely at night—the climactic showdown commences at sunrise—this is one of John Ford's most striking black-and-white films. All those rich black shadows seem only to deepen the legend.

11 **SHE WORE A YELLOW RIBBON** *(1949, Turner, not rated)* Monument Valley never seemed more thematically huge than in John Ford's moving ode to old cavalrymen. As John Wayne rides out on his

RIO BRAVO:
ANGIE DICKINSON, JOHN WAYNE

last mission before retirement, the towering buttes seem to stand as memorials to the frontier he helped tame—and as craggy reminders that he didn't finish the job. They are the story of his life. The middle film of Ford's unofficial cav-

alry trilogy stands tall on its own—but should be rented with *Fort Apache* and *Rio Grande* for full epic effect.

12 **RIO BRAVO** *(1959, Warner, not rated)* The jail under siege has been the setting for who knows how many Westerns. But Howard Hawks saw it as the ideal situation for some robust comic characters. John Wayne is the stalwart Sheriff John T. Chance; Dean Martin, the drunken Dude; Rick Nelson, the cocky Colorado; and Walter Brennan, the grumpy Stumpy. Their byplay is so entertaining that it's almost a letdown when the boys put aside their differences to shoot it out with the bad guys.

13 **THE OX-BOW INCIDENT** *(1943, FoxVideo, B&W, not rated)* Henry Fonda rides into a cattle town just in time to be swept up in an angry lynch mob. The rest of the movie takes place in the nearby foothills, where Fonda and his partner (Harry Morgan) watch in horror as the mob condemns and executes three suspected rustlers. Because of its basically passive hero and its apparent refutation of frontier justice, the film is not considered by connoisseurs to be a "true" Western. Okay, so maybe it isn't—but it's a memorable one.

14 **DESTRY RIDES AGAIN** *(1939, MCA/Universal, B&W, not rated)* James Stewart's Destry is an improbable hero: skinny, softspoken, and so pure about keeping the peace that he doesn't even carry a gun. But the fun is in watching him tame a lawless town, using just his wits and his charm. Even more fun is Marlene

83

Dietrich as frontier chanteuse Frenchy, who belts out bawdy barroom songs and has the movie's best fight. Director George Marshall teases genre conventions but respects them too much to trash them. His comic Western stays within the rules and is all the funnier for it.

15 THE MAGNIFICENT SEVEN *(1960, MGM/UA, not rated)* This movie made action stars of half a dozen actors—chief among them Steve McQueen and Charles Bronson—who join up with Yul Brynner to save a Mexican town from marauding bandits. The story was inspired by Akira Kurosawa's *The Seven Samurai*, which had been inspired by the Hollywood Westerns. Director John Sturges brings the idea back home in a blaze of glory.

16 ONCE UPON A TIME IN THE WEST *(1969, Paramount, PG)* Somewhere in here there's a story about the struggle for land that lies in the path of the railroad. But obscuring mere plot details are the outsize shadows cast by a trio of strangers: one good (Charles Bronson), one bad (Jason Robards), one evil (Henry Fonda). Sergio Leone serves up this epic conflict with an operatic Ennio Morricone score and his most mythic spaghetti-Western mise-en-scène: a dusty sunbaked pseudo-Southwest in which ranch houses and railcars are as big inside as the great outdoors.

17 McCABE & MRS. MILLER *(1971, Warner, R)* Robert Altman's version of how the West was won looks and feels like no other. Its landscape is bleak, its people unkempt, its interiors dark and smoky. Warren Beatty is gambler-dreamer McCabe; Julie Christie is displaced madam Mrs. Miller. Together they turn a muddy mining camp into a boom town, then watch mining-company thugs attempt a hostile takeover. The tour de force finale finds antihero McCabe in an ironically heroic position: alone, outnumbered, facing his moment of truth. Set in a cruelly beautiful snowstorm, it's a *High Noon* for the cynical '70s.

18 BUTCH CASSIDY AND THE SUNDANCE KID *(1969, FoxVideo, PG)* Paul Newman and Robert Redford play the West's best-looking outlaws in this witty rewriting of history. Having outlived their era, Butch and Sundance get chased right out of the West by the modernized railroad detectives. On the lam, they gallop into a series of comic adventures that ends in an epic shoot-out with a small army of Bo-

PHOTOFEST

BUTCH CASSIDY AND THE SUNDANCE KID:
PAUL NEWMAN, KATHARINE ROSS,
ROBERT REDFORD

HERB 'N' COWBOYS

Mario Van Peebles may have beefed up *Posse* by casting rap stars and putting hip-hop songs on the soundtrack, but it was Herb Jeffries, the original African-American singing cowboy, who brought black music to the Old West. In 1937, Jeffries starred in Hollywood's first all-black, full-length Western, *Harlem on the Prairie*. A handful of hour-long quickies followed (in which he used his real last name, Jeffrey): *Two-Gun Man From Harlem* (1938), *The Bronze Buckaroo* (1939), *Harlem Rides the Range* (1939), and 1938's *Twenty Notches to Tombstone*. The plots were simple: Run the bad guy off the land and get the girl, though today's audiences might find the implications of a near-white hero defeating the evil, darker-skinned villain offensive.

Jeffries patterned Bob Blake, his fearless alter ego, after his own childhood heroes, movie gunslingers W.S. Hart and Tom Mix. Like them, he became a matinee idol, albeit for the smaller black audience. "I used the same formula," he says. "I didn't smoke or drink or shoot anybody unless it was in self-defense."

With budgets of just $150,000 each, his movies were shot outside Hollywood in Victorville, Calif., in five to seven days. "We got up at the crack of dawn and had to chase the sun over the hill," says Jeffries, who did his own stunts. His cowboy experience later helped him land bit parts in the '60s TV Western *The Virginian*. But singing was his real calling. After writing songs for all his pictures, Jeffries toured with Duke Ellington and recorded the 1941 hit "Flamingo." He made a country album for Warner Bros. in 1993, and, at 83, still tours around the world.

Although he's pleased, Jeffries says he's not surprised by the return of the black Western. "Cowboys are never dated," he insists. "A horse doesn't wear a license plate."
—*Heather Keets*

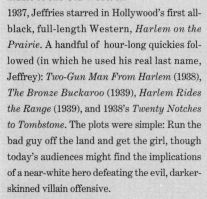

livians. Director George Roy Hill captures their final moment in a sepia-toned freeze-frame. It's almost like seeing a legend being born before your eyes.

19 JEREMIAH JOHNSON (1972, Warner, PG)
Set against an awesome landscape, Sydney Pollack's mountain-man saga is like a legend in its elemental, formative stage—raw, rough-hewn, not yet larger than life. Renouncing civilization, ex-soldier Johnson (Robert Redford) wrests a little piece of the wilderness from hungry wolves, grizzly bears, and inhospitable Indians. Along the way he doesn't talk much, and the movie doesn't miss it.

20 LITTLE BIG MAN (1970, Fox Video, PG)
Adapted from the Thomas Berger novel, Arthur Penn's film was one of the first

Westerns to look at the "winning" of the West from the Indians' point of view. And yet its ironic hero is the decidedly pale-faced Dustin Hoffman. Raised by Cheyennes but destined to be a man without a tribe, Hoffman's Jack Crabb embarks on a picaresque odyssey en route to his fate as the only white survivor of Custer's Last Stand. A sprawling collision of satire, slapstick, and shocking bloodshed, the film effectively shattered all known Western traditions. The genre hasn't been the same since.

21 DANCES WITH WOLVES (1990, Facets, PG-13) Irony of ironies: When Little Big Man took the Cheyenne Indians' point of view, it helped hasten the death of the classical Western. But when director-star Kevin Costner celebrated the Sioux in this multiple-Oscar winner, he almost single-handedly revived the genre. The film's real achievement isn't that it explores the flip side of Western myth but that, in doing so, it makes the frontier seem like virgin movie territory again. Whether hunting buffalo, smoking with the chief, or dancing with a wolf, Costner almost makes you believe he's the first white man to do it.

22 THE SHOOTIST (1976, Paramount, PG) As an old gunfighter dying of cancer—but determined to go on his own terms—an ailing John Wayne found the fitting coda for his 48-year career. Directed by Don Siegel, the film is somberly shaded, with glints of gallows humor. We watch as this living legend makes peace with himself, puts his affairs in order, and cleans his gun in preparation for one last glorious showdown. James Stewart and Lauren Bacall add grace notes to a lovely swan song.

23 THE VIRGINIAN (1929, Facets, B&W, not rated) Based on Owen Wister's myth-affirming novel, this cowboys-and-rustlers story was the first important Western of the talkie era. Star Gary Cooper's long, lanky frame shaped the mold for the archetypal Western hero. But for all its historical importance, this chestnut holds up as entertainment, too. Highlighted by roguish humor, aw-shucks romance, and one manfully moving scene at a hanging tree, the movie is nearly as vital now as it was at the dawn of the sound age.

24 THE GUNFIGHTER (1950, FoxVideo, B&W, not rated) Seeking to rekindle an old flame—and meet the son he's never

LITTLE BIG MAN: DUSTIN HOFFMAN

KOBAL COLLECTION

86

known—famous gunfighter Gregory Peck stays too long in a town full of men who want to shoot down his legend. The story's a well-worn cliché now, but this is the original, and still definitive, version. As he hunches over his whiskey in a nearly deserted saloon, Peck's haunted eyes and heavy-hanging mustache etch a telling portrait of loneliness and regret.

25 **THE NAKED SPUR** *(1953, MGM/UA, not rated)* Director Anthony Mann made a passel of minor classics; perhaps the best was this tautly woven tale. Mann's favorite star, James Stewart, plays an amateur bounty hunter escorting killer Robert Ryan through the breathtaking Rocky Mountains. Along for the ride are Janet Leigh, as Ryan's loyal girlfriend, and Ralph Meeker and Millard Mitchell, as two money-grubbers who've declared themselves Stewart's "partners." The constantly shifting alliances make those mountain trails even more precipitously treacherous.

26 **WINCHESTER '73** *(1950, MCA/Universal, B&W, not rated)* When James Stewart gets bushwhacked and loses his favorite firearm, he sets off in grim pursuit to get it back. Meanwhile, the rifle repeatedly changes hands, in a rapid-fire chain of events that bracingly dramatizes the kill-or-be-killed code of the West. In Anthony Mann's hands, every plot turn clicks like the tumblers in a Wells Fargo safe.

27 **BUCK AND THE PREACHER** *(1972, Columbia TriStar, PG)* Ever the pioneer,

BUCK AND THE PREACHER:
SIDNEY POITIER

Sidney Poitier made movie history by directing the first black Western released by a major studio. Poitier also stars as the trail guide Buck, who leads wagon trains of ex-slaves to the frontier promised land. Teaming with Harry Belafonte's con-man "preacher" (who keeps a gun in his hollow Bible), Buck joins the ranks of all true Western heroes, shooting it out with a gang of racist marauders—and coming out on top. Among its other overdue revisions, this movie features the refreshing sight of Indians riding to the rescue. Call it poetic license—or poetic justice.

28 **THE GOOD, THE BAD, AND THE UGLY** *(1967, MGM/UA, R)* The man with no name reached mythic proportions in the third collaboration between Clint Eastwood and Sergio Leone. Stylized over the top, the movie pits Eastwood's antihero against two even less heroic outlaws (Lee Van Cleef, Eli Wallach) in a cutthroat quest for a buried cache of gold. With its huge close-ups, stark desert vistas, and sprawling battle scenes, the film loses something on video. But what remains is a uniquely iconoclastic vision of what it took to win the West.

29 HIGH PLAINS DRIFTER *(1973, MCA/Universal, R)* Clint Eastwood's title character is another kind man with no name: He rides out of the shimmering desert heat to take his revenge on a desolate town with a guilty past. Eastwood is either a ghost or a dead man's avenging twin. But though his identity is ambiguous, everything else is strikingly vivid. Eastwood the director pays homage to Sergio Leone, but the most inspired images are his own: His vision of the whole town painted red and renamed Hell established him as a director to be reckoned with.

30 CAT BALLOU *(1965, Columbia TriStar, not rated)* Jane Fonda kids her early ingenue image as Catherine Ballou, a schoolmarmish maiden who turns outlaw to avenge her father's death and win back his ranch. Riding with her is a motley gang who can't shoot straight—among them gunfighter (and Oscar winner) Lee Marvin, a falling-down drunk on an equally shaky horse. Done balladstyle, with Nat "King" Cole and Stubby Kaye as a banjo-strumming Greek chorus, this farce kicks up a ruckus with Western clichés and turns them into a breath of fresh air.

MYSTERY/ SUSPENSE

1 VERTIGO *(1958, MCA/Universal, PG)* A clinical depiction of psychosis that stars Jimmy Stewart, and the closest Alfred Hitchcock came to splattering his own neuroses across the screen. It's a simple plot, really: Phobic police detective falls for friend's wife, torments self with guilt when she dies, then flips out over girl who looks just like her. With a swooning Bernard Herrmann score and sphinxlike Kim Novak, this can be read as a metaphor for the way that men—and film directors—manipulate women to match some ivory ideal in their heads. And it's a hell of a thriller, too.

THE MALTESE FALCON: HUMPHREY BOGART

2 THE BIG SLEEP *(1946, MGM/UA, B&W, not rated)* Don't worry about keeping the story line straight: Raymond Chandler couldn't either—and he wrote it. Philip Marlowe, however, has it figured out, and that's what counts. As Marlowe, Humphrey Bogart is the ultimate private eye—sharp, cool, and tough in the clinches. But he does have his hands full with Lauren Bacall as a sultry rich girl in trouble, Martha Vickers as her thumb-suckingly vixenish little sister, and Dorothy Malone as a seductress in a bookshop. Howard Hawks nimbly navigates the twisting, turning script, written by, among others, William Faulkner.

3 THE MALTESE FALCON *(1941, MGM/UA, B&W, not rated)* Everyone wants the precious statue known as the Black Bird—but nobody knows who has it. As Peter Lorre, Sidney Greenstreet, and other shady characters converge on a sound-stage-created San Francisco, Humphrey Bogart's Sam Spade finds himself the man in the middle. Pretty soon he's the center of attention, outfoxing these double-dealers at their own game. First-time director John Huston masterfully pulls together the plot threads. Of course, he had masterful source material, courtesy of mystery writer Dashiell Hammett.

4 THE 39 STEPS *(1935, Facets, B&W, not rated)* This is the British Hitchcock film that made America and Hollywood sit up and take notice of the masterful director (it was known as "the mortgage lifter" for indebted movie houses). All the trademark motifs are here—the innocent man (Robert Donat) wrongly accused of murder, the nest of spies led by an upper-class smoothy, the icy blond (Madeleine Carroll) who thaws under the hero's bluff warmth. Crackerjack entertainment, with two lastingly surreal touches: a missing finger and a music-hall performer who does his job fatally well.

5 LAURA *(1944, FoxVideo, B&W, not rated)* Otto Preminger's creamy suspense-romance is one of the kinkier movies to come out of Hollywood. Detective Dana Andrews skirts necrophilia as he falls in love with murder victim Laura Hunt. But—surprise—she's alive, and played by Gene Tierney, so it's up to him to find out who wanted her dead in the first place. There are plenty of suspects, and they're all pretty twisted; even sweet Laura herself is something of a basket case. Featuring David Raksin's swooning title theme—maybe the most famous movie music ever.

6 THE THIN MAN *(1934, MGM/UA, B&W, not rated)* Nobody tackles a mystery with more style than Nick and Nora Charles, those independently wealthy amateur detectives who solve murders while trading witty banter and tossing down martinis. They're so screwball funny (and sexy) that they don't really need the murder plots to keep us (or themselves) entertained. Yet William Powell's Nick is never more dashing than when he's in danger, and Myrna Loy's Nora is never more delightful. And pet pooch Asta is always ready to lend a paw. The first, and best, of a scintillating series.

89

7 REAR WINDOW *(1954, MCA/Universal, PG)* James Stewart peeps into the apartments across the way and discovers a wife killer (Raymond Burr, timid and lethal). This may be Hitchcock's best-crafted movie. Watch it twice: once for the sheer enjoyment of it, the second time to notice how each of those apartments contains a variation on Stewart's fears of marriage to girlfriend Grace Kelly—and to see how closely his peeping resembles the way we watch movies.

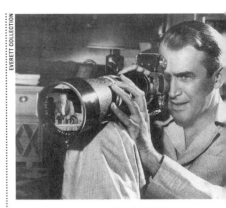

REAR WINDOW: JAMES STEWART

8 THE POSTMAN ALWAYS RINGS TWICE *(1946, MGM/UA, B&W, not rated)* From the moment John Garfield sees Lana Turner in her white short shorts and turban, it's only a matter of time before he agrees to help her kill her husband. James M. Cain, who wrote the novel, was a master of marital murder, but this one is special. Under Tay Garnett's direction, Garfield and Turner don't just throw off heat; they actually seem in love. When final justice is served, their fate seems almost tragic.

9 THE SILENCE OF THE LAMBS *(1991, Facets, R)* Anthony Hopkins' Hannibal Lecter is among the most malevolent madmen in movie history. And he's only one of two psycho killers terrorizing this film. Jodie Foster (who took home her second Oscar for this role) plays an FBI agent who needs Lecter's help to catch a serial killer. Cutting between the killer at large (Ted Levine) and the killer in custody (Hopkins), director Jonathan Demme serves up one dread chill after another. But nothing is scarier than what Hopkins can do with that coldly insinuating voice and those ice-blue eyes. Brrr.

10 NORTH BY NORTHWEST *(1959, MGM/UA, not rated)* Alfred Hitchcock's most lighthearted wrong-man confection borders on the actively surreal. Cary Grant is a poised Manhattan ad exec who gets mistaken for a U.S. intelligence agent, framed for a murder in the lobby of the U.N., and attacked by a crop duster in the Midwest, only to end up hanging with Eva Marie Saint from Mount Rushmore while a homosexual thug (Martin Landau) stomps on his hand. The title is from *Hamlet,* and it doesn't mean a damned thing.

11 NOTORIOUS *(1946, FoxVideo, B&W, not rated)* Ingrid Bergman is a spy in the house of love in Hitchcock's gorgeously cruel melodrama. The emphasis is more on tormented romance than on espionage thrills: While you'll squirm in suspense as Bergman marries ex-Nazi Claude Rains and searches his house for secrets of the Reich, Hitch is more interested in her relationship with boss Cary

Grant. It's a portrait of love as emotional S&M, and, in the censor-be-damned kiss sequence, it's amazingly sexy.

12 KISS ME DEADLY *(1955, MGM/UA, B&W, not rated)* Mickey Spillane's Mike Hammer was never much of a sleuth, but he sure knew how to slug his way to the bottom of a mystery. Here Hammer (played hard as nails by Ralph Meeker) gives a ride to a scared hitchhiker; the next thing he knows, she's dead. Being Mike Hammer, he's got to find out why. Director Robert Aldrich busts the private-eye genre out of the button-down '50s with a dazzling display of camera angles. True to its underworld milieu, the movie's as hip, jazzy, and jagged as a broken beer bottle.

13 THE BIG HEAT *(1953, Columbia TriStar, B&W, not rated)* Glenn Ford is relentless as a cop who snoops around a fishy suicide case until his wife is killed by a car bomb meant for him. Then he gets really intense. Quitting the corrupt police force, Ford goes after the mobsters behind the murder. Along the way, he gets help from Mob moll Gloria Grahame, who wants to get even with boyfriend Lee Marvin for throwing hot coffee in her face. A scalding movie in more ways than one, directed by master Fritz Lang.

14 IN THE LINE OF FIRE *(1993, Columbia TriStar, R)* Clint Eastwood is compellingly fallible as an aging Secret Service man matching wits with a psycho stalking the President. Increasing the stakes, the movie saddles its hero with guilt for not having saved JFK—as if the normal fears and self-doubts wouldn't have been awesome enough. Of course, John Malkovich's reptilian performance helps make this more than just another assassination-plot movie.

15 STRANGERS ON A TRAIN *(1951, Warner, B&W, not rated)* Hitchcock sure knew how to cast a killer—but few of them were creepier than Robert Walker as the wacko rich kid Bruno Anthony. Meeting Farley Granger on a train, he playfully suggests a murder swap: He'll kill Granger's estranged wife if Granger will kill Walker's domineering dad. Imagine Granger's surprise when Walker carries out his end of the deal. Your turn, old boy! The climax, on a whirling carousel, is as visually exciting as it is dramatically satisfying.

16 CHARADE *(1963, MCA/Universal, not rated)* Audrey Hepburn barely hangs on to her famous poise as an American in Paris pursued by men who think she

IN THE LINE OF FIRE: **CLINT EASTWOOD**

91

has their gold. Enter Cary Grant as a mystery man who charms her off her feet while coming to the rescue. Or is he one of the bad guys? You're never quite sure, and that's part of the fun—along with the bull-in-a-china-shop villainy of James Coburn and George Kennedy and the droll, deadpan performance of Walter Matthau as a CIA man. Or is he one of the bad guys?

17 BODY HEAT *(1981, Warner, R)* Lawrence Kasdan's neo–film noir may be largely pastiche, but William Hurt and Kathleen Turner are playing it for keeps. Everyone remembers the passion with which Hurt threw that chair through the plate-glass door to get at his femme fatale. Watch this one again to see how much feeling he puts into murdering Richard Crenna. This is the real thing.

18 THE LADY FROM SHANGHAI *(1948, Columbia TriStar, B&W, not rated)* "When I start out to make a fool of myself, there's very little can stop me," says protagonist Orson Welles, recounting the details of how he was framed for murder. As film noir goes, this is a decidedly artsy affair; Welles' stylized visuals are deliriously dreamlike. Finally, the style *is* the substance. From Rita Hayworth's shocking platinum hair to the famous hall-of-mirrors shoot-out, this film is a stunner.

19 AND THEN THERE WERE NONE *(1945, Facets, B&W, not rated)* Agatha Christie's classic gathers 10 guilty guests together in a gloomy private-island mansion, then starts killing them off one by one.

But who's the murderer? Is it their unseen host, or one of them? The trick, as always in a Christie mystery, is to try to outguess the movie's sleuths. The fact that the sleuths are also the suspects and are comically insulted to be under suspicion only adds to the fun. René Clair directs a classy ensemble led by Walter Huston and Barry Fitzgerald.

20 MURDER ON THE ORIENT EXPRESS *(1974, Paramount, PG)* The ultimate all-star whodunit. Richard Widmark is murdered on the snowbound *Orient Express*, and it's up to Hercule Poirot (an almost unrecognizable Albert Fin-

THE LADY FROM SHANGHAI:
ORSON WELLES, RITA HAYWORTH

ney) to find the guilty party. Among the likely suspects: Lauren Bacall, Ingrid Bergman, Sean Connery, Anthony Perkins, Vanessa Redgrave, and Michael York. The cast alone would have made this worth the trip.

21 MARATHON MAN *(1976, Paramount, R)* This highly charged thriller (adapted

AN ALIEN COP, ITS WIFE & HER LOVER

On those nights when the new releases are rented out, video stores seem to carry just one film— with 5,000 copies in stock. And all B movies on tape appear to have the same title and plot. To see what we mean, match the title (left) with the appropriate plot summary (right). —*Nisid Hajari*

1.	*Caged Fear*	A.	Reporter hunts ruthless politician.
2.	*Haunting Fear*	B.	Ruthless businessman hunts guests.
3.	*Midnight Fear*	C.	Sheriff hunts ruthless businessman.
4.	*The Fear Inside*	D.	Sheriff hunts homicidal maniac.
5.	*Class of Fear*	E.	Town hunts homicidal maniac.
6.	*Blind Vision*	F.	Undercover cop hunts homicidal maniac.
7.	*Murderous Vision*	G.	Detective hunts serial killer.
8.	*Double Vision*	H.	Detective and psychic hunt serial killer.
9.	*Double Cross*	I.	Burnt-out cop hunts serial killer.
10.	*Double Trouble*	J.	Reporter and editor hunt serial killer.
11.	*Double Impact*	K.	Detective hunts terrorists.
12.	*Final Impact*	L.	Detective hunts homicidal vampire.
13.	*Final Embrace*	M.	Planet attacked by homicidal monster.
14.	*Deadbolt*	N.	Agoraphobe attacked by homicidal roommate.
15.	*Dead Certain*	O.	Med student attacked by homicidal roommate.
16.	*Dead Space*	P.	New kid attacked by homicidal peers.
17.	*Deadly Bet*	Q.	Kickboxer attacked by Vegas gangster.
18.	*Deadly Game*	R.	Kickboxer trains new kickboxer.
19.	*Deadly Conspiracy*	S.	Kickboxer discovers grisly murder.
20.	*Out for Blood*	T.	Kickboxer avenges wife's murder.
21.	*Blood on the Badge*	U.	Kickboxer avenges brother's murder.
22.	*Bloodfist IV*	V.	Photographer avenges brother's murder.
23.	*Blood Clan*	W.	Kickboxing twins avenge father's murder.
24.	*Pale Blood*	X.	Fist-fighting twins bust smuggling ring.
25.	*Kill Line*	Y.	Woman avenges twin sister's murder.
26.	*Killer Image*	Z.	Woman driven insane by husband's affair.
27.	*The Killing Mind*	AA.	Woman jailed for husband's crime.
28.	*Love Kills*	BB.	Woman's lovers killed by homicidal maniac.
29.	*To Catch a Killer*	CC.	Woman takes a homicidal lover.
30.	*Whisper Kill*	DD.	Homicidal maniac stalks music-video world.

93

Answers: 1. AA; 2. Z; 3. D; 4. N; 5. P; 6. BB; 7. H; 8. Y; 9. A; 10. X; 11. W; 12. R; 13. DD; 14. O; 15. I; 16. M; 17. Q; 18. B; 19. C; 20. T; 21. K; 22. S; 23. E; 24. L; 25. U; 26. V; 27. F; 28. CC; 29. G; 30. J

CLEAN UP THIS WORLD BY SUNDOWN

There's one sure way to communicate the message that environmentalism is good: Show that people who hurt the environment are bad. Combining black hats and green consciousness, a number of post–Cold War action-adventure movies feature villains who are enemies of the earth.

THE NAKED GUN 2½: THE SMELL OF FEAR *(1991)* **Villain:** Oil-company magnate Quentin Hapsburg. **Treachery:** Kidnaps a prominent scientist scheduled to deliver a pro-energy-efficiency policy speech and replaces him with an evil doppelgänger. **Resolution:** Hapsburg falls out a window and is mauled on the sidewalk by a lion; real scientist gives his speech.

TEENAGE MUTANT NINJA TURTLES II: THE SECRET OF THE OOZE *(1991)* **Villain:** Shredder. **Treachery:** Uses toxic waste to mutate wolf and snapping turtle into monsters to destroy hero turtles; threatens to use ooze for future mutations. **Resolution:** Shredder becomes huge after ingesting a vial of the substance, but he's killed while fighting the heroes.

THE RESCUERS DOWN UNDER *(1990, animated)* **Villain:** Hulking poacher McLeach. **Treachery:** Ensnares a rare eagle for profit; holds kangaroos, koalas, and other animals captive for their skins. **Resolution:** McLeach is pushed into a river full of crocodiles, then goes over a waterfall; brave mice save the eagle.

IT ZWIBBLE: EARTHDAY BIRTHDAY *(1990, animated)* **Villain:** Garbage-loving Queen of the Dump. **Treachery:** Her minions litter a stream and misdirect invitations to an Earth Day party thrown by dinosaurs. **Resolution:** Magic dust brings children to the celebration; Queen craves more garbage in which to wallow.

STAR TREK VI: THE UNDISCOVERED COUNTRY *(1991)* **Villain:** General Chang, chief Klingon warmonger. **Treachery:** He symbolizes the Klingons' contempt for their environment, which leads to ozone-layer depletion and subsequent destruction of power-generating moon Praxis. **Resolution:** Chang is phaser-blasted away in battle with the *Enterprise*.

—*Doug Brod*

94

by William Goldman from his novel) is paced by Dustin Hoffman as a graduate student and runner-in-training being pursued by Laurence Olivier as a Nazi war criminal on the run. For those who care, there's a complex plot having to do with hidden jewels and concentration-camp victims—but ultimately the chase is all that really matters. In the most talked-about scene, Olivier employs a torture technique to which we can all relate: taking a dentist's drill to Hoffman's teeth. Just the sound of this scene gets most people screaming.

22 **WAIT UNTIL DARK** *(1967, Warner, not rated)* Poor Audrey Hepburn's in trouble again. Her husband has unwittingly brought home a heroin shipment hidden in a doll, and the smugglers will do anything to get it back. Hepburn is alone and oblivious and—oh, yeah—she's blind. The deservedly famous finale pits ruthless Alan Arkin against terrified Hepburn in a little apartment. Then the lights go out. If you don't jump the first time you watch this scene, you must be dead already.

23 **PLAY MISTY FOR ME** *(1971, MCA/Universal, R)* In his directing debut, Clint Eastwood gives himself an atypical role. As a late-night deejay stalked by a recent one-night stand, he's practically passive—until he must race to rescue his girlfriend Donna Mills in her pitch-dark house, high above the Pacific. But the real star here is Jessica Walter, who is Eastwood's nightmare date: Gradually evolving from possessive to manic-obsessive, she's as scary as Jack the Ripper—and just as handy with a knife.

24 **THREE DAYS OF THE CONDOR** *(1975, Paramount, R)* Post-Watergate paranoia propels this thriller, released at the height of our national mistrust—the same year the CIA was accused of planning to kill newspaper columnist Jack Anderson. Ironically, the film's hero (Robert Redford) is a CIA man: an innocent researcher who accidentally uncovers a dirty company secret. He comes back from lunch to find his coworkers slaughtered, then spends the rest of the film on the run through a Christmastime New York that is quickly closing in on him. Sydney Pollack directs, with a stranglehold.

25 **COMA** *(1978, MGM/UA, PG)* Doctor Geneviève Bujold turns resident detective when comatose patients start disappearing from her hospital. On paper, Robin Cook's book requires a strenuous suspension of disbelief. On screen, doctor-turned-director Michael Crichton peels away the plot layers with such surgical skill that you're as helpless to resist as a person on an operating table. Try watching the chamber-full-of-bodies scene without at least a little shudder.

26 **BLOOD SIMPLE** *(1984, MCA/Universal, R)* Writer-director Joel Coen and writer-producer Ethan Coen burst onto the movie scene with this mock film noir, and although they've loaded it up with genre jokes and camera tricks, they've also given it a gripping script. John Getz and Frances McDormand are

95

ACTION & MORE

actually sympathetic as the illicit lovers marked for murder, and Dan Hedaya is memorably mean as the cuckolded husband whose murder plot backfires. But M. Emmet Walsh walks off with the film as a sleazeball private eye who double-crosses everyone and kills nearly all of them for good measure.

FATAL ATTRACTION:
GLENN CLOSE, MICHAEL DOUGLAS

27 **CAPE FEAR** *(1991, MCA/ Universal, R)* In the first *Cape Fear,* upright Gregory Peck fights fire with fire to rid himself of mad stalker Robert Mitchum. In this Martin Scorsese remake, Nick Nolte plays a less sterling hero who finds himself sinking to Robert De Niro's level, with help from various corrupt cops and lawyers. Everyone here is guilty. It's not a question of good over evil; it's more like survival of the fiercest. Fittingly, the final confrontation takes place in a swamp, during an apocalyptic rainstorm. It's bloodily bleak.

28 **FATAL ATTRACTION** *(1987, Paramount, R)* Glenn Close is electrifying as every married man's worst nightmare.

After spending a wild weekend with somebody else's husband (Michael Douglas), she stalks him with a single-minded intensity that gets more warped as it goes. The boiled bunny is her most vivid atrocity, but some of her subtler mind games linger a lot longer. Adrian Lyne's direction is a bit calculated—but then, so is a steel trap.

29 **MISERY** *(1991, Columbia TriStar, R)* Seen strictly as a quasi-horror thriller, *Misery* should keep you on the edge of the couch without grossing you out. And as a nifty piece of filmmaking, which literalizes the stereotype of the tortured artist, it won't insult your intelligence or good taste, either. In this film version of the Stephen King novel, James Caan is Paul Sheldon, a commercially successful writer of formula romance novels who goes to the Colorado Rockies to write a real book for a change. After a car crash, he is nursed to health/taken prisoner by his "No. 1 fan," world-class psychopath Annie Wilkes (Kathy Bates, who picked up an Oscar for her splendid performance). His battle to survive the violent schizophrenic mood swings of his tormentor provides the film with an eerie and intellectually engaging terror. You keep wondering, "What would I do if I were Paul?"

30 **DEAD AGAIN** *(1991, Paramount, R)* In this engrossing romantic thriller, amnesiac Emma Thompson is tormented by nightmares of a murder committed before she was born. Then she meets dreamboat Kenneth Branagh (*Henry V*), a private detective who takes a stab at resolving her transcendental trauma. Soon the two feel as if they've known each other all their lives, and in fact they have: Under the spell of hypnotist Derek Jacobi, they discover that they're reincarnated lovers linked by a crime of passion. With its stylized black-and-white sequences and fast-paced melodramatic plot, this homage to film noir is both intense and purposely self-conscious—and on the small screen, where remote-happy viewers are already used to genre jumping, star director Branagh's time-shifting technique is particularly effective.

Reviews written by Michael Sauter, as well as Ty Burr, Bruce Forer, and Jill Rachlin.

A DIRECTOR UNDER THE INFLUENCE

HERBERT GEHR/LIFE

From Brian De Palma to Danny DeVito, every director who has tried a crane shot has been labeled "Hitchcockian"—and it's true, Alfred Hitchcock was certainly one of the movies' most influential innovators. What nobody points out, though, is that even Hitch was influenced by other directors. Notably:

F.W. Murnau: His purely visual storytelling approach inspired Hitchcock, beginning with his 1926 thriller, *The Lodger.*

D.W. Griffith: Hitch appropriated chase and last-minute rescue motifs for many films, from *Blackmail* (1929) to *Family Plot* (1976).

Luis Buñuel: Hitch's penchant for dream sequences came from Surrealism, particularly Buñuel's 1928 *Un Chien Andalou* (made with Salvador Dalí, a collaborator on 1945's *Spellbound*).

Sergei Eisenstein: The crosscuts between the amorous couple (Grace Kelly and Cary Grant) and fireworks in *To Catch a Thief* (1955) pay homage to Eisenstein's use of montage.

Henri-Georges Clouzot: Reportedly envious of Clouzot's 1955 thriller, *Diabolique*, Hitchcock fashioned *Psycho* (1960) as a similarly bleak black-and-white film.

Michelangelo Antonioni: Blown away by *Blow Up* in 1966, the aging master of suspense began regularly screening current films. Discovering a new freedom, Hitch included nudity and a graphic strangulation in 1972's *Frenzy.* —*Tim Purtell*

97

SCI-FI & MORE

AROUND THE TIME movies started going onto video and into the home, so did the genres of science fiction and horror, led by 1977's *Close Encounters* (suburbia ain't alone anymore—see No. 4) and 1978's *Halloween* (suburbia ain't safe anymore—see No. 20). Coincidence? To quote *The Twilight Zone*: *Dee*dle-deedle-*dee*dle-deedle.

Both genres have their limitations. Horror fads come and go (think of all those famous monsters, possessed children, and diced teenagers), while sci-fi can't help but suffer in comparison with the *real* future when it arrives. The related fantasy genre has it easier: If horror wants to remind us of our mortality, and science fiction wants to sober us into thinking about the larger consequences, fantasy is a mental vacation—sort of like Bermuda with hobbits.

And yet all three styles persist, even on the home screen with the lights on. We still shriek and clutch each other when Mrs. Bates enters the bathroom, we stretch our minds to accommodate *2001* (see No. 10), and we're awed by the playful razzle-dazzle of *Star Wars* (see No. 7). Perhaps daydreams and nightmares are just what the movies do best. If so, here are the best of the best.

1 **PSYCHO** *(1960, MCA/Universal, B&W, R)* The film that cut movie history in half: When that knife came swooping past the shower curtain at Marion Crane (Janet Leigh), Hitchcock was announcing that from then on, no one was safe, that a heroine could be butchered before the movie was half over, and that a nice young man like Norman Bates (Anthony Perkins) might have some serious skeletons in his closet. Shot in chintzy black and white on a TV budget, *Psycho* marks the point where the contemporary movie era—the age of sensation over sentiment—began.

2 **JAWS** *(1975, MCA/Universal, PG)* "You're gonna need a bigger boat," the shark hunter said. That's for sure. This landmark thriller was made by Steven Spielberg the hungry young tyro as opposed to Spielberg the beloved family entertainer, and the difference between the two is palpable. The premise is as simple as boy meets girl; here it's huge killer shark meets thriving resort town. Roy Scheider as the town's manic top cop, Richard Dreyfuss as the brilliant but callow fish expert, and Robert Shaw as the enigmatic old salt all create vivid characterizations that make this movie more than the world's scariest water ride.

3 **KING KONG** *(1933, Turner, B&W, not rated)* Forgive its clipped, hammy acting and the titular behemoth's labored ascent up the Empire State Building, and you still have an enormously entertaining urban myth. Mirroring the film's shameless huckster, who delights in showing the public the Eighth Wonder of the World, directors Merian C. Cooper and Ernest B. Shoedsack seem to take great pleasure in showcasing their gimmicky twist on *Beauty and the Beast*. With astounding (for their time) special effects by Willis O'Brien.

4 **CLOSE ENCOUNTERS OF THE THIRD KIND** *(1977, Columbia TriStar, PG)* Unlike *E.T.* or *Hook*, Steven Spielberg's UFO drama delivers wonder from a *grown-up*'s point of view: It plays like a Frank Capra movie with a big budget and a metaphysical grandeur. Richard Dreyfuss is fine as our Everyman—his actor's fussiness is balanced by the film's grand scale—but the director is really the star here. His magical Hollywood optimism is evident in everything from the toys that come to life in Cary Guffey's bedroom to the mind-blowing bulk of the mothership. A reedited "Special Edition" is available on videotape, and it's the preferred version.

KING KONG: **FAY WRAY AND FRIEND**

5 **NIGHT OF THE LIVING DEAD** *(1968, Republic, B&W, not rated)* From out of nowhere—well, Pittsburgh, actually—George Romero and company galvanized the country by making the goriest, most creepily claustrophobic horror film of its time. Other movies have crassly upped *Night*'s gross-out quotient, but none has been as deeply, resonantly disturbing as this. A disparate group of people take refuge in an abandoned house when the countryside is suddenly besieged by flesh-eating zombies. By the time the absurd explanation for the zombies comes around, you won't care about how ridiculous it is; you'll be captivated by the suffocating tension. The movie's threadbare black-and-white look was probably more a function of its budget than a deliberate strategy, but boy, does it work—the grainy film stock feels as old as death itself.

6 **FREAKS** *(1932, MGM/UA, B&W, not rated)* One of the most disturbing exploitation films ever made, this tale of life among circus sideshow performers packs a horrific punch more than 60 years after it was made. Populating the film with real-life midgets, pinheads, and sundry other unfortunates, director Tod Browning (*Dracula*, 1931) creates a climate of dread heightened by an unforgettable banquet scene and one of the most shocking finales ever filmed.

7 **STAR WARS** *(1977, FoxVideo, PG)* George Lucas took his private tales of space-age heroes and villains and turned them into everybody's Big Myth. *Star Wars* changed the movies: After a decade of counterculture

narrative, it reintroduced the notion of spectacle; it transformed the special-effects industry and made audiences realize films could take them *anywhere*; and it helped create the modern Hollywood marketing behemoth. In essence, this is the greatest of all movie ma-

STAR WARS: PETER MAYHEW, MARK HAMILL, ALEC GUINNESS, HARRISON FORD

chines: What we remember isn't so much the plot—or even the characters—as the high-flying *exuberance* of the whole package.

8 **THE BRIDE OF FRANKENSTEIN** *(1935, MCA/Universal, B&W, not rated)* The original *Frankenstein* is pretty great, but the sequel is where director James Whale—one of Hollywood's most gifted eccentrics—really cut loose. Startlingly, this is primarily a *comedy*, albeit of a dark tongue-in-cheek hue. Boris Karloff and Colin Clive are back as monster and creator respectively, and Elsa Lanchester plays both Karloff's birdlike intended and (in a prologue) author Mary Shelley herself. Still, it's Ernest Thesiger who steals the creepshow as the mildewed, maleficent Dr. Pretorious.

KOBAL COLLECTION

101

9 ALIENS *(1986, FoxVideo, R)* Here's one of those anomalies: a sequel that manages to leave its admittedly great source film in the cinematic dust. Director James Cameron applies his breathtaking command of action filmmaking to craft a horror movie that moves the viewer emotionally. Sigourney Weaver is back as Ripley, doing battle with—literally—the mother of all space creatures on a return trip to the shoulda-been-forbidden planet. (Another sequel, *Alien³*, was lost in space.)

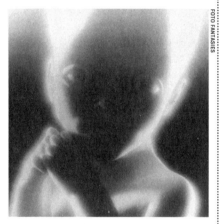

2001: A SPACE ODYSSEY

10 2001: A SPACE ODYSSEY *(1968, MGM/UA, G)* For some, Stanley Kubrick's adaptation of an Arthur C. Clarke short story was a mindblower; for others, a head-scratcher. Whatever your opinion, the movie is inarguably vast and metaphysically ambitious. From the Strauss-scored Dawn of Man to computer HAL warbling "Bicycle Built for Two" as it dies to Dave Bowman's (Keir Dullea) cryptic experiences with the alien monolith, *2001* challenges and dazzles. It's also one of the few wide-screen films that need to be seen on video in a letterboxed version; not for nothing is Kubrick known as a perfectionist.

11 ALIEN *(1979, FoxVideo, R)* The crew of a spacecraft is set upon by a hungry otherworldly creature in director Ridley Scott's astonishing update of 1950s monster movies. Remarkable alien design by the Swiss artist H.R. Giger, genuinely shocking scare scenes, one neat-looking monster, and the infamous and oft-copied stomach-bursting sequence combine to make this one of the most influential of all sci-fi thrillers.

12 FRANKENSTEIN *(1931, MCA/Universal, B&W, not rated)* The party line is that the 1935 sequel, *Bride*, is better, and it's correct. But that's no excuse to skip this one, especially since current video versions reinstate bits that were deemed unacceptable even before the Production Code. A scene of the monster throwing a child into a lake was excised partly at Boris Karloff's insistence—he felt it was out of synch with the character he'd so meticulously crafted. If you haven't seen this, prepare to be knocked out by the complexity and poignancy of his performance.

13 HENRY: PORTRAIT OF A SERIAL KILLER *(1990, MPI, unrated)* John McNaughton's devastating docudrama, based on the life of the notorious Henry Lee Lucas, is one of the most disturbing movies ever made. Exploitative yet artful, this stripped-down narrative matter-of-factly recounts the savage spree of a deviant and his corrosive home life with

FOTO FANTASIES

partner-in-terror Otis. Gritty, unflinching, and ultimately very sad.

14 INVASION OF THE BODY SNATCHERS *(1956, Republic, B&W, not rated)* It has been interpreted as an anti-McCarthy tract, but that's too specific. The reason *Invasion* keeps getting remade is that it warns against creeping conformism of *any* kind—and so fits perfectly into whatever year you happen to watch it. Don Siegel shot it as a sturdy little B film, with Kevin McCarthy (no relation to Uncle Joe) slowly realizing that his fellow townsfolk are being replaced by soul-dead aliens at an alarming rate. Don't go to sleep—"you're next!"

15 THE TERMINATOR *(1984, LIVE, R)* It recharged Arnold Schwarzenegger's career (because he showed he could

THE TERMINATOR:
ARNOLD SCHWARZENEGGER

take a joke, he suddenly wasn't one), but the real breakthrough was writer-director James Cameron's. The time-crossing plot is ingenious, and the action set pieces unstoppable, but Cameron's smartest move was to give a waitress

named Sarah Connor (Linda Hamilton) the burden of carrying on the human race. It's that wild dislocating of the day-to-day (think of naked cyborg Arnold overlooking L.A. at the beginning) that makes *Terminator* more than a brilliant demolition derby. Not a blockbuster in theaters, it was one of the first movies that found its success in the "after-market" of pay cable and video.

16 THE WOLF MAN *(1941, MCA/Universal, B&W, not rated)* Has there ever been a movie monster as worthy of sympathy as poor, schlumpy Larry Talbot (Lon Chaney Jr.), whose animal nature gets the better of him when the full moon comes out? Some of the classic Universal horror movies play as camp today; this isn't one. Talbot's relationship with his unbelieving father (Claude Rains) has psychological depth, the transformation scenes are a peach, and, best of all, it's *scary.*

17 THE DAY THE EARTH STOOD STILL *(1951, FoxVideo, B&W, G)* All together now: *Gort...Klaatu...Barada...Nikto!* Highclass science fiction with a message, *Earth* sought to put raging Cold War paranoia into a galactic perspective. Michael Rennie is the alien who lands in Washington with a warning for mankind: Pursue peace or else. The Army guys shoot him, of course (but only wound him). Patricia Neal conveys the proper terrestrial awe for her ET housemate, while Bernard Herrmann's electronic score moans and mutters.

18 BACK TO THE FUTURE *(1985, MCA/Universal, PG)* Back in 1985, this seemed a gen-

103

uine miracle amid a glut of smirky, smutty teen comedies. The difference wasn't just in the fantastic conceit of sending Marty McFly (Michael J. Fox) back to 1955, where he has to play matchmaker to his own parents or he'll never be born. It was that director Robert Zemeckis and his longtime cowriter, Bob Gale, treated their characters with affection and their audience with intelligence, slamming through every absurdist time-travel permutation and trusting that we'd hang on all the way.

19 **ISLAND OF LOST SOULS** *(1933, MCA/Universal, B&W, not rated)* This classic runs only 71 minutes, and, truth to tell, it creaks plenty. But it has so many great bits—Charles Laughton's sleek portrayal of the twisted Dr. Moreau, trying to hurry evolution through science, and man-beast Bela Lugosi's readings of "the law" are highlights—that it can't conceivably be dismissed. The bad guys here are sappy romantic leads Richard Arlen and Leila Hyams; the movie grinds to a halt almost every time they open their mouths. But that's what fast-forward buttons are for.

20 **HALLOWEEN** *(1978, Media, R)* The original slasher picture, John Carpenter's tale of an escaped maniac's small-town rampage charted the rocky course for horror in the '80s. It's not much more than a simplistic body-count tally, but this stylish movie favored honest, thrilling scares over extreme gore.

21 **RE-ANIMATOR** *(1985, LIVE, R and unrated)* With remarkably inventive and

assured direction from Chicago theater's Stuart Gordon, here's a horror comedy that miraculously is as scary as it is funny. A contemporary take on an H.P. Lovecraft story about a mad scientist who discovers a serum that brings corpses to life, the film doesn't miss any opportunity to spew gore, gristle, and entrails across the screen. Though certainly not for all constitutions, the movie is a gleefully tasteless meditation on the merits of envelope pushing.

22 **TIME BANDITS** *(1981, Facets, PG)* Magical midgets drag an English child through a time warp in his closet. Next stop: encounters with John Cleese as Robin Hood, Sean Connery as Agamemnon, Ralph Richardson as God, and David Warner as the funny but ineffectual Devil. Directed by Terry Gilliam, this was one of the biggest hits associated with the Monty Python troupe, and only a characteristically mean-spirited ending keeps it from the status of a children's classic.

HALLOWEEN: **TONY MORAN**

BRINKE OF VIDEO STARDOM

Wearing pink shorts, a white T-shirt, and a perky ponytail, actress Brinke Stevens looks eerily like one of the innocent coeds she plays—at least in the first few scenes, before she sprouts fangs. "I usually start out normal and pretty, and about halfway through I get possessed, go insane, or turn into a vampire," says Stevens, scream queen of video quickies and one-woman underground industry.

In *Nightmare Sisters*, her transformation from mousy sorority girl to vampy vampire takes about half an hour. In *Teenage Exorcist*, she's a prim yuppie who moves into a mysterious old house and, faster than you can say "Linda Blair," starts thrashing about in a murderous rage—and a skimpy black leather getup. It's only fitting, then, that Stevens underwent a real-life metamorphosis from marine biologist with a master's degree to B-movie babe.

Stints as an extra in more than 100 movies finally led to her first speaking/screaming role in 1982's *Slumber Party Massacre*, in which she fell victim to a driller killer. With the rise of the VCR, B-grade Hollywood was then in the midst of a rabid gore cycle, providing abundant opportunities for nubile young women. "They always needed 14 girls to play victims," Stevens says. "I got good at screaming." Through videos such as *Sorority Babes in the Slimeball Bowl-O-Rama*, *Transylvania Twist*, and *The Haunting Fear*, she's also become adept at shower scenes and at delivering lines without lisping, despite the fangs Poli-Gripped to her teeth. "But I still can't eat with them," she says.

Off screen, as of the early '90s, the 30ish Stevens has made a cottage industry out of exploiting her exploitation-flick status. She personally writes the newsletter that goes to the 2,500 dues-paying members of her fan club and appears at fright-film conventions wearing flowing wigs and slit-to-there dresses with plunging necklines—the better to hawk her videos and autographed photos. She produced and hosted *Shock Cinema*, a four-volume "making-of" cassette series aimed at nondiscriminating horror-film viewers. In 1992, callers could hear the smoky-voiced actress read scary bedtime stories on her 900 phone line—which won an award as the best 900 number in the country—and her byline has appeared in such magazines as *Fangoria*, *Horrorfan*, and *Femme Fatales*. She wrote *Teenage Exorcist*, and her screenplays for two mainstream erotic thrillers have made Hollywood rounds. Stevens has even trademarked a character, Evila (no relation to the campy Elvira), a seductive vampire who is part of the mini-empire built upon Stevens' on-screen neck biters. Taking this a step further, Stevens stars in her own comic book, *Brinke of Eternity*. "Though I haven't tried to break out of B movies, the opportunity hasn't been offered either," Stevens says. "So rather than expand vertically, I expanded horizontally."

—*Pat H. Broeske*

105

23 **DAWN OF THE DEAD** *(1979, Republic, not rated)* Since the movie is set in a suburban shopping mall, it's not hard to get the point of George Romero's second zombiethon. That said, this devastatingly brutal and funny commentary on our consumer culture remains the ne plus ultra of sociological horror. Arguably the goriest film made up to its time, *Dawn* revels in the freedom of its indie origins and spotlights production values that belie its very modest million-dollar budget. Not for the squeamish, but this successful hybrid of exploitation and art is an essential genre staple.

24 **THE INVISIBLE MAN** *(1933, MCA/Universal, B&W, not rated)* It's rather disheartening to contemplate that this definitive compendium of wit and horror does its job in a scant 71 minutes—current Hollywood films nearly twice *The Invisible Man*'s length can't come close to matching its delightful inventiveness. It launched character actor Claude Rains' movie career, even though, as a once-benign scientist whose foray into invisibility transforms him into one of the screen's most insolently Nietzschean villains, he remains unseen for most of the film. Some of the special effects look a little ragged around the edges, but most of them are still breathtaking today. Plus, director James Whale stacked the cast with many favorite eccentric bit players.

25 **A CLOCKWORK ORANGE** *(1971, Warner, R)* Stanley Kubrick's tale of ultraviolence and its discontents (adapted from Anthony Burgess' novel) is one of the chilliest films ever made; even Kubrick's super-cool *2001: A Space Odyssey* is an ickily sentimental lovefest by comparison. Alternating scenes of still-stomach-churning mayhem with bits of absurdly broad black humor, the story of near-irredeemable future thug Alex and his technological "rehabilitation" arouses mixed feelings even in its staunchest admirers, which is as it should be. Brilliantly shot and scored, and highlighted by a genuinely brave performance by Malcolm McDowell, this is required viewing as opposed to a casual Saturday-night rental. Go the latter route and you're guaranteed to shoot your evening to hell, which is where the film takes place.

26 **THE INCREDIBLE SHRINKING MAN** *(1957, MCA/Universal, B&W, not rated)* After passing through a radioactive cloud, Scott Carey (Grant Williams) finds himself getting a wee bit wee. Jack Arnold's film gets larger and larger in scope as Carey gets smaller and smaller in body. With compelling bluntness, *Man* touches on frustration (Carey has to live in a dollhouse), native mettle (he has a terrifying showdown with a spider), and ultimate acceptance of the mystery at the center of the universe. Pretty heady for a junky '50s sci-fi flick.

27 **THE EXORCIST** *(1973, Warner, R)* If you think about it, this movie has a whole lot to answer for. As well as setting a new standard for cinema shock treatment, it spewed a slew of crummy knockoffs exploiting religious paranoia. Looking at it now, you'll wonder

106

THE INCREDIBLE SHRINKING MAN: GRANT WILLIAMS

how it ever got an R rating—today's more uptight ratings board would slap an NC-17 on this thing before the first 20 minutes were up. And quite a bit of the movie is genuinely morally objectionable. It's equally scary, though; director William Friedkin's a wily manipulator, and he pulls zero punches in the story of the demonic possession of a sweet 12-year-old girl. The mere sight of exorcist Max von Sydow's freezing breath in the film's harrowing climactic scene raises goose bumps that are likely to last for days, even if you're watching on a muggy summer night.

28 REPULSION *(1965, Video Dimensions, B&W, not rated)* A great feminist horror film —and it was directed by Roman Polanski. Most of the movie is speechless, taking off when hairdresser Catherine Deneuve's sister splits for a weekend with her sleazy married boyfriend, leaving the increasingly neurotic beautician to her own devices. Her solution to the progressively desperate harassment she receives from various males is to kill them, but she's hardly the villain here. Filled with unforgettable images, *Repulsion* unfolds with the ruthless logic of a too-real nightmare.

29 THE TEXAS CHAINSAW MASSACRE *(1974, Castle Hill, R)* It might surprise you to learn that this infamous shocker isn't terribly gory—that "family" film *Indiana Jones and the Temple of Doom* shows a lot more spilled blood and internal organs than this. A crew of genuinely unpleasant post-hippies on a day trip to an old family house fall afoul of a clan of ex–slaughterhouse workers, who proceed to make brutal work of them. The near-mutant Leatherface, gibber-

ROSEMARY'S BABY:

JOHN CASSAVETES, MIA FARROW

ing and squealing incoherently as he dismembers his victims, is the embodiment of inhumanity. The pitch-black humor that director Tobe Hooper drops throughout the movie is the precise opposite of comic relief.

30 **FORBIDDEN PLANET** *(1956, MGM/UA, G)* Only in the '50s would they think of turning Shakespeare's *The Tempest* into a shiny sci-fi drama. (Can't you hear the story pitch? "Spaceships! Robby the Robot! Anne Francis! If the Bard were alive today, that's how he'd do it!") Leslie Nielsen, a lifetime before the *Naked Gun* movies, is an el blando hero who stumbles onto a planet peopled by Dr. Morbius (Walter Pidgeon), his babe of a daughter (Francis), their pet robot, and—Shakespeare's Caliban Freudian-ized—the "monster from the id."

31 **TERMINATOR 2: JUDGMENT DAY** *(1991, LIVE, R)* By 1991, everyone knew Arnold would be back, so the underdog edge

was gone. Remarkably, James Cameron recouped by making Schwarzenegger the good guy, by inventing a new bad guy in the unstoppably liquid T-1000 cyborg (Robert Patrick), by putting a prickly mother-son (Linda Hamilton and Edward Furlong) relationship between them, and—most important—by inaugurating a new age of computerized special effects.

32 **THE HAUNTING** *(1963, Movies Unlimited, B&W, not rated)* A group of psychic researchers—including the luminously sexy Claire Bloom and *Twin Peaks* shrink Russ Tamblyn—spend a few terrifying days and nights ghost-hunting in a haunted New England house. Based on a novel by Shirley Jackson, and directed by Robert Wise, a veteran of the great Val Lewton–RKO horror film unit of the '40s, *The Haunting* is still the most frightening psychological ghostfest ever made, even though the spirits are heard but never seen. In retrospect, it has been surprisingly influential: Its creepy black-and-white realism, weird camera angles, and rustic settings can now be seen as a huge if unacknowledged influence on George Romero's *Night of the Living Dead.* Don't watch it alone.

33 **THE FLY** *(1986, FoxVideo, R)* The original 1958 DNA-switcheroo is an enjoyable potboiler, but David Cronenberg's remake sustains real horror from start to queasy finish. Look past the baboons turning inside out and the mutating flesh, and there's a startlingly intense love story here—journalist Geena Davis must decide whether to stand by scientist Jeff Goldblum as he wastes away into larval inhumanity. As a state-of-the-art gross-out, it's impressive, but as a metaphor for terminal disease (Cronenberg's father died a slow, painful death), it's nearly unbearable.

34 **INVASION OF THE BODY SNATCHERS** *(1978, MGM/ UA, PG)* If the '50s original is a parable of McCarthyism, the politics of Philip Kaufman's hip, San Francisco–set remake are more reliably lefty. The always thoughtful Kaufman used the pod metaphor to lampoon a wide range of social trends, but his observations never get in the way of the shocks. The lead casting of Donald Sutherland, who's never spookier than when he's coming off sincere, is genuinely inspired; the casting of Leonard "Mr. Spock" Nimoy as a shrink is goofily inspired.

35 **ROSEMARY'S BABY** *(1968, Paramount, R)* Because Roman Polanski upped the ambiguity quotient of Ira Levin's bestseller, *Baby* continues to chill after other, more obvious movies have aged into silliness. Is Rosemary Woodhouse (fragile Mia Farrow) the victim of a witches' coven in league with her ambitious husband (John Cassavetes) to impregnate her with the spawn of Satan? Or is the poor dear just…nervous? The menace is all the sharper for the prosaic Manhattan settings and the familiar old Hollywood faces (Ruth Gordon, Ralph Bellamy) whose smiles seem to hide true evil.

36 **JURASSIC PARK** *(1993, MCA/Universal, PG-13)* Although it lacks the spiky characterizations of *Jaws*, this Steven Spielberg film still stands as the thrill ride par excellence. *Jurassic* is a mile-

109

MURRAY CLOSE

JURASSIC PARK: **TYRANNOSAURUS REX**

THE DEAD ZONE: CHRISTOPHER WALKEN

stone for showing us what generations of kids have only dreamed about: living, breathing, *eating* dinosaurs. Okay, so they exist only on a computer drawing board; Spielberg's genius is to meld them convincingly with a filmed real world. The *T. rex* attack is among the most visceral few minutes in movies, and it points the way toward the future of the art. Make of that what you will.

37 **NEAR DARK** *(1987, HBO, R)* Director Kathryn Bigelow's ultrastylish, ultraviolent vampire flick plays like a sick revisionist Western, with horror stalwart Lance Henriksen as the leader of a clan of bloodsuckers on a sanguinary sojourn through country back roads. Rounding out the exceptional little-name cast are Adrian Pasdar, quietly intense as an inductee, and Jenny Wright, otherworldly as the beauty who grows attached to him.

38 **THE DEAD ZONE** *(1983, Paramount, R)* Reining in Stephen King's adolescent excesses and infusing a sense of dread, hit-or-miss horror auteur David Cro-

nenberg crafted about as serious and spooky an adaptation as King may ever get. Based on a 1979 novel, the film tells of a gifted man who can see people's destinies just by touching them. With his dead eyes and embalmed presence, Christopher Walken is perfect as the freaky protagonist.

39 **BRAZIL** *(1985, MCA/Universal, R)* A real curio: It's as if a 1930s British bureaucrat had daydreamed himself into the worst future imaginable. Although Terry Gilliam's black comedy owes a lot to Orwell's *1984*, it has a creepy, duct-obsessed lunacy all its own. Jonathan Pryce is the hero-wimp vainly caught between the monolithic government and dreams of freedom, and Robert De Niro pops up as a plumber for the underground resistance. The sets alone have the power to bend one's brain.

40 **THE BIRDS** *(1963, MCA/Universal, PG-13)* From Daphne du Maurier's slight short story, Hitchcock pulled his least sentimental, most unnerving horror show. It's really about apocalypse, and the human race's vanity in thinking that it deserves any better. Tippi Hedren, Rod Taylor, Suzanne Pleshette, and Jessica Tandy are all trapped in daily cages of propriety, privilege, and resentment. Then, out of nowhere, birds start going for people's eyes. An honest nightmare, from the never-explained premise to the synthesized screeches on the soundtrack.

41 **THE ADVENTURES OF BUCKAROO BANZAI ACROSS THE 8TH DIMENSION** *(1984, Movies*

Unlimited, PG) Director W.D. Richter meant it to be confusing—as though *Adventures* were the 27th installment in an ongoing serial, and you'd missed the previous 26. The only recourse is to let this droll sci-fi–action insanity take over your brain. You get good aliens, bad aliens, Peter Weller as a Zen rock star/surgeon/race-car driver, Jeff Goldblum as a heroic New Jersey doctor in a cowboy suit, and John Lithgow rolling his fruity eyeballs

CARNIVAL OF SOULS: CANDACE HILLIGOSS

as bad guy Dr. Emilio Lizardo. Just one question: Why *is* there a watermelon there?

42
CARNIVAL OF SOULS *(1962, Facets, B&W, not rated)* It's a fallacy that all the poetic stuff in this Midwestern-made obscurity–turned–cult classic got in there by accident. Turns out industrial filmmaker Herk Harvey was consciously influenced by the likes of Bergman and Cocteau when he concocted this eerie tale of a snooty church organist (Candace Hilligoss) who dies in an auto accident—except she doesn't know she has. Hence, she's at a loss to explain why she becomes invisible to the gener-

al public at inconvenient times, or why she's attracted to the abandoned fairground where other undead types urge her to join their dance. What makes the highfalutin touches work is their sheer awkwardness—the discordant notes they strike are eerier than any slickly executed flourishes would be. Watching this movie, you're laughing at the corniness of it all one minute, frightened out of your wits the next.

43
THE STEPFATHER *(1987, Columbia TriStar, R)* In which the nuclear family achieves fission. All serial killer Terry O'Quinn wants from his new brood is "a little order," but if he were really serious he wouldn't have married into a family with a teenage daughter reaching puberty. Joseph Ruben's knowing direction and O'Quinn's uncanny performance elevate *The Stepfather* above the routine; when O'Quinn asks, "Who am I here?" before clubbing Shelley Hack with a phone receiver, he takes us closer to genuine dementia than any actor has since Anthony Perkins donned Mom's clothes.

111

44
PLANET OF THE APES *(1968, FoxVideo, PG)* "It's a madhouse! A madhouse!" The first shock of this movie is the sight of Chuck Heston's bare butt—a real pro, he doesn't use a dorsal double the way Kevin Costner did in *Robin Hood*. As an astronaut who lands on a world where apes rule and humans are herded like animals, Heston's in for a lot of surprises, most of them unpleasant. The script piles on the allegorical preachiness (it was cowritten by Rod Serling, so what do you expect?),

MIXED BLOOD

SUCKER PUNCH

Early on in *Dracula*, Gary Oldman grabs an enormous gothic goblet, sidles up to a bleeding cross, fills his cup with the hearty brew from the gushing altar, and swallows the contents in one thirsty gulp.

But what is that stuff Gary's guzzling, really? A drinkable fake-blood formula called KD-151 Blood Jellies, Jams, and Syrups, made for the entertainment industry by makeup artist Ken Diaz.

"[Francis] Coppola was very intent on showing blood living, coursing through the veins," says *Dracula* makeup-effects designer Greg Cannom. Originally, "It was supposed to be a trickle," he says. "But when shooting began, Coppola kept shouting, 'More blood! More blood! More blood!!!' We just ended up going for it." After all the biting, sucking, slurping, and oozing was over, Cannom had gone through more than 10 gallons of bogus hemoglobin for the actors alone.

To make a batch yourself at home, try this recipe for blood syrup:

♦ 1 bottle light corn syrup
♦ Generous amount red food coloring
♦ Smaller amount yellow food coloring
♦ 1 dash each of green and blue food coloring
♦ Optional: Heaping spoonful titanium oxide (powder found in toothpaste); pinch of Methyl-Paraben (a preservative)
Mix until bloody.

Go ahead, suck one down. —*Juliann Garey*

but the ape world created by top Hollywood craftsmen—especially the incredible makeup that completely obscures the features of Kim Hunter, Roddy McDowall, and Maurice Evans —is utterly convincing. And that last shot is still priceless.

CARRIE: SISSY SPACEK, WILLIAM KATT

45 THEATRE OF BLOOD *(1973, MGM/UA, R)* Someone show this movie to Janet Reno. The attorney general might have to rethink her position on media violence when she realizes all the ultra-icky means of murder used here are lifted straight out of Shakespeare, one of the pillars of Western culture. Vincent Price is the ham actor who fakes his own death and applies said means to a group of catty critics who he feels denied him a prestigious prize. Clever stuff, complemented beautifully by one of the snootiest British casts ever assembled for a horror movie.

46 CARRIE *(1976, MGM/UA, R)* Anyone who didn't quite fit in during high school (i.e., all of us) has to feel for poor, drab Carrie White (Sissy Spacek),

caught between a fanatic mom (Piper Laurie) and tauntingly popular schoolmates. Of course, not all of us were telekinetic…. Brian De Palma embellishes Stephen King's horrific tale with cruelly brilliant touches, but it's Spacek's wallflower vulnerability that grabs you like a hand from the grave.

47 THE NAVIGATOR: A TIME-TRAVEL ADVENTURE *(1988, Facets, PG)* During the

Middle Ages, the bubonic plague moves closer and closer to a country hamlet. The desperate townspeople follow the advice of a visionary young boy, who leads them through a hole in the earth and brings them out into…a modern-day New Zealand city! Sounds like a particularly bent *Twilight Zone* episode, but in the hands of director Vincent Ward *(Map of the Human Heart)*, this is a risky, breathtaking tale of miracles, faith, and the vagaries of historical context.

48 EVIL DEAD 2: DEAD BY DAWN *(1987, LIVE, unrated)* When producer Dino De

Laurentiis gave him a bigger budget, Detroit wunderkind Sam Raimi remade rather than sequelized his legendary independent horror flick—with astonishing results. Looking like it was photographed by a speed freak, the movie has a ferocious momentum informed by Raimi's love of cartoons. There's also a riotous turn by the stoic Bruce Campbell as the cabin-bound hero who battles demons summoned from the *Book of the Dead*. It features artfully staged physical humor inspired by the Three Stooges and multicolored blood—maybe Raimi thought

BLADE RUNNER:
DARYL HANNAH, HARRISON FORD

that would win the film a more audience-friendly R rating; it didn't, and the film went out unrated. Raimi did make a sequel: 1993's slapsticky *Army of Darkness.*

49 PEEPING TOM *(1960, Home Vision, not rated)* Producer-director Michael

Powell wrecked his career with this portrait of a camera-obsessed killer. British critics were outraged, and with good reason: *Tom* forces viewers to acknowledge the prurient kick they get from cinematic violence, making them accomplices to the deceptively mild-mannered movie cameraman (Carl Boehm) who murders women to capture their terrified expressions on film. As Boehm does to his victims, *Peeping Tom* holds a mirror up to the audience, creating a harrowing meditation on voyeurism.

50 BLADE RUNNER *(1982, Warner, R)* Ridley Scott's future-shock film noir was

a commercial failure, but its influence

113

has turned out to be surprisingly wide and deep. In fact, this is most people's idea of what tomorrow's "wired world" will look like: corporate, dystopian, kludgy. "Blade runner" Harrison Ford is on the trail of renegade robot replicants, the only trouble being that they seem so much more *human* than he. Look for the reissued director's cut, which deep-sixes the film's worst flaw: Ford's bored narrative voice-over.

51 DRACULA *(1931, MCA/Universal, B&W, not rated)* The movie that launched a thousand parodies—and typecast a career. Bela Lugosi plays the bloodthirsty Transylvanian count in director Tod Browning's gothic fever dream. Bearing little resemblance to Bram Stoker's original novel—based instead on a Balderston-Deane play—the film is all mood and menace, with a seductive Lugosi etching an unforgettable antihero. Creaky and overly theatrical by today's standards, the film nevertheless remains a motion-picture milestone.

52 THE TIME MACHINE *(1960, MGM/UA, PG)* Rod Taylor heads into the far beyond and finds mankind devolved into two competing species: the vacant, amoral Eloi and the monstrous Morlocks. Producer-director George Pal gives the H.G. Wells novel that started it all (with its less-than-optimistic view of human progress) the full MGM classic treatment. Wells purists may balk, and Pal's then state-of-the-art effects do look cheesy by today's Industrial Light & Magic standards, but *The Time Machine* retains an appealing Victorian

charm. Taylor, the Mel Gibson of the '60s, is a pleasure to watch.

53 ROBOCOP *(1987, Orion, R)* "I f---in' love that guy!" slimy yuppie Miguel Ferrer enthuses after the bullet-blasted Detroit cop is transformed into a metal-plated, computer-controlled law-enforcement machine. So did moviegoers—this gory, nastily satirical sci-fi

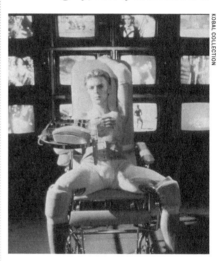

KOBAL COLLECTION

THE MAN WHO FELL TO EARTH:
DAVID BOWIE

thriller spawned two (wildly inferior) sequels and a syndicated TV series. Dutch director Paul Verhoeven's first major American film was his finest Hollywood moment; his use of video imagery in the transformation scenes is particularly innovative. Peter Weller is suitably deadpan in the title role.

54 BACK TO THE FUTURE PART III *(1990, MCA/Universal, PG)* In the third installment of this series, writer Bob Gale and director Robert Zemeckis figured out

114

a way to get "future boy" Marty (Michael J. Fox) and his pal Doc Brown (Christopher Lloyd) into the 1880s West. Whereupon the creators' love of old movies and modern moviemaking overwhelms the tortuous when-is-this-anyway? plotting. As Fox makes like a pint-size Clint Eastwood and Lloyd gets a love interest in Mary Steenburgen (time-twisting as she did in 1979's *Time After Time*), *III* mixes comedy, Western, and sci-fi into a radiantly confident cocktail.

55 **THE MAN WHO FELL TO EARTH** *(1976, Columbia TriStar, R)* Nicolas Roeg's puzzle style of moviemaking became even more fragmented when *Man* was cut by 20 minutes before release; thankfully, the original is now available on tape. The restored scenes give an acrid poignancy to the tale of Thomas Jerome Newton (David Bowie), an intergalactic

PHOTOFEST

STAR TREK II: RICARDO MONTALBAN

Candide who comes to Earth seeking help for his dying planet and is slowly, irredeemably corrupted. Demanding, pretentious, and worth it, this stunning conundrum gives Bowie his best role.

56 **THE HOWLING** *(1981, Columbia TriStar, R)* The dizzying barrage of in-jokes and horror homages in this film don't diminish its scariness—they actually enhance it. That's because director Joe Dante approaches this contemporary werewolf saga from a fan's perspective, where less enthusiastic moviemakers wink at the audience to show they're above it all. Dee Wallace plays a TV reporter who finds a coven of lycanthropes living the good life at a California spa. The joys of werewolf sex are rather explicitly depicted, and unlike a lot of horror films that followed this one, *The Howling* doesn't end with a complete cop-out. Slight but engrossing.

57 **STAR TREK II: THE WRATH OF KHAN** *(1982, Paramount, PG)* The fabled TV sci-fier made the transition to the big screen with decidedly mixed results. The second time seems to have been the charm, as this film eschews much of the TV series' fortune-cookie philosophizing while successfully replicating the show's engaging camp qualities and humor. And at its center is a robust performance by Ricardo Montalban as the lion-maned leader of rebels.

58 **THEM!** *(1954, Warner, B&W, not rated)* Giant mutant ants are running wild in the desert, and only state trooper James Whitmore, FBI agent James Arness,

POLTERGEIST: HEATHER O'ROURKE

and charming mad scientist Edmund Gwenn can stop them. The mechanical beasties aren't entirely convincing, but this archetypal '50s monsters-on-the-loose flick can still tingle your carapace, thanks to taut direction, an intelligent script, a believable cast, and a nail-biting climax in the sewers of Los Angeles. And don't blink, or you'll miss a bit part played by the young Leonard Nimoy.

59 **TOTAL RECALL** *(1990, LIVE, R)* When naysayers decry violence in the movies, they usually turn to such genre staples as the *Friday the 13th* and *Nightmare on Elm Street* films. But, in fact, this elaborate excursion is probably the goriest R-rated movie yet released. Arnold Schwarzenegger stars as a 21st-century man who travels to Mars to team up with a rebel faction and do bat-tle with a corporate megalomaniac. It's an intriguingly complex tale (based on a Philip K. Dick story), beautifully made, with literally eye-popping special FX.

60 **A NIGHTMARE ON ELM STREET** *(1984, Media, R)* The movie that spawned the deplorable series isn't the teenage gore cartoon its sequels were. It's a trenchant examination of the murderous powers of the subconscious. The scene in which teen-dream killer Freddy Krueger makes his harrowing entrance—tossing and slashing a dreaming nubile all over (and we mean all over) her room—will make you forget the jokey Krueger of subsequent incarnations right quick. Despite its halfhearted denouement, *Nightmare* represents the last gasp to date of innovative thinking in Hollywood horror.

61 THE 5,000 FINGERS OF DR. T *(1953, Columbia TriStar, not rated)* If the early '50s were really so bland, how do you explain this screwy musical fantasy, designed and coscripted by Dr. Seuss himself? *Lassie*'s Tommy Rettig plays a kid who dreams that his martinet piano teacher (Hans Conried) has imprisoned 500 boys in a kind of *Who-ville* castle for a recital on a piano the length of a freight train. From the kid's surreal beanie to the Busby Berkeley–for–tots finale, *Fingers* is a triumph of gaga production design—a toy chest bulging with Technicolor strangeness.

62 DEAD OF NIGHT *(1945, Facets, B&W, not rated)* A varied and unsettling compendium of five scary tales (from four directors), this plays like *The Twilight Zone* with a British accent. They could have kept the fusty comic golf episode, but three others will haunt you: a paranoid ventriloquist (Michael Redgrave) whose dummy gets the better of him; a mirror whose murderous past reflects on its new owners; and, in the story that links the tales, a mild-mannered man helplessly caught in the miasma of his own nightmares.

63 SUSPIRIA *(1976, Facets, not rated)* The last thing you want to do with this movie is try to make sense of it. A dizzying, hallucinogenic fantasia of colorful grotesquerie, it has a nominal plot involving a German ballet school run by devil worshipers (or something) and the travails of a young American ballerina (Jessica Harper) who's their latest student and perhaps next victim. But the story line is merely an excuse for director Dario Argento to exercise his genuinely perverse imagination and equally impressive camera virtuosity.

64 CURSE OF THE DEMON *(1958, Facets, B&W, not rated)* Is hyperrational psychologist Dana Andrews really the victim of a sorcerer's curse, or is it all in his head? The film's producer probably threw in a few shots of the title critter so audiences would feel they'd got their money's worth, but the rest of Jacques Tourneur's eerie, atmospheric skin-crawler leaves the demon mostly to your imagination. Screenwriter Charles Bennett was one of Alfred Hitchcock's ablest collaborators, and this may in fact be the finest Hitchcock movie that Hitchcock never made.

65 DON'T LOOK NOW *(1973, Paramount, R)* Donald Sutherland and Julie Christie repair to Venice in an attempt to rebound from the accidental drowning of their daughter. There they plunge into a concatenation of mysteries: Who is killing people along the canals? What do those weird middle-aged sisters—including the blind one who claims to be psychic—want with the couple? And is that the ghost of his child Sutherland sees flitting down an alleyway? Nicolas Roeg directs it like a jigsaw puzzle whose pieces suddenly make shattering sense.

66 POLTERGEIST *(1982, MGM/ UA, PG)* This movie took the haunted house out of the remote, shadowy, rural distance

***A BOY AND HIS DOG*: DON JOHNSON**

and plunked it down smack dab in the middle of safe, sunny suburbia. Such a beautifully simple idea, it's amazing no one thought of it earlier. The plot is simple too: After a housing development is built on a grave site, various disgruntled ambassadors of the undead make their displeasure known in the home of real estate agent Craig T. Nelson. They animate trees, completely ruin the backyard swimming pool-in–progress, and abduct the family's adorable little daughter (the late Heather O'Rourke). Although it's a ruthlessly efficient scream machine, *Poltergeist* won't haunt you the way the best horror flicks do. Know-it-all cineasts will have fun detecting the alternating hands of producer Steven Spielberg and director Tobe Hooper, who wasn't nearly as prone to the cutes as his boss was.

67 **WHITE ZOMBIE** *(1932, Facets, B&W, not rated)* A perhaps accidentally great flourish of baroque horror in the silent tradition, this talkie features Bela Lugosi as a spooky zombie entrepreneur in Haiti. Seemingly innocuous objects—a scarf used to wrap a voodoo doll, a rose (containing poison), and others—take on a fetishistic significance in this strangely poetic work, the first zombie film. Made for nearly nothing (Lugosi himself, fresh from his *Dracula* triumph, reportedly earned only $800 for his participation), it's not particularly frightening but is convincingly eerie.

68 **COCOON** *(1985, FoxVideo, PG-13)* A group of Florida retirees are rejuvenated—literally—when they discover a swimming pool next door impregnated with pods from another planet. If that plot reflects America's obsession with youth a little too bluntly, rest assured that it's all smoothed out in the playing. Veterans Don Ameche, Hume Cronyn, Jessica Tandy, and Maureen Stapleton give their characters a grace that comes from truly understanding what second chances mean; in their company, upstarts like Steve Guttenberg and Tahnee Welch look positively fetal.

69 TOPPER (1937, Facets, B&W, not rated) Cary Grant and Constance Bennett are tipsy socialite ghosts who wreak havoc with the home life of Milquetoast Roland Young. *Topper* is based on a book by Thorne Smith, an unjustly neglected pop novelist of the 1920s who specialized in racy supernatural fantasies about the very rich—amazingly sophisticated stuff for its day. A lot of his, er, spirit survives in this film adaptation. In fact, those familiar with only the G-rated '50s TV *Topper* will be surprised by the adult carryings-on. Loads of fun, but avoid the colorized version, which has the sickly look of a faded postcard.

70 THE OMEN (1976, FoxVideo, R) In the post-*Exorcist* '70s, when it was considered cool to make shocking mainstream horror films, director Richard Donner nabbed high-profile stars Lee Remick and Gregory Peck to play the parents of Damien, the son of Satan. *The Omen* has perfectly pitched chills, including moviedom's niftiest beheading and a frightening dog-attack scene. (It begat three fairly lousy sequels, but don't hold that against it.)

71 A BOY AND HIS DOG (1975, Facets, R) Harlan Ellison (on whose novella this film is based) has reportedly disowned this funny, mean-spirited, and supremely weird low-budget tale of survival in the postnuke future. But don't let that stop you. Don Johnson stars as a horny young man who wanders through a strange underground community with his telepathic canine. Half *Road Warrior* precursor, half *Twilight Zone* episode, this politically incorrect hoot is definitely not for all tastes.

72 ERASERHEAD (1978, Facets, B&W, not rated) The closest the movies have ever come to the feel of an actual nightmare, David Lynch's debut feature remains defiantly uncategorizable. Henry (Jack Nance) is a glum antihero who wanders a barren black-and-white landscape in

119

ERASERHEAD: JACK NANCE

which chicken dinners crawl around on the plate, angels live under the radiator, and infants are mutant hell spawn. If you can get into its dreamy, drawn-out spell, the movie eventually reveals itself as a comedy of the darkest, most surreal pitch imaginable. Certainly Buñuel would have laughed.

73 TALES FROM THE CRYPT *(1972, Facets, not rated)* The best of the British omnibus movies of the '70s (which included, among others, *The Vault of Horror, Asylum*, and *Tales That Witness Madness*), this one collects five stories from E.C. Comics of the '50s. The first and most shocking episode has Joan Collins murdering her hubby and receiving her seasonal payback on Christmas Eve. The other tales deliver their fair share of scares and well-engineered ironic endings. Don't confuse this with the inferior HBO series.

74 DEAD RINGERS *(1988, Media, R)* Taking as his source the seamy and all-too-real murder-suicide of twin gynecologists, director David Cronenberg comes up with a horror movie whose scares are of the emotional stripe—and more frightening for it. Jeremy Irons plays the brothers (the camera trickery is so subtle that you barely appreciate the skill of the performances), while Geneviève Bujold is the woman who upsets their fatally hermetic little world.

75 TREMORS *(1990, MCA/Universal, PG-13)* The mutant-monster classics of the '50s get a fond comeuppance in this droll screamer. A one-phone desert town is visited by a passel of giant, nasty, hungry underground worms that can sense the vibration of the lightest footstep. The cast is eclectic—from Kevin Bacon and Fred Ward to country-and-western

PHOTOFEST

TREMORS: FRED WARD, FINN CARTER

SCI-FI & MORE

EVIL TO THE MAX

Some religious sects believe that both God and the devil reside in all of us. Take Max von Sydow: In *Needful Things*, the famed Swedish-born actor played Satan as a small-town shopkeeper—28 years after he was Christ in *The Greatest Story Ever Told*. How did the 180-degree switch come about? "Because I'm a foreigner, I'm offered the foreigner in the story," says von Sydow. "Frequently the foreigner is villainous. But I don't mind, if the villain is interesting." To play the Ultimate Villain, he says, "you have to invent the logic and the reality of this particular character." Von Sydow's tips on how to give good evil:

1. Be unfailingly pleasant. "If they see the devil with horns and claws and fangs, they will put up their defenses. But if he's nice, they will go along with him, they will open up, and they will not defend themselves because they won't feel threatened."

2. Manipulate, manipulate, manipulate. "He blackmails nice, ordinary people, or he tempts them with all his little wonderful things. Once they agree to do him a favor, suddenly they realize, 'What did I do? Was it really that innocent?' Then they are hooked—he can make them dance along to his music."

3. Exploit people's appetites. "If they feel attraction to someone or to good food or good wine or whatever, the devil should encourage that, and then make them pay later."

—*David Nagler*

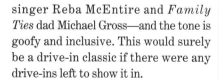

121

singer Reba McEntire and *Family Ties* dad Michael Gross—and the tone is goofy and inclusive. This would surely be a drive-in classic if there were any drive-ins left to show it in.

76 **THE CONQUEROR WORM** *(1968, HBO, not rated)* In what is arguably his best performance, Vincent Price plays an unrepentantly sadistic inquisitor in 17th-century England who takes advantage of civil war to stage his own personal auto-da-fé. A soldier whose wife has been raped by Price's assistant vows revenge. This was young British director Michael Reeves' last film (he died of an accidental drug overdose shortly after completing the movie)—a shame, because he was a unique talent. His vision can be discerned even in the lousy video versions circulating in the U.S. Note: The original title, *Witchfinder General*, was changed to *The*

Conqueror Worm (even though the story line has no relation to any of Poe's works) for American theatrical release.

77 THE WICKER MAN *(1972, Facets, not rated)* Not so much a horror film as a thoughtful consideration of Christian ethics versus more earthier pagan practices, this will disappoint shock addicts but delight connoisseurs of the quietly outré. Future *Equalizer* star Edward Woodward is suitably self-righteous as the devoutly religious police inspector investigating mysterious disappearances on a Scottish island. Seems that Christianity isn't popular on his remote outpost, as Woodward unpleasantly discovers. Christopher Lee gives one of his suavest performances as the hedonistic pagan squire.

78 Q—THE WINGED SERPENT *(1982, MCA/Universal, R)* This outlandish tale of a Mexican serpent-god that attacks Manhattan—chomping at nude tar-beach sunbathers, then taking refuge in the pinnacle of the Chrysler Building—is a scream. Writer-director Larry Cohen, no stranger to strange horror (having made the *It's Alive* monster-toddler movies), coaxes a deliriously intense performance from the mush-mouthed Michael Moriarty as an opportunist shlub who wants to give up the monster's whereabouts to police for a price.

79 HORROR HOTEL *(1960, Sinister, B&W, not rated)* With his portrayals of Dracula in numerous British shockers, the handsome Christopher Lee was the embodiment of sexy, piercing evil. In this little-known, compact thriller, he's the essence of creepy menace as a professor with ulterior motives who guides a university student researching witchcraft in a Massachusetts town. The film plays beautifully on TV, where its stagy dramatics get pushed to the background in favor of its spare atmospherics.

80 THE COMPANY OF WOLVES *(1984, Movies Unlimited, R)* What do you get when you mix *Little Red Riding Hood*, Sigmund Freud, *The Werewolf of London*, and Bruno Bettelheim—then toss in Angela Lansbury as a grandma straight out of Grimm? This puzzle-box fantasy from *Interview With the Vampire* director Neil Jordan is a tart, luxurious marriage of medieval fairy tale and kinky coming-of-age symbolism, with a wild sense of play that offsets its sizable pretensions.

81 I WALKED WITH A ZOMBIE *(1943, Turner, B&W, not rated)* That's a lousy title for this voodoo chiller, one of the most spectral B movies ever made. Reworking the plot of *Jane Eyre* in a Haitian setting, producer Val Lewton and director Jacques Tourneur (both fresh from the original *Cat People*) dropped their nurse heroine (Frances Dee) into a plantation family cursed by lust, jealousy, and creepy zombie fever. Like all of Lewton's films, this one gets more frightening the less it shows.

82 STARMAN *(1984, Columbia TriStar, PG)* Who else but John Carpenter, genre mixmaster extraordinaire, would even *try* to meld science fiction and women's

AN AMERICAN WEREWOLF IN LONDON:
DAVID NAUGHTON

melodrama? Against the odds, this rises above contrivance and cliché to become a tender intergalactic romance. Jeff Bridges (Oscar-nominated for this) plays an alien who takes on the form of Karen Allen's dead husband for a terrestrial reconnaissance mission. As they elude the feds and travel back roads, *Starman* becomes a study of the walking wounded reaching toward each other across unimaginable distances.

83 **THE WITCHES** *(1989, Warner, PG)* Jim Henson was no dummy: As executive producer of this delightful fantasy, he hired eccentric director Nicolas Roeg, not known for his work in the area of kids' entertainment, to helm this adaptation of a Roald Dahl story. The result is a wickedly funny film with a lot of breathtaking cliffhangers for its child hero (who's turned into a mouse when he stumbles upon a witches' convention at a resort hotel) and a lot of sly humor for adults. Anjelica Huston is perfectly cast as the svelte head of the coven.

84 **AN AMERICAN WEREWOLF IN LONDON** *(1981, LIVE, R)* Long the monster that got no respect in the movies (*The Wolf Man* and *The Howling* are the only other werewolf pictures worth watching), the lycanthrope enjoyed a comeback with John Landis' comic tale of a student who gets attacked in the English moors. David Naughton top-lines, but the real star is the grisly Oscar-winning transformation effects by Rick Baker, which changed the face of horror makeup in the '80s.

85 **SLEEPER** *(1973, MGM/UA, PG)* This is perhaps the spottiest of Woody Allen's "early, funny" films, but just when you think it's run out of steam, he pulls out an inspired gag that keeps you going through the bare patches. Here he plays a health-food-store owner cryogenically frozen in the '70s and revived in a future where Rod McKuen is considered a great poet. Reliable foil Diane Keaton's best moment is when she sings the "Rebels Are We" song Allen lifted from his previous *Bananas*.

86 **VILLAGE OF THE DAMNED** *(1960, MGM/UA, B&W, not rated)* The first film to capitalize on parents' fears that their children are perhaps not quite theirs. In this film, it's because they're not. The setup, in which a whole town passes out for a couple of hours and every able woman therein wakes up pregnant, is a bit of a stretch, but once the kids are born it's solid terror all the way. The uniformly blond, blue-eyed tots (the impregnators were aliens, see) can read the thoughts of adults, and whenever the grown-ups think or do something the youngsters don't like... oh, my. Multiple resonances aside, this

123

SEEMS LIKE OLD TIMERS

Makeup! It's a classic horror-flick trick to make up young actors to get them to look much older. But how realistic is that makeup? Let's take a look at some actors who once *played* oldsters, then *became* them. —*Tim Purtell*

Charlton Heston in *The Ten Commandments* (1956) and in 1990 at age 67

Sam Jaffe in *Lost Horizon* (1937) and in the early '60s in his early 70s

Bob Hope in *Road to Utopia* (1945) and in 1990 at age 87

Dorothy Lamour in *Road to Utopia* (1945) and in 1984 at age 70

Orson Welles in *Citizen Kane* (1941) and in 1985 at age 70

Rosalind Russell in *Sister Kenny* (1946) and in the mid-'70s in her mid-60s

Joseph Cotten in *Citizen Kane* (1941) and in 1976 at age 71

Bing Crosby in *Road to Utopia* (1945) and in 1972 at age 68

124

packs a lot of walloping, literate suspense into its 77 minutes.

87 **BRAIN DAMAGE** *(1988, Paramount, R)* A chatty parasitic slug named Aylmer attaches itself to the necks of passersby and trades a hallucinogenic secretion for its prime dinner: fresh brains, from wherever the host can, er, dig them up. This cheap, fast, gross, and extremely funny horror-comedy by Frank Henenlotter *(Basket Case)* manages to be both a subterranean antidrug parable and a sleazy B flick without losing its cool. That's some kind of trashy feat.

88 **THE UNINVITED** *(1944, MCA/Universal, B&W, not rated)* One of the classiest of Hollywood ghost stories, this has a touch as delicate yet as penetrating as the scent of mimosa that figures so strongly in the story. Ray Milland and Ruth Hussey are a brother and sister who buy a gorgeous old Cornwall mansion by the sea—only to find out that it's haunted by at least one ghost. Gail Russell is the young lass whose family quarrels extend beyond the grave (and you think you have problems).

89 **THE THING** *(1951, Turner, B&W, not rated)* One of the great flying-saucer flicks, this one concerns a frozen thing found by scientists in the Arctic. After they accidentally thaw it out, the creature (an unrecognizable James Arness) attacks them, and they must find the key to its cell structure to subdue it. The climax cooks. Howard Hawks is credited as producer, but his directorial influence comes through in the feeling of

Paul Muni in *The Life of Emile Zola* (1937) and in 1959 at age 64

Bette Davis in *What Ever Happened to Baby Jane?* (1962) and in 1987 at age 79

Edward G. Robinson in *Dr. Ehrlich's Magic Bullet* (1940) and in 1973 at age 80

Marlon Brando in *The Godfather* (1972) and in 1991 at age 67

125

camaraderie among the group that extends to the lone woman. This version leaves more to the imagination than John Carpenter's 1982 remake.

90 THE GHOST AND MRS. MUIR

(1947, FoxVideo, B&W, not rated) Definitely not to be confused with the jokey, shallow TV sitcom it inspired, Joseph Mankiewicz's romantic fantasy is a charmer of the first order. Gene Tierney is the widow who moves into a seaside cottage, and Rex Harrison bristles becomingly as the deceased ship's captain who doesn't want to give up his old haunt. It wasn't the first or last time Hollywood discovered how sexy a couple could be when they're not allowed to touch each other.

91 BATMAN RETURNS *(1992, Warner, PG-13)* Tim Burton followed up the dark, vague, virtually plotless *Batman* with this lavish, sardonic episode that perfectly captures the tone of the Dark Knight's comics. With a game cast, including Danny DeVito as a runty and pathetic Penguin and Michelle Pfeiffer as a tempting Catwoman, Burton and Co. manage to fashion the superhero movie to end all superhero movies.

92 TIME AFTER TIME *(1979, Warner, PG)* Malcolm McDowell stars as H.G. Wells in this funny and clever film in which the author of the *The Time Machine* chases Jack the Ripper (the delightfully devilish David Warner) from the Victorian era back to the future (in this case, contemporary San Francisco), where he falls in love with a spunky woman (Mary Steenburgen). McDowell

and Steenburgen's on-screen chemistry was no act, and they wed after making the film (but divorced 10 years later).

93 TRILOGY OF TERROR *(1975, Facets, not rated)* Three tales of four anguished women, cowritten for television by horror vet Richard Matheson, directed by *Dark Shadows* creator Dan Curtis, and starring a superb Karen Black. While the first two episodes (one about a seductive teacher, the other concerning a pair of mysterious twins) are above-average chillers, the third, in which a woman is pursued in her high-rise by a tribal doll that comes to life, is the most terrifying 25 minutes ever shot for TV.

94 THE LAIR OF THE WHITE WORM *(1988, LIVE, R)* Trust Ken Russell to adapt a Bram Stoker story and make sure all the kinky subtexts are hanging out where everyone can see them. This time the result is a goofy take on Saturday-matinee snake-goddess-cult serials. Amanda Donohoe plays a proper British lady who moonlights as a high priestess (you should see what she does to one of the Boy Scouts), and Catherine Oxenberg is a beautiful, dim victim who's almost fed to the beastie that Donohoe keeps in her basement.

95 SLAUGHTERHOUSE-FIVE *(1972, MCA/Universal, R)* That Kurt Vonnegut Jr.'s oddest book was actually made into a movie is startling. That it has aged so well—when nearly everything from that era now looks like hippy-dippy headcheese—is a sweet surprise. Michael Sacks is the hapless Billy Pilgrim,

126

unstuck in time and Ping-Ponging from his past (the World War II firebombing of Dresden, Germany), through his present (suburban American boredom), and into his future (kidnapped by aliens and living under a glass dome with Valerie Perrine). Hey, it could happen.

96 **DARK STAR** (*1974, Facets, PG*) If John Carpenter's directorial debut looks like a student film, that's because it is. It's also a very funny science-fiction parody in which four astronauts and one alien go around the bend from boredom and lack of toilet paper. Presenting space travel as a never-ending car trip with people you can't stand, it wickedly deflates the pomposity lurking behind almost every episode of *Star Trek*.

97 **BLACK SUNDAY** (*1960, Sinister, B&W, not rated*) Not to be confused with the dull-as-dust thriller about blowing up the Super Bowl, this Italian-made horror film was trimmed and saddled with a less effective musical score by its American handlers (although you can hear the original music on the Sinister tape). Even expurgated, though, this moody tale of a reincarnated witch out to wreak havoc on her dissolute descendants (the ineffable Barbara Steele in a dual role) is a horror milestone. It launched the career of idiosyncratic director Mario Bava, who went on to make a string of peculiar horror gems. This one's the best.

98 **THE PRINCESS BRIDE** (*1987, Columbia TriStar, PG*) This is not a patch on William Goldman's beloved cult novel, a book that works both as a straight-up fairy tale and a hilarious commentary on same. Yet Rob Reiner's film is still enormous, affectionate fun. Robin Wright and Cary Elwes skirt blond blandness as the nominal good guys Buttercup and Westley, but Chris Sarandon (prissy evil prince), Christopher Guest (epicene swordsman), and Mandy Patinkin (effusive avenger) save the day.

99 **LE DERNIER COMBAT** (*1983, Facets, B&W, R*) A thinking yahoo's *Mad Max*, this first feature film from French director Luc Besson (*La Femme Nikita*) is a remarkable post-holocaust play-off between a meek little guy (Pierre Jolivet) and a big brute (Jean Reno). There's no dialogue (chemical weapons ruined the survivors' vocal cords), but gleaming black-and-white photography and surreal touches like a rain shower of fish keep the viewer enthralled.

100 **LIQUID SKY** (*1983, Facets, R*) Once considered on the cutting edge of New York punk filmmaking, this grubby little wonder now plays like a quaint period piece. But what a period! A teeny-weeny spacecraft crashes in lower Manhattan and stores up fuel in the form of chemicals produced by the human brain during orgasm or heroin highs. Luckily for our extraterrestrial, there's plenty of both around the apartment of the pallid, put-upon heroine (Anne Carlisle). Nastily funny, this is one alien-attack flick in which you're actively rooting for the alien.

Reviews written by Doug Brod, Ty Burr, and Steve Simels.

127

MUSIC

ONCE, THEY MADE MUSICALS. Now they make music videos. The difference? Musicals made a show of optimism, music videos make a show of cynicism, and other than that, not much, when you look closely. The similarities are far more important. There's the notion that people can express themselves in song—spontaneously, articulately, with a full orchestra or rock band chiming in from just outside the frame. The way songs are used is the same too—as mating dances, bitter laments, or private musings. Musical numbers have always been both a dream of a perfect world and the most direct way of showing us what's going on inside a character's head.

The genre has developed and changed in a clearer arc than almost any other, and because so many musicals are available for rent, you can get a sense of Hollywood history from Busby Berkeley pep through MGM swank all the way to rock & roll swagger. This list mines 100 gems from that history. Whether you favor Fred and Ginger (see *Top Hat*, No. 7) or Frank N. Furter (see *The Rocky Horror Picture Show*, No. 14), you'll find something to sing about here.

1 **WEST SIDE STORY** *(1961, MGM/ UA, not rated)* A preposterously ambitious Hollywood hybrid of ballet, operatic melodrama, and tabloid relevance—derived from Shakespeare, yet—that successfully brings the traditional musical form to its peak (and virtual end). With unforgettable Leonard Bernstein–Stephen Sondheim songs and Jerome Robbins choreography, this street-gang update of *Romeo and Juliet* endures by eschewing Broadway razzmatazz for an overripe morbidity that almost feels like rock & roll. With Natalie Wood, George Chakiris, Rita Moreno, and Richard Beymer.

2 **WOODSTOCK** *(1970, Warner, R)* The benchmark of concert movies is also one of the most entertaining documentaries ever made. Michael Wadleigh's exhaustive, Oscar-winning three-hour tapestry surveys the sights, the sounds, and the "philosophy" of the hippie festival at Yasgur's farm. Though available on tape, the movie is best seen on wide-screen laserdisc, which preserves the innovative split screens and digitally remasters the electrifying performances, including Joe Cocker's devastating "With a Little Help From My Friends"; Crosby, Stills and Nash's beautiful "Suite: Judy Blue Eyes"; and Jimi Hendrix's stunning "Purple Haze."

A KINGLY APPETITE FOR VIDEO
ELVIS' TAPE COLLECTION

Long before the King ascended to the big screen himself, he was obsessed with movies. As a teenage usher at Memphis' Loew's State Theater, Elvis Presley memorized lines from *King Solomon's Mines* and *The Prince Who Was a Thief*. A decade later, he would frequently rent the Memphian Theatre for private screenings. His eclectic tastes ranged from Peter Sellers vehicles (particularly *Dr. Strangelove*) to the artsy *Letter From an Unknown Woman.*

Eventually, the rock & roll pioneer became an early video maven. In Graceland's gaudy, mirror-ceilinged TV room, Elvis had a professional three-quarter-inch VCR hooked into a trio of TV sets. "The damn thing weighed nine tons," says Lamar Fike, a former member of Presley's inner circle. Some videos from the King's collection have been on display at Graceland: *Oral Roberts: We the People*, *The Return of the Pink Panther*, part of the Ali-Norton fight, 1971 New York Giants highlights, *The Godfather*, *Executive Action*, and *Monty Python* episodes.

His Velvet Majesty's interest in the then-revolutionary video recorder was apparently sporadic. At the very least, according to Fike, Elvis may have been the first person who couldn't figure out how to get his VCR to record: "He had one of us do it for him." —*Nisid Hajari*

MUSIC

THE LAST WALTZ: VAN MORRISON, BOB DYLAN, ROBBIE ROBERTSON

SINGIN' IN THE RAIN *(1952, MGM/ UA, G)* Practically everybody's favorite movie musical. A breezy and still-funny take on the early days of Hollywood via writers Betty Comden and Adolph Green, with Gene Kelly, Donald O'Connor, Debbie Reynolds, and Cyd Charisse in peak form—and a zippy score by movie-musical pioneers Nacio Herb Brown and Arthur Freed.

HELP! *(1965, MPI, G)* After *A Hard Day's Night*, the Beatles and director Richard Lester were being compared (not unreasonably) with the Marx Brothers, and with their second collaboration they made the debt explicit. No cinema vérité this time out: Here the boys are dodging cultists trying to get back a magic ring from Ringo. And when they're not performing some

of the best rock tunes of the mid-'60s, Lester gets them into hilarious comic set pieces of a distinctly Marxian bent, including a "Help!"-is-on-the-way montage (lifted from *Duck Soup*) that can make you hyperventilate with laughter.

THE LAST WALTZ *(1978, MGM/UA, PG)* Martin Scorsese, who honed his concert chops coediting *Woodstock*, filmed this glorious record of The Band's final performance on Thanksgiving 1976. Though The Band has since played on (without guitarist Robbie Robertson), a host of guest stars, such as Van Morrison and Bob Dylan, lend a sense of closure to the proceedings. And with the simultaneous ascent of punk and disco at the time of its release, the picture remains a signaling of the end of an era for folk rock.

MUSIC

TOP HAT: GINGER ROGERS, FRED ASTAIRE

6 **THE BAND WAGON** (1953, MGM/UA, not rated) Librettists Comden and Green kept the title; the original star, Fred Astaire; and the best Arthur Schwartz–Howard Dietz songs of a hit 1931 Broadway revue—but then fashioned a completely new story that slyly spoofs Astaire's aging image, director Vincente Minnelli's artier tendencies, Cyd Charisse's acting ability, and the '50s Broadway scene in general. Nanette Fabray and Jack Buchanan add appropriate dashes of theatrical pepper.

7 **TOP HAT** (1935, Turner, B&W, not rated) The very top among all the Fred Astaire–Ginger Rogers musicals. Eye-popping Art Deco sets, clever dialogue, loony secondary characterizations, top-notch songs (by Irving Berlin), and, of course, those seductive "Cheek to Cheek" dances.

8 **SWING TIME** (1936, Turner, B&W, not rated) An ultraclose challenger to Top Hat as the best of the Astaire-Rogers vehicles. The fun starts when Fred tries to pick up dance teacher Ginger by pretending he can't dance. (So much for realism.) They then spin and tap their way merrily through a bunch of romantic complications to the best score Jerome Kern and Dorothy Fields ever wrote together.

9 **ELVIS: ONE NIGHT WITH YOU** (1968, Music Video, not rated) The unedited version of Elvis' comeback TV special, and probably the last glimpse of the King before the rot set in. This isn't the best music Presley ever made—in fact, there's showbiz glitz aplenty here, some of which disturbingly presages the bloated '70s Las Vegas period. But in the main, Elvis' feral energy is pretty overwhelming, as is the emotional intensity of the jam-session stuff—an emetic clearly meant to purge his soul of years of self-loathing, going-through-the-motions, music-as-product crap. Deservedly legendary.

10 **CARMEN** (1984, Columbia TriStar, PG) Perhaps the only opera film that really works. Director Francesco Rosi shot this version of the Bizet classic on location in Italy, and the whole thing is so artfully realistic that you never once wonder why the characters are constantly singing. Of course, it helps that Placido Domingo and Julia Migenes-Johnson can act as well as they vocalize, not to mention that Migenes-Johnson is one of the few opera divas who's as sexy as the character she's portraying.

11 **THE KING AND I** (1956, FoxVideo, G) The most visually stunning and exotic of all the movie adaptations of Rodgers

and Hammerstein's musicals—especially in the letterboxed laserdisc edition (the panned-and-scanned version chops off telling details and the eye-boggling sweep of the CinemaScope production numbers). Yul Brynner won an Academy Award as the sexy, feudalistic king of 19th-century Siam who gets more than he bargained for from his children's modern-minded tutor, Deborah Kerr (singing voice dubbed by Marni Nixon).

12 CABARET *(1972, Warner, PG)* Director-choreographer Bob Fosse brilliantly pulls off the seemingly impossible: soberly (and unblinkingly) setting a saucy, snappily paced romantic musical in '30s Berlin as the Nazis come to power. In her Oscar-winning role, Liza Minnelli is the free-spirited American expatriate seeking divine decadence in the wrong place, as Joel Grey (he won an Oscar too) holds a cabaret mirror to the encroaching spectre around her—and the world. Arguably John Kander and Fred Ebb's best score.

13 GUYS AND DOLLS *(1955, FoxVideo, not rated)* Damon Runyon's seedily lovable gamblers, honky-tonk dames, and prim missionaries along Times Square may have about as much relation to New York reality as Oz has to Kansas, but Marlon Brando, Frank Sinatra, Jean Simmons, Vivian Blaine, Stubby Kaye, and a great supporting cast make you forget that in this boisterous musical caper. It's not always as cartoonishly clever as the Broadway show, but Frank Loesser's terrific score never falters.

14 THE ROCKY HORROR PICTURE SHOW *(1975, FoxVideo, R)* Though its eventual video release quashed its legendary status as the definitive midnight movie, this kitschy, risqué, and joyfully horrific musical comedy has more memorable songs (such as "The Time Warp" and "Sweet Transvestite") than most "straight" musicals. That the soundtrack is closer to the '50s schmaltz of *Grease* than to the acid and glam rock that ruled its day bespeaks the movie's roots as a long-running British stage production.

15 STOP MAKING SENSE *(1984, Facets, not rated)* As good as most of Talking Heads' records were, David Byrne's musical postgraduate anxiety attacks were often criticized for being a tad too clever. Luckily, Jonathan Demme's film record of a Heads concert pretty much blows these quibbles away. Directing with at least as much visual flair as he demonstrated in *The Silence of the Lambs*, Demme gives us a band that seems positively transported by what it's playing. This may not be the best rock-concert film ever, as some have claimed, but it's

133

GUYS AND DOLLS:
MARLON BRANDO, FRANK SINATRA

STOP MAKING SENSE: DAVID BYRNE

probably the closest the movies have ever come to showing the unfettered joy of collaborative music making.

16 **TOMMY** *(1975, Columbia TriStar, PG)* Ken Russell was the perfect choice to direct the film version of the Who's classic rock opera about a deaf, dumb, and blind kid who finds salvation in pinball. Outrageous images, a fantastic cast (including Ann-Margret rolling around in a room full of baked beans), and Pete Townshend's remarkable songs make this one of rock's premier head movies. And while some may find the film ridiculous to the point of being grotesque, its pull as sheer spectacle and its ferocious musical performances (from the likes of Tina Turner and Keith Moon) are undeniable.

17 **MEET ME IN ST. LOUIS** *(1944, MGM/UA, not rated)* The epitome of a colorful, heartwarming family musical—as a good thing. Judy Garland, Lucille Bremer, and Margaret O'Brien are sisters growing up in St. Louis at the time of the 1904 World's Fair, facing up to domestic dilemmas and romantic predicaments to a lilting score by Hugh Martin and Ralph Blane. Other pluses: Vincente Minnelli's direction and George Folsey's color photography.

18 **SHOW BOAT** *(1936, MGM/ UA, B&W, not rated)* The classic movie version of the landmark 1927 Jerome Kern–Oscar Hammerstein musical that pioneered the inclusion of serious dramatic ideas and social commentary within a musical. For all its trailblazing frankness on racial injustices of a century ago, shameful stereotypes remain. But Irene Dunne, Paul Robeson, Helen Morgan, Allan Jones, and Charles Winninger contribute genuinely unforgettable

TOMMY: ELTON JOHN

characterizations, James Whale's direction is tightly paced, and the score is forever gorgeous.

19 **SHOW BOAT** *(1951, MGM/ UA, not rated)* Some of the story's been changed from the '36 version—not always for the better, except for a more poignant ending. This time there's glowing Technicolor and more lavish sets, costumes, and musical numbers to go with the great Kern-Hammerstein score. Ava Gardner and Howard Keel stand out in a cast that also includes Kathryn Grayson, Joe E. Brown, William Warfield, and Marge and Gower Champion.

20 **THE SOUND OF MUSIC** *(1965, FoxVideo, G)* The sort of musical that gives old-fashioned charm a good name. Sure, it gets stickily sentimental in spots, but its famous hills are alive not only with Rodgers and Hammerstein's irresistible songs but also with spectacular Alpine location shots, imaginative cinematography, and Julie Andrews' most winning performance. (She even manages to avoid being upstaged by all those kids.)

21 **SATURDAY NIGHT FEVER** *(1977, Paramount, R)* An unabashedly romanticized look at the discomania of the '70s youth culture, but played and danced with just the right bite and style by John Travolta and Karen Lynn Gorney to the soundtrack music by the Bee Gees. It captures the restlessness of a whole generation's search for something more than the emptiness of just "Stayin' Alive" with or without music.

SINGER-DIRECTORS

THEIR WAY

Barbra Streisand may be the exception that proves this rule about singers-turned-directors: *Keep your night job.* While several vocalists have enjoyed much-publicized stints in the director's chair (David Byrne, Prince), others have toiled away on more obscure (and generally poor) projects—but not without leaving their unique mark on each film.

Singer and Film: Frank Sinatra, *None but the Brave* (1965). **Directorial Touch:** Frames actors dead center in most shots of pacifist war drama, leaving most of screen empty.

Singer and Film: Bob Dylan, *Renaldo and Clara* (1978). **Directorial Touch:** Biopic has Ronnie Hawkins as Dylan, himself as Renaldo.

Singer and Film: Neil Young, *Rust Never Sleeps* (1979). **Directorial Touch:** Concert film combines huge props symbolizing artist's humility with many close-ups of himself.

Singer and Film: Joni Mitchell, *Refuge of the Roads* (1984). **Directorial Touch:** Mixes underlit concert footage of herself with scenes from Luis Buñuel's 1961 *Viridiana*.

Singer and Film: Ray Davies, *Return to Waterloo* (1984). **Directorial Touch:** Replaces most of the dialogue in parable of Thatcher's Britain with his own music.

—*Nisid Hajari, Tim Purtell*

THE HARDER THEY COME: JIMMY CLIFF

22 **MONTEREY POP** *(1968, Movies Unlimited, not rated)* This documentary of the seminal 1967 rock festival is disappointing from a contemporary vantage point: A lot of important bands (the Byrds, Buffalo Springfield) who actually played at Monterey are nowhere to be seen; many of the bands that are showcased frankly stink (Country Joe and the Fish, the Animals); and the editing is often sloppy. But the best performances—the Who, Jimi Hendrix, Otis Redding—have lost none of their revolutionary power, and *Monterey Pop* remains invaluable as a time capsule of an era that now seems as remote as the Mesozoic.

23 **FUNNY FACE** *(1957, Paramount, not rated)* She's Audrey Hepburn, doing her own singing and dancing (delightfully, too) as a gamine bookworm turned into a top fashion model by photographer Fred Astaire in ever-so-romantic Paris. The title and most of the songs are from a 1927 Gershwin musical (which Astaire also starred in), but the rest is all new, including director Stanley Donen's striking color images, which

evoke the most sophisticated trends of '50s fashion photography. And the inimitable Kay Thompson steals every scene she's in.

24 **THE PIRATE** *(1947, MGM/ UA, not rated)* A flop when first released, this fantasy-parody of old-time swashbucklers has built a well-deserved cult following over the years. It's packed with some of the most lavish, exciting dances Gene Kelly ever filmed, as well as colorful, imaginative production ideas from director Vincente Minnelli. Then there's a witty Cole Porter score, Judy Garland at her drollest, and the dancing Nicholas Brothers at their sharpest.

25 **THE HARDER THEY COME** *(1972, Facets, R)* A poor Jamaican country boy (Jimmy Cliff, in a world-class performance) comes to the big city and becomes a reggae star and a hunted criminal at more or less the same time. This realistic-looking slice-of-life melodrama helped introduce the rest of the world to Jamaican music (its fabulous soundtrack features Toots and the Maytals, the Melodians, and Cliff himself, among others), and its No.-1-on-the-charts/ No.-1-on-the-Most-Wanted-list gimmick is strikingly contemporary in the era of Snoop Doggy Dogg and Tupac Shakur.

26 **THE BUDDY HOLLY STORY** *(1978, Columbia TriStar, PG)* Gary Busey's uncanny (not to mention Oscar-nominated) performance as early rock's quavery-voiced, bespectacled legend anchors this exceptional, straightforward musical drama. His fine singing and the real playing of filmic Crickets Don Stroud and Charles Martin Smith add a verisimilitude rarely found in rocker bios.

27 ON THE TOWN (1949, MGM/UA, not rated) In this musical-comedy expansion of Leonard Bernstein and Jerome Robbins' popular 1943 ballet, *Fancy Free*, Gene Kelly and Frank Sinatra are sailors seeking fun and romance on a 24-hour pass in New York with help from Betty Garrett, Ann Miller, and Vera-Ellen. Directors Kelly and Stanley Donen filmed some of this Hollywood musical on location, and the ways they capture the chipper spirit of the Big Apple help compensate for the regrettable abridgment of Bernstein's original score.

28 THE GREAT ROCK 'N' ROLL SWINDLE (1980, Warner, not rated) Punk's first great movie. With the Sex Pistols' charismatic manager and provocateur, Malcolm McLaren, as its guide, this potpourri of offensive set pieces and fiery performance footage fancifully chronicles the other side of musical rebellion—the image making and the hype. Highlight: the showstopping Sid Vicious delivering a snarling "My Way" guaranteed to curl Ol' Blue Eyes' toes.

29 THE COMMITMENTS (1991, FoxVideo, R) The Roddy Doyle novel about the formation, local success, and ultimate dissolution of a white Dublin soul group has been crafted by director Alan Parker into a hilarious, marvelously detailed portrait of youthful idealism and musical passion. And while it's basically just the story of a cover band, there's no denying the brio the talented cast brings to many musical numbers, per-

ON THE TOWN: FRANK SINATRA, JULES MUNSHIN, GENE KELLY

forming such classic R&B standards as "Try a Little Tenderness" as if they owned them.

30 EASTER PARADE *(1948, MGM/UA, not rated)* The only star-teaming of Fred Astaire and Judy Garland takes a playful, Pygmalion-like story and surrounds it with no fewer than 17 of Irving Berlin's best songs. It's practically one showstopper after another, especially "Steppin' Out With My Baby," in which Astaire dances in slo-mo (in the foreground) against a fast-stepping chorus (in the background).

31 LITTLE SHOP OF HORRORS *(1986, Warner, PG-13)* Granted, it seems unlikely —a gazillion-dollar musical remake of a cheapie horror flick Roger Corman originally made in about three days. But against the odds it works: Alan Menken and Howard Ashman's Off Broadway score has genuine rock energy, the performances are a hoot (particularly Steve Martin's impersonation of Elvis as a sadistic dentist), and Levi Stubbs (of the Four Tops) is unforgettable as the voice of a man-eating plant from outer space. Feed me, Seymour!

32 GOLD DIGGERS OF 1933 *(1933, MGM/UA, B&W, not rated)* The spunkiest of Busby Berkeley's song-and-dance "funtasias" for Depression-era audiences. It holds up as saucy, pre-Code entertainment and as sharp (if unintentional) sociology, especially the "Pettin' in the Park" and "Remember My Forgotten Man" numbers. Berkeley's pioneering addition of

neon lighting to his typical geometric patterns for "The Shadow Waltz" is still stunning. Joan Blondell, Ginger Rogers, Ruby Keeler, and Dick Powell head the cast, and the likable songs are by Harry Warren and Al Dubin.

33 ANOTHER STATE OF MIND *(1983, Movies Unlimited, not rated)* A slam-dancing *Real World*, this video documentary follows two young L.A. punk bands, Youth Brigade and Social Distortion, on their first North American tour. Originally full of spirit, sass, and not a little naïveté, roughly a dozen travelers see their ambitions eventually squelched by the cabin fever and personality conflicts that erupt within their beaten-up school bus. The only picture to capture the idealism and hypocrisy of rock's last rebels, this is the definitive document of the U.S. hardcore scene.

34 AN AMERICAN IN PARIS *(1951, MGM/UA, not rated)* The story's not much—the romantic ups and downs of an ex-GI who stays in Paris after World War II to study painting. But what a colorful, Oscar-winning palette of sights and sounds director Vincente Minnelli creates via some of George Gershwin's best songs and instrumental works—climaxing in a 17-minute pop ballet that ingeniously reflects the painting styles of Van Gogh, Dufy, Renoir, Utrillo, and Toulouse-Lautrec. With Gene Kelly, Leslie Caron, Oscar Levant, and French music-hall star Georges Guetary.

35 A STAR IS BORN *(1954, Warner, PG)* Judy Garland's last hurrah in a

THE GIRL CAN'T HELP IT: EDMOND O'BRIEN, JAYNE MANSFIELD, TOM EWELL

Hollywood musical—and vivid proof that few have ever matched her in the genre. This musical remake of a popular '30s tearjerker about rises and falls in movieland (a third remake with Barbra Streisand is best forgotten) lets James Mason shine as much as Garland, and the Harold Arlen–Ira Gershwin score never strikes a false note. The video version restores many long-cut scenes and songs, but it is not letterboxed (thus undercutting director George Cukor's full-screen images, especially in the musical numbers).

36 THE DECLINE OF WESTERN CIVILIZATION II, THE METAL YEARS *(1989, Columbia TriStar, R)* Director Penelope Spheeris followed up her fine punkumentary with this hilarious look at L.A.'s neo–heavy-metallurgists. Though this is os-

tensibly a musical documentary, the on-stage antics pale in comparison with the telling interview segments with musicians whose development may have been arrested but they rock free. The highlight: W.A.S.P. guitarist Chris Holmes' frightening, alcohol-drenched in-pool interview under the not-so-watchful eye of his deck-bound mom.

37 THE GIRL CAN'T HELP IT *(1956, FoxVideo, not rated)* This brash, goofy Jayne Mansfield vehicle has more than just the star's pneumatic charms and Frank Tashlin's delightfully cartoonish direction going for it. It also showcases some top rockers of the '50s, including Gene Vincent, Eddie Cochran, and Little Richard, in crisp, exciting performances that add flash to this story of a gangster moll's transformation into a chanteuse.

KIDS AT PLAY

Fueling movies like *The Commitments* is that classic teenage dream (usually fantasized during third-period algebra) of playing in a ginchy rock band. But why did Alan Parker cast unknowns when he could have hired stars who really *have* played in garage combos? Here are just a few of the celebs who once sang "Brown Sugar" off-key on a semiprofessional basis.

Diane Keaton (Actress) **Rock & Roll Gig:** Lead singer for the Roadrunners, New York City area, late '67 and early '68. **Repertoire:** Aretha Franklin and Jefferson Airplane. **Memory:** According to Roadrunners bassist Guy Gillette, Keaton "could really belt back in those days."

Bobcat Goldthwait (Actor-comedian) **Rock & Roll Gig:** Sixteen-year-old lead singer of the Dead Ducks, Syracuse, N.Y., circa 1978. **Band Influences:** Ramones, early Who, Charlie Daniels. **Band Career:** High school dances. **Memory:** "I was using pretty much the same delivery as today. A lot of angst."

Pat O'Brien (Sportscaster) **Rock & Roll Gig:** Keyboard player, Dale Gregory and the Shouters, Sioux Falls, S.D., circa 1963–66. **Band High Points:** Topped Sioux Falls charts with 45 of "Did Ya Need to Know"; opened for the Hollies and hung out with them at bass player's father's pool. **Memory:** "Basically, I'm still in the same business now."

Chevy Chase (Actor) **Rock & Roll Gig:** Drummer and keyboardist for the Chamaeleon Church (right)—one album on MGM Records, 1968 (above). **Other Band Members:** "I don't remember their names." **Earlier Musical Experience:** College band with Donald Fagen and Walter Becker of Steely Dan. **Memory:** "We sounded a little like the Association. We wore Nehru jackets and sang faggy little tunes." —*Steve Simels*

38 **HEAD** *(1968, Facets, not rated)* Or *The Monkees Take a Trip.* The Prefab Four's sole cinematic foray (cowritten by Jack Nicholson!) is a wildly incoherent mélange of vignettes both musical and hallucinogenic, showcasing the ersatz Beatles' considerable comedic talents and knack for delivering a good tune. Brilliant proto–rock videos, the musical numbers (such as "Can You Dig It" and "Circle Sky") deftly marry spaced-out pop ditties with elaborately and imaginatively conceived imagery.

39 **KISS ME KATE** *(1953, MGM/ UA, not rated)* As the first big musical filmed in the then-hot 3-D process, it's filled with visual gimmicks (such as handkerchiefs and other props forever being tossed directly toward the camera) that become plain silly in the flat video version. But they don't undermine the sizzling spirit of Cole Porter's songs, combining a tale of modern marital battlers with Shakespeare's slam-bang *Taming of the Shrew*. With Kathryn Grayson, Howard Keel, Ann Miller, and Bob Fosse.

40 **THE MUSIC MAN** *(1962, Warner, G)* Are musical con men as American as apple pie? Robert Preston makes it seem so as he lights up the screen as Meredith Willson's red, white, and brassy bandmaster selling the promise of "76 Trombones" to a 1912 Iowa town. It's all as bright, exuberant, colorful, and tuneful as a Fourth of July celebration, with on-target help from Shirley Jones, Buddy Hackett, Paul Ford, Hermione Gingold, and little Ronny Howard.

41 **MY FAIR LADY** *(1964, FoxVideo, G)* She may be the most overesteemed of musical ladies, but she still has a lot of sparkle and, yes, class as played by Audrey Hepburn (singing voice courtesy of Marni Nixon). But the movie belongs as much to Rex Harrison, as the phonetics prof who transforms a cockney waif into a proper English lady and finds himself transformed in quite another way. Alan Jay Lerner and Frederick Loewe's gorgeous score both softens and freshens the bite of Shaw's original *Pygmalion*.

42 **WE'RE ALL DEVO** *(1983, Rhino, not rated)* Devo, an Akron, Ohio–bred futuropop quintet, was the first band to take full advantage of the possibilities that a quirky visual style can have on modern rock music. Constantly redefining their look in each clip, these conceptual punsters came up with brilliant mini-movies that were funny, experimental, theatrical, and never dull. The 13 clips in this generous historical anthology, some of which predate MTV's dawning, provide biting social commentary to boot.

43 **GIGI** *(1958, MGM/UA, G)* The most sumptuous of Vincente Minnelli's musicals—and well-deserving of its nine Oscars. Leslie Caron is a sheer delight as Colette's young rebel who unhinges the slyly wicked world of rakes and courtesans in fin de siècle Paris, with unintentional help from Maurice Chevalier, Hermione Gingold, and Louis Jourdan. With a score by Lerner and Loewe, this was one of the few big musicals created for the screen and later transported to the Broadway stage.

44 **HOLIDAY INN** *(1942, MCA/Universal, B&W, not rated)* Although best known for propelling "White Christmas" to the megahit list, this movie has about a dozen other good Irving Berlin songs, pegged to different annual holidays. And since most of them are in the feet and vocal cords of Fred Astaire and Bing Crosby, they're all treated royally as the guys compete for the same girl (Marjorie Reynolds).

45 **ROCK 'N' ROLL HIGH SCHOOL** *(1979, Facets, PG)* Teenmovie legend Roger Corman produced this throwback to '50s juvenile-delinquent epics, which stars New York punks the Ramones; it's a riotous delight. Perky P.J. Soles plays a rebellious teen who enlists her favorite rock band to help rally the student body against a tyrannical principal. Beware the god-awful 1990 sequel, *Rock 'N' Roll High School Forever.*

46 **PHANTOM OF THE PARADISE** *(1974, FoxVideo, PG)* A fantastical glam retelling of the cinematic and theatrical horror show directed by Brian De Palma and composed by and costarring homuncular middlebrow songwriter Paul Williams?! An impossible-sounding collaboration, to be sure, but one that succeeds as both pop parody and evocation of pop excess. De Palma's arrestingly overbaked visuals and Williams' clever, parodic songs provide a unique twist on the oft-told tale of Faustian soul-selling.

47 **THE PAJAMA GAME** *(1957, Warner, not rated)* Factory labor relations may seem an unlikely basis for a bright and bouncy musical, but with Doris Day as the proto-feminist union rep and John Raitt as the management honcho, it turns out to be capital (or is that capitalistic?) fun. Broadway veteran George Abbott and codirector Stanley Donen have paced everything briskly, and Bob Fosse's dances include his classic "Steam Heat."

48 **LA BAMBA** *(1987, Columbia TriStar, PG-13)* Fifties rocker Ritchie Valens could have been the subject of a conventional biopic à la *The Buddy Holly Story*—Valens and Holly were killed in the same plane crash, after all. One would think there's not much to say about the life of a 17-year-old, yet director Luis Valdez staged this account of Valens' short but triumphant life as (among other things) a study of sibling rivalry and class prejudice. Even when it goes Hollywood romantic, it still feels more real than any other film in its genre. Icing on the cake: great musical sequences, including a spellbinding turn by Howard Huntsberry as the late Jackie Wilson.

49 **GENTLEMEN PREFER BLONDES** *(1953, FoxVideo, not rated)* Surprise: It's the brunette, Jane Russell, who steals the show— from Marilyn Monroe, no less. But Monroe is still purringly terrific, as both she and Russell sashay through Anita Loos' saucy account of two Americans who set Paris most unsquarely on its derrière. The Jule Styne–Leo Robin songs add plenty of snap, crackle, and punch.

50 **HAIRSPRAY** *(1988, Columbia TriStar, PG)* Bad-taste auteur John Waters goes soft,

KOBAL COLLECTION

THE PAJAMA GAME:
DORIS DAY, JOHN RAITT

LA BAMBA: LOU DIAMOND PHILLIPS

disco-y hit theme song twice in the package remains one of rock music's greatest mysteries.

52 **SEVEN BRIDES FOR SEVEN BROTHERS** *(1954, MGM/UA, G)* Probably the most macho musical ever made. It's a strikingly original, witty, and fast-moving account of how seven hardworking brothers on the Oregon frontier get themselves seven wives. Michael Kidd's dances are all knockouts, especially the exuberant barn-raising number. Howard Keel, Jane Powell, and Russ Tamblyn head the cast, Stanley Donen directs, and the songs are by Johnny Mercer and Gene DePaul.

53 **LOVE ME OR LEAVE ME** *(1955, MGM/UA, not rated)* A remarkably frank portrait of '20s and '30s songbird Ruth Etting— and a tautly terrific mixture of solid drama and equally solid music (by Irving Berlin, Rodgers and Hart, and others). Doris Day may not much resemble Etting either physically or vocally, but she turns in a stunning performance as the singer whose involvement with a Chicago racketeer nearly destroys them both. And with James Cagney as the pigheaded hood, the dramatic sparks really fly.

sort of, with this wonderfully vibrant period piece about dance-crazed teens confronting civil rights issues and puppy love in early-'60s Baltimore. Peppered with the offbeat casting of real pop stars Ric Ocasek, Debbie Harry, and Sonny Bono, it's an invigorating nostalgic kaleidoscope that also manages to resurrect some lost classics of early-'60s soul.

51 **GREASE** *(1978, Paramount, PG)* Take a well-regarded, nostalgic stage show, add two of the era's biggest pop-culture icons (Olivia Newton-John and John Travolta as teen lovers), and you have a lively, good-humored romp with energy and color to spare. Why the producers of the 24-song soundtrack album felt it necessary to include Frankie Valli's

54 **THE RUTLES: ALL YOU NEED IS CASH** *(1978, Music Video, not rated)* Years before *Spinal Tap*, Monty Python's Eric Idle helped concoct this dead-on rockumentary on the rise of a Beatles-like British pop group. Daft humor, impeccable period detail, and note-perfect soundalike song parodies make this made-for-TV special the sine qua non of Merseybeat

THE RUTLES: ALL YOU NEED IS CASH:
JOHN HALSEY, NEIL INNES, ERIC IDLE,
RIKKI FATAAR

artifice, leaving the likes of Gerry and the Pacemakers and the Dave Clark Five in the dust.

55 **FUNNY GIRL** *(1968, Columbia TriStar, G)* She's Fanny Brice, the great singer-comedienne of vaudeville and early radio fame, whose offstage life was anything but funny. Barbra Streisand's Oscar-winning portrayal (and movie debut) tells us more about Streisand's own musical, comedic, and dramatic talents than about Brice's, but this is still a rollickingly entertaining if none-too-accurate "bio-musical." Jule Styne and Bob Merrill wrote the terrific score, and William Wyler directed.

56 **OKLAHOMA!** *(1955, Fox-Video, G)* The Rodgers and Hammerstein corn is still as high as an elephant's eye, and some of the original show's intimacy and simplicity got lost in the transfer to a Hollywood big-screen superproduction. But director Fred Zinnemann and a well-chosen cast (Shirley Jones, Gordon MacRae, Charlotte Greenwood, Gloria Grahame, Gene Nelson, Rod Steiger) keep the songs, dances, and story (something about a ranch romance in the Oklahoma Territories of the early 1900s) all moving along sunnily.

57 **PURPLE RAIN** *(1984, Warner, R)* Prince, one of pop music's most mercurial performers, made his film debut in this semiautobiographical comic drama that perfectly captures his narcissistic, enigmatic, and hedonistic persona. Some of the most electrifying performance sequences ever captured (of songs like "Let's Go Crazy") overpower the often trite dramatics.

58 **ROMAN SCANDALS** *(1933, Facets, B&W, not rated)* The real Ruth Etting (see No. 53) sings her heart out in a now-classic slave-market scene, with dozens

FUNNY GIRL:
OMAR SHARIF, BARBRA STREISAND

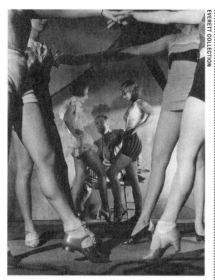

42ND STREET: RUBY KEELER, WARNER BAXTER, GINGER ROGERS

of nude Busby Berkeley chorines (including a young Lucille Ball) decorously chained together with only the strategic placement of their ultralong wigs saving them from the censors. In his funniest movie—spoofing the parallels between civic corruption in ancient Rome and in '30s America—Eddie Cantor shows why he was one of the few top Broadway and radio singer-comedians to also achieve Hollywood stardom.

59 **42ND STREET** *(1933, MGM/UA, B&W, not rated)* Neither as naughty nor as bawdy as its title song says. You know the plot of this granddaddy of all backstage musicals: how the chorus unknown saves the show on opening night. Despite lines and situations that have long since become clichés, a spry and spunky cast give it the kind of zip few copycats have matched, and Busby Berkeley's numbers are still in a class

by themselves. With Ruby Keeler, Dick Powell, Ginger Rogers, Warner Baxter, and Bebe Daniels.

60 **THE IDOLMAKER** *(1980, MGM/UA, PG)* Conventional wisdom (not necessarily accurate) has it that rock hit an all-time low between 1959 (Buddy Holly's death) and 1964 (the arrival of the Beatles). Maybe that's why director Taylor Hackford made this fictionalized biography of Bob Marcucci, the Svengali who created late-'50s/early-'60s teen idols Fabian and Frankie Avalon, with a late-'70s–influenced score: Real period music might have been unlistenable. Notwithstanding the soundtrack anachronisms, however, *The Idolmaker* is one of the few reasonably realistic cinematic studies of the mechanics of the music business, and the late Ray Sharkey, as the Marcucci character, gives a brilliantly believable performance as a genius hustler, an only-in-America cross between Phil Spector and Sammy Glick.

61 **COVER GIRL** *(1944, Columbia TriStar, not rated)* She's Rita Hayworth at her Technicolor loveliest, dancing up a gorgeous storm with Gene Kelly. A routine backstage story is dressed up with sassy one-liners by Eve Arden, some candid twists involving pre-lib magazine-cover models, and a gilt-edged score by Jerome Kern and Ira Gershwin that includes "Long Ago and Far Away." Nan Wynn dubbed Hayworth's sultry singing voice.

62 **ROYAL WEDDING** *(1951, MGM/UA, not rated)* The nuptials are Princess (soon-to-be-Queen) Elizabeth's in 1947, and actual

145

THE KING AND THEM

The real measure of a screen phenomenon could be the degree to which it's vainly—sometimes pathetically—mimicked. If so, there's no better evidence of Elvis Presley's cinematic impact than the wave of swiveling wannabes who followed in the wake of his move to Hollywood. For instance:

Cliff Richard in *Expresso Bongo* (1959) The most successful of several British Elvis clones (remember Billy Fury or Dave Berry?), Richard had his first starring role in this generally amusing satire, in which he becomes an overnight sensation after being spotted by a small-time talent agent (Laurence Harvey). Pleasant surprise: Richard is genuinely charismatic and can almost act. **B–**

John Ashley in *How to Make a Monster* (1957) Teen near-star Ashley (*Frankenstein's Daughter*) was low-budget studio American International Pictures' in-house Elvis for several years, even though he had no discernible musical or acting ability. Here, he croaks his way through "You've Got to Have Ee-ooo"—though whatever ee-ooo was, Ashley didn't have it. **C–**

Dick Contino in *Daddy-O* (1959) Contino, an aging crooner trying to cash in on the rock & roll boom, sported a bad rug and affected a sort of Jack La Lanne–on-a-bender look for this teen-flick nonsense about drag racing and drug smuggling. Fortunately, Contino sings several ersatz rock numbers—music by none other than John Williams (*Star Wars*)—that are memorably awful, and costar Sandra Giles looks swell in a succession of pointy bras. **C+**

Jimmy Clanton in *Go, Johnny, Go!* (1959) Despite his status as a footnote to rock history (his only hit: 1958's "Just a Dream"), Clanton was one of the few faux Presleys with any talent. He was also goofy-looking, which may explain why this fictionalized account of his discovery by legendary deejay Alan Freed devotes more time to great musical numbers by Chuck Berry, Ritchie Valens, Eddie Cochran, and Jackie Wilson than to its nominal star. **B+**

Arch Hall Jr. in *Wild Guitar* (1962) A hick rock hopeful comes to Hollywood with a guitar on his back and secures a record deal in about four hours, which sums up the realism quotient of this no-budget exposé of the music business. Adding insult to injury, star Hall (imagine Glen Campbell run through a trash compactor) sings several self-penned ditties that make "You've Got to Have Ee-ooo" sound like "A Day in the Life." **D** —*Steve Simels*

147

STORMY WEATHER: BABE WALLACE, LENA HORNE

newsreel coverage is intercut with a story about a dance team (Fred Astaire and Jane Powell) who also find romance amid the festivities. Powell sings and dances with more pizzazz than she'd ever previously shown, and Astaire's showstoppers include a classic in which he dances up and down the walls and across the ceiling. Burton Lane and Alan Jay Lerner wrote the top-notch score.

63 **STORMY WEATHER** *(1943, FoxVideo, B&W, not rated)* One of the few major-studio musicals with an all-black cast. And, guilty though it may sometimes be of reflecting dated racial stereotypes, there's an almost steady parade of lively numbers involving such musical legends as Bill "Bojangles" Robinson, Lena Horne, Fats Waller, Ada Brown, Katherine Dunham, Dooley Wilson, Cab Calloway, and the incredible Nicholas Brothers.

64 **THE JOLSON STORY** *(1946, Columbia TriStar, not rated)* Al Jolson's *The Jazz Singer* may have given movie musicals their first voice, but most of his subsequent '30s pix were real dogs. Then along came this none-too-accurate but entertaining biopic, and Jolson the stage-hogging egomaniac was forgotten for Jolson the charismatic singer. That's Jolie's own voice on the soundtrack as Larry Parks does him justice on film.

65 FAME *(1980, MGM/UA, R)* Alan Parker's drama traces the dreams and disappointments of students at New York's prestigious High School of Performing Arts with a dynamic combination of urban grit and visual verve. With Oscar-winning music as well as a star-making performance by Irene Cara, the film inspired a long-running TV show that, though slicked up, managed not to trash the source material.

66 ZIEGFELD FOLLIES *(1946, MGM/UA, not rated)* Easily the classiest of the '40s all-star revues. The peg is legendary showman Florenz Ziegfeld (William Powell), looking down from the great beyond and putting on a lavish show, with Vincente Minnelli supervising direction of the cream of MGM's roster. Fred Astaire gets the three best numbers, including one with Gene Kelly. Other "acts"—with more hits than misses—spotlight Lena Horne, Fanny Brice, Esther Williams, Judy Garland, Lucille Ball, and Cyd Charisse.

67 THE GAY DIVORCÉE *(1934, Turner, B&W, not rated)* Fred Astaire and Ginger Rogers' first starring hit—with what is still the blithest dance of seduction they ever did (to Cole Porter's "Night and Day"). Sharp dialogue and a wonderful cast of supporting players (including Edward Everett Horton and Betty Grable) even make the silly plot about romantic misunderstandings enjoyable.

68 YOU WERE NEVER LOVELIER *(1942, Columbia TriStar, B&W, not rated)* The title perfectly fits Rita Hayworth, who also proves to be one of Fred Astaire's best dancing partners here. There are a few too many story complications (partly spoofing Latin American marriage customs), but also a lovely Jerome Kern–Johnny Mercer score to keep things moving right along. Nan Wynn again dubbed Hayworth's singing voice.

69 X: THE UNHEARD MUSIC *(1985, Movies Unlimited, R)* Though a bit premature in documenting its subject—the seminal L.A. punk band X (filming began in 1980)—this probing look at the influential group is chockablock with thrilling in-concert performances and artful pseudo-rock-video treatments. Not surprisingly, two of the charismatic group's members, bassist-singer John Doe and singer Exene Cervenka, have since started careers as film actors.

70 FOOTLIGHT PARADE *(1933, MGM/UA, B&W, not rated)* Who killed vaudeville? It wasn't James Cagney. In his first screen musical, he's a producer trying to save his dancers' jobs with live musical prologues for new "talkie" movie houses. Never mind that his spectacular numbers, courtesy of Busby Berkeley, are on too grand a scale even for the colossal Radio City Music Hall—they're still great fun. Joan Blondell, Ruby Keeler, and Dick Powell help spark the clever, wisecracking plot, and the songs are by Harry Warren, Al Dubin, Sammy Fain, and Irving Kahal.

71 FOLLOW THE FLEET *(1936, Turner, B&W, not rated)* Fred Astaire and Ginger

Rogers play successfully against their usual sophisticated images in this one, as a sailor and a dance-hall hostess in prewar San Francisco. They even get to do the only deliberately gagged-up dance routine of all their movies—and it's a honey. So is the Irving Berlin score. Randolph Scott and Harriet Hilliard (before she became Mrs. Ozzie Nelson) have sizable roles, and Lucille Ball and Betty Grable the itsiest of bit parts.

72
THE HARVEY GIRLS *(1945, MGM/UA, not rated)* Or *How Some Spunky Waitresses Tamed the West*. This lively, lighthearted romp boasts a high-voltage cast (Judy Garland, Ray Bolger, Angela Lansbury, Cyd Charisse, Marjorie Main, Virginia O'Brien) and an alter-nately lusty and poignant Harry Warren–Johnny Mercer score. Its most famous sequence: "On the Atchison, Topeka and the Santa Fe," with its great shots of the train coming into town and the exuberant musical celebration that follows.

73
HIGH SOCIETY *(1956, MGM/UA, not rated)* Take a Broadway and movie hit (*The Philadelphia Story*), recast it with a true Philadelphia blue blood (Grace Kelly), then switch the locale to Newport (scene of top jazz festivals in the '50s), and turn it into a musical. It all works neatly, thanks to the breezy teaming of Frank Sinatra and Bing Crosby as Kelly's costars, with brief but bright support from Louis Armstrong.

HIGH SOCIETY: FRANK SINATRA, GRACE KELLY

Cole Porter's score includes his mammoth movie hit "True Love."

74 **THIS IS ELVIS** *(1981, Warner, PG)* The King gets the royal treatment with this neat, unusual documentary, which combines film clips, interviews, and concert footage with dramatic reenactments to paint a vivid portrait of the evolution of celebrity. From Tennessee bumpkin to Las Vegas cartoon, pop culture's most enduring (some would say still-living) legend is presented as a force of nature.

75 **STATE FAIR** *(1945, FoxVideo, not rated)* Sure enough, "It's a Grand Night for Singing" in the first version (not 1962's stinkeroo remake) of Rodgers and Hammerstein's original film musical. Reportedly written with a dictum from producer Darryl Zanuck to match the homespun qualities of *Oklahoma!* (then Broadway's biggest blockbuster), the movie focuses on the romances of Jeanne Crain and Dana Andrews, and Dick Haymes and Vivian Blaine, at an Iowa farmers' fair. It's all unashamedly hokey, warmly sunny, and musically glorious.

76 **QUADROPHENIA** *(1979, Rhino, R)* The Who's 1973 album—a look back at the early-'60s Mods vs. Rockers English youth culture—always felt like an aural movie treatment (far more so than their earlier *Tommy*), and director Franc Roddam's adaptation captures it just about perfectly, from the amphetamine-fueled frustration of its lower-class protagonists to the frighteningly aphrodisiacal power of mindless violence. Great music and lots of fine performances, including

VIVA LAS VEGAS:
ANN-MARGRET, ELVIS PRESLEY

a memorable cameo by Sting, who has the energy and charisma of a punk-rock Gene Kelly.

77 **BLUE SKIES** *(1946, MCA/Universal, not rated)* The wartime budget restrictions that put a crimp in 1942's *Holiday Inn* were considerably loosened for Paramount's first big postwar musical with the same stars, Fred Astaire and Bing Crosby—this time in Technicolor and with nearly 20 more Irving Berlin songs (some new, some old). While not surpassing its predecessor, it's still quite a dapper entertainment—at its most dazzling when Astaire precision-dances with 10 mirror images of himself to "Puttin' on the Ritz."

78 **VIVA LAS VEGAS** *(1963, MGM/UA, not rated)* Elvis Presley must have felt weird about this tribute to the town where, in the '50s, he had bombed as badly as anyone can bomb. But if he did, it doesn't show here, perhaps because Ann-Margret was one of the few Presley costars with sexual charisma equal to his. A camp hoot overall, to be sure, but sparks fly when the two perform together, and the Doc Pomus–Mort Shuman title song is an iconic classic.

79 **HAIR** *(1979, MGM/UA, PG)* Director Milos Forman *(One Flew Over the Cuckoo's Nest)* did a wonderful job of opening up the groundbreaking Rado-Ragni-MacDermot hippie musical for the screen, while coaxing impassioned performances from the likes of John Savage and Annie Golden. Even if it did come a few years too late, the film provides ample proof of just how great the songs are.

80 **THE GREAT ZIEGFELD** *(1936, MGM/UA, B&W, not rated)* An Oscar winner for Best Picture and at its time the most superlavish of all Hollywood musicals—in keeping with the style and image of the Broadway impresario whose life it chronicles (with many liberties, of course). The dramatic elements (involving William Powell, Luise Rainer, and Myrna Loy) get a bit sticky, but the production numbers are spectacular, and the legendary Fanny Brice has several choice sequences.

81 **PINK FLOYD THE WALL** *(1982, MGM/UA, R)* Emotionally cold, unyieldingly nihilistic—not the usual words you'd apply to a great musical. Yet Alan Parker's take on Roger Waters' rock opera is all of these. This virtually dialogueless tale of a rock star's descent into insanity is manic in its intensity and breathtaking in its visuals (including fluid and arresting animation by Gerald Scarfe). And there's a reason the record has sold more than 9 million copies in the U.S. alone.

82 **BIRD** *(1988, Warner, R)* Director Clint Eastwood's take on the life of Charlie Parker, the genius saxophonist who revolutionized contemporary jazz, doesn't really get the essence of the man, but that's probably unknowable anyway. Fortunately, what's here is good enough that you won't mind the unsolved mystery—it's a deeply felt tribute with incredible music (those are Parker's actual solos on the soundtrack, although the backings were rerecorded in gorgeous Dolby stereo) and strong performances (yes, that's Samuel E. Wright, better known as the voice of Disney's Sebastian the crab, as Parker colleague Dizzy Gillespie).

151

BIRD: **FOREST WHITAKER**

MUSIC TO THEIR EYES

You can take the music-video director off MTV, but just try keeping MTV out of that same director's movies. David Fincher's background in clipdom—he did Madonna's "Vogue"—may not have informed the musical direction of his deep-space thriller, *Alien³*, but it certainly inspired the film's quick-cutting, virtuosic visuals. He's just one of many music-vid auteurs to venture onto the big screen, bringing with them some rock & roll baggage. And here are some others you can now see at home.

MARY LAMBERT Music Videos: Madonna's "Material Girl" and "Like a Prayer" **Feature Film:** *Siesta* (1987) Daredevil (Ellen Barkin) who believes she may have killed someone has a weird and sexy odyssey through Spain. **B**
Mark of Their MTV Years: Pointless cameo by scary diva Grace Jones, who accessorizes by wearing a rat on her shoulder.

RUSSELL MULCAHY Music Videos: Duran Duran's "Hungry Like the Wolf" and Kim Carnes' "Bette Davis Eyes" **Feature Film:** *Highlander 2: The Quickening* (1991) Expensive, eco-conscious hackwork pitting futuristic swashbucklers (Christopher Lambert and Sean Connery) against assassins who threaten the Earth. **C–**
Mark of Their MTV Years: With their incongruous rock-god locks, Lambert and Connery wouldn't look out of place jamming in a Whitesnake cover band.

RICHARD STANLEY Music Videos: Renegade Soundwave's "Probably a Robbery" **Feature Film:** *Hardware* (1990) Imitative postapocalyptic thriller in which a junkman unwittingly gives his sculptress girlfriend the remains of a killer robot with the power to reactivate itself. **C+**
Mark of Their MTV Years: Seminal punk Iggy Pop cast as voice of a manic deejay; Lemmy, bassist and singer for Motörhead, as a cabdriver.

JULIEN TEMPLE Music Videos: Janet Jackson's "When I Think of You," Neil Young's "This Note's for You" **Feature Film:** *Earth Girls Are Easy* (1989) Three fuzzy aliens crash-land in a Southern California swimming pool and are taken under the wing of a dippy manicurist (Geena Davis). Resembles those other beach-party movies—the ones that didn't star Frankie and Annette. **C**
Mark of Their MTV Years: Cowritten by the costar, MTV's non-Downtown Julie Brown—the one who *didn't* host Club MTV. —*Doug Brod*

152

BELLS ARE RINGING: DEAN MARTIN, JUDY HOLLIDAY

83 **ERIC CLAPTON UNPLUGGED** *(1992, Warner Reprise, not rated)* In some ways, Clapton's entire post-Cream career has been an attempt to get back to the less-is-more emotional directness of the Delta bluesmen who inspired him. Which is why the small-audience, basically acoustic *Unplugged* format suits him so perfectly—in his heart of hearts, he surely prefers this kind of late-night, smoky-jazz-club intimacy to the arena-scale bombast he usually dispenses because of the mandates of his stardom. By now, of course, this version of "Layla" is a little overexposed, but who cares when the rest of the concert is still so winning?

84 **GIRL CRAZY** *(1943, MGM/UA, B&W, not rated)* Although this Gershwin show has been rehashed the most (1965's *When the Boys Meet the Girls* and 1992's *Crazy for You*), this zesty version has yet to be bettered—and it's also the best of the many movie teamings of Mickey Rooney and Judy Garland (with Judy really making the most of the great Gershwin songs). The slam-bang "I Got Rhythm" finale was staged by Busby Berkeley. With June Allyson, Nancy Walker, and Tommy Dorsey's orchestra.

85 **BELLS ARE RINGING** *(1960, MGM/UA, not rated)* And they're worth ringing—for Judy Holliday's gem of a performance (reprising her last great Broadway role), for Comden and Green's clever story, for Jule Styne's wonderful score, and for Vincente Minnelli's stylish direction (best captured in the letterboxed laserdisc edition). Holliday plays a telephone-answering-service operator who keeps meddling in the affairs of some of the clients—with zany results. Helping to keep everything moving along spiritedly are Dean Martin, Jean Stapleton, and Holliday's real-life squeeze, jazz saxophonist Gerry Mulligan.

86 A DAMSEL IN DISTRESS *(1937, Turner, B&W, not rated)* This *Damsel* was long underappreciated because it gave Fred Astaire, after seven films with Ginger Rogers, a partner (lovely young Joan Fontaine) who wasn't known as a dancer. Overlooked were its fine Gershwin score, a clever P.G. Wodehouse plot, elegant direction by George Stevens, an Oscar-winning fun-house dance sequence choreographed by Hermes Pan, and George Burns and Gracie Allen hoofing alongside Astaire in several numbers (and holding their own quite nicely, thank you).

87 MICHAEL NESMITH IN ELE-PHANT PARTS *(1981, Pacific Arts, not rated)* Nesmith, the Smart Monkee, is one of the men who actually invented MTV, for which he rarely gets the credit—blame?—he deserves, even though it clearly qualifies him as the D.W. Griffith of music video. This long-form collection of comedy bits and mini-movies of his own quirky Southern California rock tunes is sedate compared with later MTV fodder—there's a notable lack of bimbos in chains, for example—but it's as handsomely made as anything around now, and a lot less pretentious. Best moment: an opening montage trashing Nesmith's image as hippie minstrel by turning his

NEW YORK, NEW YORK:
LIZA MINNELLI, ROBERT DE NIRO

1970 hit "Joanne" into the theme for the Japanese monster movie *Rodan*.

88 THERE'S NO BUSINESS LIKE SHOW BUSINESS *(1954, FoxVideo, not rated)* And there's no song like an Irving Berlin song to rescue a movie musical whenever the plot gets a little too heavy—which it does here as it follows a show-biz family through the years. Mama Ethel Merman belts out her numbers as only she could, Marilyn Monroe sends the temperature soaring in the "Heat Wave" sequence, and Donald O'Connor, Mitzi Gaynor, Dan Dailey, and Johnnie Ray all get to shine too.

89 NEW YORK, NEW YORK *(1977, MGM/UA, PG)* Widely underrated as both a musical and a serious drama when first released, this is a searing dissection of how conflicting career drives derail the love of two musicians—a singer (Liza Min-

MUSIC

nelli) and a jazz saxist (Robert De Niro). The musical numbers are first-rate, with Minnelli at peak pow level in the title number. The video version restores a long-cut musical sequence (with Minnelli and Larry Kert) that adds meaningful perspective to the whole story.

90 RETURN TO WATERLOO (1984, Movies Unlimited, PG-13)
An hour-long, disturbingly surreal day in the life of a British businessman (Kenneth Colley, of the *Star Wars* movies) who may or may not be a rapist-killer. There's hardly any dialogue here; head Kink Ray Davies' directorial debut tells its story almost solely through his songs (some of which turned up later on the Kinks' album *Word of Mouth*). Still, for all its retro-'60s arthouse pretensions, *Return to Waterloo* is more sophisticated and moving than anything you've ever seen on MTV.

91 BILLY ROSE'S JUMBO (1962, MGM/UA, G)
The last of the supermusicals of MGM's "golden age"—and one of the most unjustly underrated. Based on Billy Rose's legendary mid-'30s Broadway mixture of circus and musical extravaganza, the movie has a peerless Rodgers and Hart score. Doris Day, Jimmy Durante, and Martha Raye keep the old-fashioned story line moving right along, and Busby Berkeley's numbers add just the right wit and whimsy.

92 GOING HOLLYWOOD (1933, MGM/UA, B&W, not rated)
A sleeper of a light-hearted musical comedy—modest in its production numbers and refreshingly good-humored while slyly spoofing the star worship that movies spawned. Marion Davies is the romantically determined fan in pursuit of a popular crooner (a youthful Bing Crosby virtually playing himself). The classic "Temptation" is just one of the Nacio Herb Brown–Arthur Freed songs introduced in this one.

93 SPRINGTIME IN THE ROCKIES (1942, FoxVideo, not rated)
The story's routine (about romantic misunderstandings among show folk), but Betty Grable never photographed more beautifully—or sexily. The plentiful musical numbers —involving Grable, Carmen Miranda, Charlotte Greenwood, John Payne, and Harry James' orchestra—are all designed for the bright Technicolor hues that distinguished most of Fox's '40s musicals, though rarely this stunningly. And who can resist Miranda's "Chattanooga Choo Choo" in Portuguese?

94 MAYTIME (1937, MGM/UA, B&W, not rated)
A genuine sweetheart of an old-fashioned operetta—one that can win over even those who think they hate the genre. Jeanette MacDonald and Nelson Eddy are at their least arch, and John Barrymore adds just the right amount of thespian spice. The Sigmund Romberg score (with help from Tchaikovsky) is unfailingly melodic, and MGM's production is as opulent as you can get in glorious ol' black and white.

95 YANKEE DOODLE DANDY (1942, MGM/UA, B&W, not rated)
The wartime flag-waving may be gnawing, but then the subject of this rousing (if only par-

155

ALL THEY DO IS ACT NATURALLY

Elvis, Paul McCartney, Madonna—no matter who the performer and what the era, one fact remains: *Rock stars can't act.* Here's why:

Their job is vulgar excess, not disciplined control. Professional actors spend years "refining their instrument." Rockers spend years *playing* theirs—or smashing them to bits, or setting them on fire. This is why Roger Daltrey seems so thrilling singing "Won't Get Fooled Again" and so dippy running around in diapers in Ken Russell's *Lisztomania.*

DALTREY   LAUPER

Their dialogue sounds real only when it's their own. It's hard to maintain that hip, rebellious independence when you're spouting a hack screenwriter's lines. By being her own ditsy self in interviews, Cyndi Lauper originally came off as a delightful found object. But in the prefab comedy *Vibes,* her neo–Betty Boop shtick just seemed tinny.

YOUNG   STING

Who wants to see these people act normal? If rowdy rock excess looks ridiculous on film (see "Vulgar Excess," above), the flip side—a musician essaying a kitchen-sink role—can be just plain boring. Examples: Phil Collins as the drab Buster, Art Garfunkel on the losing end of *Carnal Knowledge,* and Neil Young as a monosyllabic biker mechanic—all-too believably—in *'68.* Exceptions: Joan Jett in *Light of Day* and Levon Helm in anything.

DYLAN   PRINCE

Playing a character is not the same as being one. Except for David Bowie—whose act has always consisted of role-playing—rock stars seem to think MTV mannerisms will serve in place of Method. Sting has wanly pursed his lips through *The Bride, Dune,* and *Stormy Monday,* and Kris Kristofferson has shoveled his laid-back mellowness in so many movies he has practically worn a rut in the ground.

There's a reason these people *sing.* Does anybody have any idea what Bob Dylan is saying in *Hearts of Fire?*

Posturing looks really, really silly in close-up. One word: Prince.   —*Ty Burr*

tially accurate) biopic was never very subtle either: George M. Cohan, the egomaniacal actor-producer-songwriter who reigned on Broadway for most of this century's first half. James Cagney is a powerhouse in his Oscar-winning portrayal, and Cohan's songs are paraded nonstop in all their patriotic glory.

96 **YELLOW SUBMARINE** *(1968, Facets, G)* This animated fantasy, inspired by what is in retrospect one of the Beatles' ickiest records, holds up a lot better than most psychedelic artifacts. For one thing, the script (cowritten by *Love Story*'s Erich Segal, of all people) is frequently quite witty; for another, some of the musical numbers ("Eleanor Rigby" in particular) are mated to visuals that actually live up to the songs. Of course, the film loses a certain grandeur on the small screen, but the soundtrack—background music by George Martin along with the Beatles stuff—almost compensates. A period piece, but a charming one.

97 **KING OF JAZZ** *(1930, MCA/ Universal, not rated)* Most of the first musical talkies creak by today's standards, and this revue—which has little to do with jazz as we know it today—certainly creaks in its nonmusical spots. But the extravagant multilevel production numbers have rarely been surpassed, especially the Paul Whiteman Orchestra's bold, oddball, surreal version of Gershwin's "Rhapsody in Blue." With Bing Crosby, John Boles, Laura LaPlante, and more.

98 **KRUSH GROOVE** *(1985, Warner, R)* The definitive rap movie has yet to be made.

In the meantime there's Michael Schultz's lively comedy tracing the commercialization of the street sound. Genre superstars like Run-D.M.C. and Kurtis Blow share the spotlight with snot-nosed up-and-comers the Beastie Boys for this thinly veiled account of the origins of the influential media company Rush Productions. A guaranteed smile for the open-minded.

99 **SWEET DREAMS** *(1985, Facets, PG-13)* Patsy Cline, who died in 1963, was part country, part rock & roll, and all woman. Cline's tumultuous marriage to Charlie Dick is the central issue in *Sweet Dreams*, a film as lusty and spirited as the great singer herself. Director Karel Reisz downplays the particulars of Cline's success in favor of character development, letting the original recordings stand for themselves rather than serve as career signposts. As Cline, Jessica Lange is radiant; Ed Harris makes Charlie both lovable and despicable.

100 **THE STORY OF JAZZ** *(1994, BMG, not rated)* If your budget allows you to buy only one jazz video, this should be the one: Though perhaps not the best, it's comprehensive, squeezing a century of musical history into 90 absorbing minutes. Visually, it benefits from well-chosen, at times oddly moving footage of forgotten early musicians and enthusiastic amateur dancers. Principal writer Chris Albertson's thorough grounding in jazz tradition is a real plus.

Reviews written by Roy Hemming, Doug Brod, and Steve Simels, as well as Chip Deffaa and Ira Robbins.

157

FOREIGN

FOREIGN-LANGUAGE FILMS used to be the absolute pits to watch on tape. The only prints available to U.S. distributors were scratchy abominations that had been on the revival and college circuits for decades. You were never sure whether you were renting a dubbed or a subtitled version, and it was a toss-up as to which was worse: the dubbed, for making Yves Montand sound like Gomer Pyle, or the subtitled, for the maddening consistency with which tiny white letters were overlaid on white tablecloths and walls.

Fortunately, all that has changed in the past few years. The distributors have got their acts together, and newfangled enhanced subtitles available on both classic and recent foreign-language films make following the dialogue a pleasure rather than a game of hangman. And make no mistake: The films on this list *are* a pleasure to watch, if only for reminding us that the Hollywood way of movie-making doesn't have to be the only way. Think of these films as courses in a banquet, each spiced with whole new countries of flavor, that fill you up in unexpected ways. Hamburgers are pretty good too, but why eat them every day?

1 **CRIES AND WHISPERS** *(1972, Home Vision, R)* Working with three colors—red (blood), black (despair), and white (joy)—Ingmar Bergman and his longtime cinematographer, Sven Nykvist, turn film into a chamber music of images to tell the quiet, harrowing story of a woman (Harriet Anders-

CRIES AND WHISPERS:
INGRID THULIN, LIV ULLMANN

son) dying of cancer who is desperate to ease her passage from this world but cannot find comfort from her two ambivalent sisters (Liv Ullmann and Ingrid Thulin). There is no more direct or poetic statement about the terrors of mortality, the need for love, and the possibility of one moment of grace upon the earth.

2 **8½** *(1963, MPI, B&W, not rated)* A richly comic, daringly imaginative, and intellectually gripping look into artist's block by Federico Fellini, made after he achieved international success with *La Dolce Vita*. Marcello Mastroianni plays Guido, a film director who cannot move a creative muscle after a huge success and is compelled to look at his past for clues as to how to continue with his life.

The result is as close as film ever gets to stream of consciousness. Honest and emotionally elegant.

3 **THE EARRINGS OF MADAME DE...** *(1953, Facets, B&W, not rated)* In Max Ophüls' ominous masterpiece, about the feelings of people who are only superficially superficial, camera movement expresses how the characters feel. Madame De... (Danielle Darrieux), a vain and spoiled society woman, sells earrings given to her by her husband (Charles Boyer), which return to her through an Italian diplomat (Vittorio De Sica) with whom she falls madly in love. Few other films are so consistently imbued, from first frame till last, with such a ravishing style (Ophüls pulls off some of the most dizzyingly complicated shots on record) and such a haunting sense of the inexorable.

4 **THE BATTLESHIP POTEMKIN** *(1925, Republic, B&W, silent, not rated)* Sergei Eisenstein's account of a shipboard mutiny and the ensuing massacre on the steps of Odessa on the Black Sea gives the impression of continuously being in exciting motion. How? By using more than 1,300 separate shots within the short space of 67 minutes and, in the process, defining film grammar: the juxtaposition of images to create extraordinarily swift and changing emotional effects.

5 **THE NIGHT OF THE SHOOTING STARS** *(1982, Facets, R)* Working in a style that blends neorealism and humanism with a sense of melodrama they claim comes from Giotto's paintings, Paolo and Vittorio Taviani create a masterful tapestry woven out of one woman's World War II memory, which she uses as a lullaby for her baby. The film has an uneasy, fluttery quality; the realities of war alchemize into a fantastical tale, and the believable becomes astoundingly incredible.

6 **THE RULES OF THE GAME** *(1939, Home Vision, B&W, not rated)* Jean Renoir's intricate tragicomedy about a hunting weekend at a château where everyone's life, from the gamekeeper's to the host's, is caught in crucial transition. It's an ineffable mixture of farce, lyricism, and horror, fashioned on the eve of the second world war. Jeered at its release for many reasons—including having both an Austrian (Nora Gregor) and a Jew (Marcel Dalio) in its cast—it was cut, recut, then

banned outright. After the negative was destroyed by Allied bombs, it was reconstructed, beginning in 1956, from various pieces of found footage.

7 **THE PASSION OF JOAN OF ARC** *(1928, Facets, B&W, silent, not rated)* Carl Theodor Dreyer's painstaking dramatization is taken from the actual historical records, of the Maid of Orléans' trial and burning at the stake. As Joan, stage actress Maria Falconetti, in her only film role, gives one of those performances that inspire pity and terror. The movie is an ordeal, yet somehow exalting, raising human suffering to a level of strange eloquence.

8 **UGETSU** *(1953, Video Yesteryear, B&W, not rated)* Kenji Mizoguchi's astonishingly fluid ghost

161

KOBAL COLLECTION

8½: **MARCELLO MASTROIANNI**

fable follows the ambitions of two peasants in feudal Japan, one of whom is bewitched by the spirit of a woman who died before she could love. The men abandon their wives; one is raped and becomes a prostitute, the other senselessly killed while her husband experiences rapture in the arms of his phantom lover. A poignant, mist-drenched elegy for the transitory nature of things.

9 COME AND SEE *(1985, Facets, not rated)* Elem Klimov's retelling of the 1943 German invasion of Byelorussia is extraordinary for its

AGUIRRE, THE WRATH OF GOD:
KLAUS KINSKI, HELENA ROJO

perspective: A teenager (Alexei Kravchenko) views the mounting genocide with childlike wonder, yet with a will to survive it all. Few films match Klimov's for its sheer horror—or number of

deaths. Nor does any other movie juxtapose death with beauty so incessantly.

10 HIROSHIMA, MON AMOUR *(1959, Facets, B&W, not rated)* Alain Resnais' intensely erotic, groundbreaking film about memory and horror, in which a French actress (Emmanuèle Riva) and a Japanese architect (Eiji Okada) begin a casual affair, features raw and contrapuntal dialogue by Marguerite Duras. The personal anguish of the two entwined lovers—she had her head shaved for sleeping with a German soldier, and he feels guilty for having avoided his city's atomic holocaust—symbolizes the pain spawned by the far-reaching atrocities of the last great war.

11 FELLINI SATYRICON *(1969, MGM/UA, R)* Federico Fellini's free adaptation of Petronius becomes a bus tour through the fertile and outlandish landscape of the director's imagination—a film orgy for the senses that is best not made sense of. Erotic, excessive, self-indulgent, subversive, though smeared with compassion for the freaks and outcasts of nature who populate it like denizens of some great collective dream.

12 MIRACLE IN MILAN *(1951, Home Vision, B&W, not rated)* Vittorio De Sica's fantasy is irresistibly good-hearted. Toto the Good (Francesco Golisano), a foundling who lives among the destitute in a shantytown outside Milan, helps fight the capitalists with the aid of a guardian angel (Emma Gramatica) who swoops down to earth with her magic dove. Simply one of the sweetest films ever made.

CHAINING OUR YANKS

The stereotyped characterization of Japanese businessmen as cold, heartless bottom-liners in American movies such as *Rising Sun* does nothing to promote goodwill between the U.S. and Japan. But what about America-bashing in Japanese movies? After decades without much anti-American sentiment in their movies, the Japanese began to turn a critical eye on the U.S. in the '80s, as the following films attest.

THE BUSHIDO BLADE *(1980)* **Target:** Ugly, unwelcome explorers. **Vehicle:** A routine martial-arts adventure that takes a pretty dim view of Commodore Perry (Richard Boone) and his historic 1853 mission to open Japan. **Depiction of Yanks:** Arrogant, materialistic, vulgar, and unhygienic, they spend leisure time watching racist minstrel shows. The nominal sympathetic lead (Frank Converse) only becomes a hero when he accepts the ancient wisdom of the samurai.

MACARTHUR'S CHILDREN *(1985)* **Target:** Postwar American occupation. **Vehicle:** U.S. troops take control of a Japanese village at the end of World War II, dismantling traditional Japanese culture. **Depiction of Yanks:** Soldiers are overzealous agents of social disruption and humiliation.

163

TAMPOPO *(1986)* **Target:** American crudity. **Vehicle:** An arty comedy that has something to do with food and sex. **Depiction of Yanks:** A fat, bald American makes a pig of himself while scarfing up a plateful of noodles.

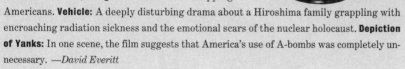

BLACK RAIN *(1988)* **Target:** Atomic-bomb–dropping Americans. **Vehicle:** A deeply disturbing drama about a Hiroshima family grappling with encroaching radiation sickness and the emotional scars of the nuclear holocaust. **Depiction of Yanks:** In one scene, the film suggests that America's use of A-bombs was completely unnecessary. —*David Everitt*

13

AGUIRRE, THE WRATH OF GOD *(1972, New Yorker, not rated)* In chronicling the story of a power-driven demagogue (Klaus Kinski) on a 16th-century expedition toward El Dorado, the legendary city of gold, Werner Herzog made a movie the way cathedrals were built in the Middle Ages. Shot with immense difficulty in Peru (amid squabbling between the director and star), it has both a grandeur and an immense folly: Herzog fashions an adventure story but demythologizes it at the same time. Seldom has a film been bathed in as much glistening beauty.

14 **LANDSCAPE IN THE MIST** *(1988, New Yorker, not rated)* In Theodoros Angelopoulos' road movie—a modern, dreamlike variation on *The Odyssey*—an adolescent girl (Tania Palaiologou) and her brother (Michalis Zeke) make their way to Germany to find a father they have heard about but never met. The journey of these babes in the woods toward the illusion of a father is completely heartrending, as plaintive as the sound of an oboe, yet rigorously unsentimental. A profound, deeply affecting work.

15 **L'AVVENTURA** *(1960, Home Vision, B&W, not rated)* In Michelangelo Antonioni's seminal work, a woman (Léa Massari) from a well-heeled boat party becomes lost near a Sicilian island, and eventually everyone gives up the search for her, including a friend (Monica Vitti) who becomes involved with the missing woman's lover. The film, abandoning traditional "story," becomes instead an interior existential drama about the inability of people to communicate and an austere meditation on the brittle nature of human relationships.

16 **SMILES OF A SUMMER NIGHT** *(1955, Home Vision, B&W, not rated)* Later revamped by Stephen Sondheim as *A Little Night Music*, Ingmar Bergman's peerless and patrician comedy of manners looks on balefully as a group of assorted lovers weekend at a country estate, fall in and out of love, and generally make fools of themselves. This airy outing with tragic undertones was his last comic work before he began to send in the frowns.

17 **NAPOLÉON** *(1927, MCA/Universal, B&W, silent, G)* The career of the Little Corporal (Albert Dieudonné) is told through a series of magnificent set pieces, ending with a wondrous wide-screen triptych. Abel Gance was one of the few filmmakers to turn pyrotechnics into poetry: Watch for the tour de force cross-cutting between a small boat at sea during a storm and the sea of bodies at the Reign of Terror's revolutionary convention, culminating in a vertiginous pendulum swoop of the camera over thousands of faces.

18 **IVAN THE TERRIBLE, PARTS I & II** *(1944–46, Facets, B&W/color, not rated)* Sergei Eisenstein's immense treatment of the life of the notorious 16th-century czar, played by Nikolai Cherkassov in the Bolshoi style of arched eyebrows and rolling eyes, is a visual grand opera unlike any other. The camera moves with studied grace through a cobweb of fantastic sets or sweeps through expansive landscapes to Sergei Prokofiev's thunderous score, creating an almost trancelike effect.

19 **MURIEL** *(1963, Facets, not rated)* Alain Resnais returns to his theme—how the past makes prisoners of us all—in this complex study of a widow (Delphine Seyrig) and her former lover (Jean-Pierre Kerien) who cannot come to grips with their own personal history. The widow's stepson (Jean-Baptiste Thierée), in turn, is haunted by Muriel, a girl he saw tortured to death in the Algerian War. Time past keeps intruding on reality, spoiling it for any small enjoyment. Shattering.

20 **L'AGE D'OR** *(1930, Facets, B&W, not rated)* Salvador Dalí contributed to the screenplay of Luis Buñuel's surrealist masterpiece, which denounces everything from religion to sexual propriety to the basic family structure of society. An archbishop gets thrown out of a window, a blind man gets kicked, a child is shot by a gamekeeper, and a farm cart is led through a drawing room. For pure subversive imagination, few films since have matched this.

21 **ZERO FOR CONDUCT** *(1933, Facets, B&W, not rated)* Jean Vigo's anarchic, surreal film about a revolt in a boys' school is perhaps as close as film ever gets to the pristine economy of great poetry: Its imagery is often inexplicably pleasurable. The famous dormitory pillow fight with the "snow" of feathers is the first truly rhapsodic use of slow motion on film, and to achieve "an unreal sonorousness," composer Maurice Jaubert transcribed the music he wrote for the scene backward. An imaginative work that has influenced countless others.

22 **EVERY MAN FOR HIMSELF AND GOD AGAINST ALL** or **THE MYSTERY OF KASPAR HAUSER** *(1975, New Yorker, not rated)* Werner Herzog's wonderfully strange, true chronicle of a "wild child" named Kaspar Hauser found in the village square of Nuremberg in 1828, barely able to walk or talk. After being assimilated somewhat into society, he was murdered as mysteriously as he appeared. To play him, Herzog chose a sometime actor and mental patient, Bruno S., who gives an astonishing performance. A

165

bizarre and beguiling investigation into the values of "civilization."

23 **IKIRU** *(1952, Home Vision, B&W, not rated)* Akira Kurosawa's finest film is, ironically, not one of his samurai spectacles but a quiet drama about a mild-mannered bureaucrat (Takashi Shimura), who, upon learning he is dying, attempts to bring some special meaning to his life. To that end, he helps build a playground in an impoverished part of a city, and it is with a sense of accomplishment that he goes to his grave.

24 **LA GRANDE ILLUSION** *(1937, Home Vision, B&W, not rated)* Jean Renoir's classic of pacifism, set in a World War I POW camp, features Jean Gabin as a lowly mechanic, Marcel Dalio as a Jewish banker's son, and Erich von Stroheim

and Pierre Fresnay as enemy officers who share an aristocratic background. Memorable for its simplicity of emotion and symbolism—especially the geranium that signifies the enduring friendship of the two officers—and a spareness of style that is completely humble.

25 **THE BICYCLE THIEF** *(1948, Nostalgia, B&W, not rated)* In Vittorio De Sica's ingenuous tale, the theft of a poor man's bicycle, his sole means of employment, takes on epic emotional proportions. The viewer follows the hapless fellow (played with disarming naturalism by nonprofessional Lamberto Maggiorani) through a series of misadventures until he is all but beaten by a heartless social system. But the film is more than social commentary, resonating as the story of a man alone in the world, trying as nobly as he can to survive.

PHOTOFEST

EVERY MAN FOR HIMSELF AND GOD AGAINST ALL: **BRUNO S.**

FOREIGN

JULES AND JIM: HENRI SERRE, JEANNE MOREAU, OSKAR WERNER

26 **VIRIDIANA** *(1961, Facets, B&W, not rated)* Nobody throws dinner parties like Luis Buñuel. The scrofulous assortment of the lame, halt, and blind whom the pious Viridiana (Silvia Pinal) brings back to her dead uncle's estate pig out on leg of lamb and cavort to Handel's "Hallelujah Chorus" on the hi-fi. This utterly blasphemous and corrosive satire of Holy Mother Church, with its shot of the partying beggars in a wicked visual parody of the Last Supper, was banned by both the Vatican and the Spanish government.

27 **JULES AND JIM** *(1962, Home Vision, B&W, not rated)* François Truffaut's exuberant story of a triangle—the essentially bourgeois Jules (Oskar Werner) and Jim (Henri Serre) and the manic, bohemian Catherine (Jeanne Moreau), whom they both love—just before and after World War I, as they make their ways "in life's whirlpool of days…round and round, together bound." No other film so headily captures the extravagant and reckless poetry—and desperation—of the Jazz Age.

28 **NOSFERATU** *(1922, Republic, B&W, silent, not rated)* "Is this your wife?" the desiccated vampire (Max Schreck) asks while holding a portrait in his talons. "What a splendid throat!" The subject of F.W. Murnau's masterpiece is dread and the atmosphere is 19th-century miasma, charged with unique intensity as the pointy-eared bloodsucker steals into Bremen carrying plague before light overcomes his darkness and the true love of a woman undoes him.

29 **METROPOLIS** *(1926, Kino, B&W, silent, not rated)* Fritz Lang's city of the fu-

EUROPEAN FILMS, THE AMERICAN WAY
AUTEURS DE FORCE

It's strange enough when arty European directors like Paul Verhoeven come to America and make popcorn fodder like *RoboCop*. Just imagine what would happen if the cinematic tables were turned and Hollywood's hit makers tried to make Euro art-house films, such as:

CINEMA PARANOIDO Spike Lee (*Malcolm X*) directs this story of young, idealistic Tito (Lee himself), who dreams of opening a movie theater devoted only to unwritten, unshot movies by African-Americans who Tito feels should rightfully have been filmmakers. When attendance sags, Tito organizes a boycott against local members of his potential audience. With Danny Aiello as the old Italian projectionist.

CRY HARD John McTiernan (*Die Hard*) teams Miranda Richardson and Bruce Willis in this action-packed IRA bloodfest. But there's a surprise: Portraying a mysterious hairdresser/assassin, Jaye Davidson is blown away before having a chance to express any emotion whatsoever.

STRICTLY BALLGAME Ron Howard (*Far and Away*) helms this affectionate film about a small-town guy with one driving passion: Wiffle ball. The movie is sprinkled with star cameos, including Robert De Niro as a former big league player–turned–tarpaulin king and Gary Cooper (via special effects) as Lou Gehrig. Starring Clint Howard.

MY PRETTY FEET The laughs keep coming in this Garry Marshall (*Pretty Woman*) tale of a fun-loving paraplegic (Patrick Swayze) and his lusty nurse (Marisa Tomei). Co-starring Rosie O'Donnell as Swayze's wise-cracking mom.

BARBRA STREISAND'S HOWARDS END This literary drama of class conflict is given added poignancy by the director's own performance as an Edwardian matriarch. The beauty of the English countryside is enhanced by frequent close-ups of Streisand (*The Prince of Tides*), whose character is never off screen, even after her death. Jason Gould costars.
—*Douglas A. Mendini*

ture, inspired by New York in the 1920s, keeps its workers, their heads bowed, in a subterranean sprawl of machinery while above ground the masters delight in decadence. It was a foreboding of Nazi Germany, from which Lang later fled. A visionary and innovatively stylistic work, the film is a triumph of celluloid choreography, as masses move through the frame like great swells of Wagnerian music.

CINEMA PARADISO: SALVATORE CASCIO

30 **CINEMA PARADISO** *(1988, HBO, not rated)* Giuseppe Tornatore's memoir of growing up in a small Sicilian town, where the local cinema and its projectionist (Philippe Noiret) serve as the center of existence and knowledge for young Salvatore (Salvatore Cascio), is a movie for people who love movies. Tornatore's rapturous, confessional work both acknowledges and celebrates the pain and joy of remembrance, finishing in a grand flourish with what is possibly the greatest montage in the history of movies.

31 **TOUS LES MATINS DU MONDE** *(1991, Touchstone, not rated)* A profound meditation, visually like a series of still lifes, on the springs of creativity, this is perhaps the most moving of all stories about the relationship between teacher and pupil. Gérard Depardieu plays the successful 17th-century composer Marin Marais, who recalls his ascetic mentor, the reclusive Sainte Colombe (Jean-Pierre Marielle). Depardieu's son, Guillaume, is the young Marais, who learns that pain—and particularly the pain of loss—may be the true path to expression and understanding.

32 **WEEKEND** *(1967, New Yorker, not rated)* Jean-Luc Godard's self-proclaimed "Film Found on a Dump" is an immense traffic accident and tie-up seen as a metaphor for society that includes almost 10 minutes of car horns and what may be the greatest single tracking shot in film. This is a vision of the world gone utterly insane, from one woman screaming, "My Hermès handbag!" to cannibalism to a landscape littered with corpses and cars smeared with blood.

33 **THE MARRIAGE OF MARIA BRAUN** *(1978, New Yorker, not rated)* A masterpiece of irony about the "economic miracle" experienced by Germany after the war stars the stunning Hanna Schygulla as Maria Braun, a victim of her own success and one of those people who keep expecting happiness but miss what there is of it while they wait. Directed by Rainer Werner Fassbinder in a lush style that is part camp, part melodrama, part raw realism.

34 **AMARCORD** *(1973, Facets, R)* A fond, rambunctious, and bittersweet memoir by

169

Fellini (the title translates as "I remember" in his hometown dialect) about growing up in Fascist Italy, directed in a near-cartoon style to Nino Rota's bumptious music. There is a tremendous affection for the characters in his past—a mammoth tobacconist, a blind accordionist and his dog, an anonymous mad motorcyclist, and a crazy old uncle who climbs a tree and shouts, "I want a woman!" for hours on end—that is utterly infectious.

35 **UMBERTO D.** *(1952, Facets, B&W, not rated)* Umberto D. (Carlo Battisti, a college professor who had never acted before) is old and meagerly pensioned, and lives alone with his dog. He is quietly determined to live out the rest of his life with something approaching dignity. Director Vittorio De Sica has an extraordinary compassion for him. To watch the old man in his attempts to survive is at first heartrending, then, after a while, closer to inspiring.

36 **TOKYO STORY** *(1953, New Yorker, B&W, not rated)* Yasujiro Ozu's gentle but ultimately acerbic story of two old folks (Chishu Ryu and Chieko Higashiyama) who come to visit their children in the big city, only to find that the kids don't have time for them. But the film, which is as gracefully made as a tea ceremony, is much more about the passing of time and the serenity of old age in the face of both disruption and chaos. The two actors are miracles of charisma.

37 **IN A GLASS CAGE** *(1986, Cinevista, not rated)* This gripping story of transference between a torturer and his victim from little-known Spanish director Agustin Villaronga is so visceral that people have been known to feel physical pain while watching it. A young man (David Sust), once abused by a German concentration-camp doctor (Gunter Meisner) who is now paralyzed and trapped in an iron lung, makes his former master his slave. Horror mounts with almost unbearable momentum.

38 **THE SEVENTH SEAL** *(1956, Video Dimensions, B&W, not rated)* The black-cloaked figure of Death (the horribly anemic-looking Bengt Ekerot) plays a medieval knight (Max von Sydow) a tough game of chess for the knight's soul in Ingmar Bergman's classic allegory. The knight's spiritual journey leads him through villages razed by the Black Death, and it is those scenes of God's unfathomable ways that stick in the memory with precision.

39 **THE LAST LAUGH** *(1924, Facets, B&W, silent, not rated)* F.W. Murnau's film about a portly old doorman (the great Emil Jannings, wearing a marvelous bushy white mustache and a sad smile underneath it) who loses his job and dignity and is left with only his uniform from the Atlantic Hotel, the symbol of his pride of position. The story still has the power—through its unsentimental depth of feeling—to move us grandly.

40 **LA STRADA** *(1954, Home Vision, B&W, not rated)* Fellini's poetic account of the mysteriousness of intimate relationships between human beings. Giulietta Masina, in a beautifully acted perfor-

***VAMPYR*: JULIAN WEST**

mance, is the simpleminded waif Gelsomina, and Anthony Quinn is the bullying and cloddish circus strongman Zampanò, who both abuses and needs her. The story follows the progress of their tacky sideshow through provincial towns and, like Nino Rota's music, just won't leave your head afterward.

41 **VAMPYR** *(1931, Kino, B&W, not rated)* The most modern of older fright films, Carl Theodor Dreyer's vampire movie, with its prowling camera and indistinct connection to reality, is firmly in touch with the mysterious and inexplicable. The theme, as in all of Dreyer's films, is suffering, and it reaches a kind of apogee when the hero witnesses his own funeral from inside the coffin, which has been fashioned with a small window.

42 **THE SEVEN SAMURAI** *(1954, Home Vision, B&W, not rated)* Akira Kurosawa's sophisticated epic—a Japanese Western—has a rousing comic tone but also depth of thought and feeling. Villagers hire seven samurai to protect their homes from marauding bandits. The samurai, with their rigorous code of moral behavior and unflinching notions of dignity and compassion, work for a handful of rice a day. They fend off bandits—the battle scenes are magnificent exercises in action directing—because it is what they do; it is all they know, and they take extreme pride in it.

43 **M** *(1931, Sinister, B&W, not rated)* Peter Lorre has his greatest role as the Milquetoast child murderer (based on a

M: PETER LORRE

real-life Düsseldorf killer) who can't help but follow his compulsions. He flees his hunters, who literally back him into a corner. And then we watch him sweat it out. Fritz Lang's film has no musical score (though who can forget the tune from *Peer Gynt* the murderer whistles each time he strikes?), but it uses sound brilliantly. Lang and Lorre's real achievement, however, is to make us feel revolted by M's crimes yet sympathetic to his wretched plight.

44 **KAOS** *(1984, MGM/UA, R)* A four-part film by Paolo and Vittorio Taviani, based on stories by Luigi Pirandello, that shows the sensuous beauty of landscapes and faces. A prologue and epilogue link these Sicilian tales, whose subjects range from a man who is liter-ally moonstruck to another about a grown man abandoned by his mother. The line between the real and the fantastic acquires an incredible tension, and the emotional breadth of the tales is beautifully, bracingly far-ranging.

45 **SEVEN BEAUTIES** *(1975, Facets, not rated)* A brilliant black comedy, told with flashbacks, about a small-time Neapolitan mafioso, Pasqualino (Giancarlo Giannini), who will do anything, including making submissive love to a concentration-camp commandant, to survive. Director Lina Wertmüller's grim, ungenerous view of human nature remains provocative. And the comedy—Pasqualino chopping up a corpse to fit it into a bag and a Spanish anarchist POW (Fernando Rey) committing suicide by jumping into a vat of excrement—is unmatched in its darkness.

46 **LA RONDE** *(1950, Facets, B&W, not rated)* A witty and elegant series of vignettes from director Max Ophüls. "I adore the past," says narrator Anton Walbrook. "It is so much more restful than the present…and so much more reliable than the future." And in the film (which opens and closes with the young, stunning Simone Signoret as an eager-to-please prostitute), life and love, buoyed by Oscar Straus' lilting score and Ophüls' dollying camera, have the headiness of a merry-go-round.

47 **FANNY AND ALEXANDER** *(1983, Columbia TriStar, R)* Ingmar Bergman's late-life masterpiece is a rousing, sumptuous celebration of family life—a gathering amid green velvet and plump red Victorian trappings for Christmas Eve dinner—but it's also a look at the chronic pain that life engenders. There's a Grimm's-fairy-tale quality to Bergman's swan song, especially when Fanny and Alexander go and live with a stern bishop and his forbidding housekeeper. The finale, however, is sweetly redemptive.

48 **THE 400 BLOWS** *1959, Home Vision, B&W, not rated)* François Truffaut's autobiographical tale of 12-year-old Antoine Doinel (Jean-Pierre Léaud), the classic misunderstood kid, for whom the only thing worse than life at home is life in the schoolroom. The film has a prankish lyricism and a real, poignant regard for its hero. And it boasts one of the most famous closing shots in movie history—

a freeze-frame of the pained Antoine on the beach—reportedly because the director simply ran out of film.

49 **THE CONFORMIST** *(1971, Paramount, R)* A multi-layered psychosexual portrait of Marcello (the superbly self-effacing Jean-Louis Trintignant), a would-be assassin in 1938 Italy, who must choose between two women—the sexually ambivalent Dominique Sanda and the animalistic, empty-headed Stefania Sandrelli. Director Bernardo Bertolucci surrounds Marcello's bland emotion and thought (conformity is seen as the seed of fascism) with all the visual splendor the movie medium can offer.

50 **ORDET** *(1955, Facets, B&W, not rated)* A hypnotic, austere adaptation of Kaj Munk's miracle play examines a crisis of faith amid two factions of Christianity—one dark and somber, the other humane and forgiving—in a Jutland farming community. Rather than camouflage the story's origins, director Carl Theodor Dreyer chooses to celebrate them with long takes worthy of the gravity of the subject matter.

51 **SHADOWS OF FORGOTTEN ANCESTORS** *(1964, Home Vision, not rated)* Set in the Carpathian Mountains, a place forgotten by God and the rest of the world, Sergei Paradjanov's film is a delirious work of magic realism with imaginative bursts of color and violence (at one point, blood splatters over the lens). Paradjanov's camera, in telling a tragically romantic story, is astonishingly renegade: 360-degree pans, vertiginous

173

FORBIDDEN GAMES: GEORGES POUJOULY, BRIGITTE FOSSEY

overheads, guerrillalike hand-held movement, and rhapsodic zooms—and none of it to be forgotten.

52 **FORBIDDEN GAMES** *(1952, Facets, B&W, not rated)* Paulette (Brigitte Fossey), a little girl whose parents are killed during a German air raid in the film's graphic opening, is brought to live with a callous peasant family, where her only ally is their son (Georges Poujouly). Misunderstanding the nature of war and death, they steal crosses for their cemetery of dead animals, creating their own little Rousseauistic universe amid the horrors of family and war. René Clément's antiwar film is far more frightening than any bullets or bombs.

53 **NIGHTS OF CABIRIA** *(1957, Facets, B&W, not rated)* For a while it looks like Cabiria (Giulietta Masina), an aging and optimistic Rome streetwalker, is an-gling to become the World's Most Adorable Whore. But Federico Fellini's seemingly artless film builds to a heartbreaking crescendo. Director and actress take you so far inside the character that you begin to see the world from her point of view. Images linger long afterward.

54 **OPEN CITY** *(1945, Facets, B&W, not rated)* Furtively planned while the Nazis were still occupying Rome and made just two months following the city's liberation, the film is a dramatic document of the Italian resistance to fascism and the first neorealist film to reach an international audience. Aldo Fabrizi plays a priest working for the underground, based on a real-life priest who was executed; and the feral, passionate Anna Magnani is magnificent as the pregnant Pina. The unbearable authenticity achieves a tough, crude power.

55 **THE CABINET OF DR. CALIGARI** *(1919, Republic, B&W, silent, not rated)* This is the landmark silent movie of German Expressionism. The viewer sees the action through the warped perspective of an insane doctor; it's like looking through a lens of madness. The angular sets are still striking; in fact, no other film's art direction has ever come up with so original a visualization of dementia. With Werner Krauss as the madman, Conrad Veidt as his somnambulistic helper, and Lil Dagover as the sexually harassed woman.

56 **TOO BEAUTIFUL FOR YOU** *(1989, Orion, R)* Few films capture the melancholy and excitement of romantic obsession as well as Bertrand Blier's demanding, nonlinear tale: A man (Gérard Depardieu) cheats on his beauteous wife (Carole Bouquet) with his plain secretary (Josiane Balasko). The action, seen from three different points of view, shifts mercurially between what the characters actually experience and what they fantasize. We watch as the present quickly slips into the past, and this affair, like all others, becomes an exercise in instant nostalgia.

57 **Z** *(1969, Facets, not rated)* Constantin Costa-Gavras' highly charged political drama about the assassination of a humanist leader (Yves Montand) in a turbulent country resembling Greece. The attempts at a cover-up are undone by a tenacious magistrate (Jean-Louis Trintignant). It has the rat-a-tat-tat rhythms and momentum of an action movie, and its nonstop dialogue creates the effect of ammunition being fired.

58 **THE CHILDREN OF PARADISE** *(1945, Home Vision, B&W, not rated)* Director Marcel Carné and writer Jacques Prévert made this life-in-the-theater and unrequited-love classic with the mixed blessings of the Nazis. Jean-Louis Barrault plays the mime who falls hopelessly in love with the elusive, complex Garance (played by the luminous Arletty). "Garance, Garance": The name has a haunting ring years after you hear it.

59 **GET OUT YOUR HANDKERCHIEFS** *(1978, Facets, R)* In Bertrand Blier's ode to the odd, the tone lies somewhere

between farce and fairy tale. The preternaturally beautiful Solange (Carole Laure) has retreated into some mysterious corner of herself, and not even the sexual ministrations of a second man (Patrick Dewaere), at the prompting of her husband (Gérard Depardieu), can "bring back her smile." It takes a 13-year-old genius at a summer camp to do the job, which, like so much of this billowy movie, is completely unexpected.

175

WILD STRAWBERRIES:
GUNNAR BJÖRNSTRAND, INGRID
THULIN, VICTOR SJÖSTRÖM

60 **WILD STRAWBERRIES** *(1957, Video Yesteryear, B&W, not rated)* In his last acting role, Victor Sjöström, Sweden's first internationally acclaimed director, gives one of the great screen performances, as the withdrawn Professor Isak Borg, who, returning to his hometown to receive an honorary degree, recalls and reexamines his past, and the icy cynicism within him begins to melt into forgiveness. Ingmar Bergman's film is fraught with now-famous symbols and dream sequences, including the clock without hands and Borg watching a coffin carrying his own corpse falling off of a horse-drawn hearse.

61 **RASHOMON** *(1950, Home Vision, B&W, not rated)* Akira Kurosawa's meditation on the relative nature of truth. A woman is raped and a man is killed in a sun-dappled forest one day. Four characters offer differing versions of what happened, and by the time we hear them out, we may not know all that much more, but we will be the wiser about human nature. A fluid, troubling work.

62 **L'ATALANTE** *(1934, New Yorker, B&W, not rated)* Jean Vigo's poetic, romantic tale (his only full-length feature), set aboard a Seine barge, which becomes a microcosm of life, stars Jean Dasté and Dita Parlo as lovers and Michel Simon as the licentious mate. A film drenched in misty atmosphere, it's a kind of cinematic tone poem. There are scenes—such as that of the lovers sleeping in separate quarters and making imagined love to each other—that leave their mark on the memory forever.

63 **MY LIFE AS A DOG** *(1985, Paramount, not rated)* Twelve-year-old Ingemar (the delectably winsome Anton Glanzelius) identifies most strongly with Laika, the first dog in space, who starved to death. His mother is dying of tuberculosis and Ingemar's own dog has been put to sleep. There's a bleakness in this Lasse Hallström comedy about growing up absurd. And rarely has a film so essentially serious been so completely entertaining.

64 **TAXI BLUES** *(1990, New Yorker, not rated)* The best film yet made about Russia's painful transition from communism. Piotr Zaitchenko plays a hard-

ORPHEUS: JEAN MARAIS, FRANÇOIS PERIER

FOREIGN

working cabbie along Moscow's wide, lonely, mean streets who's taken for a ride by a freewheeling and somewhat crazy, Westernized jazz musician (Pyotr Mamonov). The taxi driver begins to question what his entire history has meant in Pavel Lounguine's raw and mournful movie.

65 **LOLA MONTÈS** *(1955, Facets, not rated)* The story of the famous courtesan (Martine Carol) who becomes a circus novelty is Max Ophüls' means for examining the transitory nature of fame and fortune. While the actress playing the heroine is less than fascinating, the film nevertheless represents the triumph of manner over matter, as Ophüls' camera performs its dizzy dance of death.

66 **DEATH IN VENICE** *(1971, Warner, PG)* Director Luchino Visconti, with help from cinematographer Pasqualino De Santis and costume designer Piero Tosi, turns Thomas Mann's novella of romantic obsession into a lush and sensual experience. Dirk Bogarde is Aschenbach, the composer vacationing and dying in gorgeous, sweltering Venice, pining for Tadzio, the ideal of youthful beauty, to the strains of Mahler's Fifth Symphony.

67 **ORPHEUS** *(1949, Sinister, B&W, not rated)* A retelling (and reversal) of the Orpheus and Eurydice myth set in a bohemia of cafés, poets, musicians, and writers where everything functions symbolically, including a talking car. Jean Marais is the poet who demands an explanation for his dream life, journeying to the underworld to follow Death (Maria Ca-

177

sarès), an alluring harpy in evening gloves and tight black gown. Revisionist art has seldom been as much fun.

68 DIABOLIQUE *(1955, Sinister, B&W, not rated)* Genuinely creepy, Henri-Georges Clouzot's shocker is set in a dingy provincial boys' school, where Simone Signoret and Véra Clouzot (who have a suggestively intimate relationship) murder the headmaster, with whom they've both been involved. And then his body disappears. Dark, twisty, unlovely stuff, much copied by later movies. Watching it makes you feel like you've touched something cold and sticky.

69 DIVA *(1981, Facets, R)* Ostensibly about the obsession of a young postal worker (Frédéric Andrei) with a gorgeous black opera singer (Wilhelmenia Wiggins Fernandez), Jean-Jacques Beineix's stunning directorial debut also has gangsters, a dead prostitute, two Taiwanese record pirates, a Vietnamese shoplifter, and a loft decorated with wrecked automobiles, among some other inexplicably enjoyable objects and people. The first film to mix late-'70s punk sensibility with genre fiction in a bright, abrasive, poetic, pop way.

70 CHRIST STOPPED AT EBOLI *(1983, Facets, not rated)* The film takes place in a village so remote and backward that even Christ would not have ventured to it (hence the title), and is one of the few to treat peasant life without condescension and piety. Director Francesco Rosi imbues Carlo Levi's memoir with an almost palpable sense of teeming life.

The magnetic Gian Maria Volonté is the writer who remembers living there in exile and discovering as much about himself as he does about the ancient, superstitious culture in which he seeks refuge from Mussolini and his Fascists.

71 LA DOLCE VITA *(1960, Republic, B&W, not rated)* Convincing and memorable decadence along Rome's Via Veneto, as seen through the eyes of a jaded gossip columnist (Marcello Mastroianni) and masterminded by Federico Fellini. The highlights include a statue of Christ taking a helicopter ride, Anita Ekberg bathing in a fountain, homosexuals dressed up as fairies, and that devastating final scene, with its still-startling shot of the innocent girl on the beach.

72 DELICATESSEN *(1992, Paramount, R)* In this lip-smackingly good and rudely imaginative vision of the future, in which protein is scarce and unholy terror stalks a decaying apartment building, tenants try to avoid being one another's dinners. These denizens, including one woman whose suicide attempts keep hilariously backfiring, are filmed to heighten their grotesqueness and are among the strangest characters ever to step in front of a camera.

73 SHOESHINE *(1946, Facets, B&W, not rated)* Two shoeshine boys in Allied-occupied Rome get involved in a black-market operation to buy a horse they love and are sent to juvenile prison, where they are separated and appallingly mistreated. Shot in an actual prison, Vittorio De Sica's film nevertheless has a

BREATHLESS: JEAN-PAUL BELMONDO, JEAN SEBERG

dreamy quality, as if the events were not really happening, because what we see is too much to bear. As one boy is inexorably played against the other by the system, the film reaches a heartbreaking, indelible conclusion.

74 **THE VANISHING** *(1988, Fox Lorber, not rated)* In one of the most terrifying films ever made, a woman (Johanna Ter Steege) "disappears" at a gas station during a vacation, and her boyfriend (Gene Bervoets) becomes obsessed with finding out what happened to her. She has vanished at the hands of a madman (Bernard-Pierre Donnadieu) who may have killed her. A game of existential cat and mouse ensues between the two men and leads to an unforgettable finish. George Sluizer's brilliant rendering of the ultimate nightmare.

75 **BREATHLESS** *(1959, Facets, B&W, not rated)* Jean-Luc Godard's homage to the American B pictures of the 1940s and '50s ushered in the French *Nouvelle Vague*, or New Wave. Jean-Paul Belmondo is the gangster on the lam from the police and Jean Seberg his amoral American girlfriend, who eventually betrays him. The film's casual yet completely assured style—it's one of the first films with real *attitude*—has been copied over and over, as has the notion of an antihero, here so powerfully embodied by Belmondo.

76 **THE LOVERS** *(1958, New Yorker, B&W, not rated)* Its love scenes caused an absolute furor in its time: Jeanne Moreau, the wife of a priggish and smug provincial publisher (Alain Cuny), finds rapture in the arms of a lover (Jean-Marc Bory) she meets accidentally. Louis Malle's erotic paean to sexual liberation includes a half hour of balletic bliss, to the strains of Brahms, while the lovers take a stroll through a memorably moonlit garden.

77 **MON ONCLE ANTOINE** *(1971, Home Vision, not rated)* A luminescent film about coming of age in Quebec, set at Christmas in an asbestos-mining town, where a young boy has died at an isolated farmhouse, and another boy, Benoît, in his first confrontation with death, helps his undertaker uncle with the corpse. For Benoît, it is a time of painful revelation: He discovers his uncle is a drunk and his aunt is sleeping with a store clerk (played by the director, Claude Jutra). Nothing is what it once seemed to be, and part of Benoît has died as well.

78 **KAMERADSCHAFT** *(1931, Facets, B&W, not rated)* G.W. Pabst's film, a call for brotherhood between nations, opens with the Prelude to Wagner's *Die Meistersinger von Nürnberg* and is based on a true incident: a mine disaster in a French town near the French-German border, after which German miners came to help. The sound-editing techniques (there is no musical score following the Prelude, just the heavy-breathing, natural sounds of the mines) are still wondrous, and Pabst uses crowds with the same mathematical grandeur and visual sweep as Lang or Eisenstein.

79 **MISS JULIE** *(1950, Facets, B&W, not rated)* One of the most imaginative renderings of a famous play onto film, Alf Sjöberg's adaptation of the August Strindberg work expands the action visually so that the material becomes a new experience. Anita Björk plays the repressed Julie and Ulf Palme the valet who tempts her out of herself. In the midsummer sequences, the viewer shares the madness that takes hold of Miss Julie and uncorks her bottled-up self.

80 **KAGEMUSHA** *(1980, Fox-Video, PG)* When a warlord (Tatsuya Nakadai) dies, his *kagemusha*, or double, who is a petty thief, is put in his place and must assume the weight of power and responsibility for which he was never meant. Ablaze with color and resounding with stirring images of battle, Akira Kurosawa's ironic cautionary tale says, eloquently, that masquerades are doomed to failure.

81 **JU DOU** *(1989, LIVE, PG-13)* This tale of doomed love unfurls with almost morbid inexorability as a series of beautiful, kinetic still lifes. A fabric-dyeing mill in the 1920s is the setting for Ju Dou's (Gong Li) humiliation by an abusive husband and her consuming passion for his nephew. The movie's stately sense of the dramatic frames a window through which a distant scene comes vibrantly close to Western view.

WOMEN ON THE VERGE OF A NERVOUS BREAKDOWN: CARMEN MAURA, ROSSY DE PALMA

181

82 **PIXOTE** *(1981, Facets, not rated)* Hector Babenco's brutal film takes its place among the great movies dealing with childhood. The 10-year-old Pixote (Fernando Ramos da Silva) is among 3 million Brazilian children who live by crime, and Babenco used impoverished and illiterate children for an authentic cast. He follows Pixote's progress from reform school to becoming a pimp to the ultimate despair—the death of all laughter within him.

83 **WOMEN ON THE VERGE OF A NERVOUS BREAKDOWN** *(1988, Orion, R)* Pedro Almodóvar's breakneck farce is a gorgeous piece of pop filmmaking and is about nothing more than having a good time, but seldom has any director brought as much flair to the business of partying. In it, Almodóvar also celebrates the artificial, fantasy aspects of film: The backdrops look as fake as the pretzel-like plot twists are unbelievable. The beautifully frantic Carmen Maura is the put-upon heroine.

84 **CLAIRE'S KNEE** *(1970, Facets, not rated)* Everything's summery in Eric Rohmer's little lyric about a man's infatuation with a patella. The about-to-be-married hero (Jean-Claude Brialy) is obsessed with the moral implications of touching a young girl's knee before his marriage. When he finally does, you'd think Tristan had gulped his first draft of the magic love potion. Rohmer's script flares with high-toned intelligence, and cinematographer

Nestor Almendros basks in the beauty of France, making it look like a Renoir painting.

85 **LAST YEAR AT MARIENBAD** *(1961, Facets, B&W, not rated)* Critics have nearly gotten hernias trying to explain director Alain Resnais and screenwriter Alain Robbe-Grillet's time-memory-illusion extravaganza about a dressy, enigmatic woman (Delphine Seyrig) whom a man (Giorgio Albertazzi) may or may not have met years (months? days? minutes?) ago at a luxe spa. Robbe-Grillet swears the couple never did meet; Resnais vows he couldn't have made the film unless they had. Let the viewer decide.

86 **THE BATTLE OF ALGIERS** *(1966, Facets, B&W, not rated)* Gillo Pontecorvo's portrayal of the events leading up to the 1957 Algerian War is a political statement that has guts and yet is also exciting as film. The documentary feel has a marvelous spontaneity (aided by some terrific hand-held camera movement) that pulls the audience into the material and to the people who are involved in the guerrilla activities. Meticulously detailed, with harrowing torture and bombing sequences, the film has an epic sweep that recalls the grandeur of early Russian and German cinema.

87 **EYES WITHOUT A FACE** *(1959, Sinister, B&W, not rated)* Pierre Brasseur is a plastic surgeon who tries unsuccessfully to restore daughter Edith Scob's hideously disfigured face with skin grafts from abducted girls, procured for him by Alida Valli. The mask worn by the daughter so she won't have to look at herself gives her the aspect of a mannequin—or sad Barbie doll—who's living through hell. With a fluid rhythm and nocturnal scenes, director Georges Franju gives the schlock material an ethereal quality unique to horror films.

88 **BABETTE'S FEAST** *(1987, Orion, G)* Based on an Isak Dinesen story set on Denmark's remote Jutland coast, this mouthwatering film is a highly literary paean to food, glorious food, filled with moments of high comedy and wistful charm. Stéphane Audran plays the housekeeper for a couple of old maids from a pious religious sect who gets to light up their dreary lives with one spectacular smorgasbord. A film for that "strange little muscle," the tongue.

89 **BLOOD OF A POET** *(1930, Home Vision, B&W, not rated)* Abandon all literal-mindedness, ye who enter here. Jean Cocteau's experimental film, in four sections, occurs in a fraction of a second, the time it takes a chimney (crumbling in the first shot) to fall to the ground (the last one). Astounding images abound: a drawing of a mouth that comes alive, a poet who goes through a mirror, a snowball fight in which a child is killed, and a game of cards with Destiny.

90 **TORMENT** *(1944, Facets, B&W, PG)* A terrifying study of a sadomasochistic schoolteacher (Stig Järrel) and the far-reaching effect he has on an innocent pupil (Alf Kjellin) and the girl (Mai Zetterling) the pupil loves. The script, by the young Ingmar Bergman, directed by Alf Sjöberg, seems an act of vengeance against bad teachers. But Järrel's moonfaced, bespectacled fellow will haunt anyone who has ever hated the man or woman at the front of the classroom.

91 LA CAGE AUX FOLLES *(1978, MGM/UA, R)* A screamingly funny farce in which two middle-aged lovers—Albin, a purse-lipped drag entertainer called Zaza (Michel Serrault), and Renato, more conservative and "masculine" (Ugo Tognazzi)—try to pass among heterosexuals. The point is not so much that it can't be done as that it *shouldn't* be done, and Serrault's giddy performance, timed to the nanosecond, is a joy. No one is likely to forget such scenes as the one in which Renato tries, hopelessly, to teach Albin to "butter [his] toast like a man."

92 THE SHOP ON MAIN STREET *(1965, Home Vision, B&W, not rated)* A powerful Czech movie about the persecution of the Jews during World War II, with Josef Króner as an Aryan appointed controller of a button shop owned by a happy, polite, slightly deaf old Jewish woman (Ida Kaminska) who doesn't really know what's going on. The expulsion of the Jews, in contrast with earlier Sunday promenades that feature hats being tipped and sweet music in the air, is nightmarish and the betrayal of the old shopkeeper unspeakably saddening.

93 YOL *(1982, Columbia Tri-Star, not rated)* Codirected by screenwriter Yilmaz

LA CAGE AUX FOLLES: **MICHEL SERRAULT**

EVERETT COLLECTION

IN THE REALM OF THE SENSES: EIKO MATSUDA, TATSUYA FUJI

Güney from his prison cell and edited into final shape after his escape, this Turkish film has an intense center of gravity: the longing for home. Five political detainees are given a week's leave, and each heads home (*yol* means "way of life"). Their journeys are told and woven with great power. When one young Kurd reaches his guerrilla-ravaged village, he kneels to the ground and reverently kisses it. One has to go all the way back to early Russian cinema to find a comparable image.

94

EUROPA, EUROPA *(1991, Orion, R)* German political pressure may have kept this film from being nominated for an Academy Award in 1991, but this French-German coproduction will surely be remembered long after most

of that year's winners are forgotten. Directed by Agnieszka Holland and adapted from Solomon Perel's autobiography, it tells the story of a German Jewish teenager who survives the Nazi era through a combination of luck, happenstance, and deception, including several years passing as an ideal "ethnic German" in a Hitler Youth school. The often nerve-racking drama is leavened occasionally with unexpected comic touches, though Holland's penchant for symbolism sometimes gets a bit heavy-handed.

95

LA JETÉE *(1964, Facets, B&W, not rated)* Chris Marker's haunting half-hour science-fiction film of life after World War III, where one man, able to travel back and forth in time and obsessed with the image of a young woman on the jetty at Orly Airport, is told (with the exception of one astonishing moving image) entirely through the use of still photographs. Marker's film, in which life has come to a literal standstill, is uniquely disturbing: Death becomes the absence of movement; life, the power held in an image.

96 **DAY FOR NIGHT** *(1973, Warner, dubbed, PG)* François Truffaut's film about the intricacies, drudgery, and drama of making a film (an innocuous thing called *Meet Pamela*), where crises range from car trouble to the raging hormones of the cast to a kitten that won't take direction. Jacqueline Bisset plays an actress making her first film since having a nervous breakdown, and Valentina Cortese is divine as a tippling vet who keeps blowing her lines. Throughout, the camera moves as sensually as a woman taking off her stockings.

97 **CLOSELY WATCHED TRAINS** *(1966, Fox Lorber, B&W, not rated)* A droll, erotic, and ultimately shocking black comedy about life at a small Czech train station during World War II. Director Jiri Menzel expertly juggles pathos and absurdity as a young dispatcher (Vaclav Neckar) learns about love, pain, and the whole damn thing. There's a generosity of spirit—even toward the Germans—pervading this film that is very accomplished and all too rare.

98 **THE WANNSEE CONFERENCE** *(1986, Home Vision, not rated)* A harrowing documentary-style enactment of a January 1942 Third Reich meeting that was called to decide the fate of the troublesome Jews. This high-powered business meeting, where extermination is casually rationalized, proceeds with a bone-chillingly ordinary quality, what philosopher Hannah Arendt termed "the banality of evil." And the barking of a German shepherd outside the meeting becomes a reminder that such dogs herded Jews to their deaths.

99 **IN THE REALM OF THE SENSES** *(1976, Fox Lorber, NC-17)* Nagisa Oshima's disturbing (to say the least) chamber drama of erotic obsession is based on a true story of a woman arrested in Tokyo in 1936 in possession of her lover's severed genitals. The fictional lovers (Tatsuya Fuji and Eiko Matsuda), having exhausted their sexual repertoire, begin strangling each other to sustain their pleasurable sensations, bringing sex to a deadly conclusion. Some kind of great movie, certainly with plenty of contemporary resonance.

100 **THE SPIRIT OF THE BEEHIVE** *(1973, Connoisseur, not rated)* Set in post–Civil War Spain, the film features a heartbreaking Ana Torrent as a little girl who befriends a wounded fugitive, believing him to be the Frankenstein monster. Directed by Victor Erice, it's at once a parable of life under Franco, a lament for lost innocence, and an exquisite evocation of childhood imagination. On all levels, it's haunting.

Reviews written by Lawrence O'Toole, as well as Roy Hemming, Melissa Pierson, and Michael Sauter.

185

K I D S

WHO MADE HOME VIDEO the megabillion-dollar industry it is today? Kids did, of course. Actually, their parents did, once they realized that renting a Disney classic beat plonking the little ones in front of the tube and letting MTV scoop out their minds. And in the early '90s, when studios decided to increase the number of tapes they offered for sale (as opposed to rental), "kidvid" again led the pack, which makes perfect sense when you understand that the average small child likes to repeat a favorite movie experience over and over and over again, until the VCR heads wear down to nubs or Mom and Dad destroy the tape—whichever comes first.

We understand the pain that comes from hearing "It's a Small World" 932 times before dinner. And we won't even talk about Barney. What we offer in these two kidvid lists—the 50 best live-action and the 50 best animated—are tapes that will keep them pacified and you sane, that you can watch *with* your children and enjoy as much *as* your children (although perhaps, in the tradition of our No. 8 animated pick, *The Adventures of Rocky and Bullwinkle*, on another level entirely).

LIVE ACTION

1 **E.T. THE EXTRA-TERRESTRIAL** *(1982, MCA/Universal, PG)* The most popular family movie of all time—and for good reason. The story is heart-swellingly fantastical: A stranded space alien is befriended by a young boy (Henry Thomas), who tries to help E.T. get back home. Full of surefire Steven Spielberg trademarks, awesome special effects (in particular, E.T. him/her/itself), and a story that ever so gradually hooks viewers and climaxes at breakneck speed.

2 **THE WIZARD OF OZ** *(1939, MGM/UA, G)* No, it certainly isn't Kansas—it's a golden age of Hollywood backlot heaven for kids of every age, complete with plucky heroine Dorothy (Judy Garland), lovably creepy Munchkins, truly timeless song masterpieces (by Harold Arlen and Yip Harburg), and a witch so wicked that after seeing her once you love hating her for the rest of your life.

3 **MARY POPPINS** *(1964, Disney, G)* Nanny Mary Poppins (Julie Andrews, in her screen debut) blows into a proper London household with her whimsical ways—and unusual friends like Bert, the chimney sweep (Dick Van Dyke)—transforming the boring lives of her charges and their stiff parents. Irresistibly sweet songs—"A Spoonful of Sugar," "Chim Chim Cheree," "Let's Go Fly a Kite"—and animated segments keep the 139-minute movie from lagging for a second.

4 **KING OF THE HILL** *(1993, MCA/Universal, PG-13)* Steven Soderbergh's lyrical coming-of-age drama shows how the world actually looks through a child's eyes. Set in St. Louis during the Depression, this tale of an innocent, resourceful boy (Jesse Bradford) who drops through the net of middle-class life takes you back to a time when everything in your existence—neighbors, schoolmates, first crushes, even the buildings on your block—seem filled with a potent singularity and wonder.

5 **BENJI** *(1974, Movies Unlimited, G)* Sure, the story is silly and the acting over-the-top. But *Benji* features every little kid's favorite kind of star—a cute li'l pup—in one of the most remarkable cinematic dog performances ever. In fact, it puts most of Lassie's work to shame. The pint-size mutt scurries through his paces in an amazing series of stunts and tricks that makes this dumb movie lovable, qualifying it as great family viewing.

6 **THE MIRACLE WORKER** *(1962, MGM/UA, B&W, not rated)* An inspiring true story about the friendship between Helen Keller, a deaf and blind child (Patty Duke), and Annie Sullivan, the teacher (Anne Bancroft) who brought her out of the figurative darkness. Both Duke and Bancroft took home Oscars for their performances. A 1979 made-for-TV version—with Patty Duke playing Annie Sullivan—is good, but the original is better.

7 **LITTLE WOMEN** *(1933, MGM/UA, B&W, not rated)* In an age when family values are constantly

THE ADDAMS FAMILY: RAUL JULIA, ANJELICA HUSTON

invoked, here's a vintage film that shows them in action. This definitive version of Louisa May Alcott's Civil War story about the happiness and sorrow of the March sisters—led by Katharine Hepburn as Jo—was nominated for three Academy Awards.

8 **THE ADDAMS FAMILY** *(1991, Paramount, PG-13)* At last, a functional family! Not your typical role models, Gomez and Morticia Addams (Raul Julia and Anjelica Huston) rule their brood with love and gentle persuasion, rather than harsh words or guillotine blades. It works: Wednesday and Pugsley are always polite and presentable. Younger kids may have trouble following the larcenous plot, but there's more than enough here to keep everyone in the house laughing together.

9 **BORN FREE** *(1966, Columbia TriStar, G)* The '60s story of how a game warden and his wife raise a lion cub in Kenya is even more meaningful in light of the pro-environmental stance among today's youngsters. As the grandmother of the save-the-animals genre, *Born Free* holds up incredibly well and is far better than most of its offspring.

10 **NATIONAL VELVET** *(1944, MGM/UA, G)* Years before Elizabeth Taylor made headlines with her vast number of husbands, she was a child star, and this was her *Home Alone.* Perhaps the oldest kid-and-a-horse movie, it's still the champ. Mickey Rooney, with his youthful "let's put on a show" exuberance, helps angelic young Liz enter her horse in the Grand National race. For all its predictability, the story is still suspenseful, and looks great in beautiful Technicolor.

11 ABBOTT AND COSTELLO MEET FRANKENSTEIN *(1948, MCA/Universal, B&W, not rated)*

ABBOTT AND COSTELLO MEET FRANKENSTEIN:
LOU COSTELLO, LON CHANEY JR.

190

Bud Abbott and Lou Costello teamed up in almost 40 stupidly fun movies that have tickled generations of children. Every one of the films contains classic bits, but this one holds together best. As Dracula, Bela Lugosi has designs to put Lou's brain into the Frankenstein monster, but the dotty duo won't believe the wolf man when he tells them they're in danger.

12 THE AUTOBIOGRAPHY OF MISS JANE PITTMAN *(1974, Facets, not rated)* This Emmy-winning made-for-TV movie traces the struggle of African-Americans from the era of slavery to the civil rights movement through the eyes of a 110-year-old woman. In the title role,

Cicely Tyson brings the personal to the political, which will leave a lasting impression on children.

13 OLD YELLER *(1957, Disney, G)* Based on the classic novel that has been required reading in many schools, *Old Yeller* was one of the first boy-and-his-dog movies—and none have improved on it. The heartrending climax is probably too tough for younger viewers to take. For older kids, the book report can be done from this faithful retelling.

14 HONEY, I SHRUNK THE KIDS *(1989, Disney, PG)* Getting there is a no-brainer, but once the kids are shrunk, this movie's charm quotient skyrockets. There's great fun in watching the mini kids encounter everyday items and deal with them from a different perspective: Cheerios as a water ride, the backyard as a jungle, the family dog looming larger than *Tyrannosaurus rex*. Best of all, the kids return to normal just before, not after, the effects get stale.

15 THE ADVENTURES OF HUCK FINN *(1993, Disney, PG)* Since 1920, there have been no fewer than eight film versions of Mark Twain's novel. Disney's is lively and sensitive, with lush cinematography and an exuberant score. At the outset, Huck (Elijah Wood) promises the audience a "split-lickin' good time," and he delivers.

16 THE KARATE KID *(1984, Columbia TriStar, PG)* Eight years after directing *Rocky*, John G. Avildsen re-created

the underdog story for the Clearasil set. Teen idol Ralph Macchio is a bit earnest in the title role, but this movie works because of Noriyuki "Pat" Morita's offbeat performance as Mr. Miyagi, the karate master whose unorthodox training techniques pay off.

17 **HOMEWARD BOUND: THE INCREDIBLE JOURNEY** *(1993, Disney, G)* It's déjà vu all over again. Disney updated its 1963 animal road movie by combining *Look Who's Talking* with *The Incredible Journey*. The funny thing about this hybrid—in which the audience hears the animals' conversations as they lead a grand adventure—is that it works. Don Ameche, Michael J. Fox, and Sally Field supply the voices for an engaging trio of misplaced pets. Their snappy banter keeps the trek moving at a lively pace.

18 **SOUNDER** *(1972, Paramount, G)* The story of a family of sharecroppers in Depression-era Louisiana is told without sentimentality, though we see them cope with their share of adversity. Paul Winfield and Cicely Tyson were each nominated for an Oscar, as was the understated but powerful movie. Taj Mahal provides a fine soundtrack—and a strong on-screen performance.

19 **THE MUPPETS TAKE MANHATTAN** *(1984, FoxVideo, PG-13)* Playwright Kermit and his Muppet troupe take a bite out of the Big Apple and wind up with a bad taste in their mouths. Turns out, it's filled with worms, namely, greedy producers, stiff competition, and financial hardship—and Miss Piggy even gets mugged in Central Park. At least they're not dis-

191

HONEY, I SHRUNK THE KIDS: ROBERT OLIVERI

criminated against for being puppets. Part of the fun is its cinematic sightseeing tour and, though kids won't get them, its numerous cameos—almost as many as in *The Player.*

20 THE SECRET GARDEN *(1993, Warner, G)* This darkly lavish version of the Frances Hodgson Burnett children's story makes clear its link to gothic romance: Basically, it's *Jane Eyre* retooled for the sandbox set. In Kate Maberly, director Agnieszka Holland found the perfect young actress to play Mary Lennox, the cynical orphan who brings herself and the gloomy estate of her uncle (John Lynch) into bloom when she discovers a hidden bower. Holland's lush color scheme loses some oomph on video, but it's hard to imagine the little loner in your house not taking this one to heart.

21 THE PARENT TRAP *(1961, Disney, not rated)* Divorce, practically unthinkable back in the '60s, is almost a given in the '90s. That's precisely why kids will sympathize with the efforts made by twins (played by Hayley Mills) to get their folks back together. Psychological correctness aside, this is a silly good time.

22 THE YEARLING *(1946, MGM/ UA, G)* This classic story speaks to the downside of domesticating wild animals. In this case, love doesn't conquer all, a hard-learned fact that makes the outcome of this family drama a three-Kleenex affair. Far removed from the senseless killing of animals and people that often occurs in many of today's films, and no one can blame the father (Gregory Peck) for the task he must perform.

23 WHITE FANG *(1991, Disney, PG)* The adventures of a boy (Ethan Hawke) and his dog in Alaska. No surprise that the dog steals the show. In true Jack London fashion, the tale is action-packed, and bloodshed abounds in some of the dogfight scenes. Still, not even repeated viewings will make this a tired tale.

24 WILLY WONKA AND THE CHOCOLATE FACTORY *(1971, Warner, G)* An ambitious adaptation of the Roald Dahl fantasy in which a winsome child, along with four hilarious spoiled brats, wins a tour of the world's greatest chocolate factory. Outrageous sets, broad characterizations, and a determined march to a happy ending add up to make this a tuneful fave.

25 THE ABSENT-MINDED PROFESSOR *(1961, Disney, B&W, G)* "Flubber," a perfectly ridiculous name for a flying rubber substance, was the result of a bad lab day for absentminded professor Fred MacMurray. The prehistoric special effects won't trick young viewers in the '90s, who are steeped in far more complex wizardry. But the good-natured story and scene-stealing performance by greedy businessman Keenan Wynn still hold up.

26 ADVENTURES IN BABYSITTING *(1987, Disney, PG-13)* All too rare, this is a comedy with a female lead, and Elisabeth Shue does the job well. Don't be fooled by the title: This is not about mishaps

GRADE SCHOOL CLASSICISM

They don't have pictures of scruffy li'l dogs or Smurfs or fuzzy puppets on the boxes. But video-cassettes of old Hollywood movies—the ones video stores file under "Classics"—often appeal to kids much more than the second-rate, product-plugging cartoon fluff that's constantly marketed to them. Though made for adults, American movies of the '30s, '40s, '50s, and '60s had to meet strict standards of moral conduct under the industry's old Production Code. (Sustained profanity, nudity, and all the other hallmarks of modern grown-up films were verboten until 1968, when the Motion Picture Association's ratings code was introduced.) As a result, vintage Hollywood films exude an air of chaste, glamorized make-believe that today's grown-ups find quaint—and that children embrace immediately. Want proof? Try any of the following on a grade-schooler:

Hitchcock's chase trilogy: The master of suspense filmed virtually the same cross-country chase three times, in *The 39 Steps, Saboteur,* and *North by Northwest*. All of them have whiz-bang pacing, creepily low-key villains who demonstrate why you should *never* follow that smiling man with the ice cream cone, and plots built on the ultimate childhood bugaboo: being blamed for something you didn't do.

The Hope-Crosby *Road* **films:** Five are on video, and in jaunts from Rio to

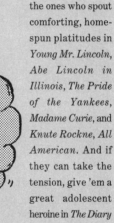

Bali to Hong Kong, Bob and Bing perfectly capture the bickering, childlike banter of best pals who seem to do everything together.

Anthony Mann Westerns starring James Stewart: Kids instantly connect with Stewart's stalwart courage and clumsy, just-got-my-growth-spurt gait, traits best seen in four morality tales that unfold in easy-to-grasp visual terms—*Winchester '73, Bend of the River, The Man From Laramie,* and *The Naked Spur*.

Biopics: Eight-year-olds are enchanted by Hollywood's idealized role models, especially the ones who spout comforting, homespun platitudes in *Young Mr. Lincoln, Abe Lincoln in Illinois, The Pride of the Yankees, Madame Curie,* and *Knute Rockne, All American*. And if they can take the tension, give 'em a great adolescent heroine in *The Diary of Anne Frank*.

Gangster-on-the-lam movies: Why are young minds so blown away by Cagney in *White Heat,* Bogie in *High Sierra,* and both toughs in *Angels With Dirty Faces*? Because there's violence, action, and guns but no gore. And nothing exorcises fears about crime and punishment like seeing these charismatic rats fall to "da coppers" in the end. —*Steve Daly*

193

at home. It's a romp through Chicago's nightlife for the babysitter and her underage charges.

27 SHORT CIRCUIT *(1986, Fox-Video, PG-13)* Anthropology meets technology and creates a robot with a heart, a brain, and a sweet personality. Who would go back to the cold, lonely weapons factory if he could live with Ally Sheedy? Sweet and funny, and far better than the sequel it begat.

28 BEETHOVEN *(1992, MCA/Universal, PG)* Family meets dog, family loses dog, family finds dog. Formulaic, true, but that's why formulas work. The fluffy, drooling Saint Bernard in the title role is just what you want in a fluffy drooler. And Charles Grodin does a wonderful turn as the man who would be master.

29 MARCH OF THE WOODEN SOLDIERS *(1934, Nostalgia, B&W, not rated)* If it's a true classic, it doesn't matter how old it is, and this Laurel and Hardy vehicle has legs. Extraordinary sets and broad characters mark this tale, as the brave citizens of Toyland defend their home against the evil invading boogeymen. (Also known as *Babes in Toyland*.)

'FREE WILLY' STAR JASON JAMES RICHTER

A BOY AND HIS ORCA

Lassie. Flipper. E.T. Behind every pop-culture beast, it seems, is a devoted boy. Take *Free Willy*, the film about a melancholy whale and the lad who befriends him. Below, its 13-year-old star, Jason James Richter, talks about fame, the perils of celebrityhood, and what a whale's tongue feels like.

Q: What were your first impressions of Willy?
A: Well, his real name is Keiko, and he was really cool. We made a deal: As long as he didn't bite my hand off, I'd be his best friend. He even let me pet his tongue! It felt like Bazooka bubble gum.

Q: After *Free Willy*, what will be your biggest challenge?
A: Dealing with the press and figuring out who my real friends are. Also, I have to figure out how not to get harassed every time I go to the Taco Bell.

Q: Of all the actors and actresses out there, whom would you most like to meet?
A: I wish I could meet Spencer Tracy. I loved that movie *A Guy Named Joe*. But he's dead.

Now it would probably be Sean Astin. Not only was he in *The Goonies*, but he was in *Encino Man*!

Q: What kind of movie would you like to do next?
A: If the material is good, anything. But I won't do stupid horror movies. Or trash, like *Hoffa*. —*Kenneth M. Chanko*

30 TREASURE ISLAND *(1950, Disney, PG)* "Based on the Robert Louis Stevenson classic" and "filmed in England" are attributes that don't exactly put *Treasure Island* in *Indiana Jones'* league, but there's enough color, action, and violence in it to hold any older kid's attention. Though it sounds sexist to say so, it's more of a boy's movie. Homework alert: Disney changed the novel's ending to a more upbeat commercial climax, so don't get caught.

31 THE BLACK STALLION *(1979, MGM/UA, G)* A hauntingly beautiful tale of a boy's special relationship with a mysterious horse. Kelly Reno gives a believable performance as the boy, and Mickey Rooney shines as a trainer who helps turn "the Black" into a winner.

32 SWISS FAMILY ROBINSON *(1960, Disney, G)* This was a breakout movie because of the parents' roles. Instead of the usual one-dimensional dupes that cluttered the movies of the '60s, John Mills and Dorothy McGuire play a sensitive, whimsical, and concerned dad and mom shepherding their shipwrecked family. They help keep this movie fresh—as do typically exhilarating Technicolor action sequences.

33 FREE WILLY *(1993, Warner, PG)* This serious-minded eco-adventure will be an eye-opener for preteens raised on inane canine comedies. The surprisingly touching film follows a troubled 12-year-old boy who bonds with a 7,000-pound orca. You'll laugh, you'll cry

BEETHOVEN:

NICHOLLE TOM, CHRISTOPHER CASTILE, SARAH ROSE KARR

195

...then your kids might hit you up for a Greenpeace donation.

34 FERRIS BUELLER'S DAY OFF *(1986, Paramount, PG-13)* The title tells the tale: Ferris (Matthew Broderick) plays hooky from school, drives a cool car, gets the girl, and ignites Chicago with his antics. John Hughes' hippest teen film fulfills every kid's fantasy of how to spend a day cutting class.

35 FREAKY FRIDAY *(1977, Disney, G)* Mary Rodgers adapted her novel, about a mother and daughter who switch roles, to fit the Disney mold. As the daughter, Jodie Foster shows why she was destined to become a star, and Barbara

Harris takes a nice turn as her mom. Despite its '70s setting, the plot still works. That's why Hollywood keeps using it. More up-to-date versions include *Like Father, Like Son* and *Vice Versa.*

36 **THE RED PONY** *(1949, Republic, not rated)* A compelling story from the novel by John Steinbeck, *The Red Pony* is as sad and poignant as *The Yearling*, but it turns gruesome. After the horse's demise, the film continues beyond the tragedy to show nature taking its course. It isn't pretty. The gore isn't gratuitous, but it's difficult to watch.

37 **MY SIDE OF THE MOUNTAIN** *(1969, Paramount, G)* A young Henry David Thoreau devotee (Ted Eccles) leaves home to take up residence in the Canadian Rockies for a year, developing his special gift for befriending the local animals. The antithesis to *Home Alone*, it's equally entertaining in its way.

38 **TEENAGE MUTANT NINJA TURTLES** *(1990, LIVE, PG)* Four turtles, named for Italian Renaissance painters, who sport *Karate Kid* headgear and scarf down pizza. Who says there are no new ideas? It may not have won any Oscars, but if awards were given for merchandising, this would have won Best Picture. You won't be able to keep your kids away from this one, even if you know tae kwon do.

39 **WHERE THE RED FERN GROWS** *(1974, LIVE, G)* A moving family drama set in 1930s Oklahoma. A determined boy (Stewart Peterson) scrapes together enough money to buy two puppies. They all grow up together as he trains them to be champion hunting dogs.

40 **THE ERNEST GREEN STORY** *(1992, Disney, not rated)* A stiff lesson in race relations with all the promise of the civil rights movement that has yet to materialize. Hopefully, this inspired true story of the first young black man (Morris Chestnut) to graduate from a previously all-white high school in Little Rock, Ark., will underscore the need for more tolerance and acceptance.

41 **A FRIENDSHIP IN VIENNA** *(1988, Disney, not rated)* The memory of the Holocaust has been infused with new life, thanks to Steven Spielberg's Oscar-winning epic, *Schindler's List*. This well-crafted made-for-TV movie will give your kids a smaller, less-jarring view of this historical atrocity without the nightmares. Not as bleak as the true-life *Diary of Anne Frank*, and the cast of TV actors is somewhat more recognizable.

42 **THE INCREDIBLE MR. LIMPET** *(1964, Warner, not rated)* You know the old story: Boy (in this case, a really old one—Don Knotts) meets girl, boy turns into fish, fish helps sink a Nazi submarine. Dippy mix of live action and animation and a too-stupid-to-really-care-about story mesh to make a surprisingly fun family movie.

43 **THE MAN FROM SNOWY RIVER** *(1983, FoxVideo, PG)* A coming-of-age Western from Down Under, teaching the necessity of

LETTER-PERFECT MOVIES

Who says TV is bad for kids? Sly parents can get young people to hone their reading skills through video—by engrossing them in some entertaining movies that just happen to use written words in their plots. Here are a few of the movies you can get on tape that are appropriate for a variety of ages and reading levels.

MY LIFE AS A DOG *(1985, not rated)* A poignant film about a young boy growing up in Sweden during the late '50s. Be sure to ask for the subtitled, not the dubbed, version. Appropriate for readers 10 and up who can handle sophisticated themes.

JUMPIN' JACK FLASH *(1986, R)* Perfect for teens with reading difficulties, it's got adventure, laughs, and romance—all conveyed via computer screen. Star Whoopi Goldberg reads the words as they appear on her screen to help viewers/readers follow the plot as well as the text.

WARGAMES *(1983, PG)* Matthew Broderick plays a hacker who breaks into a top secret government computer. Messages appear on the computer screen throughout the movie, adding to the plot twists. Ages 10 and up.

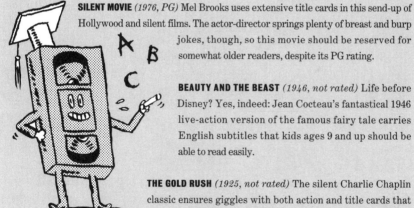

SILENT MOVIE *(1976, PG)* Mel Brooks uses extensive title cards in this send-up of Hollywood and silent films. The actor-director springs plenty of breast and burp jokes, though, so this movie should be reserved for somewhat older readers, despite its PG rating.

BEAUTY AND THE BEAST *(1946, not rated)* Life before Disney? Yes, indeed: Jean Cocteau's fantastical 1946 live-action version of the famous fairy tale carries English subtitles that kids ages 9 and up should be able to read easily.

THE GOLD RUSH *(1925, not rated)* The silent Charlie Chaplin classic ensures giggles with both action and title cards that are simple enough for all readers. *—Rebecca Ascher-Walsh*

coexistence between man and beast. It also offers opulent Australian scenery, beautiful wild stallions running free, and an offbeat dual role by Kirk Douglas. In the end, our hero (Tom Burlinson) gets the girl and the horse(s).

44

HARVEY *(1950, MCA/Universal, B&W, not rated)* What kid can't relate to an imaginary friend? This film was intended for an adult audience, but its gentle demeanor and main character, Elwood

OUTDATED RATINGS

X-ING OUT OLD Gs AND Rs

Time changes everything, including movie ratings: The Motion Picture
Association of America had much different standards when it began
issuing ratings in 1968. "It's fair to say that if [the X-rated 1969 release]
Midnight Cowboy came out today, it would probably get an R," admits
MPAA president Jack Valenti. "It might even get a PG-13." But not all
of the MPAA's standards have been relaxed: Some early-'70s PG films
would be PG-13 today; in 1984 the MPAA decided to give this more
restrictive designation to any film involving drug use. Here are seven examples of movies on video
we think would get different ratings if they were released in theaters now. —*Frank Lovece*

MOVIE	THEN	NOW?	WHY
THE GREEN BERETS (1968) John Wayne, David Janssen	G	R	Graphic war violence; flaming bodies; village slaughtered. Video box claims "Not Rated."
PLANET OF THE APES (1968) Charlton Heston, Roddy McDowall	G	PG	Bloody shooting deaths, hanging human carcasses, and a gosh-darned expletive.
THE BOSTON STRANGLER (1968) Henry Fonda, Tony Curtis	R	PG	TV-movie-tame true-crime drama; two near-subliminal shots of a woman's breast.
PLAY MISTY FOR ME (1971) Clint Eastwood, Jessica Walter	R	PG-13	Deejay stalked by groupie; it's *Fatal Attraction* minus graphic sex. One mention of marijuana.
MCCABE & MRS. MILLER (1971) Warren Beatty, Julie Christie	R	PG-13	Brief shot of nude bathers, one F-word. Opium-smoking sole reason for the 13.
THE ANDROMEDA STRAIN (1971) Arthur Hill, David Wayne	G	PG	Disturbing thriller of deadly space virus on Earth. Dead children, a gruesome wrist slicing.
INDIANA JONES AND THE TEMPLE OF DOOM (1984) Harrison Ford	PG	PG-13	Scene of ripped-out heart got the PG-13 bandwagon rolling.

P. Dowd (James Stewart, in a brilliantly understated performance), make it a true find for younger viewers. Despite the skepticism of friends and family, Dowd stands by his invisible friend, who happens to be a six-foot-tall rabbit. If pop psychology had existed then, this movie would have been less insightful because today this kind of behavior is encouraged—well, at least in 6-year-olds.

45 KIDNAPPED *(1960, Disney, PG)* Another Robert Louis Stevenson classic—did he write any other kind?—brought to the screen as another flashy action-adventure (starring Peter Finch, Peter O'Toole, and Disney staple James MacArthur). The outcome was another success for the hit factory.

46 ALL CREATURES GREAT AND SMALL *(1978, FoxVideo, not rated)* Based on James Herriot's best-selling books about a young veterinarian in rural England, the slow-paced stories may not grab children accustomed to today's fast-paced, fast-forward fare, which caters to short attention spans. But it is worth the effort for those with a little patience.

47 HOME ALONE *(1990, FoxVideo, PG)* Eight-year-old Kevin (the role that made Macaulay Culkin a superkid) has the survival instincts of a Marine. To thwart the bad guys (Joe Pesci and Daniel Stern) trying to break into his home, Kevin employs a succession of ingenious and excessively brutal techniques. If he learned this stuff from television, Janet Reno may have a case. Just make sure your kids know what not to try at home.

HARVEY: JAMES STEWART AND FRIEND

48 HEIDI *(1937, FoxVideo, B&W, not rated)* In this version of a classic tear-jerker, orphan Heidi (Shirley Temple) is sent to live with her mean grandfather (Jean Hersholt) in the Alps. Eventually her sunny charm melts his cold heart—and then their troubles begin. There's a little bit of everything in this one: laughs, cries, even a musical number.

49 INTO THE WEST *(1993, Touchstone, PG)* A disconsolate widowed father (Gabriel Byrne), his two precocious moppets, a majestic white horse, and Emerald Isle folklore make this movie thoroughbred family entertainment. This captivating adventure also touches on emotional issues not found in formulaic kids' fare.

50 OLIVER! *(1968, Columbia TriStar, G)* The Best Picture Oscar winner for 1968, this rollicking musical version of Dickens' *Oliver Twist* enlivens the story of an orphan who learns a life of crime when he's taken in by a band of pickpockets.

Reviews written by Linda Movish, Ty Burr, Ellen Cannon, and Owen Gleiberman.

199

ANIMATION

1 **BEAUTY AND THE BEAST** *(1991, Disney, G)* This animated Disney feature is the one most endowed with appeal-for-all-ages ingredients: There's Belle, a feminist heroine; Gaston, the egomaniacal, pumped-up villain; lilting Alan Menken melodies and adroit Howard Ashman lyrics; stunning computer-graphic backgrounds in the ballroom scene; and Disney's all-time-high lineup of indelible supporting characters, led by saucy candlestick Lumière, fussy clock Cogsworth, maternal teapot Mrs. Potts, and Chip, the sprightly kid cup. It all barrels by at an MTV-era pace designed to stand up to well-deserved repeat viewings.

2 **PINOCCHIO** *(1940, Disney, G)* Obsessively detailed drawings create a thoroughly believable world, and outside the benevolent sphere of dad Geppetto's workshop that world is not a pretty place. Poor sinner Pinoke falls into the clutches of one evil figure after another—a charlatan fox, an abusive puppeteer, a sinister donkey broker—despite the best efforts of cheery guardian Jiminy Cricket. In fact, the sensibility lurking beneath the happy-go-lucky score is so serious, it would be wise to set aside postmovie family time to answer kids' inevitable questions: What's a conscience? And what's so wicked about being an actor?

3 **A SALUTE TO CHUCK JONES** *(1949– 60, Warner, not rated)* Jones is the Warner cartoon director who gave Bugs Bunny deadpan timing,

BEAUTY AND THE BEAST

played the hare brilliantly against the sore loser Daffy Duck, invented *Road Runner,* and sent Daffy as Duck Dodgers to the "twenty-fourth and a half century." In this eight-cartoon sampler, you'll find comedy as inspired as anything in Chaplin or Keaton, from the pantomime in "One Froggy Evening," the tragic tale of an amphibian who refuses to sing and dance for anyone but his master, to the wide-eyed mugging of "Feed the Kitty," in which a bulldog tries to hide a tiny feline from his owner.

ALADDIN

4 **THE LITTLE MERMAID** *(1989, Disney, G)* The way-down-under musical that marked the resuscitation of Disney feature cartoons for a much broader, more adult audience in the '90s. If you haven't seen it lately, surprise! It now looks primitive compared with *Beauty and the Beast* and *Aladdin.* But no matter how resolutely two-dimensional the hard-edged graphics sometimes seem, the gotta-be-me teen-romance story line and the Howard Ashman–Alan Menken songs (especially guardian crab Sebastian's celebratory showstopper, "Under the Sea") have marvelous depth.

5 **BETTY BOOP SPECIAL COLLECTOR'S EDITION, VOLS. 1 AND 2** *(1931–36, Republic, B&W, not rated)* Shimmying on gartered gams and cooing sweet come-ons (Mae Questel's high-pitched vocals make her sound like Mae West on helium), jazz baby Betty got away with frisky behavior until the Production Code lowered her hem and raised her neckline in 1934. Both incarnations are represented here, and today the sexuality (if not the sexism) in the pre-Code shorts seems pretty harmless.

What shines through in these mostly pristine prints (a dozen cartoons on each tape) is the delightful inventiveness of the Fleischer studio's animation, where anything goes and every object bounces to the beat. Highlight: bizarre hallucinations set to Cab Calloway licks in volume one's "Snow White."

201

6 **THE SNOWMAN** *(1982, Columbia TriStar, not rated)* There's next to no dialogue in this exquisitely rendered British adaptation of Raymond Briggs' picture book. Gestures, expressions, and a haunting orchestral score tell the story as a boy ushers his come-alive creation around the house (while Mom and Dad sleep), then flies Superman-style with the homesick fellow back to the North Pole to visit his snow pals. The melancholy ending will stir grown-up intimations of mortality in youngsters; for adults, it brings back the childhood wonder and pain of finding—and losing—a perfect playmate.

7 **ALADDIN** *(1992, Disney, G)* What man, woman, or child wouldn't want to hang out forever with

Robin Williams' big, blue wish factory of a genie? If the mile-a-minute topical gags and celeb caricatures become inscrutable to future generations, the sheer energy in Disney's blitzkrieg-speed take on the *Arabian Nights* should prove timeless. While kids will probably hit rewind most often to re-watch the Genie's breathless introductory song, "Friend Like Me" (part of another socko Ashman-Menken score, with assists by Tim Rice), the movie's true marvel of compression is the riotous "Prince Ali" number: It manages to burlesque the public relations biz, the Macy's Thanksgiving Day Parade, teen idoldom, and political demagoguery—all in under three minutes.

8 THE ADVENTURES OF ROCKY AND BULLWINKLE, VOLS. 1–12 *(1959–61, Buena Vista, not rated)* Visually, these tapes couldn't be cruder. But the smart pun-upmanship that flies from the lips of Jay Ward's made-for-TV 'toons puts most condescending kidvid dialogue to shame; just the *voices* of Rocket J. Squirrel (plucky kid) and Bullwinkle J. Moose (sweet moron) are endlessly amusing. Each tape contains a multipart main story and some extras,

THE ADVENTURES OF ROCKY AND BULLWINKLE

FOTO FANTASIES

like a smart-alecky segment of "Fractured Fairy Tales" or a hat trick from Bullwinkle. Our top pick: volume one, "Mona Moose," in which Canadian Mountie Dudley Do-Right goes undercover to catch Snidely Whiplash, and his girlfriend Nell once again declares that she's in love with Dudley's horse.

9 DUMBO *(1941, Disney, G)* Or, *The Ugly Duckling* under the big top. Every scene's a virtuoso flourish of perfectly judged animation, music, and sentiment in one of the shortest of all Disney features (64 minutes): big-eared Dumbo accidentally toppling a pyramid of mean-old-lady elephants; the little guy getting drunk and imagining "Pink Elephants on Parade"; a passel of jiving crows (they're not at all PC, though somewhat less offensive than many other black caricatures of the era) teaching him to fly. Parental Kleenex alert: You'll probably blubber harder than your children when a locked-up Mrs. Jumbo caresses her son with her trunk through the bars of her cage.

10 DAFFY DUCK: THE NUTTINESS CONTINUES... *(1937–56, Warner, not rated)* A peerless portrait skewed not to the early-career, completely insane Daffy but to the fully evolved, sneaky, jealous, egotistical Daffy. Most of these eight shorts are directed by Chuck Jones, who makes the drake unforgettably inept as a gunslinger ("Drip-along Daffy"), a swashbuckler ("The Scarlet Pumpernickel"), and the victim of a practical-joker animator (the practically existentialist "Duck Amuck"). For those who can't get enough duck: Check out MGM/UA's *Daffy!*, his best from 1938 to 1948.

UNSETTLED SCORE

If the story of *Aladdin*'s music were told in a song, the ditty would have more verses than "99 Bottles." Composer Alan Menken found himself in perpetual rewrite after first submitting the songs with lyricist Howard Ashman in 1988. After Ashman died of AIDS in '91, Menken continued solo, then teamed with Tim Rice (*Evita*). Along the way, twice as many finished tunes were dropped as made it into the movie. Here's what happened to some of the rejects:

"You Can Count on Me" (Menken) **Scene:** Song introduces Aladdin. **Sample lyric:** "You can count on me/I'll come through for you." **Why it went:** Too pokey an intro for Aladdin and his monkey, Abu, who should seem fleet and rascally (replaced by "One Jump Ahead").

"Proud of Your Boy" (Ashman & Menken) **Scene:** Aladdin vows to his mom that he'll shape up. **Why it went:** Katzenberg pronounced the mom character "a zero" in early story sessions. She was scratched, the song went with her, and Aladdin became an orphan.

"Babkak, Omar, Aladdin, Kasim" (Ashman & Menken) **Scene:** Aladdin and his street pals in a Bob Fosse–style dance number. **Sample lyric:** "Four friends, no phonies/Me and my cronies/ Babkak, Omar, Aladdin, Kasim!" **Why it went:** Too many supporting characters to weave into the story; the three friends were cut.

"How Quick They Forget" (Ashman & Menken) **Scene:** Pals lament in barbershop harmony that Aladdin has abandoned them after becoming a prince. **Why it went:** The pals went (see above).

"Humiliate the Boy" (Ashman & Menken) **Scene:** Jafar strips Aladdin of his princely clothes. **Sample lyric:** "We'll emasculate him slowly, all the better to enjoy/How delicious to humiliate the boy." **Why it went:** Considered too caustic. After it was cut, other Jafar songs (some listed below) were tried.

"My Time Has Come" (Menken) **Scene:** Enter the villain, who tells how hideous his life has been and how he is going to make others miserable, too. **Why it went:** Too slow and introspective.

"Why Me" (Menken & Rice) **Scene:** Same as "My Time Has Come." **Sample lyric:** "In my formative and hungry years/I was unappreciated by my peers/As their slings and arrows flew/I would ponder—wouldn't you/Why me?" **Why it went:** Song didn't advance the story; directors wanted something with a big chorus.

"My Finest Hour" (Menken & Rice) **Scene:** Jafar bats the Earth around with the Genie. **Sample lyric:** "My finest hour, the globe in thrall/The world's my plaything and I'll bounce it like a ball." **Why it went:** Directors decided it was too late in the movie for an extended showstopper for the villain. —*Steve Daly*

203

11 BAMBI *(1942, Disney, G)* Long before *The Lion King* grew up fatherless, Disney's adorable little deer-prince grew up motherless in this lushly rendered circle-of-life story, still a pinnacle of "realistic" animation. You don't move past the densely layered multiplane forest backgrounds, you journey *through* them; the animals look so naturalistic, they could be in a documentary. Warning: When Bambi's mom is killed by hunters (implied through music, sound effects, and editing), be prepared for tears, fears, and questions from the under-8 set.

12 FANTASIA *(1940, Disney, G)* Disney's visionary grand-daddy to MTV, marrying animated visuals to orchestral music, took three decades to find its audience (it was a 1969 reissue in the wake of *Yellow Submarine*'s success that finally put it over). Never mind the interludes with stuffy critic-composer Deems Taylor lecturing in live action about the classical compositions that inspired each of the film's eight segments. Check out the *moves* on that dew sprite and those wiggly mushrooms and the pirouetting hippo and—yikes!—that army of possessed, bucket-wielding brooms guaranteed to give small kids bad dreams. Don't keep this movie from tykes over 5, though; discovering *Fantasia* deserves to be a landmark childhood moment.

13 RUPERT AND THE FROG SONG *(1985, Pioneer, not rated)* Cute Beatle Paul McCartney had a hand in making this equally cute animated featurette, an eco-fable about Rupert the bear falling under the spell of the croaked tune of the title. Wife Linda helped concoct the story, while Paul contributed the song. A big hit on the animation-festival circuit, it also became the biggest-selling video ever released in England.

14 COLUMBIA PICTURES CARTOON CLASSICS *(1948–56, Columbia TriStar, not rated)* While the Disney studio completely dominated the feature-animation field after World War II, a rebel team of Disney expatriates known as UPA (United Productions of America; Columbia's in the title because it was the distributor) grabbed the short-subject spotlight with angular, highly stylized work that wowed critics and snagged lots of Oscars. The highlights in this UPA survey include seminal Gerald McBoing-Boing and Mr. Magoo shorts (much funnier than the myopic coot's later TV 'toons), plus a Salvador Dalíesque rendition of Edgar Allen Poe's "The Tell-Tale Heart," creepily narrated by James Mason.

15 A SALUTE TO FRIZ FRELENG *(1949–58, Warner, not rated)* He's the Warner Bros. cartoon director who handled most of Sylvester and Tweety's spats and brainstormed the final design of little Speedy Gonzales, whose de facto debut is here along with seven other shorts showcasing Freleng's way with music and gags. Among the funniest are "Birds Anonymous," which treats Sylvester's desire to eat Tweety like alcoholism, and "High Diving Hare," one of Freleng's grand Bugs Bunny–Yosemite Sam matchups.

BUGS BUNNY CLASSICS

16 **A CHARLIE BROWN CHRISTMAS** *(1965, Hi-Tops, not rated)* The first *Peanuts* TV special was also a breakthrough in holiday cynicism: Lucy avers that Christmas is "run by a big Eastern syndicate, you know." (This is not the tape for the kid who still believes in Santa.) Charlie eventually finds the season's "true meaning" in a New Testament reading from Linus, but, whatever your denomination, it's Vince Guaraldi's score of boppish original tunes and jazz takes on a seasonal standard ("O Tannenbaum") that really makes this minimally animated program a soul nourisher.

17 **THE MANY ADVENTURES OF WINNIE THE POOH** *(1966–74, Disney, G)* There's more of the round 'n' cuddly Disney style than

that of illustrator Ernest Shepard in these adaptations of A.A. Milne's storybooks, but why quibble: Sterling Holloway's vocal take is Poohfection, and Paul Winchell's Tigger sounds equally right. This tape edition, which combines the first three *Pooh* theatrical featurettes—*Winnie the Pooh and the Honey Tree* (1966), *Winnie the Pooh and the Blustery Day* (1968), and *Winnie the Pooh and Tigger Too* (1974)—is no longer sold by Disney, but you can rent it in stores; the individual tales are now sold separately. Beware the avalanche of Disney *Pooh* cassettes that are composed of subsequent TV show material; they're not nearly as good.

18 **BUGS BUNNY CLASSICS** *(1941–48, MGM/UA, not rated)* Seven cartoon shorts

NOT SO HAPPILY, AFTER ALL

She doesn't live in a palace, and she never married Prince Charming. But Adriana Caselotti, the original voice of Disney's Snow White, is pretty charming herself. At the age of 77, she spoke to us from her home in Southern California about her lone movie role:

Q: What was it like to work on such a groundbreaking picture?

A: I didn't understand this thing until the opening night. They never let me see any rushes. We started on the film in 1934, when I was 18, and it went on until I was 21. [The studio] would call me in, and I was paid $20 a day whenever I worked. In the middle of the production, they ran out of money. They didn't know if they'd ever be able to continue, and I wasn't called for a year. Walt had to go to the Bank of America to borrow another $250,000 to finish the film.

Q: It's amazing how much you still sound like the movie's Snow White.

A: You know, I live the part. All day long I'm singing the songs. I go around cooking and singing. And [neighborhood] kids come and ask me to do a show for them in front of the wishing well. I have a big wishing well outside of the house.

Q: What was the movie's premiere like?

A: It was on December 21, 1937, at the Carthay Circle in Los Angeles. I went with Harry Stockwell, who was the voice of the prince. The girl asked us for our tickets. I said, "I'm Snow White and this is Prince Charming, and we don't need any ticket." She said, "I don't care if you're the Old Witch, you need tickets

to get in here." We waited until she wasn't looking and snuck upstairs into the balcony.

Q: What are your memories of Walt Disney during production?

A: He would only say something if we were doing something wrong. But he never would have had me there if I hadn't been okay, because he was really a perfectionist. To me, he was just about the greatest man artistically. He seemed to understand what was correct in anything that had to do with art, with music.

Q: How did you feel when Disney chose not to use your voice for the animated Snow White who presented a cartoon award during the 1993 Oscar telecast?

A: I was hurt by that. This would have been my opportunity to show that at 77, I can still sound exactly the way I did in 1937. I was very unhappy about it, and when I called up the newspapers the next day, boy, I got results. The *Los Angeles Times* wrote it up. Army Archerd wrote it up in *Variety*. He said, "She sounded like Snow to me." That made me feel so good. But I am not angry at the Disney company about it. I am very happy for having been given the opportunity to be the voice of Snow White. I get so much happiness out of it that I live in a cloud. I've never come out of it. —*Steve Daly*

aren't nearly enough to define "classic" Bugs adequately, but this compilation is a great place to start. The brassy, Bronx-meets-Brooklyn bunny gets the best of an Edward G. Robinson lookalike in "Racketeer Rabbit," puts out a boxer's lights in "Rabbit Punch," and crosses Acme disintegrators with Marvin the Martian for the first time in "Haredevil Hare." For a gourmand menu of shorts starring the later, more urbane, 1949–57 Bugs, see Warner's collection *Bugs Bunny's Wacky Adventures.*

19

101 DALMATIANS *(1961, Disney, G)* Why is this pleasant, modest little canine adventure so much more enduring than other Disney cartoon features of its era, such as *The Sword in the Stone* or *Sleeping Beauty?* Maybe it's because *Dalmatians* revels in domestic bliss— lingering on archetypal images of love between master and dog, husband and wife, pooch parents and newborn pups —in an era when most screen families are trendily dysfunctional. And as Pongo and Perdita track down fur-worshiping Cruella De Vil, the "mad old lady" who steals their 15-puppy brood to make a dog-skin coat, they act uncannily more human than the moms and dads in most live-action movies, sharing their confusion, weariness, and worry with a poignancy you'd never find in, say, *Home Alone.*

20

SNOW WHITE AND THE SEVEN DWARFS *(1937, Disney, G)* Can a young heroine who lives to cook and clean and primps so she'll look her best when some handsome man comes to carry her away still

be called the fairest of them all? That's the mother-daughter debate likely to rage in households where *Snow* sits next to videos of Disney's more recent musical romances, *The Little Mermaid* and *Beauty and the Beast.* Yet however creaky some of its conventions, *Snow's* supporting cast of little people still has the same fresh appeal, thanks to Disney's genius for making cartoon characters seem so alive.

21

WHERE'S SPOT? *(1993, Disney, not rated)* Spun off from Eric Hill's lift-the-flap books, this gentle video aimed at the 4-and-under set (a decidedly neglected segment of the kidvid audience) follows a concerned canine mom as she searches for her pup, Spot. Along the way, she discovers easily identifiable animals hidden behind doors, cupboards, trees, and so on. The theme music is as placid as an old Seals and Crofts tune, and the bold colors and simple words loll reassuringly along. Parenting alert: Toddlers used to handling the picture books may attempt to find a flap to open on the TV screen (in this video, Spot's mom does the opening for you). Also on video are *Spot Goes to the Farm* and *Spot Goes to a Party.*

22

MAURICE SENDAK'S REALLY ROSIE *(1975, CC Studios, not rated)* Author-illustrator Sendak *(Where the Wild Things Are, In the Night Kitchen)* wrote and directed this charming revue in which urban eccentric and self-proclaimed star Rosie has the neighborhood kids try out for parts in a pretend movie. They audition by reciting odd, mock-morose Sendak poems, set to some very

207

'70s music by Carole King (who also provides Rosie's vocals). The ditties, especially the silly "Chicken Soup With Rice," make fine sing-alongs for preschoolers who've overdosed on Raffi's "Baby Beluga."

23 **THE GOLDEN AGE OF LOONEY TUNES, VOL. 4: BOB CLAMPETT** *(1942–46, MGM/UA, not rated)* Clampett was by far the wildest Warner cartoon director, forever contorting Daffy Duck, Porky Pig, and a gallery of proto-underground-comix goons into the most grotesque incarnations conceivable. This seven-cartoon collection showcases one of his loopiest, "The Great Piggy Bank Robbery" (starring Daffy as Duck Twacy), along with a dead-on *Fantasia* parody hosted by Elmer Fudd ("A Corny Concerto"), and a twisted yet touching and faithful Dr. Seuss adaptation ("Horton Hatches the Egg").

24 **TEX AVERY'S SCREWBALL CLASSICS, VOLS. 1 AND 2** *(1943–52, MGM/UA, not*

THE REN & STIMPY SHOW:
THE CLASSICS, VOL. 1

rated) Bending the physics of movie reality was director Avery's obsession. He made a number of shorts with Droopy the dog and his nemesis, the Wolf, but none of his characters had much identity; anything-for-a-laugh inventiveness is the real star in these survey collections of Avery's years at MGM (he also worked at Warner Bros. and for Walter Lantz). Amphetamine pacing makes for high hilarity whenever a character does a double take, and you'll be stunned by the adult sexiness Avery got into a busty chorine named Red. Viewing tip: Treat this as supersugary eye candy. Watch more than two in a row and your head will swim.

25 **THE REN & STIMPY SHOW: THE CLASSICS, VOL. 1** *(1993, Sony Wonder, not rated)* What Wednesday and Pugsley Addams probably watch on their VCR. Soothing as nails on a blackboard, John Kricfalusi's warped cable-TV creations aren't really funny (and in most parents' opinion aren't suitable for very young children). But there's no denying that hyper Chihuahua Ren, who carries on like a homicidal mental patient, and his cat pal, Stimpy, who's moronically enamored of his body's ickiest private functions, are exquisitely, dementedly well drawn. Two of the three shows here, "Stimpy's Invention" (Ren wears a helmet that makes him forcibly happy) and "Space Madness" (Ren goes insane and eats soap in zero gravity), are indeed classics of graphic grotesquerie. Do they rot impressionable minds? Hey, c'mon, you used to sing "15 Tons of Greasy Grimy Gopher Guts" in the backseat of the bus, and you turned out all right.

SUPERMAN CARTOONS: THE COMPLETE COLLECTION

26 **CINDERELLA** *(1950, Disney, G)* Maybe not the most appropriate pick for families going through divorce or remarriage, but for those who can take the naked cruelty on display—poor Cinderella vividly mistreated by her cold stepmother and stepsisters—it all comes out right in the end. Her woes are eased by some of the Disney organization's catchiest songs ("Bibbidi-Bobbidi-Boo," "A Dream Is a Wish Your Heart Makes"), and a delightful supporting cast of mice whose Chipmunk-like, electronically sped-up voices also help break the considerable tension.

27 **THE SECRET OF NIMH** *(1982, MGM/UA, G)* Who will help a widowed mouse save her hole-in-the-ground household from the ravaging tractors of spring plow-

ing? The visuals are superlative, the tone adult, and the vocal work inspired (especially Dom DeLuise as a daft crow) in this first, best feature-film effort from Disney defector Don Bluth. Sadly, he went on to increasingly juvenile diminishing returns with *An American Tail*, *The Land Before Time*, and the wretched, outright misfires *All Dogs Go to Heaven*, *Rock-A-Doodle*, and *Thumbelina* (which have racked up healthy business on video; do the little ones a favor and don't follow the lemmings).

28 **SUPERMAN CARTOONS: THE COMPLETE COLLECTION** *(1941–43, Video Dimensions, not rated)* The Fleischer Studios' series of shorts was the best thing to happen to the Man of Steel until Christopher Reeve came along. Some of the

WWII espionage plotlines haven't dated well (one short, "Japoteurs," features some mighty demeaning Asian caricatures). But the elaborate, realistic shading on Supe and Lois Lane, the Wellesian camera angles, the masses of mad-scientist hardware, and a wealth of meticulous, realistic Metropolis backgrounds make these cartoons a lavish-as-Disney visual treat (they cost a fortune at the time to make). Try to avoid the numerous tape editions made from shabby, public-domain 16 mm prints; they're usually so dark you can't make out the action. Video Dimensions' comprehensive, 17-short collection comes from superior 35 mm prints.

29 THE RESCUERS (1977, Disney, G) Nearly perfect entertainment for the under-8 set. This is a subtly crafted movie, the last Disney film shaped by veteran animators who had been at the studio for decades but left or died beginning in the late '70s. (Just compare the brassy, overloaded sequel, *The Rescuers Down Under*, and you'll appreciate their expertise.) Miss Bianca (that's Eva Gabor speaking) and Bernard (Bob Newhart), button-cute rodents on a mission to save a kidnapped little girl, always move in ways that spell out what they're saying, so even the youngest viewer can follow, and spindly-limbed villainess Madame Medusa (Geraldine Page) provides deftly choreographed hysterics in the mold of *101 Dalmatians*' Cruella De Vil. Fast-forward alert: Skip the sung-as-voice-over songs.

30 THE WIND IN THE WILLOWS, VOLS. 1–4 (1983, HBO, not rated) Kenneth Grahame's beloved characters Ratty, Mole, and Toad work wonderfully well here as stop-motion animated figures. They look like actual woodland creatures, toddling along in clothes through believable and elaborate Edwardian sets. Disney did an entertaining all-cartoon take on the same stories in 1949, which is also out on tape, but it's not quite as flavorful, nor remotely as English.

31 THE JUNGLE BOOK (1967, Disney, G) Something just about every child today can relate to, by direct or indirect experience: a custody battle, as persnickety Bagheera (the voice of Sebastian Cabot) and genial bachelor slob Baloo the Bear (Phil Harris) compete to win young Mowgli's respect and affection before he's turned over to "the man-village" to grow up. Wonderfully loose and character-driven, with unforgettable speaking turns by George Sanders (as tiger Shere Khan) and Sterling Holloway (as sinister serpent Kaa). Harris' musical elucidation of "The Bare Necessities" may be the sweetest marriage of personality and song in the Disney canon.

32 TWEETY & SYLVESTER (1942–48, MGM/UA, not rated) Biggest belly laughs in the whole Warner Bros. cartoon lineup. This eight-short set rounds up the riotous first solo bows of the big, sloppy cat and itty-bitty birdie (the designs weren't quite right yet, especially a naked-looking *pink* Tweety), their first team-up, and standout face-offs like Sylvester's musical-meow torment of slumbering Elmer Fudd in director Friz Freleng's "Back Alley Oproar." No cartoonist should be able to milk this

210

much prime comedy from mutual speech impediments, but, boy, does he.

33 MORE OF DISNEY'S BEST: 1932-1946 *(1932–46, Disney, not rated)* Six short cartoons teeming with shots as painstakingly elaborate as those in the best Disney features, and with reason: Walt pushed his artists hard through the '30s to develop the visual command that found full flower in *Snow White*, *Pinocchio*, and *Fantasia*. Highlights include "Three Little Pigs" (1933), one of the earliest Technicolor cartoons and the first to feature fully realized personalities; Mickey's battle with a convincingly huge giant in "The Brave Little Tailor" (1938); and "The Old Mill" (1937), the first short to employ the depth-simulating multiplane camera.

34 LADY AND THE TRAMP *(1955, Disney, G)* Will pampered cocker spaniel Lady be pushed aside once her human "parents" have a real baby? Footloose lothario Tramp thinks so, and the mutt tries to lure Lady away from domesticity with romance. (Note that, under the stars, Tramp and Lady *sleep together on screen*!) Disney's most acutely observed catalog of doggie behavior—it captures exactly how canines eat, how they trot, how they stretch in the morning—just as knowingly depicts Homo sapiens rites of passage like being babysat by relatives you don't like, handling bullies who blame you for things you didn't do, and making room for a new sibling.

35 RIKKI-TIKKI-TAVI *(1975, LIVE, not rated)* Cobra in the bathroom—look out!

Adapting a story from Rudyard Kipling's *The Jungle Book*, Chuck Jones brings a wonderful visual grasp of how animals move to this half-hour TV special about a wiry, snake-sniffing pet mongoose who protects a family in India. For rural rug rats about to invade the backyard, it's also a useful cautionary about nature's nastier creatures. Orson Welles reads a narration taken straight from Kipling's prose, and unlike Disney's loose retelling, it reflects imperialist England's fascination with caste and conquest.

36 BEN AND ME *(1953, Disney, not rated)* A four-decade-old Disney featurette that's a gem of historical revisionism: It celebrates the little mice it says were the *real* brains behind the great men of history, from a Dutch painter and a group of Pilgrims to American statesman Benjamin Franklin. Disney fixture Sterling Holloway provides the voice of tiny Amos, who takes hapless old Ben in hand by repairing his printing press, fashioning bifocals for him from two sets of broken spectacles, and editing his newspaper into a model of enlightened reporting. History lessons were never so much fun.

37 THE POINT *(1971, LIVE, not rated)* Born round in a pointy world, little outcast Oblio is banished to the Pointless Forest, where he learns he does *so* have a reason for being. This boldly graphic TV movie—it resembles a Saul Steinberg *New Yorker* cartoon crossed with *Krazy Kat*—owes a lot to the countercultural thrust of *Yellow Submarine*, a relationship even more, well, pointed on video, where Ringo Starr is the narrator (his vocals replace Dustin Hoffman's original broadcast-version voiceover). Harry Nilsson's sweet score makes a lovely lullaby.

38 **PLYMPTOONS** *(1991, Tapeworm, not rated)* You've probably seen these brief, astounding colored-pencil cartoons as MTV station breaks or in the channel's animation show *Liquid Television*. These are "Plymptoons," created by warped artist Bill Plympton. Included on this video are the shorts "25 Ways to Quit Smoking," "Your Face," and equally droll, gross-out gagfests such as "How to Kiss." Too eerily off-kilter for young kids, it's a blast for preteens and adults.

39 **THE DAYDREAMER** *(1966, Columbia TriStar, not rated)* How did Hans Christian Andersen become a writer? Using a mix of stop-motion animation and live action, producer Arthur Rankin Jr. and director Jules Bass (they made *Rudolph the Red-Nosed Reindeer* and countless other TV specials) show how runaway Chris imagines himself at the center of the tales that would later become *The Little Mermaid*, *The Emperor's New Clothes*, *Thumbelina*, and *The Garden of Paradise*. In the Rankin-Bass tradition, all the jerky little figurines have celebrity voices (including Cyril Ritchard, Boris Karloff, Tallulah Bankhead, Hayley Mills, and Ed Wynn).

40 **MICKEY AND THE BEANSTALK** *(1947, Disney, not rated)* Donald Duck and Goofy may not get title billing, but they're on screen just as much as the mouse in Dis-

ney's amusing rewrite of the Jack saga. Like several other *Disney Mini-Classics* video titles, this was originally a segment in an old grab-bag feature (*Fun and Fancy Free*), and it's got the lavish look that goes with such budgets. The beanstalk's nighttime blooming is wonderfully imagined, and tricks of scale make the dum-dum giant look darn big.

41 **HOW THE GRINCH STOLE CHRISTMAS!** *(1966, MGM/UA, not rated)* One of the first animated adaptations of a Dr. Seuss tale was helmed by *Looney Tunes* legend Chuck Jones, whose dry wit and affinity for villainous characters made him an apt choice indeed. The result: an instant Christmas classic with terrific gags, swell songs, and, most memorably, a Grinch you could identify with—Jones was hip to the fact that even children can get a little ambivalent about the holiday season.

HOW THE GRINCH STOLE CHRISTMAS!

42 **POPEYE CARTOONS** *(1936–39, Republic, not rated)* The '50s and '60s Popeye cartoons are dreck to avoid like the plague. For a real trip, check out these longer-than-usual Max Fleischer shorts, wherein our spinach-eating sailor meets up with the likes of Ali Baba, Aladdin, and Sinbad—mostly played by his longtime nemesis, Bluto. They're replete with surreal grotesques and made in exceptionally lavish Technicolor.

43 **HANNA-BARBERA PERSONAL FAVORITES: THE FLINTSTONES** *(1960–66, Turner, not rated)* Cartoon purists may hate us for even *considering* including a videotape from Hanna-Barbera, the kings of "limited" TV animation. But who could resist creators William H. and Joe B. personally introducing four *Flintstones* episodes, chockablock with dozens of those dopey Stone Age inventions like an animal garbage disposal and a mastodon-trunk vacuum cleaner? Witness the birth of Pebbles, Barney's being mistaken for a superspy, Fred being played by a drawing instead of by John Goodman with a bad haircut, and visits from guest stars Ann Margrock (vocals by Ann-Margret) and that little green alien, the Great Gazoo (Harvey Korman).

44 **HORTON HEARS A WHO!** *(1970, MGM/UA, not rated)* The team that made such a splash for the Grinch tackled the much sweeter Dr. Seuss character Horton this time out. The compassionate elephant seeks out the source of a faint peep, reasoning that "a person's a person, no matter how small." His skeptical companions, though, give him much grief for his efforts. While Horton himself is a sweetheart, narrator Hans Conried is more than up to conveying the acid contempt of Horton's scoffers.

45 **CHARLOTTE'S WEB** *(1973, Paramount, G)* Hanna-Barbera, a concern never known for its overweening artistic ambitions, tried something different with this adaptation of E.B. White's beloved children's classic. While it falls way short of the animation mark established by Disney, it's quite pleasant in its way, largely as a result of the expert vocal talents of Debbie Reynolds, Agnes Moorehead, Henry Gibson, and a suitably snide Paul Lynde.

46 **GULLIVER'S TRAVELS** *(1939, Nostalgia, not rated)* The Fleischer studio's attempt to beat Disney at the feature-film game (this was its answer to 1937's smash *Snow White and the Seven Dwarfs*) proved ruinous; over the years, however, it has developed a cult reputation. The obviously rotoscoped rendering of the giant Gulliver is an annoyance, as

213

THE NAME GAME

You're so proud: The kids are getting independent, picking out their own clothes, even their own videos. But be forewarned: A little over-the-shoulder guidance in the video store can prevent some unhappy surprises at home. Often, the movie on a cassette isn't quite as kid-oriented as the title or the packaging implies. Take the innocent-sounding *The Little Girl Who Lives Down the Lane*, which turns out to be the tale of a teen with a taste for human flesh. For some other eye-openers, read on:

BEDTIME STORY *(1963, not rated)* **What the title sounds like:** Something to watch in Dr. Denton's, clinging to a stuffed animal. **What the package shows:** A bad Hirschfeld caricature of three people playing tug-of-war. **What it really is:** Two con men go to great lengths to bilk a naive, gorgeous woman.

BIRDY *(1984, R)* **What the title sounds like:** A boy and his pet parakeet. **What the package shows:** With a little ingenuity and a lot of Elmer's glue, a boy really flies. **What it really is:** The story of a schizophrenic who pursues his desire to be a bird.

A BOY AND HIS DOG *(1975, R)* **What the title sounds like:** Old Yeller II. **What the package shows:** A happy face within a cloud. **What it really is:** A telepathic canine helps a young punk forage for food and women.

THE HANDMAID'S TALE *(1990, R)* **What the title sounds like:** Something penned by the Brothers Grimm. **What the package shows:** Natasha Richardson, pretty in red. **What it really is:** Two parts Stepford Wives, one part Hitler's master plan.

THE LOST BOYS *(1987, R)* **What the title sounds like:** Peter Pan's old gang got their own fea-ture. **What the package shows:** Teenagers looking cool in black and white. **What it really is:** The Crips and the Bloods have nothing on this gang: They're vampires.

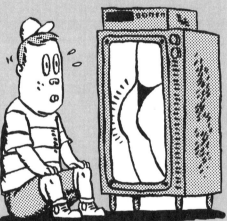

A TIGER'S TALE *(1988, R)* **What the title sounds like:** A *National Geographic* documentary filmed on location. **What the package shows:** Ann-Margret as a heavenly creature. **What it really is:** A high school senior gets involved with his girlfriend's mother.

PROM NIGHT *(1980, R)* **What the title sounds like:** Gidget gets a corsage. **What the package shows:** Jamie Lee Curtis, in close-up. **What it really is:** A slasher film, and the school halls are flowing with blood. —*Linda Movish*

214

are the chirpy songs, but overall this is a rich, colorful, clever entertainment.

47 **BABAR: THE MOVIE** *(1989, LIVE, G)* Some of today's more republican parents may not approve of elephant king Babar on account of his being a monarch. The point they miss is that he's also an elephant, and a damn cute one, at that. This feature, in which Babar goes to war against rhino invaders, is a little splashier than other animated adaptations of Laurent de Brunhoff's tales. But it still has that polite, slightly bland charm that's rather a tonic after a day spent, say, shopping for *Mighty Morphin Power Rangers* toys.

48 **RUDOLPH THE RED-NOSED REINDEER** *(1964, LIVE, not rated)* Generations of kids grew up thinking Burl Ives was a talking doll, thanks to his turn as the narrator of this stop-motion animated TV special. Sophisticated recent efforts in this realm, such as *Tim Burton's The Nightmare Before Christmas*, have made this TV treasure look a little quaint, but it's still very appealing—youngsters who have already been exposed to more advanced fare still get scared by the Abominable Snowman scene.

49 **THE SWEATER** *(1991, Smarty Pants, not rated)* The lushly animated title story, one of three in this wonderful collection, humorously conveys a man's memory of what he put up with as a 10-year-old forced to wear a jersey of a hockey team despised in his town. *The Ride*, a wordless film, focuses on a chauffeur's daydream about what could happen to his

RUDOLPH THE RED-NOSED REINDEER

absentminded boss. *Getting Started* is a look at the perils of procrastination.

50 **THE GREAT MOUSE DETECTIVE** *(1992, Disney, G)* The appeal of this animated, all-mice version of Sherlock Holmes is, well, elementary. When a toymaker is kidnapped from his workshop, his desperate daughter turns to Basil of Baker Street (the voice of Barrie Ingham) for help. He and his portly associate, Dr. Dawson (Val Bettin), set out to save the girl's father—only to end up ratting out London's furriest fiend, Professor Ratigan (Vincent Price). Younger children will be mesmerized by the battle of wills between these rodent warriors, but be prepared: Even in lilliputian scale, the final, somewhat violent scenes could frighten young children.

Reviews written by Steve Daly, as well as Glenn Kenny, Jill Rachlin, and Jeff Unger.

215

DOCUMENTARY

WE WATCH "regular" (fiction) movies to visit places we can't imagine otherwise. We watch documentary (nonfiction) films to see where we've been, how we live, and what some of us are doing about it. Because the very nature of film is, on a certain level, documentary—it captures an image of the physical world in real time—it's not surprising that some of the greatest films and filmmakers are in this field. Their work has unusual staying power. In a sense, we return to these movies as if to prove the past really happened. Robert Flaherty unveiled *Nanook of the North* (No. 14) in 1922—and every kid still knows his subject's name. Leni Riefenstahl's *Triumph of the Will* (No. 4) makes you understand with brutal clarity why people followed Adolf Hitler. Michael Apted's *35 Up* (No. 37) lets us check up on 14 British schoolchildren as they grow into weary middle age. Of course, our list of the 100 greatest documentaries (most of which are not rated by the MPAA) isn't all trenchant, hard-hitting stuff. Who knows? You may need *Table Manners for Everyday Use* (No. 80) more than you think.

1 **HARLAN COUNTY, USA** *(1977, Facets, PG)* Barbara Kopple's Oscar-winning account of a 1973–74 coal miners' strike in eastern Kentucky is a landmark achievement in documentary journalism. Beginning with the Brookside Mine workers' decision to strike for a new contract, Kopple uses the bare-bones story to capture the stark drama of the miners' daily lives, their picket-line confrontations with gun-toting guards, the culture of the Appalachian hollows where the miners live and work, and the national politics of the United Mine Workers union (UMW presidential candidate Joseph "Jock" Yablonski was assassinated during the course of Kopple's coverage). It all flows seamlessly, with the dramatic punch and human power of a superior fiction film.

2 **BERLIN—SYMPHONY OF A GREAT CITY** *(1927, IHF, B&W, silent)* Without a spoken word, shot in grainy black and white, and aiming to capture the rhythms of 1920s Berlin from dawn to dark, *Symphony* provides spectacular evidence of the power of nonfiction film narrative. Director Walther Ruttmann's cameras are everywhere and see everything, and his use of montage technique transforms the 70-minute film into monumental urban drama.

3 **RING OF FIRE** *(1988, Mystic Fire)* The best travel-adventure series ever made, these four hour-long tapes are Lorne and Lawrence Blair's record of their 10-year exploration of Indonesia's Spice Islands and other South Seas islands. Beginning in the

TRIUMPH OF THE WILL, 1935

EVERETT COLLECTION

mid-'70s, the British filmmakers meet, among other interesting people, the headhunters who reportedly ate Michael Rockefeller, the professional python hunters of Bhutaan, a man who ignites paper through powers of concentration, and—oh, yes!—much more. A staggering testimony to the magic of this world.

4 **TRIUMPH OF THE WILL** *(1935, Movies Unlimited, B&W)* Commissioned by Der Führer himself, Leni Riefenstahl took her cameras to Nuremberg for the 1934 Nazi party convention and filmed the emerging glory of one of history's greatest horrors. An exercise in exaltation, it shows Hitler in a nimbus of light and his well-scrubbed followers, young and old, nearly beside themselves with enjoyment of his avuncular nature. With the help of music that causes a catch in the throat, the film is history's best-crafted and most darkly effective piece of advocacy advertising.

5 **NIGHT AND FOG** *(1955, Video Yesteryear, B&W)* In 32 brief minutes, director Alain Resnais (*Hiroshima, Mon Amour*) offers a counterpoint to Riefenstahl's work, brilliantly achieving what dozens of other documentaries and feature films have labored hours for: evoking the horrors of Nazi concentration camps and conveying the message for succeeding generations that it could easily happen again. Resnais creates his essay of evil like a master composer at the keyboard, using still photos, wartime footage, and contemporary film of the abandoned camps to sum up the Holocaust in a few powerful images.

6 **THE VOYAGER ODYSSEY: 1977–1989** *(1990, Malibu) Odyssey* defies every cliché of space-exploration documentaries, combining leading-edge computer animation and digital special effects with NASA photography to create a gorgeous, breathtaking, and, ultimately, grandly inspirational 44-minute experience. It charts the *Voyager* missions from Earth to Jupiter to Saturn to Uranus, and gracefully transforms standard space film of indistinct celestial bodies into an intimate look at countless cosmic wonders. There is no narration, only a stunning orchestral soundtrack.

7 **COMMON THREADS: STORIES FROM THE QUILT** *(1989, HBO)* In 1987, when nearly 50,000 Americans had already succumbed to AIDS, some friends gathered in a San Francisco storefront and began piecing together a quilt of panels bearing the names of those they had lost. When this documentary was made, there were more than 13,000 panels and the quilt covered 14 acres. This Oscar-winning film focuses on five of those names (a child hemophiliac, an IV-drug user, and three gay men), and directors Robert Epstein and Jeffrey Friedman put faces on the names by letting the victims' families reminisce.

8 **JANE FONDA'S WORKOUT** *(1982, A*Vision)* Fonda spoke, and a nation felt the burn. One of the best-selling videos ever, a pioneer of the video fitness boom, and a new career for the Oscar-winning actress— all because the exercises are challenging yet doable, and Fonda is an ace instructor.

ALWAYS FOR PLEASURE, 1978

9 **ALWAYS FOR PLEASURE** *(1978)*, **J'AI ÉTÉ AU BAL** *(1989)*, and **YUM, YUM, YUM!** *(1990, all from Flower Films)* Filmmaker Les Blank excels at capturing one of America's most vibrant ethnic cultures, the riotous Creole-Cajun melting pot of south Louisiana. These three films are equally superb at exploring diverse aspects of this world: the annual pre-Lenten Mardi Gras festival (*Always for Pleasure*); Cajun and zydeco music (*J'ai Été au Bal*, French for "I went to the dance"); and the glories of Cajun cooking, from Paul Prudhomme's renowned New Orleans restaurant to open fires in backwoods Louisiana (*Yum, Yum, Yum!*).

10 **THE PEOPLE VERSUS PAUL CRUMP** *(1962, Facets, B&W)* Director William Friedkin (*The French Connection*) honed his street-smart cinema vérité film style with this little-known, early-career gem of a docudrama about a Chicago man whom the filmmaker believes to have been wrongfully sentenced to death for his role in a 1953 murder-robbery. After restaging the crime for his cameras, Friedkin tags along with crusading newspaper reporter John Justin Smith as he tries to save a rehabilitated Crump—who, from his place on death row, makes his own best case—from Illinois' electric chair.

11 **DEAR AMERICA: LETTERS HOME FROM VIETNAM** *(1988, HBO)* Against the backdrop of a chronological history of U.S. involvement in Vietnam, such actors as Michael J. Fox, Robin Williams, and Ellen Burstyn read excerpts from GIs' letters to friends and family back in the real world. The visuals include images from contemporary TV coverage of the war, as well as soldiers' own foxhole-eye-view "home movies." The result is the best, most powerfully comprehensive documentary account of America's Vietnam experience.

12

THE CLOWNS *(1971, Facets)* Director Federico Fellini himself shows up a half-hour into this minor masterpiece, lamenting "the clowns of my childhood, where are they today?... The world to which [they] belonged no longer exists." He and his crew then set off to document the lost world of the great clowns of Europe, visiting circuses and circus people in Italy and France, and re-creating memories of the great clown acts of long ago. It's a funny, touching tribute to a subject with which Fellini shows an obvious kinship.

13

NIGHT MAIL *(1936, Kino, B&W)* Lasting approximately from 1930 to 1950, the British Documentary Movement produced several great works, and its technique of heroizing the ordinary has influenced films as recent as *Schindler's List*. Produced by movement founder John Grierson, *Night Mail* is among the best, spending 24 epochal minutes capturing the everyday drama of the men who work the Postal Special mail train from London to Glasgow, a central cog in Britain's national mail system.

THE PLOW THAT BROKE THE PLAINS, 1936

14

NANOOK OF THE NORTH *(1922)*, **MAN OF ARAN** *(1934)*, and **LOUISIANA STORY** *(1948, all from Home Vision, B&W)* Often called "the father of the documentary," Robert Flaherty was more romantic artist than cinematic anthropologist. He approached natural settings not as habitats to be recorded for posterity but as raw material for carefully choreographed tone poems: *Nanook*, which follows the travails of a Hudson Bay Eskimo family; *Man of Aran*, with its

NANOOK OF THE NORTH, 1922

stunning photography of the rocky isles west of Ireland and depictions of villagers on a shark hunt; and *Louisiana Story*, dramatizing the arrival of an oil derrick on a backwater bayou, as observed by a young local boy.

15

THE PLOW THAT BROKE THE PLAINS *(1936, Facets, B&W)* Grandfather of all sobering investigative documentaries, Pare Lorentz's 49-minute epic begins as a stirring celebration of Manifest Destiny, as 96 million acres of grassland are turned into wheat farms early in the century—only to give way to a grim telling of the most tragic chapter in American agriculture, the 1930s dust-bowl crisis and eventual displacement of thousands of farm families. A master-piece of fine photography and montage editing, with a score by Virgil Thomson.

16 **SALESMAN** *(1969, Facets, B&W)* Four salesmen pound the streets of New England and Florida, hawking lavishly illustrated $49.95 Bibles to people who can barely afford their next meal. At first we are repulsed by these smarmy hucksters, with their devious pieties and shameless pressure tactics. But the genius of Albert and David Maysles' seminal slice of Americana is that we are quickly in full sympathy with these haggard, lonely, frustrated men trying to scratch out what passes for a living.

17 **26 BATHROOMS** *(1985, Facets)* Infectiously charming social documentary on the evolution of the toilet/water closet, and an intimate account of how people enjoy the room, from iconoclastic director Peter Greenaway (*A Zed and Two Noughts*). There's a bathroom for each letter of the alphabet, and each letter illustrates a whimsical insight into bathroom culture ("L is for lost soap").

18 **BEST BOY** *(1979, Facets)* Filmmaker Ira Wohl records three pivotal years in the life of his retarded cousin Philly, during which the 52-year-old moves out of his elderly parents' home for the first time in his adult life. A lovely, compassionate treatment of mental disability and the challenges—and rewards—of Philly's learning to live on his own.

19 **THE THIN BLUE LINE** *(1988, HBO)* An innocent man was saved from life imprison-ment when this documentary threw new light on his murder conviction. Filmmaker Errol Morris examines the fatal shooting of a Dallas policeman, combining Philip Glass' ominous score with reconstructions of the night of the crime. Morris gives us much more than the facts; he shows the fragility of truth.

20 **SHERMAN'S MARCH** *(1987, Facets)* Filmmaker Ross McElwee went south to make a documentary on enigmatic Union general William Tecumseh Sher-man and instead came back with a mas-terpiece on contemporary mating ritu-als, whimsically subtitled *A Meditation on the Possibility of Romantic Love in the South During an Era of Nuclear Weapons Proliferation.* His filmed encounters with the flower of modern Southern womanhood offer a rich lode

SALESMAN, 1969

PHOTOFEST

of quirky character and anecdote, confirming the universal suspicion that everyone has a story to tell, and that the best movies of all are everywhere around us.

21 LOST MAN'S RIVER: AN EVERGLADES ADVENTURE *(1990, Mystic Fire)* Novelist Peter Matthiessen's guided tour of the Ten

THE THIN BLUE LINE, 1988

EVERETT COLLECTION

Thousand Islands region of Florida's Everglades is effectively an anti-travelogue, a gorgeous piece of photography during which narrator Matthiessen takes pains to enumerate the region's inhospitality to civilized man: bugs, rats, killer snakes, humidity, violence, etc. Matthiessen's wry commentary is broken by readings from his novel about a legendary Everglades bandit. *Lost Man's River* is alive with the savage beauty of a wild and lovely land and the thoughts of a man who has dwelled long on its meaning.

22 OLYMPIA, PARTS I AND II *(1938, Movies Unlimited, B&W)* Leni Riefenstahl's

staggering 215-minute feast of images from the 1936 Berlin Summer Games is usually applauded for its technical excellence, then dismissed as pro-Hitler propaganda. While the frequent fawning close-ups of Der Führer cannot be excused, Riefenstahl's true agenda is to glorify the Olympian ideal of peaceful, idyllic competition among the world's youth. The Olympics she depicts may never have existed anywhere but in the imagination of their founders, but that, in part, is her point.

23 SOUL: SOUL OF THE UNIVERSE, THE EVOLVING SOUL, and SILICON SOUL *(1993, Atlas)* Taking off from the premise that Newtonian reductionist science "robbed the world of mystery and meaning," this sweeping three-part BBC documentary then proposes that recent advances in astronomy and physics have led scientists to "rediscover soul at the heart of the universe." It next moves to reexamine the Really Big Questions: Who are we? Why are we here? What is God? An eloquent lineup of contemporary thinkers (Stephen Hawking is just one of the crowd here) offers answers, and their comments range across the spectrum of emerging theory and belief.

24 THE BATTLE OF KHARKOV *(1942, IHF, B&W)* and THE BATTLE OF STALINGRAD *(1962, IHF, B&W)* Two superlative World War II documentaries from the propaganda machines of two mortal combatants: In the former, Nazi filmmakers use spectacular battlefront footage to celebrate the German defeat of Soviet armies near the Ukrainian city of Kharkov, paving the way for the east-

223

ern-front adversaries' showdown at Stalingrad. The elegant, emotional Eisensteinish documentary *The Battle of Stalingrad* is Soviet propagandists' turn to pay tribute to the heroic soldiers and citizens (led by party boss Nikita Khrushchev) who faced down German armies in the 200-day 1942 siege of Stalingrad, the turning point in the eastern-front war.

25 HEARTS OF DARKNESS: A FILMMAKER'S APOCALYPSE

(1991, Paramount, R) The most spectacular inside look ever offered into the ineffable process of filmmaking, specifically the shooting of Francis Ford Coppola's *Apocalypse Now* (1979). Codirected by Fax Bahr and George Hickenlooper, this documentary consists of behind-the-scenes footage shot by Coppola's wife, Eleanor; recent interviews with Coppola, his associates, and principal actors; and on-the-set audiotape recordings Eleanor Coppola made of her husband without his knowledge. *Hearts of Darkness* is a comedy, a disaster movie, a profound study in ego, obsession, and personal tyranny, and a spellbinding glimpse into the making of an epic.

26 THE CIVIL WAR *(1990, Time-Life Video)* As millions of

TV viewers already know, Ken Burns' massively thorough documentary does more than just deliver the facts; it makes you emotionally relive the most hellish, crucial chapter in U.S. history. The series tells the story using vintage photographs as well as interviews with Civil War historians. Like a great book that rewards rereading, the nine-volume video set will endure.

27 ORATORIO FOR PRAGUE *(1968, Facets, B&W)* In

August 1968, Prague director Jan Němec set out to film Czechs and Slovaks reveling in hippie love, folk traditions, and the human face of socialist Alexander Dubček—all blissfully unaware that they were about to witness and become participants in a doomsday scenario. The shocked crew soon finds its cameras trained on Soviet tanks, shooting the raw footage that would first show the world that, contrary to official statements from the USSR, the Red Army was not "invited." The filmmaker's naïveté only underscores the poignant futility of his compatriots' protests.

KOBAL COLLECTION

PARIS IS BURNING, 1991

28 PARIS IS BURNING *(1991, Facets, R)* Taking its name

from one of the Harlem drag balls it documents, this is a portrait of the truly disenfranchised— black and Hispanic drag queens—and their self-created world of illusion and disillusion. Director Jennie Livingston went to the right place at the right time with her camera. Dressed in costumes fit for a Paris fashion runway, each strutting participant for a moment becomes his fantasy, and in these competition sequences, *Paris Is Burning* bristles with excitement.

29 GENERAL IDI AMIN DADA: A SELF-PORTRAIT *(1974, Movies Unlimited)* The work

of Iranian-born French director Barbet Schroeder *(Reversal of Fortune)*, *Amin* is a chilling portrait of the former Ugandan tyrant, shown to be a man stunted and made childish by absolute power. In one scene, the hefty dictator takes obvious pride in placing first in a swimming contest that no other Ugandan would dare to win. Nicely filmed by Schroeder's longtime cinematographer, Nestor Almendros (he won an Oscar for *Days of Heaven*), the documentary isn't intended to be entirely objective, but it mostly lets Amin hang himself with his own words.

30 PUMPING IRON *(1976, Facets)* Few feature-film stars have made such an impres-

sion by starring in a documentary, but Arnold Schwarzenegger lights up this 85-minute tribute to bodybuilding, as directors George Butler and Robert Fiore have the good sense to let the 28-year-old Austrian hunk take over their film with his unassuming charm and laid-back obsessiveness (he dreams of being remembered "like Jesus...for thousands of years"). Arnold is pumping up to win his sixth straight Mr. Olympia title, the pinnacle of achievement for professional bodybuilders. Competitors include Incredible Hulk–in-waiting Lou Ferrigno.

PUMPING IRON, 1976

31 VISIONS OF LIGHT: THE ART OF CINEMATOGRAPHY *(1993, Fox-Video) Visions* is a stirring

reminder that much of what we've always loved about the movies is the way they look. This intoxicating documentary offers a cornucopia of Hollywood's visual high points—and we're not just talking pretty pictures. For a thrillingly fleet 90 minutes, we're given an appreciation of just how much motion pictures have been shaped by such offscreen visual magicians as Gordon Willis, Vittorio Storaro, and Michael Chapman—most of whom come off as disarmingly modest craftsmen, men with the souls of technicians and the eyes of artists.

32 STREETWISE *(1985, Movies Unlimited)* Teenage street kids in Seattle, observed

through the ritual of their daily lives—sleep till noon, panhandle downtown, roll a few "queers," turn a trick or two, score some drugs, party into the night, find a place to crash and somebody to crash with. Directors Martin Bell, Mary Ellen Mark, and Cheryl McCall offer a

225

powerful vision of an urban teenage America with no future and little hope.

33 **FOUR MORE YEARS** *(1972, Subtle, B&W)* Adequately covering our quadrennial political conventions requires a guerrilla mentality such as that demonstrated by the TVTV gang of counterculture video enthusiasts in their assault on the 1972 Republican National Convention, which nominated Richard Nixon for a second term. Forgoing the networks' stale brew of on-air "personalities," intrusive commentary, and overly scripted segmentation, TVTV let its cameras wander, listening to participants speak with unfiltered clarity. Part '70s time capsule, part political satire, *Four More Years* (a Nixon campaign slogan) represents a landslide victory for creative news coverage.

34 **THE SEARCH FOR ROBERT JOHNSON** *(1992, SMV)* Although it deals with Johnson's life, career, shadowy murder, and rumored pact with the devil, this video doesn't get too spooky on us. While rockers Eric Clapton and Keith Rich-

28 UP, 1984

ards put in cameo appearances to acknowledge Johnson's tremendous influence on their work, the lucid narration by blues musician/keeper of the flame John Hammond Jr. focuses on the blues—including two recording sessions that, through their impact on white blues-rockers, changed the course of popular music.

35 **AMERICAN DREAM** *(1990, HBO)* Barbara Kopple *(Harlan County, USA)* returns to the union fold with a searing, blow-by-blow account of the 1985–86 Hormel meat packers' strike in Austin, Minn. Shunning oversimplified characterizations of heroes and villains, this clear-eyed, relentlessly depressing portrait prompts questions that go beyond this strike to the very viability of the American dream. If this film leaves any room for hope, it's in the salt-of-the-earth decency, courage, and thoughtfulness of the workers on both sides of this struggle.

36 **THANK YOU AND GOODNIGHT!** *(1992, Fox Lorber)* Jan Oxenberg's eulogy to her grandmother never idealizes its subject or the imperfect humans who mourn her death. Through reminiscences, re-creations, real-life scenes, and disarmingly blunt humor, this inventive documentary will make you want to call your own grandma as soon as it's over.

37 **28 UP** *(1984)* and **35 UP** *(1991, both Movies Unlimited)* Beginning in 1963, director Michael Apted *(Gorillas in the Mist)* recorded the hopes and starting-out

MICHAEL APTED: STARTING 'UP'

His feature films (*Coal Miner's Daughter, Gorillas in the Mist*) may be better known, but British director Michael Apted's most revelatory screen adventures transpire far from the Hollywood mainstream. Starting in 1963 with *7 Up*, a British TV program on the lives of 14 English schoolchildren, Apted has revisited his subjects every seven years to produce an engrossing series about the mysteries of growing up. While the second and third installments were well received in England, Apted says the series "only got really good" with *28 Up*, the 1984 award-winning documentary.

The project began when Apted, straight out of Cambridge University (where he studied law and history), got a job as a researcher, assigned to knock on doors of public and private elementary schools and look for suitable 7-year-olds to interview for *7 Up*, a deeply critical look at the inequalities of the British class and education system. Seven years later, at a friend's casual suggestion, Apted turned the one-shot *7 Up* into an ongoing experiment, this time not as researcher but director. By now, Brits have been following the lives of *7 Up*'s cherubic youngsters for the past 28 years, culminating with the most recent installment, *35 Up*.

Apted recalls the special resonance of his latest visit to his subjects in *35 Up*: "What moved me the most was that a lot of them had children the same age as when we started, so you see the circle completed—you can see

them handing on the wisdom that we've watched them acquire."

While tracking down the subjects is relatively simple ("England is a fairly small country"), cajoling them into sharing their personal lives with the camera is not so easy. "It's such an invasion of privacy for them," says Apted, 50, who lost three of the original 14 participants after they refused to be filmed.

Meanwhile, the seed of Apted's original brainchild has been planted in other countries: An American version of *7 Up*, directed by Phil Joanou (*U2: Rattle and Hum*) and produced by Apted, has aired on CBS. Like the original British version, Joanou's documentary, called *Age 7 in America*, shows children from all walks of life—along with three little girls from a Manhattan private school, a young boy living in a shelter for the homeless is profiled—but it is decidedly more ethnically diverse. "I'm sorry there wasn't more ethnic diversity in the English one," says Apted, whose only black participant, Symon, refused to be filmed in *35 Up*. "I'm sorry there weren't more women in it as well."

A similar project is also under way in the Soviet Union (with Apted serving as a consultant), and there are tentative plans to launch Japanese and German versions. What's giving directors the seven-year itch? For Apted, the appeal is simple: "It's a very entertaining, personal, and accessible way of dealing with change." —*Taehee Kim*

227

spirits of 14 British 7-year-olds, returning to them every seven years for a film update. In *28 Up*, the subjects are all around 28 years old, and Apted records the changes in their lives, capturing an extraordinary range of ambition, energy, achievement, and disappointment. Seven years later and with more ground to cover, *35 Up* sometimes feels rushed, but it's still a remarkable spectacle. We watch values take hold, faces age, dreams come true or atrophy. What's most sobering is how the subjects' 35-year-old selves seem to have been predetermined by age 7.

38 MOTHER TERESA *(1986, Ignatius Press)* The world's most renowned "living saint," winner of the 1979 Nobel Prize for peace, founder and guiding spirit of the Calcutta-based Missionaries of Charity, is the subject of an evocative profile that was five years in the making. Showing the work of the more than 1,600 missionaries in 60 countries around the world, the film illustrates Mother Teresa's commitment to carry "God's love in action" to "the poorest of the poor," and provides stirring testimony that one person can make a difference.

39 DOWN AND OUT IN AMERICA *(1985, MPI)* National concern over homelessness in a land of plenty in the 1980s was partially fed by media attention, such as this devastatingly wrenching 60-minute documentary directed and narrated by actress Lee Grant. The film discovers thematic unity among three disparate groups: tenants of New York City's squalid welfare hotels, Los Angeles street people who transform an empty lot into a commune they call Justiceville, and Minnesota farmers being evicted from farms their families have worked for generations. Grant's interviews are poignant without being patronizing and her camera work observant without being obvious.

40 HEARTS AND MINDS *(1974, MPI, R)* Coproduced by noted Hollywood cage-rattler Bert Schneider *(Five Easy Pieces)* and directed by Peter Davis, this 1974 Oscar winner is a rapid-fire, no-narration retrospective of the images (burning villages, lying Presidents, Tet offensive) that compelled Americans to question the government's Vietnam policy. It also contains examples of the vindictive self-righteousness that has brought criticism of the antiwar movement, notably a blanket depiction of veterans as insensitive baby-killers. For better and worse, *Hearts and Minds* is an exceptional pointillist snapshot of an epochal period in American culture.

41 THE STORY OF AMERICA'S CLASSIC BALLPARKS *(1991, Movies Unlimited)* Baseball is unique in the timeless appeal of the places where it is played, including the parks profiled here—the last among the 15 constructed between 1909 and 1923: Detroit's Tiger Stadium (built in 1912), Boston's Fenway Park (also 1912), Chicago's Wrigley Field (1914), and Chicago's Comiskey Park (1910, demolished since the film was shot). They're treasures of urban architecture that endure as temples of an age when baseball was a public event and its playing fields were molded to accommodate their neighborhoods.

42 HARVEST OF SHAME *(1960, FoxVideo, B&W)* "We used to own our slaves; now we just rent them." With these words, Edward R. Murrow begins his pioneering muckraking documentary exposing the miserable conditions of migrant laborers in the United States, originally broadcast as a *CBS Reports* on Thanksgiving Day 1960. A high-impact collection of individual portraits emerges, as Murrow traces the workers' annual migration from Florida to the fruit fields of the northern states.

43 GREAT GOLF COURSES OF THE WORLD: SCOTLAND *(1992, Columbia TriStar)* When is a golf video not a golf video? When it has Sean Connery narrating a worshipful tour of historic St. Andrews, the ruggedly elegant links where the sport began 500 years ago. Golf enthusiast Connery gives an informative tour, which dispels all preconceptions of swank American country clubs: These courses are landscapes capriciously interrupted by raw nature and home to golf as the old Scots intended—a sport demanding strength and finesse, as dictated by found environments riotous with natural challenges.

44 RETURN TO EVEREST, FOR ALL MANKIND, CAMERAMEN WHO DARED, and THE EXPLORERS: A CENTURY OF DISCOVERY *(1984–89, Columbia TriStar)* Over the years, the National Geographic Society has been responsible for some of the most fascinating documentaries on any topic, and these four programs are among the most mesmerizing. Even the weakest of this group, *The Explorers: A Cen-* *tury of Discovery*, offers such bracing footage of so many sublime moments that viewers can excuse it for being one long commercial for its sponsor. Meanwhile, the other three tapes prove that the society's self-congratulation is largely justified. For the proof, check out *Cameramen*, which profiles the brave (or foolhardy) souls who risk their lives climbing mountains or dodging artillery so that armchair adventurers can experience the world.

45 SONG OF CEYLON *(1934, Kino, B&W)* One of the most impressive products of the British Documentary Movement, this 39-minute film by Basil Wright offers a memorably impressionistic vision of the British colony Ceylon (now known as Sri Lanka) by presenting images and cultural themes rather than factual data. Visions of traditional native lifestyles are repeatedly contrasted sharply with the sounds and sights of invasive Western culture.

46 THE WEEK THAT SHOOK THE WORLD: THE SOVIET COUP *(1991, MPI)* The most pivotal event in world history since World War II, the abortive Soviet coup that led to the breakup of the Soviet Union is chronicled in a first-rate ABC News documentary that offers both you-are-there immediacy and big-picture perspective. While only time will reveal all the consequences of those seven days, ABC jump-starts the historical process with a gripping account of Boris Yeltsin and 10,000 Moscow citizens facing down the cabal that tried to overthrow Gorbachev and ended up destroying their country.

229

47

HOW TO START YOUR OWN SUCCESSFUL BUSINESS *(1992)*, **YOUR PERSONAL FINANCIAL GUIDE TO SUCCESS, POWER AND SECURITY** *(1991)*, and **HOW TO FIND EMPLOYMENT IN THE '90S** *(1993, all from In the Black)* The syndicated cable program *In the Black* is geared to sparking entrepreneurism among minorities, but it contains exemplary advice for anyone looking for guidance through today's financial thicket. These three videos are made up of segments of the monthly shows, and each features no-nonsense information and inspirational case histories.

48

LAND OF LOOK BEHIND *(1990, Kino) Look Behind* is what native Jamaicans call the forbidding island forest that here serves as a metaphor for the country's deeply rooted Rastafarian culture. Directed by Alan Greenberg, what began as a record of Bob Marley's 1981 funeral becomes an incendiary look at reggae/Rasta's sociopolitical underpinnings—and a very different kind of Caribbean travel video.

49

THE OLYMPIAD SERIES *(1979, Paramount)* Writer-producer-director Bud Greenspan is the poet laureate of Olympic filmmaking, and this is his 22-tape magnum opus. Equal parts social and athletic history, the segments are uniformly informative, tightly focused, and seamlessly edited to flesh out individual performers and events with telling details (for example, a figure skater participating in an early Olympics is shown cranking a record player to start her own music before skating into com-

THE OLYMPIAD SERIES, 1979

petition). They excel in seeking out the great stories among the lesser-known Olympians and constitute a cinematic achievement to match the sterling ideals of the Games themselves.

50

BURDEN OF DREAMS *(1982, Flower)* Les Blank's legendary film of the making of Werner Herzog's quirky 1982 feature *Fitzcarraldo* proves that a documentary on the making of a film can be more fascinating than the film itself. Herzog's film is about a crazed Irish entrepreneur (Klaus Kinski) obsessed with bringing grand opera to a desolate village in the Amazon jungle. Blank's film is about a crazed German movie director (Herzog) obsessed with making this movie, on location in the actual Amazon setting. Herzog gets his film; Blank gets a better one.

51 **THIN AIR: THE 1991 NEW ENGLAND EVEREST EXPEDITION** *(1992, International Mountain Equipment)* A record of eight New Englanders' ambitious attack on Mount Everest in 1991, with bare-bones equipment and a modest budget, this video also answers the everyday questions of how mountain climbers live, work, and relax. Most impressive is its strikingly offbeat vision of the world's mightiest mountain as a wasteland littered with the detritus of previous expeditions— including, on this occasion, the body of a dead Sherpa, lying frozen where his blown-away tent once was.

52 **KOYAANISQATSI** *(1982, Pacific Arts)* If humans and nature are indeed engaged in a hand-to-hand game of life and death, director Godfrey Reggio intends for this impressionist documentary (and its sequel, *Powaqqatsi*) to be the game's official highlight film. Reggio's device is a montage of stunning, free-flowing images that emphasizes juxtapositions of natural beauty and the artificial encroachments of human invention (hot rockets against cool skyscapes; jammed expressways against serene mountain vistas), all backed by the impressive music of Philip Glass.

53 **BLAST 'EM** *(1992, Academy)* A provocative peek at the paparazzi trade looks at its subject from both sides of the lens. The filmmakers follow various photographers as they stake out and shoot celebrities; meanwhile, in interviews, several paparazzi provide revealing insights about their specialized craft. The actions of these star stalkers speak as eloquently as a thousand pictures.

54 **THE ASTRONOMERS** *(1991, Movies Unlimited)* While these six hour-long tapes excel in their ground-level explanations of stratospheric concepts (gravity waves, background radiation), they are best at humanizing and explaining this most romantic of sciences by showing a range of its practitioners: the venerated elder pioneers, the current heavyweights, and the fresh-faced graduate assistants. The common source of their drive, invoked repeatedly through these tapes, is a bedrock curiosity articulated by Bell Laboratories' Tony Tyson: "More than 90 percent of everything in the universe is something that we know nothing about."

55 **INTERVISTA** *(1987, Ingram)* In the dead of night, a Japanese TV crew arrives for an on-set interview with Federico Fellini. From there, more and more faux realities unfold in this picaresque self-portrait by Fellini: the septuagenarian director filming a re-creation of his first visit to Cinecittà studios in 1940, shooting scenes for an adaptation of Kafka's *Amerika*, and cajoling old friend Marcello Mastroianni into visiting an enormous Anita Ekberg at her country home. Beneath the big-top bustle, there's a keen acknowledgment of mortality and faded glory in this bittersweet self-portrait.

56 **THE SILK ROAD COLLECTION** *(1991, Central Park Media)* A Chinese-Japanese production that is as important for what it shows and tells as for how it was done, taking 10 years and $50 million to retrace the ancient Silk Road trade route from its Oriental end south of Beijing to Rome. The result is a muscular adventure film/education documentary that depicts western China as a vast archaeological treasure house where dry desert climates, insular cultures, and xenophobic governments have conspired to preserve two millennia of lost kingdoms and fallen cities.

57 BROTHER'S KEEPER (1992, Fox Lorber) This much is certain: On June 5, 1990, William Ward, 64 and in poor health, went to sleep on the grungy mattress he shared with his 59-year-old brother Delbert, and in the morning he was dead. This much is unknown: Did Bill die in his sleep of natural causes, or was

DEREK BERG/CREATIVE THINKING LTD.

BROTHER'S KEEPER, 1992

he suffocated by Delbert? In *Brother's Keeper*, filmmakers Joe Berlinger and Bruce Sinofsky turn an unflinching camera on Delbert and his surviving older brothers, Roscoe and Lyman, and the neighbors who fund Delbert's bail and defense—not necessarily because they believe he's innocent (as the jury finally found him) but because the brothers belong to Munnsville (pop. 499), not to the big city.

58 SUPERSTAR: THE LIFE AND TIMES OF ANDY WARHOL (1991, LIVE) Ever visible yet elusive, Andy Warhol is captured here in an entertaining portrait of the artist as a popster. Writer-producer-director Chuck Workman (*Stoogemania*) steers swiftly from Warhol's humble Pittsburgh-area beginnings to the sex, drugs, and rock & roll years to his superstardom, a status gained through his gloriously banal paintings and artful self-promotion. Warhol, who died in 1987, had a chameleonlike ability to move with the times. That talent has made his art—and this documentary—a picture of ourselves.

59 AROUND THE WORLD IN 80 DAYS (1990, Public Media) and MICHAEL PALIN'S POLE TO POLE (1992, A&E) Ex–Monty Python trouper Michael Palin has produced two immensely witty and whimsical travelogues. In the first he sets out to duplicate the epic feat of global circumnavigation described in the Jules Verne novel, vowing not to use any transportation not available in Verne's time, the late 19th century. *Pole to Pole* begins at the top of the world and ends, nearly five months later, in

vast Antarctica. Along the way, Palin dodges icebergs in the Arctic Ocean, lands in the Soviet Union on the eve of its collapse, and breaks a rib braving the rapids below Victoria Falls. With both travel shows, it's probably the best time you could have on somebody else's adventure.

60 **CANE TOADS: AN UNNATURAL HISTORY** *(1988, Movies Unlimited)* Imported to Australia in 1935 to fight a destructive beetle infestation, softball-size cane toads grew to constitute a bizarre manmade environmental disaster in the northern part of that country: They eat everything, fend off predators with a natural poison, and are such persistent breeders that a male toad is here observed attempting for an estimated eight hours to mate with a female that has been dead for several days. A whimsical educational documentary of rare wit and passion.

61 **CYBERPUNK** *(1990, Mystic Fire)* The information highway is a routine daily commute for the cyberpunks, described here as "computer cowboys hacking a perilous post-human lifestyle on new technological frontiers." Much of *Cyberpunk* consists of heady comments from the movement's head cowboy, William Gibson, the award-winning sci-fi novelist (*Neuromancer*) and confessed computer illiterate who nevertheless coined the term *cyberspace*. Often mistakenly pigeonholed with irresponsible technovandals, cyberpunks say the result of their vigorous exploration of leading-edge technology will be the "ultimate, decentralized democracy."

62 **THE JIM ROSE CIRCUS SIDESHOW** *(1993, American Visuals)* Here's one for the Geek Hall of Fame: a medley of gross-out artists and oddities who took the 1993 Lollapalooza tour by storm. The first guy dangles two steam irons from his most private part, the last guy shoves his face in broken glass and has an audience member stand on his head. In between there's enough really unsavory—and really cool—action to please both Beavis and Butt-head.

63 **MINOR LEAGUES/MAJOR DREAMS** *(1993, Tapeworm)* The real soul of pro baseball lies three leagues below the majors—where teenage phenoms find out if they're for real and suspects are weeded from prospects. Observant documentarian Nathan Kaufman spent the 1991 season with a Minnesota Twins farm team, recording the dreary bus rides, junk-food orgies, locker-room pranks, public ordeals, and private crises. Most of all, he succeeds in profiling a handful of prototypical players and, through them, the undimmed dreams of athletes everywhere.

64 **JACKSON POLLOCK** *(1992, Home Vision)* Pollock was the preeminent Abstract Expressionist, producing some of the movement's most influential paintings. Alcoholic and unruly, Pollock died in an auto crash in 1956 at age 44, and we get to hear a lot about Pollock's wretched personal behavior. But the video's real value lies in the scenes devoted to his painting. Thanks to a Hans Namuth film of Pollock at work a few years before his death, we catch vivid glimpses of his

233

'ROOM' WITH A VIEWFINDER

There are no interviews in D.A. Pennebaker and Chris Hegedus' behind-the-scenes documentary *The War Room*. There's just human behavior as unraveled before the husband-and-wife filmmakers' cameras during the 1992 Clinton campaign. "I don't know what I want to know," Pennebaker says. "I'm willing to hang out and find out whatever it is they're willing to tell me."

While hanging out for 20 days and shooting 33 hours of film—later combined with news footage for the final 93-minute version—the duo found out how tense and exhilarating life in the "war room" can be. But capturing that on film took a while. At first, Hegedus says, strategists James Carville and George Stephanopoulos "went out of the room to talk, and we'd go through this elaborate charade of taking off their microphones. Slowly they got tired of doing that."

By the end, even the media-savvy Stephanopoulos took politically sensitive calls in front of the camera. "Whatever happened that we got, he wanted it to be what we got," Pennebaker says. "The idea was that, years from then, he would look back and that would be what happened." —*George Mannes*

"drip" method of composition, which revolutionized the art of painting.

65 THE LIFE AND TIMES OF SECRETARIAT: AN AMERICAN RACING LEGEND *(1990, ESPN)* One of the 20th century's legendary sports heroes, Secretariat had a career that encompassed a scant 21 events in 16 months, from July 1972 through October 1973, when he was put out to stud. But among the events were the Kentucky Derby, Preakness, and Belmont Stakes races of 1973, resulting in three victories, three track records, the first Triple Crown in 25 years, and a racehorse of uncommon character that fired the public imagination like no other in the TV age.

66 A BRIEF HISTORY OF TIME *(1992, Paramount, G)* Knowing that theoretical physics isn't everyone's cup of tea, director Errol Morris made a film adap-

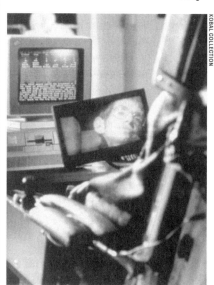

A BRIEF HISTORY OF TIME, 1992

tation of Stephen Hawking's unlikely 1988 best-seller that uses devices like a shattering teacup to illustrate the entropy of the universe. Yet for all Morris' efforts to make the theories entertaining, you don't have to digest the science to like the movie—or British cosmologist Hawking, who has a degenerative neurological affliction and expounds on black holes and the Big Crunch through a computerized voice synthesizer. A singular character

EVERETT COLLECTION

THE WAR ROOM, 1993

emerges from all the hardware, and it's bound to grab even those who don't get as excited about the mysteries of the cosmos as Hawking clearly does.

67 **TWIST** *(1993, Columbia TriStar, PG)* Tracing the unbuttoning of America through one singular dance sensation, director Ron Mann (*Comic Book Confidential*) digs up scads of campy archival footage to show how the twist served as crucial link between Elvis and the Beatles, progressing from black R&B fad to white teenage smash to New York jet-set craze to full-blown pop-culture phenomenon. He even allows a few words from the media pundit Marshall McLuhan, who called the twist a "conversation without words."

68 **THE WAR ROOM** *(1993, Vidmark, PG)* A live-wire backstage view of the 1992 Bill Clinton presidential campaign. The unabashed star of this 1993 Oscar-nominated documentary is chief Clinton strategist James Carville, a tall, bald, rascally Southerner who might be John Malkovich's wild-ass brother. Carville isn't just dedicated, he's lit: the bulb around which the Clinton campaign moths flutter.

69 **THE MAN WHO SAW TOMORROW** *(1981, Warner, PG)* Number one on the booga-booga hit parade, this feature-length production investigates the prophecies of 16th-century French physician Michel de Nostradamus. More than half of Nostradamus' 1,000 predictions have come true, says narrator Orson Welles as he introduces lurid recreations of such allegedly prophesied scenes as the death of Louis XVI and the rise of Adolf Hitler. "Was he a quack ...or was he a true prophet?" asks Welles. "Judge for yourselves."

70 **NATURE: THE VOLCANO WATCHERS** *(1990, PBS)* This documentary distills 20 years' worth of home movies by the peripatetic French husband-and-wife team of Maurice and Katia Krafft. The Kraffts established their volcanology center in Alsace in 1968 and have spent the intervening years chasing erup-

235

tions from Iceland to Hawaii. Individually, one volcanic cataclysm looks much like another, but seen sequentially in the Kraffts' films, they form a fiery tapestry that evokes the dawn of time—dwarfing man, dwarfing nature, dwarfing everything.

71 THE BEST OF PERSON TO PERSON *(1992, FoxVideo, B&W)* and THE 50TH BARBARA WALTERS SPECIAL *(1989, MPI)*
Edward R. Murrow and Barbara Walters are the TV age's most memorable interviewers of popular-culture icons, and video has delivered excellent anthologies of these two very different masters at work. In *The Best of Person to Person*, we see how Murrow—already a legendary radio newscaster—went about inventing the modern school of celebrity journalism when he launched his TV series in 1953. A couple of decades later, Barbara Walters serves up a feast of video junk food. Splicing together bits from 63 interviews (with such stars as Sylvester Stallone and Goldie Hawn, and such political figures as the Shah of Iran and Fidel Castro) to form enticingly broad categories (love and marriage, the price of fame), the tape demonstrates that the root appeal of Walters' specials is not so much getting deep dish as gaping at people foolishly trying to speak honestly about their emotional lives in a ridiculously public forum.

72 HERDSMEN OF THE SUN *(1988, Interama)* Known for setting his feature films in remote places, amid primitive peoples (e.g., *Aguirre, the Wrath of God*; *Fitzcarraldo*), German director Werner Herzog turns documentarian to record the story of the Wodaabe, a tribe of Saharan nomads whose lifestyle remains virtually unchanged since its Stone Age beginnings. And a very unusual tribe it is: Herzog's Dadaist anthropology is especially fixated on mating rituals in which the tribal men compete in beautifying themselves and the women select whom they wish to marry or merely spend the night with.

73 PAINTED SPIDER: ROCK CLIMBING IN THE '90S *(1992, Spire Productions)* These 85 minutes of foothold-by-foothold rock-climbing adventure make the case that recent advances in equipment quality may have given the climbers a fighting chance against nature, but that individual success still depends most on the timeless basics of strength, agility, and mental focus. Best of all: Peter Croft's superhumanly elegant free solo climb—no rope!—up a 900-foot Yosemite tower.

74 THE HECK WITH HOLLYWOOD *(1992, Direct Cinema)* "What the hell's a filmmaker?" Doug Block asks at the beginning of his sweaty cinema vérité peek into the lives of three defiantly non-Hollywood directors (Gerry Cook, Jennifer Fox, and Ted Lichtenheld) scrambling to compete in an overcrowded field, with undercapitalized dreams. Each of the young filmmakers has a film that has to be made, even if making the film means becoming an unrepentant hustler in the process. Block's own vision is bitterly satirical yet wholly sympathetic to the creative impulse to commit ideas to celluloid.

75 **EXPLORING ANTARCTICA** *(1991, Questar)* Exemplifying the highest achievements of travel documentary video, *Exploring Antarctica* is fascinating in large part because its subject terrain is so forbidding. No human set foot on the desolate, inaccessible, ice-wrapped continent until 1821 or fully explored it until the early 20th century. Along with its sense of slack-jawed wonder, this video also brings keen insight to the conservationist challenge that humankind faces in protecting this pristine continental laboratory.

76 **MARLENE** *(1986, Columbia TriStar)* A fittingly bizarre eulogy to the most baroque of stars, this production was complicated by the fact that 80-year-old Marlene Dietrich allowed herself to be interviewed on audiotape but flatly refused to be filmed. Director Maximilian Schell comes through with a penetrating meditation on the masks of glamour, using standard film clips as a counterpoint to Dietrich's quavery, brutally unsentimental musings on the soundtrack. If only because her screen persona was so opaque, this is the rare star bio that is crucial to an understanding of its star.

77 **A LEAGUE OF THEIR OWN: THE DOCUMENTARY** *(1988, Columbia TriStar)* Mixing newsreel and actual game footage with interviews from a reunion of the All-American Girls Professional Baseball League, this lively half hour captures the irrepressible spirit of the pioneer athletes who, between 1943 and 1954, played ball as ruggedly as men.

78 **COUSIN BOBBY** *(1992, Cinevista)* Like the fiery Harlem minister it profiles, this documentary is both uplifting and

237

COUSIN BOBBY, 1992

angry and is rendered more intriguing by the fact that the clergyman happens to be Jonathan Demme's long-lost cousin. The director of *The Silence of the Lambs* gets personal here, overlaying scenes of the Rev. Robert Castle's ecumenical neighborhood crusade with Demme's own family portrait.

79 **THE WAR GAME** *(1965, Sinister, B&W)* Heavily influenced by the hyper-dramatized narratives of the British Documentary Movement, Peter Watkins' film on the possible aftereffects of a nuclear attack on Great Britain was so disturbingly realistic that its BBC sponsors at first refused to let it be shown. Watkins' docudrama mixes interviews with "nuclear experts" and factoid reports with hideously chilling scenes of the destructive impact of the initial blast, the firestorm that follows, and the living hell that awaits the survivors.

80 **TABLE MANNERS FOR EVERYDAY USE** *(1990, Landy-Vision)* This is a modest jewel among how-to tapes, as it tackles a most mundane subject with wit, charm, and skillful instruction. On-screen principals Elliott Landy and Diana Oestreich invest the video with great humor and solid common sense, performing the "do" and "don't" approach to dining situations from fancy at-home dinners to gorge-and-run fast-food lunches.

81 **DESTINATION: MOZART—A NIGHT AT THE OPERA WITH PETER SELLARS** *(1990, Kultur)* Opera traditionalists have vilified the director Peter Sellars for his up-

dated and iconoclastic stagings of Mozart's *The Marriage of Figaro* (set in New York's Trump Tower), *Don Giovanni* (set in the ravaged South Bronx), and *Così Fan Tutte* (set at a postmodern diner). But Sellars has found an audience among open-minded opera fans. Here Sellars explains himself, with support from the singers and designers who worked with him on the three controversial productions—whose excerpts show how on-target some of his ideas are.

82 **SECRETS OF MAKING LOVE TO THE SAME PERSON FOREVER** *(1991, Playboy)* Among erotic how-to tapes, this is something of a landmark for acknowledging the possibilities of long-term, sexually fulfilling monogamous relationships. Scenes of gorgeous young couples seducing each other in their backyard pools, the backseats of their cars, and even in their bedrooms are interspersed with vignettes of some normal-looking couples telling the camera about their loss of sexual interest, along with voice-over suggestions for reinvigorating a relationship.

83 **A COUSTEAU COLLECTION** *(1990, Turner)* The great explorer Jacques Cousteau set sail into the world of television and discovered new ways to raise public consciousness of the natural world. These six tapes of TV productions that aired between 1982 and 1990 capture Cousteau's gift for taking important ecological issues and making them seem both pressing and, better yet, fascinating. Along with gorgeous photography, the tapes provide passionate but always charmingly deadpan commentary on environmental issues.

84 THE BIG BANG *(1990, Movies Unlimited, R)* Now, this is high-concept: Director James Toback *(Fingers)* takes his camera and asks an assortment of people

A COUSTEAU COLLECTION, 1990

how they think the world began. The interviewees run the gamut—a nun, a gangster, a model, an astronomer, and a Holocaust survivor, to name a few. And the menu expands to include this diverse crowd's thoughts on God, orgasms, love, race, class, murder, chaos, and death. A great video to play at the end of a dinner party.

85 INCIDENT AT OGLALA: THE LEONARD PELTIER STORY *(1992, LIVE, PG)* While shooting this documentary, director Michael Apted was given the script

for a fiction film *(Thunderheart)* based on similar subject matter—Native Americans in trouble. Of the two, the documentary offers a more journalistic, though still dramatic, take on the turmoil in the Badlands. It reconstructs a 1975 gunfight that left two FBI agents dead and makes a strong case that the wrong man may be serving time for their murders.

86 THE FEAST OF THE GODS *(1990, Home Vision)* Who altered Bellini's 1514 painting *The Feast of the Gods*? And why? Using state-of-the-art techniques—infrared photography, X rays, and computer graphics—experts at the National Gallery of Art in Washington reveal how significant portions of the masterpiece were repainted sometime after the artist's death in 1516. The story unravels like a high-culture detective story.

87 DARK CIRCLE *(1982; updated in 1991, The Video Project)* The best of several antinuke documentaries, *Dark Circle* is a virtual textbook of polished muckraking that skillfully juggles sobering big-picture topics (how a nuclear reactor works), individual personal concerns (the Colorado mothers near the Rocky Flats nuclear-weapons plant worried about the health effects of the bomb-building there), and hair-raising visual images (the awesome fury of an actual nuclear-core meltdown). Narrator Judy Irving supplements these scenes with her autobiography: Born at the dawn of the Atomic Age in 1946, she slowly came to question assumptions about "our friend, the atom."

239

88 ROY LICHTENSTEIN *(1990, Home Vision)* Best known for his comic-book images writ large, artist Lichtenstein has made a career out of primary colors, black outlines, and Benday dots, striving for, as he says on this tape, "a lack of nuance." This portrait of the Pop artist is as buoyant and accessible as its subject's paintings.

89 CIRQUE DU SOLEIL: WE RE-INVENT THE CIRCUS *(1992, IVA/PolyGram)* Like the old *Ed Sullivan Show*, video can present sensational specialty acts that we might not otherwise see. In this hour-long tape, the 25-member Canadian troupe called Cirque du Soleil features a big-top assortment of aerialists, clowns, wire walkers, and balancing acts that have more in common with Balanchine than with Barnum, as performers execute stupendous feats with balletic flair.

90 THE EAGLE'S NEST *(1987, White Star)* No matter that Nazi Germany is the most thoroughly reported and analyzed social phenomenon of our time; Adolf Hitler's high-concept tyranny retains a unique capacity to fascinate us—never more so than in this four-hour documentary produced for Dutch television in 1987. Its title refers to Hitler's Bavarian mountaintop retreat (where, in fact, Hitler rarely went, fearful of being trapped in the elevator that provided the only access to the Nest), and it uses his Obersalzberg getaways as a linchpin for its perspective on the whole Third Reich experience—fleshed out with interviews of surviving Nazi intimates

and home movies of the Reich-raff at play.

91 THE SKY ABOVE, THE MUD BELOW *(1962, Warner)* Pierre-Dominique Gaisseau's dramatic documentary of an exploratory 1,000-mile 1959 trek across central Dutch New Guinea was a surprise theatrical success on its release in the early 1960s, but it loses some of its luster in light of subsequent, better documentaries and greater public awareness of diverse cultures. While Gaisseau's narration today seems breathlessly naive and some "native life" scenes appear overly staged, this should not dim the significance of his expedition's encounters with leech-infested rivers, impassible mountain gorges, and warring tribesmen.

92 COOKIN' UP PROFITS ON WALL STREET: A GUIDE TO COMMON-SENSE INVESTING *(1993, Central Picture)* The secret to successful stock investments can be found among 16 ladies, ages 65 to 90, gathered around a table in a room above a bowling alley in rural Illinois. They are the Beardstown Business and Professional Women's Investment Club, and since 1983 they have seen their portfolio earn big profits. In this documentary of their success, the women provide detail-rich interviews to inspire others to duplicate their experience.

93 QUICK CALLANETICS: LEGS, STOMACH, and HIPS & BEHIND *(1991, MCA/Universal)* Callan Pinckney has the quick solution to toning up our mushy stomachs,

BLOND REPETITION

Documentaries seem to come in all styles, from the arty Madonna concert-tour film *Truth or Dare* to the fake "rockumentary" *This Is Spïnal Tap*. But are they really so different? You decide.

THIS IS SPINAL TAP

TRUTH OR DARE

Stage malfunction traps Derek inside plastic bubble; stage crew pries him out with blowtorch.

Stage malfunction cuts off Madonna's vocals; stage crew bails her out with faulty hand mike.

241

Nigel has backstage snit over minuscule hors d'oeuvres; manager nods patiently.

Madonna has backstage snit over technical gaffe; manager nods patiently.

Derek uses cucumber wrapped in aluminum foil as stunt phallus.

Madonna uses mineral-water bottle.

Nigel and David (Michael McKean) visit Elvis' grave and sing off-key "Heartbreak Hotel" in tribute.

Madonna visits Mom's grave while on soundtrack she sings off-key rendition of "Oh Father" in tribute.

Camera follows group stumbling through Cleveland concert-hall basement trying to find stage.

Camera follows Madonna's brother Marty stumbling through Detroit hotel hall trying to find sister's room.

Cover of "Smell the Glove" album, depicting woman on all fours, prompts boycott by Kmart.

"Like a Virgin" number, with Madonna on all fours, prompts Vatican to denounce show.

—*Steve Daly*

legs, hips, and behinds within the confines of our rushed, overextended lives. These three 20-minute tapes incorporate gentle, precise deep-muscle movements (no jerking, bouncing, or forcing) that look simple but are sometimes agonizingly tough. To her credit, Pinckney begins and ends with relaxing stretches, provides clear instructions (including how to protect the back, plus specific precautions for sciatica sufferers), and stresses taking breaks.

94 MARIO LANZA: THE AMERICAN CARUSO *(1983, Kultur)* While every bit a high-minded biography of the enigmatic Hollywood musical star (born Alfred Cocozza) of the 1940s and '50s, this treatment also raises an eyebrow over Lanza's drinking and eating binges—and his sudden death in 1959, at age 38. Rumors abound that the singer's untimely demise was a Mob hit because Lanza never paid back Mafia kingpin Lucky Luciano, who reportedly backed Lanza financially.

95 HARLEY-DAVIDSON: THE AMERICAN MOTORCYCLE *(1993, Cabin Fever)* Having survived a '50s outlaw-biker stigma and '60s financial troubles, Harley-Davidson's gentle glide into the '90s slow lane of mainstream respectability is commemorated by a reverential documentary. The video tribute includes clips from such diverse Harley-hogging

MARIO LANZA: THE AMERICAN CARUSO, 1983

EVERETT COLLECTION

DOCUMENTARY

movies as the Marx Brothers' *Duck Soup*, Kenneth Anger's *Scorpio Rising*, the Three Stooges' *Playing the Ponies*, and a 1980 sci-fi spoof, *Galaxina*, in which rocket-jockey cultists worship at a cycle-topped altar.

96 INTO THE GREAT SOLITUDE
(1989, New Film) Deskbound pencil pushers who dream of chucking it all and hitting the road will find a role model in erstwhile Wall Street exec Rob Perkins. He took a 700-mile, nine-week canoe trip through the Canadian wilderness, carrying a camcorder to capture his encounter with nature and his thoughts on a "voyage of understanding [where] my only true friend is my shadow."

97 ELMORE LEONARD'S CRIMINAL RECORDS *(1993, Home Vision)* Ten of Elmore Leonard's 30-plus novels have been made into movies. Small wonder: Leonard himself is so visually attuned that he researches prospective characters by watching videotaped interviews with cops, judges, and bail bondsmen. This 61-minute BBC documentary will be a godsend for the author's fans who want to hear their guy read from *Killshot* and other favorites, eavesdrop on the kinds of people who figure in his books, and listen to Hollywood producer Walter Mirisch explain why his pal's novels make such great film material.

98 WORLD'S YOUNG BALLET
(1969, Kultur, B&W) The First International Ballet Competition was held at Moscow's Bolshoi Theater in 1969, and its gold-medal winner was a 21-year-old entrant from Leningrad's Kirov Ballet, Mikhail Baryshnikov. This Russian-made 73-minute account of the event includes the first known Baryshnikov performance footage, including rehearsals and excerpts from two dance solos, one from *La Bayadère* and the other from *Vestris*. A treasure for balletomanes.

99 THE KOREAN WAR *(1992, White Star)* The 20th century's "forgotten war" is remembered in a painstaking five-volume, 10-hour set that often seems longer than the war itself. Forgoing slick production values for get-it-right historiography, this Korean Broadcast System program superbly explains the nuances of superpower diplomatic posturing, puppet-government chicanery, and routine battlefield horror.

100 THE INQUIRING NUNS *(1967, Facets, B&W)* Take two beatific nuns (Sisters Mary Campion and Marie Arné), give them one disarmingly simple question ("Are you happy?"), turn them loose on the streets of Chicago, and you get this guilelessly provocative documentary from the social-activist Kartemquin film collective. While some responses are silly, and a few are time-warped (the Vietnam War is an oft-cited source of unhappiness), most of the passersby provide inspiring reaffirmation of the virtue of conventional wisdom.

243

Reviews written by Terry Catchpole, as well as Ty Burr, Jess Cagle, Susan Chumsky, Steve Daly, Jim Farber, Ron Givens, Elayne J. Kahn, Dotti Keagy, Allan Kozinn, Peter Kobel, Hilton Kramer, Mary Makarushka, Lawrence O'Toole, Michael Sauter, and Dave Van Ronk.

SLEEPERS

IT'S THE DILEMMA of the video age: You walk into the local rental store, see that all 60 copies of *Jurassic Park* are rented out, and scan the aisles with dread. Thousands of titles stare you down, and you haven't heard of *one* of them. How many bad movies can they make, anyway?

Wait a minute: Total obscurity doesn't necessarily mean that a film is unworthy—just that it's unknown. Lost classics hide behind lousy titles. (*Riot in Cell Block 11* has to be terrible, right? Wrong.) Neglected jewels suffer from hideous packaging; forgotten miracles are filed in the wrong section, because the stock kid's cultural memory stops at *Young Guns II*. None of it matters: *They're still good movies.*

Don't believe us? Fine, we'll prove it. On the following pages, you will find 100 great movies, many of which you've never heard of. Some were trashed when they came out and look better with age; some were too obscure to get reviewed in the first place. A motley but rewarding collection, this is one list that was too diverse to rank from "best" to "worst." Rent 'em all and do it yourself.

BAD DAY AT BLACK ROCK *(1955, MGM/ UA, B&W, not rated)* In a modern re-working of the classic Western, one-armed Spencer Tracy shows up in a Southwestern town that's got something to hide, and it has to do with the treatment of Japanese-Americans during the war. Director John Sturges captures, mercilessly, what it's like to be a stranger in an unfriendly town. Robert Ryan, Lee Marvin, and Ernest Borgnine are astonishingly evil local villains.

THE BALLAD OF CABLE HOGUE *(1970, Warner, R)* Sam Peckinpah's *The Wild Bunch* came out the year before, and audiences probably expected more slow-mo balletic violence from him. But Peckinpah decided, cinematically speaking, to "go fishin'" for fun. Jason Robards is an ornery prospector who builds a prosperous stagecoach stop and becomes an anachronism in his own time. It's a story of individuality, set under spacious Western skies, that takes its own sweet time.

BARBAROSA *(1982, Facets, PG)* Most '80s Westerns were bloated, jokey affairs. Not this unpretentious winner, which

BARBAROSA:
WILLIE NELSON, GARY BUSEY

gave Willie Nelson his best role to date, as a desperado in the dusty Rio Grande valley. Gary Busey is a farm boy–turned–sidekick in Fred Schepisi's fine, funny campfire tale of a movie.

LA BÊTE HUMAINE *(1938, Facets, B&W, not rated)* Every film buff worth his or her salted popcorn knows Jean Renoir's *Rules of the Game* and *Grand Illusion*, but this film, his feverish adaptation of the Emile Zola novel, is just as gripping. A dark moral chiller in which railroad worker Jean Gabin is cajoled into murder by hot Simone Simon, *Humaine* is a key influence on Hollywood noirs like *Double Indemnity*—and its soul runs much deeper.

THE BIG COMBO *(1955, Facets, B&W, not rated)* "First is first and second is nobody" is the motto of racketeer and human slime Richard Conte in this flashy and often unforgettable crime flick set on the seamy side of the tracks. Cornel Wilde is the detective obsessed with putting him behind bars, and Jean Wallace is the society girl Conte keeps in sexual thrall. Surely one of the first movies to feature a pair of homosexual lovers who are also thugs.

BLUE COLLAR *(1978, MCA/Universal, R)* In screenwriter Paul Schrader's directing debut, Richard Pryor plays one of three auto-factory grunts (the other two are Harvey Keitel and Yaphet Kotto) who get in way over their heads when they rob the safe at union headquarters. Starting as a realistic comedy, it very slowly turns very frightening. It's also perhaps the only film in which Pryor isn't asked to play himself; what results is the richest *acting* of his career.

THE BROOD *(1979, Facets, R)* The title refers to the rampaging mutant spawn of Samantha Eggar, but it could just as well mean the dour tone of any horror movie from David Cronenberg (*The Fly*), in which the real source of terror lies in the ways our bodies betray us. For a cheap horror flick, *The Brood* echoes on levels you may not care to acknowledge.

BURN! *(1970, Facets, PG)* Incendiary indeed. Marlon Brando gives one of his most seductively mysterious performances as an 19th-century agent provocateur sent by the British government to incite a slave uprising on a Caribbean island. Director Gillo Pontecorvo's complex film is as remarkable for its steaming, sensual surfaces as for its sophisticated political thinking.

CANDY MOUNTAIN *(1987, Republic, R)* Codirected by esteemed still photographer Robert Frank and screenwriter Rudy Wurlitzer (*Walker*), this lovely shaggy-dog story takes a cocky kid from New York to the wilds of Canada in search of a reclusive guitar maker. On the way, he meets every musical eccentric from Buster Poindexter to Leon Redbone to Dr. John, and he finds a bizarre stillness at road's end.

CARRIE *(1952, Facets, B&W, not rated)* Unpopular because of its frank treatment of unwholesome material, director William Wyler's adaptation of Theodore Dreiser's *Sister Carrie* (not to be confused with Brian De Palma's 1976 film) contains what may be Laurence Olivier's best screen performance. As George Hurstwood, the married man who runs off with Carrie (Jennifer

COMFORT AND JOY: BILL PATERSON

Jones), Olivier paints an almost unbearably painful portrait of dissolution. Carrie becomes a famous actress as Hurstwood falls deeper into the abyss of himself.

CHILLY SCENES OF WINTER *(1979, MGM/UA, PG)* John Heard wants last year's girlfriend, Mary Beth Hurt, back, and so what if she got married in the interim? Its studio originally released this film as *Head Over Heels*, but the truth lies between the two titles; this isn't so much a cerebral film or a romantic comedy as it is a mature charmer about people using absurdity to keep loneliness from the door.

COMFORT AND JOY *(1984, MCA/Universal, PG)* Scottish filmmaker Bill Forsyth's gentle comedy about a Glaswegian deejay whose life has slipped out of its normal groove is a true piece of eccentricity. A walking Murphy's law, the music spinner gets caught in the crossfire between two underworld families fighting for rights to an ice cream concession —the oddest twist ever in the shoot-'em-up genre.

247

DEATH RACE 2000: SIMONE GRIFFETH, DAVID CARRADINE

CRISS CROSS *(1949, MCA/Universal, B&W, not rated)* Robert Siodmak directed this film noir holdup movie with speed and surgical precision. Burt Lancaster is the slightly dopey armored-car guard who gets the dirt from a skirt—the extremely alluring Yvonne De Carlo as his duplicitous wife. The robbery itself, executed with the thieves wearing gas masks, is memorably surreal. And keep an eye out for a kid named Anthony (Tony) Curtis, making his movie debut.

DANCING LADY *(1933, MGM/UA, B&W, not rated)* The mind boggles: Joan Crawford, Fred Astaire, and the Three Stooges *in the same movie*? It's as if the different levels of '30s Hollywood stardom had suddenly collapsed into a wonderful ground-floor pig pile. The movie's like that too: a fine, weird MGM musical that runs the style gamut from Astaire's lithe elegance to the Stooges' socket-popping rowdiness.

DEATH RACE 2000 *(1975, Facets, R)* This zippy prototype of postapocalyptic car-chase flicks offers something *The Road Warrior* and a zillion other clones don't: a gleefully sophomoric sense of humor and a tough-guy antihero (David Carradine) with unexpected reserves of wit, tenderness, and humility. As competing drivers barrel across the U.S., racking up points by mowing down pedestrians, director Paul Bartel keeps the gore almost discreet, and Sylvester Stallone has a lowbrow field day playing Carradine's boorish rival.

DECEPTION *(1946, MGM/UA, B&W, not rated)* Bette Davis plays Beethoven's *Appassionata Sonata* while composer

Alex Hollenius (Claude Rains, at his sneering best) destroys the stemware in a jealous rage. He's furious because cellist Paul Henreid has returned and reclaimed Bette's heart. This is wonderful old kitsch in which people always seem to be wearing evening clothes, gazing out at skyscrapers, and saying such things as, "Oh, please, don't let's make a scene."

DREAMCHILD *(1985, Movies Unlimited, PG)* The girl on whom Lewis Carroll based *Alice in Wonderland* arrives in America at age 80 to participate in the author's centenary. Once there, the elderly Alice (Coral Browne) is tormented by memories of Carroll (Ian Holm), whom she realizes was passionately in love with her. This is one of the most profound movies ever made about the intermingling of art and life, and Holm is superb as the tormented, stuttering fantasist-mathematician.

EIGHT MEN OUT *(1988, Orion, PG)* How Hoboken, N.J.–based independent filmmaker John Sayles ever made this tale of the 1919 "Black Sox" scandal on his usual spare-change budget is beyond us—the thing looks like 50 million bucks. *Eight Men Out* seems to envelop all of baseball's ornery ghosts in its caustic, clear-eyed stance, but it's the human figures you'll remember: naive pitcher Eddie Cicotte (David Strathairn), errant Buck Weaver (John Cusack), compromised hero "Shoeless" Joe Jackson (D.B. Sweeney).

A FINE MADNESS *(1966, Warner, not rated)* Sean Connery took a break from Bondage to play an obstreperous, rambunctious Greenwich Village poet who likes to give the rest of the world a piece of his mind. Not normally a loose actress, Joanne Woodward really lets her hair down as his waitress wife. The movie is a wonderfully daffy portrait of someone who believes his own publicity too much. Studio honcho Jack Warner thought Irvin Kershner's satire "antisocial" and had it recut but still didn't manage to destroy it.

FIVE CORNERS *(1987, MGM/UA, R)* Before Off Broadway playwright John Patrick Shanley hit it lucky with *Moonstruck*, he wrote this flaky but urgent slice of life set in the early-'60s Bronx, in a neighborhood in which kids who have grown up together are now spinning out into disparate orbits, from the civil rights movement to jail. Jodie Foster (the same year she won an Oscar for *The Accused*), Tim Robbins, and John Turturro all stake claims for their later work.

FORBIDDEN ZONE *(1980, Facets, B&W, R)* This genuinely twisted cult flick plays like a genetic recombination of *Alice in Wonderland*, Frank Zappa, and a Betty Boop cartoon. You get Herve Villechaize as the King of the 6th Dimension, Susan Tyrrell *(Fat City)* as his cheesy consort, and a lot of great old Cab Calloway music. Composer Danny Elfman, composer of *The Simpsons* theme music, plays the devil. Uncategorizable and incredibly cool.

THE FOUNTAINHEAD *(1949, MGM/UA, B&W, not rated)* Ayn Rand's cult novel about architect Howard Roark—a visionary Überguy with no patience for petty minds—was turned by director King Vidor into a Hollywood fever dream of enduringly strange proportions. Gary Cooper plays Roark, and

249

THE FOUNTAINHEAD: GARY COOPER

Patricia Neal is the heiress who recognizes his manly brilliance (especially when he's wielding that big drill in the quarry scene). Coop and Neal fell in love off screen and it shows—but really, the whole movie swoons.

FOXES *(1980, MGM/UA, R)* A movie that dares to treat Valley girls as if they were humans? Like, *sure*. Actually, this first feature by Adrian Lyne *(9½ Weeks)* is surprisingly touching as it watches four childhood pals heading in very different directions. Ex-Runaway Cherie Currie is the party girl hell-bent for meltdown, and Jodie Foster has the best of her teenage roles as Currie's hardheaded best friend.

FREAKED *(1993, FoxVideo, PG-13)* Star and codirector Alex Winter (Bill of *Bill & Ted's Excellent Adventure*) knows the secret of a good midnight comedy: Never let your audience get bored. Consequently, this saga of a snotty young movie idol who gets transformed by freak-show entrepreneur Randy Quaid into a hideous troll has a hilariously high hit-to-miss gag ratio. You get Mr. T as a bearded lady, Brooke

Shields revealed to be a carnivorous mutant, and the first-ever flashback by a common household hammer.

THE FRESHMAN *(1990, Columbia Tri-Star, PG)* Some comedies conk you over the head from frame one. Andrew Bergman's sneak up and cajole. Matthew Broderick stars as a naive NYU film student who gets embroiled in a plot involving a Komodo dragon, Bert Parks, and a mafioso who looks a *lot* like Marlon Brando playing Don Corleone. Bergman's genius was to get Brando himself to play the part; Brando's genius was to give it his deftest, lightest shot in decades.

GET CRAZY *(1983, Movies Unlimited, R)* This mindless teen comedy has a goofy, *Airplane!*-esque spin. Set behind the scenes of a New Year's Eve concert, it offers Lou Reed's dead-on parody of Bob Dylan, Malcolm McDowell's gleeful Mick Jagger imitation, Fabian and Bobby Sherman as villain Ed Begley Jr.'s henchmen, and more skewed cover versions of "Hoochie-Coochie Man" than you can count. Gloriously dumb, essential viewing.

GLEN OR GLENDA? *(1953, Facets, B&W, not rated)* Edward D. Wood Jr., the renowned Worst Director of All Time, made this scrappy docudrama about transvestism and transsexuality. Wood (billed as Daniel Davis) plays the earnest hero, who adores his fiancée—but not as much as he loves her angora sweater. The movie is as mind-bogglingly inept as Wood's *Plan 9 From Outer Space*, but it is also—in its brain-dead way—as personal a piece of cinema as anything Ingmar Bergman ever made.

GOOD—FOR NOTHING

It's tough enough creating a good film that nobody sees. What about A-for-achievement work that lies languishing in B-for-bomb movies? A sharp screenplay, a stellar performance, breakthrough photography—all can be for naught if the rest of the show is a turkey. Let's pause to remember a few terrific aspects of less-than-terrific movies.

THE ADVENTURES OF BARON MUNCHAUSEN *(1989)* A Terry Gilliam (*Brazil*) fantasy, *Munchausen* suffers from a pallid title character and a lumbering script, but Dante Ferretti's Jules Verne–meets–ILM production design transports the viewer to the far side of the moon and back.

THE BIG BLUE *(1988)* Despite attempts to reach an international audience, director Luc Besson's ode to free diving was a hit in France, where soggy plotting is apparently no barrier to success. Carlo Varini's exquisite globe-trotting cinematography is breathtaking in any language, though.

INDEPENDENCE DAY *(1982)* Kathleen Quinlan is the nominal star of this ho-hum drama, but it was the actress in the smaller role of a vengeful battered wife who made the few people in the audience sit up. Four years later, after an Oscar for *Hannah and Her Sisters*, everyone knew who Dianne Wiest (right) was.

251

TRON *(1982)* A polychrome showcase for hot new computer animation techniques, *Tron* was supposed to be the next big thing. It wasn't, largely because they forgot to put in a story. Still, the dazzling visual effects that made up the world inside Jeff Bridges' computer—which were supervised by Richard Taylor and Harrison Ellenshaw—remain eye-bogglingly impressive.

STAVISKY *(1975)* In this historical drama, director Alain Resnais' re-creation of 1930s Paris was deadly dull. But a vivid musical score from Stephen Sondheim touches all the period bases and still manages to connect with the viewer. —*Ty Burr*

GO TELL THE SPARTANS *(1978, Fusion, R)* Hailed by critics in the same year that *Coming Home* and *The Deer Hunter* were released, *Spartans* looked beyond the anguish of individual Vietnam vets to examine the war's fundamental tactical lunacy. Preferring a four-hankie catharsis to sober analysis, audiences stayed away in droves. That's a shame: They missed one of Burt Lancaster's best performances, as an embittered military adviser who in 1964 already sees the conflict's inevitable downward arc.

GOOD NEWS *(1947, MGM/UA, not rated)* Need a pep shot? MGM's perky college-campus musical works on the nervous system like a cup of sweet, milky coffee, which seems to be the strongest drink ever sampled by the movie's squeaky-clean students. After Peter Lawford, the football star who'll have to miss the big game if he flunks French, meets June Allyson, his just-this-side-of-snippy tutor, all their romantic and scholastic problems are resolved with a few fun production numbers.

HANGIN' WITH THE HOMEBOYS *(1991, Columbia TriStar, R)* Just about the best of the rash of films made by young black and Hispanic filmmakers in the early '90s, this acerbic urban comedy from writer-director Joseph B. Vasquez follows four buddies—played by Doug E. Doug, John Leguizamo, Mario Joyner, and Nestor Serrano—as they spend a night cruising the streets of New York, looking for a good time, and dodging the issue of their futures, or lack thereof.

HEARTLAND *(1981, Facets, PG)* Conchata Ferrell comes to work as a house-

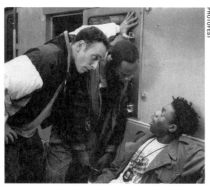

HANGIN' WITH THE HOMEBOYS:
NESTOR SERRANO, MARIO JOYNER,
DOUG E. DOUG

keeper for Rip Torn, a taciturn and stingy Scot, in the unrelenting Wyoming of 1910. This restrained period piece about the harshness of frontier life, based on a pioneer woman's diaries, has so little talk that it's almost like a silent movie. As in any good silent, however, the pictures speak volumes.

HEAT AND DUST *(1983, MCA/Universal, R)* Director James Ivory, producer Ismail Merchant, and writer Ruth Prawer Jhabvala are known for Great Books adaptations like *Howards End*, but this earlier work has a more compelling originality. Greta Scacchi is a woman who scandalizes British India in the 1920s by falling for a native prince; 60 years later her grandniece (Julie Christie) finds herself following in similar footsteps. Romantic yet lucid, it's about women making uncommon choices and learning to live with them.

HELL IN THE PACIFIC *(1968, Facets, PG)* The paradisiacal setting of a lush South Seas island threatens to turn into Club Dead as two stranded World War II soldiers try to kill each other. A resourceful American (Lee Marvin) and a Japanese (Toshiro Mifune) who is his match are men of few words, but John Boorman's direction is a textbook example of visual storytelling.

HI, MOM! *(1970, Facets, R)* One of the few counterculture satires that deserve to be called subversive, Brian De Palma's comedy features the young Robert De Niro as a Vietnam vet who becomes a Peeping Tom porno filmmaker and, finally, a bomb-wielding anarchist. The movie has a throwaway wit that has long since disappeared from De Palma's

HEAT AND DUST:
JULIE CHRISTIE, ZAKIR HUSSAIN

work, and its centerpiece sequence—a theatrical revue called *Be Black, Baby!*—is as daring and perceptive a vision of racial discord as anything in a Spike Lee film.

THE HIDDEN *(1987, Media, R)* An excellent, extremely violent sci-fi thriller that joins *The Terminator* and *Aliens* as the best of the slick action–sci-fi movies of the '80s. This one's about a surly alien that jumps from human host to human host (and one dog host) while acting out its most psychopathic impulses. Kyle MacLachlan's FBI agent is a dry run for Dale Cooper on *Twin Peaks*, but in this one he has a *reason* for being weird.

HIGH AND LOW *(1963, Facets, B&W, not rated)* Not till 1972's *The French Connection* did Hollywood produce a detective thriller as gritty and sociologically attuned as this tour de force from Japan's Akira Kurosawa. The title refers to the film's two milieus: the luxurious home of a shoe-company executive whose chauffeur's son is abducted, and the squalid haunts of the boy's heroin-addict kidnapper.

THE HIT *(1984, Facets, R)* With this sly, unpredictable gangster yarn, *The Grifters*' Stephen Frears returned to movies after 13 years directing for British TV. Everything feels fresh: Terence Stamp as the stool pigeon at peace with his impending death, John Hurt as his confounded, world-weary assassin, Laura del Sol as a hooker with a bite like a horse, and the sweepingly gorgeous Spanish scenery they pass through.

HOME OF THE BRAVE *(1949, Facets, B&W, not rated)* Producer Stanley Kramer's taboo-breaking portrait of a black World War II soldier, though somewhat dated in language and style, offers powerful insights into the psychology of racism and warfare. As a GI literally crippled by his platoon's bigotry and his own guilt, James Edwards indelibly etches the sting of each insult, and Lloyd Bridges, as his buddy, conveys the well-intentioned but ineffectual goodwill of an entire American generation.

253

THE HONEYMOON KILLERS *(1970, Facets, B&W, R)* From one-shot director

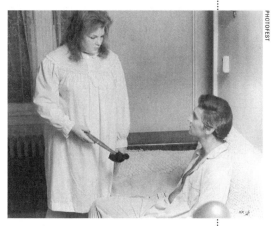

THE HONEYMOON KILLERS:
SHIRLEY STOLER AND TONY LOBIANCO

THE MANY FACES OF ALAN SMITHEE

Hollywood's jack-of-all-genres, director Alan Smithee has an oeuvre that stretches from comedy to drama to horror movies to Westerns. If you've never heard of him, it could be because he doesn't exist. Alan (sometimes Allen or Allan) Smithee is the fake name widely used by real directors who, for creative or contractual reasons, don't want to take the credit—or the blame—for certain movies. Here is an appropriately mixed bag of the ersatz auteur's films on video. —*Michael Sauter*

DEATH OF A GUNFIGHTER *(1969)* Twenty-five years ago, Smithee made a fairly promising debut with this downbeat Western. Richard Widmark stars as a determined gunslinging lawman whose brand of frontier justice has outlived its usefulness in a no-longer-Wild West. But though there's too much talk and not enough action on the way to the final shoot-out, Smithee fills the air with a growing sense of foreboding. Not since this effort has he shown such style or control. (The real Smithee: Don Siegel.) **B**

CITY IN FEAR *(1980)* Set in a contemporary Los Angeles that's being terrorized by a serial killer, this made-for-TV movie takes an often provocative look at how media hype—and the insatiable public appetite for it—can exacerbate an already explosive situation. With its incisive script and impressive cast (including the late David Janssen in his final role and Mickey Rourke in one of his firsts), this drama keeps threatening to turn into something special. But unfortunately, with Smithee stubbornly sticking to the prime-time-television stylebook, it finally has to settle

ALIAS SMITHEE: (CLOCKWISE FROM HAT) STUART ROSENBERG, DON SIEGEL, ROD HOLCOMB, PAUL AARON

for being merely a good example of its kind. (The real Smithee: Jud Taylor.) **B–**

STITCHES *(1985)* One of Smithee's real hack jobs. As top-billed Parker Stevenson leads his fellow med school cutups through the usual pranks, this moronic comedy goes out of its way to offend women, gays, senior citizens, punk rockers, Chinese exchange students, and, of course, doctors. If it weren't so laughably lame, it wouldn't be funny at all. (The real Smithee: Rod Holcomb.) **F**

LET'S GET HARRY *(1986)* Smithee's best cast gets wasted on a routine macho mission. Heading the casualty list: Robert Duvall, as a hardened mercenary leading a bunch of gung ho amateurs (among them Gary Busey and Michael Schoeffling) into the jungle to rescue buddy Mark Harmon. Traces of substance keep surfacing here, suggesting that a more ambitious movie was left on the cutting-room floor. (The real Smithee: Stuart Rosenberg.) **C**

MORGAN STEWART'S COMING HOME *(1987)* Smithee tries teen comedy, and actually shows a flair for it. Alas, he has only middling material to work with in this story of a senator's son (Jon Cryer) who's looking to win the love of his politically preoccupied parents (Lynn Redgrave, Nicholas Pryor). Cryer's attention-getting antics are mildly amusing, but the movie's best feature is Redgrave's hilarious turn as a pompous Washington wife. (The real Smithee: Paul Aaron.) **C**

GHOST FEVER *(1987)* Sherman Hemsley stars as a hapless detective serving an eviction notice on a comically haunted house. It's even more stupid than it sounds. And, like many Smithee films, this one suffers lapses in continuity that indicate heavy recutting. If anyone but Smithee had been at the helm, he'd never work in this town again. (The real Smithee: Lee Madden.) **F**

Leonard Kastle, this is an unbelievably dense and queasy look at two lovebirds who scam old ladies' money as a prelude to murdering them. Based on a true case from the 1940s, it stars Tony LoBianco as well-meaning Ray and the ineffable Shirley Stoler (who went on to *Pee-wee's Playhouse!*) as zaftig, jealous Martha, endlessly noodging the poor guy to pick up the hammer and get on with it.

HOUSEKEEPING *(1987, Columbia TriStar, PG)* The most beautiful—and misunderstood—film from director Bill Forsyth (*Local Hero*). In a ravishing wilderness town high up in the Rockies, two orphaned sisters come under the care of their wacky, free-spirited aunt (Christine Lahti). The movie is a tragicomic portrait of a woman in touch with the nonconformist impulses of the '60s a decade ahead of schedule. Lahti makes the blissed-out drifter at once a heroine and an irresponsible bum—and shows us that the two sides are inseparable.

HUMORESQUE *(1946, MGM/UA, B&W, not rated)* This is one of the great unsung melodramas, perfectly pitched between rigid masochism and yielding self-pity. Joan Crawford's a rich bitch who thaws under the caresses of her protégé, violin prodigy John Garfield. Her husband doesn't care much, and that makes it worse. Gorgeously visual (it was shot by Ernest Haller) and rampant with symbolism, it's an errant blip of genius on hack director Jean Negulesco's résumé.

INTO THE NIGHT *(1985, MCA/Universal, R)* Jeff Goldblum plays a schmuck who can't sleep, Michelle Pfeiffer—in her breakthrough role—is the chatty mystery lady who lands on his car and yanks him into a

255

whirlwind of espionage, and seemingly half the directors in Hollywood show up for jokey cameos. It looks like lightweight piffle, but this is John Landis' most mature movie, with the unlikely romance acquiring a touching gravity by the end.

JAZZ ON A SUMMER'S DAY *(1959, New Yorker, not rated)* Practically cowering from the daylight in their Age of Cool shades, some all-time jazz greats gather at a tony Yankee seaport to play the music of city streets. In the process, this record of the 1958 Newport Jazz Festival takes on the same sort of quirky clean-cut naughtiness as early issues of *Playboy*. There has never been a jazz documentary more shamelessly gushy; in gorgeous long takes, director Bert Stern treats jazz musicians (including Thelonious Monk, Louis Armstrong, and Anita O'Day) with the same smooth idol worship he brought to his Marilyn Monroe pinups. The result is just about as sexy.

THE KILLING *(1956, MGM/UA, B&W, not rated)* Years before he began making "Stanley Kubrick movies," the creator of *2001* and *A Clockwork Orange* directed this down-and-dirty caper picture, in which a pack of scuzzy crooks—Sterling Hayden and Elisha Cook Jr. among them—bring off a thrillingly elaborate racetrack robbery. Kubrick transforms the perfect-crime material into the screen equivalent of a jigsaw puzzle, leaping back and forth in time and showing the same scenes from many points of view.

LADY KILLER *(1933, MGM/UA, B&W, not rated)* Here's James Cagney at the height of his powers, viciously peppy as a gangster who lams it to Hollywood, makes good as a star, then finds his hoodlum past catching up with him. Made before the Hays Code sanitized all movies, it's a bawdy blast from the past. Poor Mae Clarke doesn't get hit in the face with a grapefruit like she did in *The Public Enemy*; no, here Cagney drags her around by her hair.

LONELY ARE THE BRAVE *(1962, MCA/Universal, B&W, not rated)* Kirk Douglas is a lonesome cowboy who hates fences and seems to belong to another century. After escaping from jail he takes off on his horse, Whiskey, only to be pursued by a laconic, sympathetic sheriff (Walter Matthau) and a posse using a helicopter. This lovely, understated film, shot in beautiful, high-contrast black and white, has a real feeling for the cowboy's stoic melancholy. And keep your eye on the truck driver, who one day would become Archie Bunker.

MACAO *(1952, Facets, B&W, not rated)* "Everybody's lonely, worried, and sorry," says tough gal Jane Russell, setting the tone for Josef von Sternberg's moody action picture (partly reshot by an uncredited Nicholas Ray), set in the Portuguese-Chinese colony. Russell sings at a joint called the Quick Reward. Robert Mitchum is her companion in world-weariness. This was as hot and suggestive as it got in the '50s.

MALCOLM *(1986, LIVE, PG-13)* A small Australian delight, this concerns a raffish bank robber (John Hargreaves) who strikes up a friendship with the title character (Colin Friels), a mildly retarded bloke with a knack for gadget-

ry. Soon the two are sending remote-controlled wastebaskets into the local bank so they can make, er, withdrawals. It's graced with a gentle performance by Friels and incredibly *happy* music by the Penguin Café Orchestra.

MARKED WOMAN *(1937, MGM/UA, B&W, not rated)* Warner Bros. was so nervy in the '30s that it barely bothered disguising Bette Davis' profession in this brutal crime melodrama. Based on the case in which mobster Lucky Luciano was brought down by his hookers, *Marked Woman* bristles with proto-feminist cynicism: Their boss is a sadist, and DA Humphrey Bogart's a wimp, so Davis and her working-girl friends walk into the fade-out by themselves.

MIKEY AND NICKY *(1976, Facets, R)* Two gangsters (Peter Falk and John Cassavetes) engage in a soul-searching, all-night talkathon. The sparring is springy and fun, and after a while it becomes

clear that one of the fellows is trying to finger the other. Directed by Elaine May, this explosive comedy is done in the improvisational style of Cassavetes' own films—and it's more successful than many of his efforts.

MIRACLE MILE *(1989, HBO, R)* Anthony Edwards makes a date with the girl of his dreams (Mare Winningham), only to discover that nuclear war is an hour away. Don't you hate when that happens? Directed for maximum love-it-or-hate-it appeal by whiz kid Steve DeJarnatt, *Miracle* posits that Armageddon will look like an epic shopping-mall riot. It's that rare thing indeed, a slapstick tragedy.

MIXED BLOOD *(1985, Media, not rated)* The only movie with a scene set in a store devoted to Menudo merchandise, Paul Morrissey's drug-war revenge comedy is so deadpan it barely has a pulse. But Marilia Pera is a campy

257

MRS. SOFFEL: MATTHEW MODINE, MEL GIBSON, DIANE KEATON

stitch as the leader of a drug gang in New York's Alphabet City, and the Bowery Boys–on–smack dialogue has the loopy, vicious ring of truth.

MONKEY BUSINESS *(1952, FoxVideo, B&W, not rated)* Not the 1931 Marx Brothers film, this little-known gem from Howard Hawks is probably the last great screwball comedy. Scientist Cary Grant and wife Ginger Rogers accidentally drink a youth serum, and while the results are a little predictable (imagine Cary in a letter sweater), the timing and performers make it screamingly funny. There's a young Marilyn Monroe as a bonus.

MRS. SOFFEL *(1984, MGM/UA, PG-13)* A nearly forgotten entry on the résumés of Diane Keaton and Mel Gibson, this true-life drama is for those who like their romance served with quiet sadness. Keaton is a prison warden's wife, circa 1901, who helps handsome Ed Biddle (Gibson) and his younger brother (Matthew Modine) escape. Directed by Gillian Armstrong *(My Brilliant Career)*, it's a story of desire helplessly beating its wings against the bars, with a chillingly lovely score by Mark Isham.

MS. 45 *(1981, International Video Entertainment, R)* Abel Ferrara *(Bad Lieutenant)* hasn't changed much since he directed this early effort—he's just shocking a larger audience now. This fierce exploitation film challenges as it panders: It turns the vigilante genre upside down by making a gun-carrying avenger out of a mute young rape victim (Zoe Tamerlis), then dares us to root her on as she grows increasingly tormented. Give a copy to a *Death Wish* fan and watch him freak.

THE NAKED KISS (*1964, Facets, B&W, not rated*) A movie that confounds all expectations. Constance Towers, a hooker who arrives in a small town pretending to be a champagne saleswoman, reforms and begins working with handicapped children. She marries the town millionaire, who's not exactly what *he* seems either. Written and directed by Sam Fuller in a sensationalistic style that would leave the editors of *The National Enquirer* slack-jawed.

1918 (*1985, Facets, not rated*) Writer Horton Foote (*The Trip to Bountiful*) has turned his memories of small-town Texas into a whole cycle of plays and films; *1918* is the heart of the bunch. Hallie Foote, playing her own grandmother, is a newlywed caught in the deadly flu epidemic of that year; Matthew Broderick is her brother. It's a home movie, in a sense, but the family is fascinating and the events indelibly moving.

THE NINTH CONFIGURATION (*1980, New World, R*) Questions like "Is it good or bad?" get left in the dust as you watch this lulu, directed by author William Peter Blatty (*The Exorcist*). The head of an Army nuthatch (Stacy Keach) turns out to be crazier than his wards, but the plot soon gives up in favor of bizarre philosophical exchanges and inscrutable passions. It's like *One Flew Over the Cuckoo's Nest* turned inside out.

ON DANGEROUS GROUND (*1951, Facets, B&W, not rated*) It only *sounds* dreadful. Robert Ryan is a sadistic New York detective, sent upstate to investigate a murder, who carries around a hatred for everyone, including himself. Ida Lupino is a blind woman at a lonely farmhouse who helps him find his humanity. Nicholas Ray's strikingly composed film, mostly shot in the flare of rural snow, is tough, taciturn, and finally very tender.

ONE-EYED JACKS (*1961, Paramount, not rated*) The only movie Marlon Brando ever directed, this psychological Western epic, in which an outlaw (Brando) seeks vengeance on a friend (Karl Malden), was greeted as a pompous, oddball failure. *One-Eyed Jacks* is nothing less than the first fully enlightened Western, and its sprawling, contemplative portrait of an America in which courage and camaraderie no longer hold sway makes it a neglected precursor to the cinema of Sam Peckinpah.

OVER THE EDGE (*1979, Warner, PG*) Set in a suburb as sterile as a moon colony, Jonathan Kaplan's juvenile-delinquent

EVERETT COLLECTION

OVER THE EDGE: **MATT DILLON**

AND THOSE WHO CAN'T, DIRECT

No matter what Robert Redford does as a director, most people still see him as a Movie Star. Well, eat your heart out, Bob: Some performers have switched to directing so successfully that no one remembers they ever acted.

KEITH GORDON *A Midnight Clear* (1992) **Thespian pinnacle:** *Dressed to Kill* (1980), as Peter, the whiz kid–turned–amateur sleuth. **Why the career change?** Though delightfully sweet in his scenes with costar Nancy Allen, Gordon was saddled with a similar nerd image in subsequent movies.

ELIA KAZAN *A Streetcar Named Desire* (1951) **Thespian pinnacle:** *City for Conquest* (1940), as Googi, a gangster. **Why the career change?** He was as dynamic as costar James Cagney, but Kazan was on the verge of stardom as a Broadway director at the time of the film's release.

BARRY LEVINSON *Bugsy* (1991) **Thespian pinnacle:** *High Anxiety* (1977), as Dennis, the hyper bellboy in Mel Brooks' Hitchcock parody. **Why the career change?** A cowriter of the film, he also overacts.

PAUL MAZURSKY *Down and Out in Beverly Hills* (1986) **Thespian pinnacle:** *The Blackboard Jungle* (1955), as Emmanuel, the smart-ass punk in this teen-angst melodrama. **Why the career change?** His Method acting pays off in a confrontation with his English teacher (Glenn Ford), but his unphotogenic mug would surely limit a big Hollywood career.

MARK RYDELL *On Golden Pond* (1981) **Thespian pinnacle:** *Crime in the Streets* (1956), as Lou, one of the gang members in Don Siegel's effective troubled-teen drama. **Why the career change?** While he handles the film's hip lingo well ("Frankie, I don't dig you"), he lacks the cool that his rebel-icon costars John Cassavetes and Sal Mineo flaunted on screen.

—*Tim Purtell*

fable was the first film to update the James Dean ethos to the permissive '70s, when the conventional forms of teen rebellion had been co-opted. It's about junior-high kids who spend their summer guzzling whiskey and playing with guns. Matt Dillon is terrific as the glamorous bad kid who leads the hero astray.

PARIS BLUES *(1961, Movies Unlimited, B&W, not rated)* In the Left Bank jazz club where trombonist Paul Newman and saxman Sidney Poitier wail, Paris seems a doped-up wonderland of racial harmony and free love. So guess what happens when smitten tourists Diahann Carroll and Joanne Woodward argue that they'd all be happier back in the States, leading civil rights protests and mowing the lawn? Duke Ellington's score grooves all the way to the big brush-off.

PAYDAY *(1973, HBO, R)* This little number leaves an unpleasant aftertaste, which probably explains why it came and went so fast in theaters. Rip Torn does wonders with the role of an addicted, low-rent country singer on tour. The movie, fueled by dead-on dialogue, follows Torn on his bender of self-destruction without either judgment or self-righteous message making. The effect is truly frightening.

PERSONAL BEST *(1982, Warner, R)* Screenwriter Robert Towne's debut as a director is both a visual celebration of women athletes and an insightful look at the relationship between competing runners Mariel Hemingway and Patrice Donnelly. One of the better sports movies ever, it's also the sole mainstream film of the early '80s to handle homosexuality without hysteria or coy timidity.

PICKUP ON SOUTH STREET *(1953, Fox-Video, B&W, not rated)* Essential pulp from Sam Fuller, the only director who walked film noir like he talked it—and, boy, could he talk it. Pickpocket Richard Widmark lifts the wallet of floozy Jean Peters, little knowing that it contains microfilm being smuggled out by her weasely Commie boyfriend. Surface McCarthyism aside, this is a great New York romance: Everyone in it is tired, suspicious, and desperate to connect.

THE PLAGUE DOGS *(1982, Facets, not rated)* A dark, terrifying, and heartbreak-

PROOF: GENEVIEVE PICOT

ing tale of two dogs who escape from a laboratory that is carrying out cruel experiments on animals only to enter an equally fierce landscape, this may be the most disturbing animated film ever made. The animals take on the sympathetic personalities of humans, who in turn lack the simplest decencies.

PROOF *(1992, New Line, R)* Call this one *sex, eyes, and photography.* Set in Melbourne, Australia, it looks at the mind games among a misanthropic blind man who likes to take snapshots (Hugo Weaving), the comely housekeeper who rearranges his furniture out of sexual frustration (Genevieve Picot), and the uncomplicated young guy (Russell Crowe) who wanders into their field of fire. It's more proof that good things come in small Australian packages.

THE REVOLT OF JOB *(1983, MGM/UA, not rated)* A Jewish couple (Ferenc Zenthe, Hedy Temessy) adopt a Christian child (Gabor Feher) in Hungary just before the Holocaust engulfs them. Quietly harrowing, the film is played out in a leisurely rhythm against the hazily gorgeous Hungarian landscape. But its real achievement is to show the progress of

261

love between the couple and the child without ever resorting to easy, tried-and-true ways.

RIOT IN CELL BLOCK 11 *(1954, Republic, B&W, not rated)* Don Siegel's tense, hard melodrama is far more than just a "prison movie." There are good guys and bad guys on both sides of *Riot*'s jailhouse standoff, but in the end the issue dividing them against each other (and themselves) is simply power. The Folsom Prison locale and no-star cast add to the brutal matter-of-factness.

THE SAGA OF ANATAHAN *(1953, Balzac, B&W, not rated)* Almost two decades after his seven shimmering films with Dietrich, director Josef von Sternberg made this final, bizarre one-shot, filmed in Japanese with a Japanese cast and crew. Based on a true incident in which 12 sailors and a woman were marooned on an island, *Anatahan* is a mocking distillation of the director's lifelong themes of human folly and the cruelties of romance. It's a gorgeously sensual movie.

SAINT JACK *(1979, Facets, R)* Moviegoers had just about given up on Peter Bogdanovich when he came through with this character study of Jack Flowers (Ben Gazzara), an American pimp in early-'70s Singapore whose decency surprises even himself. Denholm Elliott gives the performance of his career as a thoughtful, burned-out businessman, and the film has the moody sense of business transacted at midnight.

SAY AMEN, SOMEBODY *(1982, Facets, G)* A feverishly infectious documentary on gospel singers, this movie has sensational performances that make the joint jump with joy. "Gospel," says one of its oldest practitioners, Willie Mae Ford Smith, a woman with flashing gold teeth and a smile as wide as the Mississippi, "is a feeling that comes from somewhere between the bone and the marrow." Amen, sister.

SECRET HONOR *(1984, Facets, PG)* Robert Altman's film of Philip Baker Hall's one-man show is an outrageous affront to the American presidency. Taking the Nixon we discovered in the Watergate tapes and exponentially increasing the fear and loathing, Hall creates a drunken dark-night-of-the-spleen monologue that's hilarious and terrifying. It's the far side of every politician's grin.

THE SENDER *(1982, Paramount, R)* The public had tired of telekinesis by the time this stylish, subtle, and underrated horror film came out. Zeljko Ivanek gives a sensitive performance as a suicidal man brought to a psychiatric hospital, where he transfers his bad thoughts to the institute's population. The theme of repressed rage and fear lends a dramatic believability to his powers.

SHACK OUT ON 101 *(1955, Republic, B&W, not rated)* A one-set camp classic that gives you Lee Marvin as a Communist short-order cook named Slob, Keenan Wynn doing calisthenics on a diner counter, Whit Bissell recovering from a nervous breakdown, and Terry Moore acting with her pointy '50s bra as the hash-slinging heroine who finds a Red in every bed. Good bad movies don't get better than this.

THE SHANGHAI GESTURE *(1941, Mystic Fire, B&W, not rated)* Sardonic stylist

BURIED ALIVE

Sure, a film may have virtuoso direction, magnificent performances, and a grabby plot, but what good are they without the really important stuff—distribution and merchandising? All kinds of extra-aesthetic muck-ups can maim or virtually kill a film on the way from the wrap party to the premiere. Here are four movies that were made right and then were somehow done wrong.

CITIZEN'S BAND/HANDLE WITH CARE *(1977)* A rueful human comedy from the then-33-year-old Jonathan Demme (*The Silence of the Lambs*), *Citizen's Band* was dumped in drive-ins by distributors hoping to cash in on the CB-radio craze. After the New York Film Festival picked it up under a new name, *Handle With Care*, the movie acquired a hot critical reputation. But audiences still inexplicably stayed away, even when theaters let people in free to build word of mouth.

WINTER KILLS *(1979/1983)* Director William Richert fashioned this nutty exercise in political paranoia, with Jeff Bridges investigating his President-brother's assassination and John Huston as their father, a barely disguised Joe Kennedy figure. Distributor Avco Embassy reedited the film into a straight thriller and released it to wide indifference. Four years later Richert recut it, got it back into theaters, and found the cult audience he had wanted all along.

NIGHTBREED *(1990)* Horror writer Clive Barker's second stab at directing was an imaginative creature feature, but a housecleaning new regime at Twentieth Century Fox rushed it out with a junky ad campaign aimed at dice-and-slice fanatics—with a poster photo from another movie entirely! Only when video independent Media Home Entertainment released it with a new and accurate marketing blitz did Barker's creepy fantasy get pitched to its intended audience.

HENRY: PORTRAIT OF A SERIAL KILLER *(1990)* In 1985, director John McNaughton got backing from MPI Home Video to make this now-notorious art-house splatter flick featuring Michael Rooker's chilling title performance. MPI may have known it had something special, but the MPAA ratings board gave the film the kiss of death, an X. Five years later, the MPAA itself was under attack, an X looked like a badge of artistic integrity, and the company dusted off the now-unrated *Henry* for a successful theatrical release. —*Ty Burr*

263

Josef von Sternberg, flat on his back from an infection, directed this nougat of Hollywood kitsch from a cot, and the film feels as though the director had more blood rushing to his brain than usual. Ona Munson is all 10-inch fingernails as Mother Gin Sling, proprietress of Shanghai's most depraved casino, and Gene Tierney is memorably petulant as Poppy, the debutante gone crazy on sex and drugs and sin. Then there's Victor Mature in a fez as Doctor Omar.

BROTHER AND SISTER ACT

Stallone! Pfeiffer! Swayze! Their boldfaced credits blaze across the covers of cassette boxes. But get out that jeweler's loupe: It's not Sylvester, Michelle, and Patrick on display but family members Frank, Dedee, and Don, all of whom are emerging as the stars of a whole genre of movies made possible by the seemingly boundless opportunities afforded by the rental market. While their résumés may be speckled with small roles in major features, it's in low-budget independent productions and video quickies that these second-string stars shine. Here's a viewer's guide to some of the most famous names in direct-to-video movies, relatively speaking.

DEDEE PFEIFFER Star Sibling: Michelle. **Oeuvre:** *Vamp* (1986), *The Allnighter* (1987), *The Horror Show* (1989). **Notable Role:** *Red Surf* (1990), a well-acted, cookie-cutter crime drama, casts her as the frustrated pregnant girlfriend of an ex-surfing champ–turned–drug runner. She just wants him to get a real job.

JOE ESTEVEZ Star Sibling: Martin Sheen. **Oeuvre:** *Armed for Action* (1992), *Lockdown* (1990). **Notable Role:** The clumsy New Age fantasy *Soultaker* (1990) features Estevez as a beady-eyed angel of death in cowboy boots who steals the life force from a group of kids gravely injured in a car accident.

FRANK STALLONE Star Sibling: Sylvester. **Oeuvre:** *Fear* (1988), *Terror in Beverly Hills* (1988). **Notable Role:** In the silly update of Poe's *The Masque of the Red Death* (1989), he plays a guest at a deadly costume ball. Besides cracking wise, he gets to insult costar Brenda Vaccaro, with whom he has costarred three other times.

DON SWAYZE Star Sibling: Patrick. **Oeuvre:** *Driving Force* (1988), *Edge of Honor* (1991). **Notable Role:** As the squinty drug lord in the corny actioner *Payback* (1990), he cusses and gets riddled with buckshot. Writer-star Corey Michael Eubanks belongs to another show-biz dynasty: His dad hosted *The Newlywed Game*.

TERENCE FORD Star Sibling: Harrison. **Oeuvre:** *Escape From Survival Zone* (1992). **Notable Role:** His grimy, morose performance as an alcoholic news cameraman who uncovers treachery at a survivalist training compound perfectly matches the atmosphere of this lumbering, poorly made World War III flick.

ERIC DOUGLAS Star Sibling: Michael. **Oeuvre:** *The Flamingo Kid* (1984), *Delta Force 3* (1990). **Notable Role:** He stars as a troublemaking teen set straight by an unusual guidance counselor, in the bizarre, finger-wagging high school drama *Student Confidential* (1988). Costar Marlon Jackson also has a famous brother named Michael. —*Doug Brod*

It's von Sternberg's loosest film, and his loopiest—a passionate, demented, richly entertaining piece of nonsense.

SONGWRITER *(1984, Columbia TriStar, R)* Like a rambling Johnny Cash story-song, this slice of life is stronger on good-natured feel than actual plot. You won't mind, though. Willie Nelson essentially plays himself as the musician outlawed from the Nashville establishment and his own home, and Kris Kristofferson is the ex-partner he hooks up with again. Alan Rudolph directs with a relaxed touch.

STORYVILLE *(1992, Columbia TriStar, R)* James Spader couldn't pick a normal star vehicle if he wanted to, thank God. Here he's a jaded rich kid who, running for political office, gets a moral wake-up call in the form of a blackmail video. David Lynch's *Twin Peaks* partner, Mark Frost, cowrote and directed this Southern-fried melodrama; like Lynch, he isn't interested in having us believe the convoluted plot (don't worry—you won't), but he spins his weirdness with an engagingly lighter touch.

STRAIGHT TIME *(1978, Warner, R)* In Dustin Hoffman's most unappreciated performance, he plays a compulsive small-time crook who is released from prison and can't get the hang of living in the straight world. Hoffman captures the desperate logic that drives such antisocial hoods as Gary Gilmore—men who keep breaking the law because they just don't see it as real.

STREAMERS *(1983, Facets, R)* Robert Altman helps detonate the verbal grenades in David Rabe's smotheringly

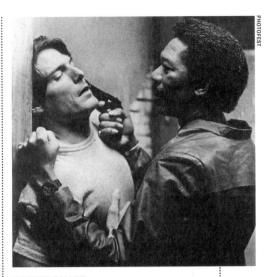

STREET SMART:

CHRISTOPHER REEVE, MORGAN FREEMAN

claustrophobic play set in a Virginia Army barracks, where several young men nervously await transfer to Vietnam. Matthew Modine leads an exemplary cast in this distressing drama of how violence and inhumanity thrive in any setting. Moral: War, like charity, begins at home.

STREET SMART *(1987, Media, R)* It starts as a fairly glib suspense drama about a slick, not-too-bright New York journalist (Christopher Reeve) getting caught in the trap of his ambitions: To meet a deadline, he makes up an exposé about a murderous pimp. But the appearance of the real thing pulls the rug out from under his plans and, in Morgan Freeman's star-making performance, drags the movie into much darker territory.

SWING HIGH, SWING LOW *(1937, Facets, B&W, not rated)* This is one of the very few movies directed by Mitchell Leisen

265

available on tape, and that is a shame. A second-rank Paramount stalwart, Leisen concocted romantic puffballs shot through with a sensuality that can still get a viewer hot and bothered. This one pits itinerant trumpet player Fred MacMurray (back when he was an honest-to-God romantic lead) and Carole Lombard in a comedy that, like all love affairs, gradually takes on somber hues.

SYLVIA SCARLETT *(1936, Turner, B&W, not rated)* In later years, both director George Cukor and star Katharine Hepburn would turn pale at the mention of this wacky youthful folly—all the more reason to seek it out. Hepburn plays a girl who disguises herself as a boy, and Cary Grant is the cockney wastrel who leads her and her father into a life of crime and vaudeville. Truly strange and quite endearing, with Grant showing for the first time the easy grace that made him a star.

THE TENANT *(1976, Paramount, R)* Roman Polanski directs and stars in this funny, sometimes terrifying thriller about a Polish expatriate who moves into a Paris apartment and begins to

SYLVIA SCARLETT: EDMUND GWENN, KATHARINE HEPBURN, CARY GRANT

THEY MIGHT BE GIANTS: JOANNE WOODWARD, GEORGE C. SCOTT

have delusions about his sinister neighbors. The third chapter in his apartment-house trilogy (after *Repulsion* and *Rosemary's Baby*), this is the most personal. Polanski's performance is a masterpiece of masochism: He burrows deep into the private, festering dread that drives people to suicide.

THEY MIGHT BE GIANTS *(1971, MCA/ Universal, G)* George C. Scott plays a New York judge who thinks he's Sherlock Holmes. He gets sent to a psychiatrist (Joanne Woodward) whose name is—oh dear—Dr. Watson. Thankfully, this touching, Paul Newman–coproduced comedy doesn't pretend that the mad are really saner than you or I. It does propose, though, that we all make our own Moriartys. A fine supporting cast of crazies helps put it over.

TICKET TO HEAVEN *(1981, MGM/UA, PG)* Ever wonder what it would be like to

CREDIT REPORT

There's no better surprise than renting an unfamiliar movie and finding that it's a gem—except for the delight of discovering performances by big stars you never expected to see. For reasons often as obscure as these unbilled turns, major actors occasionally appear in films with no credit. Here, some of the most intriguing examples.

Glenda Jackson in *The Boyfriend* (1971) Jackson plays the brittle star of a terrible Jazz Age musical who misses her chance at stardom when a visiting Hollywood director sees—and selects—her understudy (Twiggy) for a film. Ken Russell's pastiche of all the worst excesses of kitschy director Busby Berkeley puts Jackson's acting skills to a most severe test: She has to weep visibly over Twiggy's "brilliant" performance. **B–**

Robert Duvall in *The Conversation* (1974) Gene Hackman stars as Harry Caul, a wiretapper in Francis Ford Coppola's atmospheric parable about modern alienation. Duvall turns up in the key role of the Director, a man who hires Caul to get information on his unfaithful wife. Like most of the characters in the story, he is a cipher, tense and potentially menacing, a mysterious figure who may or may not be planning a murder. **A**

Gene Hackman in *Young Frankenstein* (1974) As the blind hermit, Harold, who prays for a "friend" and gets a monster (Peter Boyle) instead, Hackman delivers a marvelous parody of the sincere blind man in *Bride of Frankenstein*. The film's best moment is the famous soup scene: Unable to see his guest's bowl, Harold pours scalding hot soup in the monster's lap. **A**

Elizabeth Taylor in *Winter Kills* (1979) Almost everyone ends up dead in this crazy conspiracy comedy based on the assassination of President Kennedy. Taylor appears in a silent, voiced-over sequence as Lola Comante, a Washington hostess who supplies bedmates for the President and acts as a catalyst for his assassination. **B–**

Alec Guinness in *The Empire Strikes Back* (1980) and *Return of the Jedi* (1983) Although killed off in *Star Wars*, Guinness returns as the ghost of Obi Wan-Kenobi in both sequels. He was reportedly paid a fortune for the brief turns, but series creator George Lucas felt his guiding voice ("May the force be with you") was crucial to hero Luke Skywalker's transformation into a Jedi knight, rather than a mere Obi Wannabe. *The Empire Strikes Back:* **A** *Return of the Jedi:* **B**

Jack Nicholson in *Broadcast News* (1987) Nicholson plays a veteran TV news anchor who is one part reputation and nine parts automaton. As a drugged-out media father figure who wields power but has nothing to say, he personifies the film's point: TV news is sometimes as empty as its creators. **A** —*Tom Soter*

267

UNSUNG HEROES

If sleepers are little-known or underappreciated films, there are "sleeper people" in the movie business, too—those behind the scenes who contribute to major films without much recognition.

Hermes Pan Fred and Ginger got all the credit, but dance director Pan told them where to plant their dancing feet in most of their classic '30s musicals. He also choreographed *Silk Stockings* and *Kiss Me Kate*.

Marni Nixon Irony in action: a singing unsung heroine. Nixon provided the pipes for the stars, and when Audrey Hepburn opens her mouth to sing in *My Fair Lady*—or Natalie Wood in *West Side Story*, or Deborah Kerr in *The King and I*—it's really Nixon you're enjoying.

Gregg Toland Next time you watch *Citizen Kane*, keep in mind that Orson Welles worked out every breathtaking shot with this great cinematographer—and that Toland jumped at the chance to break the rules. He also shot *Wuthering Heights* and *The Grapes of Wrath*.

Adrian A chief costumer at MGM, he designed diaphanous wrappings for such stars as Garbo, Crawford, Harlow, and Hepburn in films including *Anna Christie* and *Grand Hotel*, influencing what women in the audience wore, or at least dreamed of wearing.

Stan Winston Winston is the gooey genius who creates characters with makeup and special effects, providing the ooh-inspiring moments of such films as *The Terminator, Aliens, Predator, Edward Scissorhands*, and *Jurassic Park*.

Max Steiner The composer most responsible for the swooning, string-laden sound of classic Hollywood, he scored films ranging from *King Kong* to *The Treasure of the Sierra Madre, Casablanca*, and *Gone With the Wind*, earning 26 Oscar nominations and winning three times.

Cedric Gibbons Gibbons practically created the position of art director, that underrated creator who oversees the entire design of a film's sets, costumes, and props. Gibbons started back with Thomas Edison but did his best work in the glory days of MGM, where he won 11 Oscars. His elegant visual stamp can be seen in *Grand Hotel, A Night at the Opera, Anna Karenina, Gaslight*, and *An American in Paris. —Jess Cagle*

become a Moonie? Check out this riveting psychodrama about an ordinary guy (Nick Mancuso), made vulnerable by the loss of his girlfriend, who is seduced into the communal, accepting circle of the Heavenly Children. Made in Canada, it's perhaps the only movie that truly evokes the frightening psychology of modern cults.

TRACK 29 *(1988, Facets, R)* Critics didn't know how to take this surreal puzzler directed by Nicolas Roeg, but that's because they think of movies as the director's creation. This film starts to make sense only if you know the work of its *writer*, Dennis Potter. Like *The Singing Detective*, it's a reality-versus-pop-culture black comedy, about a housewife (Theresa Russell) who imagines that the baby she gave up years ago has returned as randy, spooky Gary Oldman.

TROUBLE IN MIND *(1986, Facets, R)* After the triumph of *Choose Me*, director Alan Rudolph apparently went off the deep end with this fluky, impassioned modern noir set in a mythical American city. It's rich, borderline surreal, and unforgettable—if you can get into its moody mind-set. Kris Kristofferson, Geneviève Bujold, Keith Carradine, and Lori Singer tangle with one another while Marianne Faithfull and Mark Isham collaborate on a score that's just this side of heaven.

TRULY, MADLY, DEEPLY *(1991, Touchstone, PG-13)* What do the dead do? They huddle for warmth and watch videos, of course—much to the consternation of Nina (Juliet Stevenson), who had been lamenting the death of her boyfriend Jamie (Alan Rickman) before he and his chalky-faced cronies returned

***TROUBLE IN MIND*: KEITH CARRADINE**

from the Great Beyond. Made in Britain around the same time as *Ghost*, Anthony Minghella's bittersweet romantic comedy about how we need to let go of the dead strikes a clear note at a time when so many, so young, must come to acceptance after coming to grief. Stevenson's performance is stunning, and Rickman, best known for his superb villains (*Die Hard, Robin Hood: Prince of Thieves*), shows his gentler, more sensitive side as the departed.

TWICE UPON A TIME *(1983, Warner, PG)* A PG-rated cartoon fable about a despot out to give the world permanent bad dreams that's filled with nightmare images and adult wordplay? No wonder family audiences said "pass" to this fantasy from executive producer George Lucas. It's too abstract for grade-schoolers, but teens and grown-ups who like fairy tales with a Pythonesque, warp-speed edge should enjoy it happily ever after.

269

UNDER FIRE *(1983, Facets, R)* The most human political thriller in years, this look at three journalists (Nick Nolte, Gene Hackman, and Joanna Cassidy) in Nicaragua manages to score all its points and still be engrossingly suspenseful. Even the romantic subplot doesn't seem stupid. *The Year of Living Dangerously* came out the same year and is better known, but *Fire* has fewer frills and a becoming directness.

USED CARS *(1980, Facets, R)* Good-taste guardians have always hated this raunchy, high-spirited comedy, and that's all to the good. Kurt Russell is lovably venal as a car salesman with a down payment on political office, and the consistently rude script is consistently hilarious. Director Bob Zemeckis went on to the glossier *Back to the Future* trio and *Who Framed Roger Rabbit*, but this film is their equal in both laugh count and sheer spunk.

VAMPIRE'S KISS *(1989, HBO, R)* A cult has already formed for this outrageous black farce about a Manhattan trendoid (Nicolas Cage) who slips into insanity and thinks he's a vampire. The gag is that no one notices until it's way too late. It's another caustic, slapstick money loser from the pen of Joseph Minion, with a demento Cage performance that has to be seen to be disbelieved.

WHERE THE HEART IS *(1990, Touchstone, R)* This affectionate, anarchic farce from director John Boorman (*Deliverance*) deserves better than the pasting it received from critics who saw only a mess. Rich New York demolition contractor Dabney Coleman boots his profligate teenagers (David Hewlett, Uma Thurman, Suzy Amis) out the door, whereupon they start an exercise in urban squatting that eventually envelops Dad himself. Unpredictable and alive, this plays less like a movie than like a party.

WHILE THE CITY SLEEPS *(1956, Facets, B&W, not rated)* Three ambitious newspaper employees (Dana Andrews, Thomas Mitchell, George Sanders) vie to crack the case of the "Lipstick Killer," a leather-clad mother-hater who is stalking their metropolis. Fritz Lang's dirty little urban drama is a sleazy roundelay where everyone sleeps around for advancement and the compulsion for personal power within the press is revealed as the embryo of totalitarianism.

WHO'LL STOP THE RAIN *(1978, MGM/UA, R)* The dumb title certainly contributed to its initial failure. But Karel Reisz's adaptation of Robert Stone's *Dog Soldiers*, about the corruptive effects of the Vietnam war, is taut, bitter, and unremittingly cynical—you just gotta love it. Nick Nolte, Tuesday Weld, and Michael Moriarty make up one of the cinema's oddest ménages à trois as they try to move two kilos of heroin stateside and are chased by drug dealers.

WITHNAIL & I *(1987, Facets, R)* A tour de force by British actor Richard E. Grant, who plays a boozing, unemployed actor named Withnail—an impossibly narcissistic leech who never stops talking (or drinking). The movie, about how this irredeemable lout falls apart during a muddy weekend in the country, captures the toxic excess of the late '60s with such clear-eyed purity and humor that it puts Oliver Stone's *The Doors* to shame.

YOUNG AND INNOCENT *(1937, Facets, B&W, not rated)* The least known of Hitchcock's great British thrillers (the list includes *The 39 Steps* and *The Lady Vanishes*), this gives the wrong-man-accused-of-murder plot a rustic twist. Our hero (Derrick de Marney) flees into the countryside with the sweet-faced teen (Nova Pilbeam) who knows he didn't do it, and the chase climaxes with one of Hitch's most dramatic camera moves—from the back of a ballroom to the twitching eyes of a murderer.

ZARDOZ *(1974, Facets, R)* One of the craziest movies ever made, John Boorman's campily imaginative, ravishing sci-fi fantasy is set in the year 2293 in a place called the Vortex, where women are Amazons and men are nervous (and impotent). Along comes the very potent Sean Connery, ready to penetrate the Vortex in general and Charlotte Rampling in particular. Only the helplessly humorless wouldn't be enchanted.

A ZED & TWO NOUGHTS *(1985, Facets, R)* Five years before Peter Greenaway cooked up *The Cook, the Thief, His Wife & Her Lover*, he made this provocative inquisition into love, death, physical decay, Vermeer, zoos, and the alphabet. With a plot that resonates but never resolves, and camera work that gorgeously uncovers the horrors of nature, *Zed* is chilly, beguiling gamesmanship—perfect for people who love really hard crossword puzzles.

Reviews written by Ty Burr, as well as Owen Gleiberman, Steve Daly, and Lawrence O'Toole.

JOSEPH MINION: SCENARIO FOR SUBVERSION

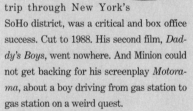

At the age of 26, in 1985, screenwriter Joseph Minion was one of Hollywood's most promising new voices. His comedy *After Hours*, which starred Griffin Dunne as a computer programmer on a nightmarish trip through New York's SoHo district, was a critical and box office success. Cut to 1988. His second film, *Daddy's Boys*, went nowhere. And Minion could not get backing for his screenplay *Motorama*, about a boy driving from gas station to gas station on a weird quest.

His then girlfriend, Barbara Zitwer, promised to produce a movie if he'd write one that was more mainstream. "Horror story," thought Minion. "There's always an audience for that." Inspired by a dead bat found on his balcony, he wrote *Vampire's Kiss* in two weeks, and it was filmed without one rewrite. "The only thing that wasn't in the script was Nick [Cage] eating a cockroach. That was his own contribution."

In *Kiss*, the New Jersey native bit into a familiar theme: A yuppie goes looking for love in New York and goes to hell instead. Critics have suggested that his monsters are AIDS metaphors, but he says, "I don't have any kind of mission. I'm just interested in people trying to connect." —*Jess Cagle*

271

LASERDISC

IF YOU'VE EVER WATCHED a movie on laserdisc, you know that it makes a VHS tape look like a puppet show. Hook a set of speakers up to the player, and you're sitting in the fifth row center of a movie palace. And the extras on many discs—from commentary by the director to still pages of the entire shooting script—can be revelatory.

That's why you'll find so many added notations in the italicized headings in this chapter, including two release dates: one for the film, one for the laserdisc. Don't let all the acronyms faze you: CLV simply means the disc plays a maximum of one hour on each side, then you have to turn it over like a record (unless you've got a top-of-the-line player that switches sides automatically). CAV is a more versatile disc format that allows you to click through screens of text or pictures a frame at a time, but also limits the total playback of real-time footage to 30 minutes per side, which means lots of interruptions in, say, a CAV disc of *Gone With the Wind*.

What follows are, essentially, the 100 Best Reasons to Own a Laserdisc Player, in the hopes that you might dip your toe in these very rewarding waters.

1 THE ULTIMATE OZ *(1939/93, MGM/ UA, 5 CAV sides plus 1 CLV side, B&W/color, not rated, $99.98; includes cut scenes, making-of tribute program, multiple audio tracks with running commentary)* The main event here is, of course, Dorothy's beloved brick-road sojourn, remastered to nearly 3-D clarity. But what makes this the true *Ultimate* in disc wizardry is the still-frame and motion-clip annex after the movie, filled with enough costume-test photos, scenery sketches, and special-effects data to prove that, yes, there was no place like late-'30s Hollywood for meticulous film craft. Alternate audio channels round up *five hours* of music and vocal takes, charting how each segment was arranged and rearranged to perfection. The whole emerald-green-boxed megillah takes a film whose pleasures you thought you'd long since exhausted and makes it exciting again.

2 TERMINATOR 2: JUDGMENT DAY— SPECIAL EDITION *(1991/93, Pioneer/Carolco/LIVE, 3 CLV sides plus 3 CAV sides, wide-screen, not rated, $119.95; running audio commentary by director and many others, massive behind-the-scenes supplement)* This is no sane person's idea of a feel-good collectible. (Gee, let's watch Arnold Schwarzenegger's monosyllabic cyborg shoot people in the kneecap *one more time!*) But laser buffs revere *T2SE* as a state-of-the-art demo disc. Remastered with the help of George Lucas' THX quality-control fanatics, the room-rattling sound and flawless picture are an instant steroid dose for your playback equipment. And if the 16 minutes edited back into the picture for this disc edition make the story a bit butt-numbing

(it's now 2 hours 32 minutes), there's also a welcome fullness to the conversations in which pubescent messiah-to-be John Connor (Edward Furlong) shapes his guardian android into the ultimate toy dad.

3 RAGING BULL *(1980/90, Voyager, 6 CAV sides, wide-screen, B&W/ color, R, $124.95; storyboards, complete screenplay, production photos)* There's no self-promotion in director Martin Scorsese's audio-track narration, just infectious passion for his work. He's a dervish when rattling off the film influences and technical challenges that inspired him in a given scene. When he falters on thematic questions—he can't talk easily about the demons that drove boxer Jake La Motta (Robert De Niro)—the disc producers splice in thoughtful remarks by Scorsese's longtime film editor, Thelma Schoonmaker. By the end of their one-two-punch lecture, you can see how Scorsese's reluctance to spell out motivations fits his vision of *Bull* as a behavioral portrait, keyed not to explanations but to observation.

4 PINOCCHIO DELUXE CAV LASERDISC EDITION *(1940/93, Disney/Image, 6 CAV sides, animated, G, $99.99; production photos, original and reissue trailers, commemorative booklet)* *Pinocchio* is the pinnacle. There's simply no animated movie that can match its obsessively detailed craftsmanship. Thanks to the staggering clarity the CAV format lends to freeze-frames and slow motion, you can easily savor the full wealth of every overstuffed shot in the movie—more artistry than could ever be absorbed in a theater. You also

CRITERION TELEVISION CLASSICS: I LOVE LUCY:
LUCILLE BALL, WILLIAM FRAWLEY, DESI ARNAZ, VIVIAN VANCE

get extras impossible to put on tape: A still-frame appendix gathers production pictures, ad posters, and sketches for scenes that were changed or cut, like a book-burning sequence with Jiminy Cricket looking on in horror.

5 **CRITERION TELEVISION CLASSICS: I LOVE LUCY** *(1952/91, Voyager, 1 CAV side plus 1 CLV side, mostly B&W, not rated, $49.95; audio commentary by cast and creators, teleplays)* Even if you know the episodes "Job Switching" (the chocolate-candy conveyor belt) and "Lucy Does a TV Commercial" (she hawks Vitameatavegamin) by heart, you've never seen them presented this lovingly. Tweaked shot by shot, these classic episodes sport such striking depth that you'll feel as if you're looking through a window. There's also nowhere else you'll see these *Lucy*s exactly as they aired, with credits that fea-

ture cartoon stick figures of Lucy and Desi and an original cigarette ad in which the stars bestow nicotine on each other by the carton. Hundreds of still frames of text and photos cover every aspect of the show from casting to costumes—all cross-indexed and peppered with short, full-motion clips that function like talking illustrations. It's not just a watch-it-once tribute; it's a working *Lucy* archive.

6 **APOCALYPSE NOW** *(1979/91, Paramount, 3 CLV sides plus 1 CAV side, wide-screen, R, $44.95)* When Francis Coppola's stoned fantasia on Vietnam finished its 70 mm, six-track-sound theatrical premiere engagements, it moved into general release in prints that garbled much of the audio detail—and early versions on home video suffered from the same low-fi muddiness. But for this disc edition, the movie's sound designer, Walter Murch, reworked the sonics from the original six-track master. Played back on a good surround setup, the remixed, four-channel *Apocalypse* (sound comes from left, right, center, and rear speakers) once again has something like the is-it-live impact of those early showings. Helicopters and gunboats don't just pound loudly through your home speakers; they take on constant, startling *direction.* Only with that aural sweep intact can the movie fire off all the sound and fury it has to offer.

7 THE LAST PICTURE SHOW *(1971/91, Voyager, 5 CAV sides, B&W, not rated, $124.95; script excerpts, screen tests)* Director Peter Bogdanovich, forced to trim *The Last Picture Show* to less than two hours in 1971, restored seven minutes to this laser-only edition of his haunting portrait of a blighted Texas town. While you won't go wrong with the original—also on tape and disc—this recut is definitely superior. For one thing, high school flirt goddess Jacy (Cybill Shepherd) becomes a more compelling character when you see her seduced on a pool table by one of her father's workmen and then rudely dumped; it helps explain why she uses sex as a weapon. Bogdanovich's alternate-audio commentary ranges from serious analysis to serious dish, and Shepherd, Cloris Leachman, and Randy Quaid also contribute surprisingly confessional remarks.

8 HERBERT VON KARAJAN: NEW YEAR'S CONCERT VIENNA 1987 *(1990, Sony Classical, 2 CLV sides, not rated, $64.98)* The peak in a series of 24 von Karajan releases, only

some of which are available on tape, this lovely performance of familiar Strauss pieces was reedited from live broadcast tapes under the late conductor's personal supervision. The digital sound captures every orchestral accent, from the pluckings of "Pizzicato Polka" to thundering percussion on the climactic clap-along, "Radetzky March." The frail, ailing maestro's conducting brilliantly illuminates the music, and ballet dancers, prancing horses, and the sumptuous interior of Vienna's Musikverein concert hall suffuse the proceedings with a holiday glow.

9 THE BUSBY BERKELEY DISC *(1933–37/92, compilation, MGM/ UA, 3 CLV sides, B&W, not rated, $39.98)* No sappy plots about backstage crises to wade through—just three hours of musical sequences staged by the master of nuttily overripe choreography. Culled uncut from nine Warner Bros. musicals of the mid-'30s, the 22 fanciful production numbers in this disc-only collection play like the erotic daydreams of a military drill instructor. The camera never stops rolling past precision-marching chorines dressed in peekaboo uniforms and feathers and bubbles and spangles and even neon lights, and it's all photographed from the wildest angles this side of *Citizen Kane*.

10 THE SEARCHERS *(1956/91, Warner, 3 CLV sides, widescreen, not rated, $39.98)*

Only this disc version frames John Ford's rectangular VistaVision shots accurately, getting in the characters who appear at the sides of the image (they're often cropped out on tape) and actually *removing* picture information from the top of the screen. As a result, instead of seeming dwarfed by huge patches of sky above him, John Wayne's Indian-hating Ethan Edwards dominates the landscapes he roams, as Ford intended. Fascinating bonus: a making-of program done in black and white for TV, with an appearance by Wayne's costar Jeffrey Hunter. Unfortunately, it treats Indians with a condescension the movie avoids.

11 LAWRENCE OF ARABIA *(1962/89, Voyager, 4 CLV sides, not rated, $69.95)* Here's one

classic you *don't* want in the most deluxe disc version available. Voyager's four-platter, $125 CAV edition appends only a smattering of behind-the-scenes photos to the restored, 217-minute cut of David Lean's desert epic, and requires you to change sides *seven times*. The cheaper CLV version we recommend has better goodies: a promotional short, some stargazer premiere footage, and a video clip of Lean launching *Lawrence*'s 1989 reissue. Columbia TriStar also offers a no-frills $39.95 disc; it's taken from the same superlative widescreen video master as the Voyager copies and makes a perfectly dazzling collectible even sans extras.

12 THE ABYSS SPECIAL EDITION *(1989/93, FoxVideo/Image, 6 sides, partial CAV, wide-*

THE BUSBY BERKELEY DISC: FROM GOLD DIGGERS OF 1933

LESTER GLASSNER COLLECTION/NEAL PETERS

OFF THE CUTTING-ROOM FLOOR

"The restored director's cut!" "The original, unrated version!" "Contains scenes never shown in theaters!" More and more videos—especially video discs—are heralding the recovery of once-scrapped footage. Some recuts subtly improve on a classic (the *Last Picture Show* disc), while others insert a few racy minutes to raunch up what was once toned down (*9½ Weeks*). And occasionally, these restorations seem like the handiwork of a compulsive filmmaker who simply can't resist the urge to noodle (*The Godfather Part III*). Here are some films on video that make the most of their added footage—along with a few whose perpetrators should have left well enough alone. —*Michael Sauter*

MOVIE		WHAT'S BEEN ADDED
DR. JEKYLL AND MR. HYDE *(1932)* Rouben Mamoulian		17 minutes*, most featuring Miriam Hopkins as a London trollop, cut to mute erotic overtones of Jekyll/Hyde split personality.
LOST HORIZON *(1937)* Frank Capra		23 minutes, several scenes of which have been recovered only as still photos, cut during World War II to tone down pacifist idealism and pro-Asia sentiment.
RED RIVER *(1948)* Howard Hawks		8 minutes, mostly of cattle drive where John Wayne and Montgomery Clift lock horns. Montage fills in 15-year narrative gap. Diary pages replace voice-over narration.
CHEYENNE AUTUMN *(1964)* John Ford		9 minutes of sequence set in Dodge City, featuring James Stewart as comical Wyatt Earp and Arthur Kennedy as Doc Holliday, cut for length.
THE MAN WHO FELL TO EARTH *(1976)* Nicolas Roeg		20 minutes, cut for length and to avoid X rating: bouts of lovemaking between extraterrestrial David Bowie and Earth girl Candy Clark; flashbacks of Bowie and family on their home planet.
NEW YORK, NEW YORK *(1977)* Martin Scorsese		Elaborate 10-minute "Happy Endings" production number, featuring Liza Minnelli and a cast of dozens, cut to reduce running time.

*All times approximate

278

Hopkins unbridled makes Jekyll/Hyde duality a more dynamic tug-of-war.

Restored scenes (including long dialogue between crash survivor Ronald Colman and High Lama Sam Jaffe) better explain Shangri-La.

Slower or not, it's the movie director Hawks intended—even if the diary pages do spill past edges of TV screen.

Sequence restored to full 20 minutes, which proves too much comic relief for an otherwise stately epic.

Fleshed-out scenes add intensity; flashback scenes add poignance; together they add greatly to this stranger-in-a-strange-land odyssey.

Recaps main story (romance between Minnelli and Robert De Niro), with a glitzy gaiety that ironically counterpoints film's outcome.

MONITOR SHOTS BY DONAL HOLWAY

screen or pan-and-scan, not rated, $99.98; THX-approved transfer) While many home-video recuts of movies merely add grace notes to an already sound story, this not-on-tape *Abyss* is the only version that makes any sense. Director James Cameron has woven 30 minutes of footage back into his original 2-hour-20-minute theatrical release, restoring a key plot thread about aliens threatening to drown humanity in tidal waves unless nuclear weapons are abolished (think *The Day the Sea Stood Still*). Even better than seeing the movie put back together is seeing it taken apart in an encyclopedic, 46-chapter making-of supplement that beautifully elucidates Cameron's technocratic style.

13 **1776** *(1972/92, Pioneer, 4 CLV sides, wide-screen, PG, $89.95; audio commentary by director Peter H. Hunt, instrumentals-only track)* Extraordinary care has been lavished on restoring this endearing founding-father chorale, expanded by a half hour to the length originally intended by the director. Almost all the additions—easy to spot because they're taken from beat-up prints that can look as timeworn as the Declaration of Independence itself—enrich the story, especially a still-timely ditty that twits conservatives.

14 **TOOTSIE** *(1982/92, Voyager, 2 CAV sides plus 2 CLV sides, wide-screen, PG, $99.95; making-of short and still-frame appendix, audio commentary by director Sydney Pollack)* It's about an actor (Dustin Hoffman) playing a woman on TV, but *Tootsie*'s panoramic ensemble scenes were made for the movies:

279

They're in Panavision, with the actors arrayed across a very broad frame. Tape copies crop out some priceless deadpan reactions from Bill Murray, Teri Garr, and Charles Durning, but all that's fixed on Voyager's letterboxed disc. Even the supervibrant, remastered color makes the flick funnier: You can tell instantly when Dorothy Michaels is having a bad-makeup day.

15 **CITIZEN KANE: 50TH ANNIVERSARY EDITION** *(1941/91, Voyager, 6 CAV sides, B&W/color, not rated, $124.95; extensive still-frame documentary, original promo trailer, early Welles short)* Aping *Kane*'s own structure, Voyager salutes it by interviewing 35 intimates: directors, actors, and cameramen who speak in short video-clip testimonials. Every production photo you've seen and some you haven't may also be found here in the still-frame appendixes, along with a meticulous history of *Kane*'s creation and impact. Lightened a touch to reveal new, teeming detail within its looming shadows, the restored film delivers the sort of I-never-noticed-that shock you'd feel looking at the cleaned-up ceiling of the Sistine Chapel.

16 **WEST SIDE STORY** *(1961/89, Voyager, 6 CAV sides, wide-screen, not rated, $124.95; video interview with codirector Robert Wise, storyboards vs. final scenes, location-scouting pictures, trailers)* Single-movie laser packages don't get more expensive than this, but they also don't get much better. A selection of casting notes (Warren Beatty gave an "excellent" audition as Tony, but "voice not right") and preproduction sketches make up a mini-seminar on how to build a musical, and a stop-and-go, clip-peppered deconstruction of the "Tonight" number is the best film-editing lesson yet crafted for disc. Budget tip: MGM/UA's $30 edition has few extras but comes from an even sharper, more vivid 65 mm source.

17 **CLOSE ENCOUNTERS OF THE THIRD KIND** *(1977 and 1980/90, Voyager, 6 CAV sides, wide-screen, PG, $124.95; text for deleted scenes)* Which is better: Steven Spielberg's 1977 movie or his some-footage-added, some-footage-removed 1980 "Special Edition"? Here's a three-disc set that lets you decide—sort of. It restores the original, slightly longer cut (never released on tape) and appends the extra "Special" scenes to the end of each disc side, so you can program your player to plop them into proper sequence. Big oversight: The liner notes don't say which scenes from the '77 version were *trimmed* in 1980. Big bonus: an ingenious three-way split-screen documentary about the film's special effects, plus a still-frame annex of more than 1,000 production photos, sketches, and storyboard panels.

18 **ALIENS SPECIAL WIDE-SCREEN COLLECTOR'S EDITION** *(1986/91, FoxVideo/Image, 7 CAV sides, wide-screen, R, $99.98; guide to restored scenes, storyboards, advertising materials, script excerpts)* Another of writer-producer-director James Cameron's home-video reedits puts back 17 minutes of scenes trimmed from theatrical prints; the best sequence shows Ripley (Sigourney Weaver) discovering that her daughter died back on Earth while she was out

CITY LIGHTS: **CHARLIE CHAPLIN**

battling the first alien. Supplemental chapters diagram *Aliens'* weaponry, ships, and set designs in the style of a military-machinery catalog, as befits a sci-fi thriller that's structured exactly like a WWII buddies-in-action flick.

19

WORK IN PROGRESS: BEAUTY AND THE BEAST *(1991/92, Disney/Image, 4 CAV sides, wide-screen, color/B&W, G, $49.99)* Before other artists color them in, animators' drawings exist as pencil "roughs," which can sometimes have more vitality than the tidied-up final product. For this cleverly engineered "workprint," carefully structured in a way no actual workprint would be, the Disney marketeers have intercut such rough passages in brief snippets during the musical numbers, and in longer segments for linking scenes. Bonus goodies include a pencil-test version of "Be Our Guest," wherein singing flatware assails not Belle but her father.

20

THE MAGNIFICENT AMBERSONS *(1942/91, Voyager, 4 CAV sides, B&W, not rated, $99.95)* Upon release, RKO Pictures shortened Orson Welles' second masterwork from nearly two hours to less than 90 minutes and destroyed the outtakes. Voyager couldn't resurrect the missing footage, but it provides the next best things: The complete shooting script and storyboards, photos from cut sequences, an audio commentary track that explains what belonged where, Welles' earlier radio-broadcast version, and a still-frame text essay on the film's production. None of this turns up *Ambersons* that crucial notch from an assemblage of glorious moments to a fully coherent movie, but it gives those moments maximum impact.

21

CITY LIGHTS *(1931/93, Fox-Video/Image, 4 CAV sides, B&W, not rated, $69.98; transcripts of altered scenes, stills of* *promo materials)* Chaplin's consummate weepie, remastered exclusively for disc with such visual fidelity you can see the wire suspending the little Tramp in the boxing-ring scenes. Presented in a "windowbox" format, which surrounds the image with a black border so that no edges in the densely packed frames get cropped, as they do on tape. Thanks to dual soundtracks, you can also hear either the original 1931 recording of Chaplin's score (tinny, but the timing is masterful) or a new, surround stereo version conducted in 1989 by Carl Davis (not always in perfect synch, but lush). Collector's note: This is one in a sterling series called "Chaplin: A Legacy of Laughter"; other volumes showcase additional Chaplin features and shorts in equally immaculate prints.

22 **DR. STRANGELOVE: OR HOW I LEARNED TO STOP WORRYING AND LOVE THE BOMB** *(1964/ 92, Voyager, 4 CAV sides, partial widescreen, B&W, not rated, $99.95; annotated early screenplay draft)* "Why does Dr. Strangelove want 10 females to each male? How does the fate of the world hang on a Coca-Cola machine? Why was General Jack D. Ripper obsessed by fluids?" So asks the original coming-attraction teaser for Stanley Kubrick's scathing antinuclear farce, presented here as the kickoff to a sublime supplemental section. The highlight: a sampling of government-produced nuclear-preparedness propaganda, from pamphlets to short films. The cheery, Kafka–on–Madison Avenue tone ("Even a thin cloth can protect [you] from radiation!") beats anything in *Strangelove* for black-humored outrageousness.

23 **TAXI DRIVER** *(1976/90, Voyager, 4 CAV sides, widescreen, R, $99.95; Bernard Herrmann's score isolated on music-only audio track, complete storyboards, essay on Herrmann's score, production photos)* Martin Scorsese, are you talkin' to *me*? Yes, it's the director himself, giving a mile-a-minute audio-track chat about how psycho cabbie Travis Bickle came to be. With a complete early draft of the screenplay and additional audio comments by scriptwriter Paul Schrader, this disc offers more insight into Manhattan lowlife types than a trip to West 42nd Street.

24 **STAR WARS TRILOGY: THE DEFINITIVE COLLECTION** *(1977, 1980, and 1983/93, Fox-Video/Image, 18 CAV sides, widescreen, digital sound, PG, $250; includes copy of Charles Champlin's book* George Lucas: The Creative Impulse, *sporadic audio-track commentary by Lucas and effects technicians, still-frame appendixes on FX techniques)* Hang the expense and the irksome side breaks (each movie is spread to five sides, plus one for supplements): This is audiovisual nirvana. The brightest scenes have the color-for-its-own-sake glow of a Technicolor musical, touches lost in any earlier tape or disc version. Even the worst-acted passages in the trilogy's choppy windup, *Return of the Jedi* (could Carrie Fisher look any more bored?), become an overwhelming visual trip. And the remastered-from-scratch Dolby Surround soundtracks bathe every scene in a totally convincing sonic *environment*. Bet you've never heard Darth Vader's leather glove crinkle when he makes a fist.

Play it loud and this disc's roaring, surround-sound, CD-caliber sonics could do to your speakers what Bruce Willis does to the terrorists who commandeer a high-rise building: blow 'em up *real good.* In contrast to cropped VHS copies, this letterboxed edition preserves all that scary empty space Willis prowls around in, and there's no electronic "squeeze" distortion, either. (That bit of transfer trickery, done just for VHS and broadcast versions to cram more of the wide-screen action into square TV screens, is why the *Die Hard* cast looks like a gallery of anorexics anywhere but on disc.)

27 THE GOLDEN AGE OF LOONEY TUNES, VOLS. 1 AND 2 *(1931–48/92, MGM/UA, 10 CLV sides each, animated, some cartoons B&W, not rated, $99.98 each)* For sheer scope, no 'toon anthology on tape can touch these best-selling sets starring Bugs Bunny, Daffy Duck, and the rest of the Warner Bros. gang. They run nearly 10 hours each. (There's a third and a fourth volume that dig deeper into esoterica.) But it's not just the size that impresses, it's the selectability, since chapter stops for each short make it easy to watch the one you want, when you want it. If you're not fan enough to know which title's what, pop in any side: Each is arranged as a mini-retrospective, tracing the evolution of, say, Sylvester or Porky Pig.

25 THE ADVENTURES OF ROBIN HOOD *(1938/89, MGM/UA, 2 CLV sides, not rated, $34.98; reissue trailer)* Forget the dashing heroics of Errol Flynn as Robin, the allure of Olivia de Havilland as Maid Marion, the soaring music by Erich Wolfgang Korngold. In this hue-drenched, beyond-vibrant disc, *Robin Hood* becomes a tale about…fashion. Scene after razor-sharp scene unveils garb of such exquisite tactility, you'll feel as mad for finery as that peacock Prince John (Claude Rains). Best news: For once, the top disc edition is the cheapest. Voyager's $50 (CLV) and $100 (CAV with supplements) versions pale, literally, by comparison.

26 DIE HARD *(1988/89, Fox-Video/Image, 3 CLV sides, wide-screen, R, $39.98)*

28 LOONEY TUNES CURTAIN CALLS *(1948–60/92, Warner, 2 CLV sides, animated, not rated, $34.98)* Of 12 single-disc anthologies drawn from the later Looney oeuvre—those postwar years when the

283

Warner Bros. cartoon auteurs hit their full graphic stride—this is the crème de la crème, the one with the magical indelibles you remember best from childhood: Elmer singing "Kill the waaabbit!" in a Wagnerian opera spoof; a frog who'll sing and dance only for his master. With timing that rivals the best of Keaton and Chaplin, the strongest cartoons here hold up to dozens of viewings—and since this is laser, they'll never turn grainy from wear or get tangled up in tape rollers.

29 THE CONNERY COLLECTION *(1962–64/92, MGM/UA, 6 CLV sides, wide-screen, PG, $69.98; original trailers)* Rocket back to Cuban Missile Crisis days with this hefty boxed set of the first three James Bond movies, wherein a young, trim Sean Connery (still with his very own hair!) disses Moneypenny in *Dr. No*, beats the crap out of Soviet agents in *From Russia With Love*, and strokes villainess Pussy Galore in *Goldfinger*. Politically incorrect overtones notwithstanding, it's a kick to rediscover the Bond series' best, leanest, most wittily violent entries, made before megabudget bloat set in.

30 THE 400 BLOWS *(1959/87, Voyager, 2 CLV sides, wide-screen, subtitled, B&W, not rated, $59.93)* François Truffaut's debut-feature portrait of a budding social delinquent is available in exactly the same wide-screen, subtitled version on tape from Home Vision. But the dual-audio-track commentary added for this disc—one track is in French, the other in English—makes it a vastly superior video keepsake. As in a compan-

ion Voyager disc of *Jules and Jim*, longtime Truffaut associates share the microphone with astute critics and commentators for a combination of biography and visual exegesis that truly reaches the level of the *magnifique*.

31 BLUE VELVET *(1986/90, Warner, 3 CLV sides, wide-screen, R, $29.98)* What hideous psychosexual depravities lurk in the dark apartment of small-town singer Dorothy Vallens (Isabella Rossellini)? You'll get the full answer on video only with this letterboxed disc, in which all the voluptuous decadence of director David Lynch's peep-slot imagery unfurls uncropped. The hyperacute digital surround sound mesmerizes too, whether blaring (you'll jump when Dennis Hopper's live-wire villain, Frank Booth, screams, "I'll f--- anything that moves!") or barely there (as when Rossellini druggily croons the title tune).

32 KING KONG/THE SON OF KONG *(1933/91, Image, 3 CLV sides plus 1 CAV side, B&W, not rated, $49.95)* Classic, shmassic—in the wake of *Jurassic*, let's admit that the first half of *Kong* plays more than ever like a prehistoric bore, with silent-movie–style acting that outhams Master Thespian. But start with side 2 of this double-bill disc set and you're instantly on the big ape's stronghold, Skull Island, in the thick of Willis O'Brien's still-thrilling, dankly atmospheric stop-motion effects work. *Son*, a flimsy follow-up, is perfectly enjoyable if you chapter-skip straight to the little white-haired simian's big scenes, again held till the latter half of the picture.

33 **SWING TIME** *(1936/86, Voyager, 4 CAV sides, B&W, not rated, $74.95; audio commentary by author John Mueller, production photos, footage of dancer Bill "Bojangles" Robinson)* Never mind dissecting fancy special-effects scenes frame by frame—this top Fred Astaire–Ginger Rogers musical is the ultimate application to date of laser's CAV format. Slow down Astaire and Rogers' dance routines to a quarter of their normal speed and you've got one of the great nature documentaries: They move like zero-gravity gazelles, their limbs rising and turning, calling and answering in a duet more intimate than you imagined was possible standing up.

34 **BYE BYE BIRDIE** *(1963/92, Pioneer, 2 CLV sides, wide-screen, not rated,* $44.95)* Years before he was head cut-up on *Hollywood Squares*, comedian Paul Lynde stole the show in *Birdie* as the uptight dad of a teen (Ann-Margret) chosen to kiss a loutish rock singer on *The Ed Sullivan Show*. Lynde's toss-of-the-head double takes never get cropped out in the wide-screen transfer, and the stereo mixes of the songs, particularly an awed choral ode to Ed ("He's my favorite human!" gushes Lynde), have amazing kick. Audio tip: Switch your left and right sound-input cables for this disc, since Pioneer got the channels backward.

35 **HOW GREEN WAS MY VALLEY** *(1941/92, FoxVideo/Image, 2 CLV sides, B&W, not rated, $39.98)* Scouring the vaults for a pristine copy of John Ford's coal-mining family saga, the folks at FoxVideo

285

BYE BYE BIRDIE: **ANN-MARGRET**

EVERETT COLLECTION

found something unexpected: a multi-track recording of the Alfred Newman score. They remixed the music into true surround stereo for disc release only, giving it a breadth wonderfully suited to Ford's expansive style. For purists, there's a full alternate soundtrack in the original mono, plus another track that gives you the music alone.

36 **CHINATOWN** *(1974/91, Para-mount, 3 CLV sides, wide-screen, R, $49.95; alternate audio track with music only)* After a few viewings, you notice that much of director Roman Polanski's noir homage takes place early or late in the daylight hours. No other video version renders Jack Nicholson and Faye Dunaway bathed in that gorgeous, slanting light as well as this disc. Irony alert: Select the music-only track when Nicholson, his nose heavily bandaged, dines with Dunaway; you'll hear a pianist playing the love song "The Way You Look Tonight."

37 **REBECCA** *(1940/90, Voyager, 5 CAV sides plus 1 CLV side, B&W, not rated, $124.95; audio commentary, Academy Awards footage)* What would Alfred Hitchcock's Oscar-winning melodrama have been like with Laurence Olivier's lover Vivien Leigh in the role of the mousy new Mrs. de Winter? Pretty awful, judging from the too-perky Leigh screen test included here (think *Scarlett Goes to Manderley*). Additional test footage demonstrates that the efforts of Margaret Sullavan, Anne Baxter, and Loretta Young to appear nervous in the part were all inferior to the bona fide anxiety projected by Hitch's ultimate choice, Joan Fontaine.

38 **MICKEY MOUSE: THE BLACK AND WHITE YEARS, VOL. 1** *(1928–35/93, Disney/Image, 10 CAV sides, one short in color, not rated, $124.99)* Further along his journey toward corporate-symboldom, you'd never see Mickey do the rude, frisky things he does here, like tormenting barnyard animals and goosing Minnie. It's a hoot to watch him steadily tamed in this enormous (four-plus hours), chronologically arranged, disc-exclusive set. A passel of extras turns the package into a primer: Hundreds of still-frame "storyboard" script sketches show how the animators planned their increasingly elaborate scenes. In style and scale, it's anything but a Mickey Mouse package.

39 **THE JAMES DEAN 35TH AN-NIVERSARY COLLECTION** *(1955–56/90, Warner, wide-screen, 10 CLV sides, not rated, $119.98, out of print; sound remastered for stereo surround, disc documentary and biographical booklet enclosed, original trailers)* Dean's first two mid-'50s features, the ultra-wide-screen *East of Eden* and *Rebel Without a Cause*, have maximum impact in the letterboxed transfers they get here; you can see how much the young Method tyro shakes up his costars. Although the laserdisc set is no longer being manufactured, making it difficult to find in stores, it's worth hunting down for its career-in-a-box completeness.

40 **BACK TO THE FUTURE** *(1985/91, MCA/Universal, 2 CLV sides, wide-screen, PG, $34.98)* The greedy-'80s punchlines are already fading into obscurity (a time-

SPARTACUS: KIRK DOUGLAS

plays like a potboiler, never more flat-footed than when Tony Curtis appears as a Bronx-accented reciter of tales from "lawn ga-go." It doesn't merit an overreverential "Special Edition" showcase, and for the most part isn't treated that way here. A thorough behind-the-scenes supplement properly treats the film as craft, not art, especially in a segment resurrecting a TV "press kit" chat filmed with star Jean Simmons; it's as blatantly unjournalistic as anything on the E! channel today.

42 **8½** *(1962/89, Voyager, 3 CLV sides, wide-screen, subtitled, B&W, not rated, $59.95; original trailer)* The movie may be about a philandering filmmaker (Marcello Mastroianni), but this disc edition couldn't be more faithful to Fellini's greatest opus. The tones are richer, the film-stock grain finer than in typical revival-house prints. None of Fellini's endlessly expressive cast winds up cropped out of the letterboxed image, and digital sound preserves the nuance in Nino Rota's integral score.

43 **JAWS** *(1975/92, MCA/Universal, 2 CLV sides plus 1 CAV side, wide-screen, PG, $39.98; trailers)* Steven Spielberg's first big splash has a lean, story-driven feel rare in his later movies. It may also be his most visually exciting work: The wide-screen shots, perfectly framed and imbued with ravishing color here, evoke the terrifying vastness of the ocean with fiendish acumen. For a treatise in suspense-scene timing, take apart editor Verna Fields' work in the CAV-formatted side 3 finale—if you can keep your palms dry enough to operate the remote.

287

traveling *DeLorean*? What's a De-Lorean, Daddy?). But technically, this will surely remain a disc for the ages, with a sparkling picture and way-cool digital Dolby Surround effects that haven't been topped. Best example: The moment when Dr. Emmett Brown (Christopher Lloyd) seemingly sends his decade-hopping car right through the TV screen and past your seat.

41 **SPARTACUS** *(1960/92, Voyager, 4 CLV sides plus 2 CAV sides, wide-screen, PG-13, $124.95; audio commentaries by cast and creative team, trailer, storyboards, deleted music cues, short about the Hollywood blacklist, production and premiere newsreels)* Visually magnificent, Stanley Kubrick's slave-revolt spectacle

44 **INTO THE WOODS** *(1990/92, Image/BPI, 3 CLV sides, not rated, $49.95)* In contrast to the other Stephen Sondheim shows taped for PBS and released on laser *(Sunday in the Park With George, Sweeney Todd)*, *Woods*, which interweaves well-known fairy tales, actually plays better under the close-up scrutiny of video cameras than it did on Broadway. Perhaps it's the intimate, advice-laden nature of songs like "Children Will Listen," turned into a heartbreaking lament by Bernadette Peters. Handy chapter markers let you instantly replay Sondheim's thorniest lyrical thickets until their meaning becomes as clear as their rhythm.

45 **THE GRADUATE** *(1967/87, Voyager, 4 CAV sides, widescreen, R, $99.95; audio commentary, production photos, ad materials, excerpts from scrapped screenplay drafts, reviews, screen tests, comparison of novel with movie)* Mike Nichols' comedy of manners has never looked so good. The plants by the bar where predatory Mrs. Robinson (Anne Bancroft) mixes her drinks are greener than a tropical jungle, and her panther-style stalking of Benjamin Braddock (Dustin Hoffman) is funniest when you can see both guilty lovers in the same wide-screen shot. The well-researched supplemental section (did you know the book's author bad-mouthed the film's marriage-be-damned finale as "immoral"?) is that rare commodity, an analysis that's as entertaining as it is educational. Budget alert: New Line/Image's 25th-anniversary edition ($39.99) looks almost as good and includes new interviews with Hoffman and Katharine Ross.

46 **NORTH BY NORTHWEST** *(1959/88, Voyager, 6 CAV sides, wide-screen, not rated, $124.95; 1959/91, MGM/UA, 2 CLV sides plus 1 CAV side, wide-screen, not rated, $39.98)* Which of these editions is best for savoring Hitchcock's cross-country chase classic? Many laser buffs can't choose, so they get both (don't laugh; it's mean to mock a subculture). Voyager's is pricey but includes storyboard–versus–finished shot comparisons for *NNW*'s standout scene, the crop-duster attack on Cary Grant, and a brief interview with Hitchcock. Colors have more kick on MGM/UA's release, and the soundtrack, remixed for stereo, keeps you more involved and more conscious of Bernard Herrmann's edgy score.

47 **INVASION OF THE BODY SNATCHERS** *(1956/86, Voyager, 3 CAV sides, wide-screen, B&W, not rated, $74.95; audio commentary, trailer, text of interview with director Don Siegel, bibliography)* When you can see the empty space *around* the spooked protagonist (Kevin McCarthy), there's more tension in this classic conspiracy thriller. Don't believe us? Check out the side 3 wide-screen demo, which shows a *Snatchers* scene letterboxed, then repeats it blown up and cropped to fill your entire TV screen. Only a pod person wouldn't be shocked at how much visual expression gets lost in the process.

48 **MIDNIGHT COWBOY** *(1969/92, Voyager, 4 CAV sides, R, $99.95; trailer, production stills, script analysis)* Leave it to laser to transform New York's sleaziest, dirtiest neighborhood into eye candy. Jon Voight, as a would-be Times Square hustler, looks achingly blue-eyed throughout, and the vibrant juice ads tacked up by his flatmate, Ratso Rizzo (Dustin Hoffman), become an emblem of the pair's longing for a better life. Capped by alternate-audio commentary from director John Schlesinger and producer Jerome Hellman, the disc shifts *Cowboy*'s focus from urban grit to the actors' profound insight into the two tragic characters.

49 **POLYESTER** *(1981/93, Voyager, 2 CLV sides, widescreen, R, $54.95; documentary short about Edith "the Egg Lady" Massey)* This disc stinks, but only because there are scents embedded in the "Odorama" card enclosed. You scratch and sniff in response to flashing numbers on the screen as housewife Francine Fishpaw (Divine) discovers the good, the bad, and the smelly in life. Director John Waters makes his audio commentary a wonderfully naughty-sweet reminiscence, which he closes with advice on how to replace a spent Odorama card: "Walk around your house. I'm sure you can find 10 smells that'll either turn you on or make you right sick." What a mind.

50 **RAIDERS OF THE LOST ARK** *(1981/92, Paramount, 2 CLV sides, wide-screen, PG, $24.95)* The biggest bargain in laserdom. Sonically, it blows any tape copy away, from that room-shaking boulder to the ghost-typhoon finale. Harrison Ford's shoot-out scenes make more sense in wide-screen, too. The sequels (*Indiana Jones and the Temple of Doom, Indiana Jones and the Last Crusade*) make fine companion collectibles,

MIDNIGHT COWBOY:
JON VOIGHT, DUSTIN HOFFMAN

especially since they're better sampled than sat through.

289

51 **THE APARTMENT** *(1960/89, MGM/UA, 3 CLV sides, wide-screen, B&W, not rated, $39.98)* Jack Lemmon, even more tic-ish than usual, stars as an insurance clerk who gets ahead by lending out his pad for executive trysts. Director Billy Wilder has him scurry through a succession of claustrophobic, barely differentiated offices, elevators, stairwells, and bedrooms, and the visual impression that he's going nowhere fast—wonderfully conveyed by the wall-to-wall walls in this wide-screen transfer—perfectly frames the script's sour view of the workplace.

52 **POLTERGEIST** *(1982/89, MGM/UA, 2 CLV sides, wide-screen, PG, $34.98;*

1994 edition, 5 CAV sides, $59.98; making-of featurette and trailers) Just how radically can a digital Dolby Surround soundtrack enhance home viewing? Crank up the volume on this letterboxed laser of Spielberg's suburban *Exorcist* and find out. The panoramic sound-effects mix says *BOO!* from every corner of the room, yet wherever you're sitting, you'll swear you hear the scared voice of little Carol Anne Freeling, spirited away by the ghosts she calls "the TV people," hovering *right next to you.*

53 **CABARET** *(1972/93, Warner, 2 CLV sides plus 1 CAV side, PG, $39.98; trailer)* True to the look that Bob Fosse's mordant '30s-Berlin mosaic had in movie theaters, this wide-screen edition crops off the top and the bottom of the image with black bands. You therefore actually see *less* than in other, non-letterboxed video versions. But what's removed adds enormously to the movie's visual power, most notably when the Kit Kat Klub's ghoulish emcee (Joel Grey) prowls the stage. With less to see of spotlights above and patrons below, there's a tighter, scarier focus on Grey's leering musical entreaties.

54 **THE KILLER** *(1989/93, Voyager, 6 CAV sides, wide-screen, subtitled, not rated, $124.95; director's audio commentary, deleted scenes, comprehensive filmography with trailers)* Gangster movies go kung fu in this gun-crazy melodrama from John Woo, Asia's answer to Peckinpah. As fate draws together a dapper assassin (Chow Yun-Fat), a cabaret singer he inadvertently blinds, and a cop disenchanted with the law, Woo piles on

ambushes by the gross. The CAV transfer lets you chart every bullet's balletic trajectory at whatever speed you like. Of course, this being a Woo movie, the director sometimes does that for you, intercutting sped-up and slowed-down motion to hurry through or linger over someone's brutal demise.

55 **GHOSTBUSTERS** *(1984/89, Voyager, 4 CAV sides, wide-screen, PG, $99.95; deleted scenes, production photos, before-and-after comparisons of shots with FX work, sketch galleries of unused ghost designs, trailers)* Bill Murray just improvised all his quips as spook chaser "Dr." Venkman, right? Wrong. Click through the shooting script page by page (that is, disc frame by disc frame) and discover how much of the first monster comedy to do monster box office was in fact scrupulously worked out in advance, including plenty of gags that didn't make the final cut. Bum contemplating gooey fallout from the detonated Stay Puft Marshmallow Man: "I wonder if there might not be a very large cup of hot chocolate somewhere in the area."

56 **LORD OF THE FLIES** *(1963/93, Voyager, 2 CLV sides, B&W, not rated, $49.95; deleted scenes, trailers, footage of production and premiere, audio track of William Golding reading and analyzing selections from his novel)* When events turn savage in this tale of a group of British schoolboys stranded on a remote island, switch to the evah-so-civilized audio commentary by director Peter Brook, producer Lewis Allen, and photographers Tom Hollyman and Gerald Feil. They're reassuringly erudite explaining how they stiff-upper-lipped it through such daunting setbacks as a nonactor cast, damaged negatives, and constant pressure to finish before autumn whisked the young performers away to school.

57 THE AFRICAN QUEEN LIMITED COMMEMORATIVE EDITION

(1951/1993, FoxVideo/ Image, 2 CLV sides, not rated, $69.98; trailer, copy of shooting script, and Katharine Hepburn memoir enclosed; disc only, $39.98) John Huston's peerless adventure-romance has always looked fine on home video, but this remastered package makes it a high-water mark for the medium. As prim missionary Rose (Hepburn) and hard-drinking captain Mr. Allnut (Humphrey Bogart) journey downriver to escape invading Germans in the Congo, the terrain no longer looks merely sharp and colorful but treacherously *real*. The cost of journeying via the deluxe set is pre-

mium, but with such delightful passengers on board, there's a lot to be said for traveling first-class.

58 THE FORBIDDEN HOLLYWOOD COLLECTION *(1932–33/93, MGM/UA, 8 CLV sides,*

B&W, not rated, $99.98; trailers) A corrupt corporate-takeover mogul, an unchecked sexual harasser, a desperate cocaine addict—is this the lineup for next week's *Inside Edition*? Nope, it's six early-talkie melodramas made before Hollywood's censorious "Production Code" clamped down on movie immorality in 1934. From a 19-year-old Loretta Young sleeping her way to a job (*Employees' Entrance*) to Barbara Stanwyck eliciting lesbian leers in jail (*Ladies They Talk About*), the tawdry goings-on still have a remarkable edge.

59 THE PLAYER *(1992/93, Voyager, 3 CLV sides plus 1 CAV side, wide-screen, R,*

LOREY SABASTIAN

THE PLAYER: **TIM ROBBINS**

JUMPING CONCLUSIONS

And in the last shot, she kills herself. No, wait—he kills her. No, no: How about, he tries to kill her, she fakes him out, then she stabs him? So went the rewrite sessions after *Fatal Attraction*'s original ending fell flat, according to director Adrian Lyne. But he's hardly the first Hollywood director—nor the latest—to have a film whose last reel went back for repairs.

WUTHERING HEIGHTS *(1939)* Viewers of the rough cut were incensed when the picture ended with Cathy (Merle Oberon) dead in the arms of her cruel lover, Heathcliff (Laurence Olivier). Director William Wyler refused to change it, so producer Sam Goldwyn commissioned a new close with the actors' stunt doubles as reunited ghosts. Opening-night crowds wept and cheered, proving, Goldwyn said, that "people don't want to look at a corpse at the end of a picture."

DR. STRANGELOVE: OR HOW I LEARNED TO STOP WORRYING AND LOVE THE BOMB *(1964)* Stanley Kubrick thought the funniest movie ever made about nuclear Armageddon would be funnier if it climaxed with a custard-pie fight. He filmed and screened the sequence but decided it was too outrageously slapstick. Also, JFK had been assassinated between the end of filming and the release, and it seemed unlikely anyone would laugh at the line, "Gentlemen, our President has been struck down in his prime."

DYING YOUNG *(1991)* The preview-card responses put the filmmakers in a double bind: Viewers didn't like Campbell Scott's leukemia-stricken character shooting himself, and they balked at Julia Roberts skipping off with interloper Vincent D'Onofrio. Though every scene still points toward the original unhappy ending, the final edit shows Roberts dumping D'Onofrio to drag Scott back to chemotherapy.

TOPAZ and **SWEET CHARITY** *(1969)* Universal produced both of these big-budget flops in the same year and tried to improve them for European release with snappier, happier closings. Now that both are on laserdiscs with both sets of endings, it's clear the auteurs' hearts weren't in the revisions. The "feel-good" capper of Hitchcock's *Topaz* shows a Soviet agent escaping but misses the droll style of Hitch's favored finale, in which a sniper fells the agent during a stadium duel. (U.S. prints ultimately closed with a third scenario, a suicide scene that Hitchcock didn't even supervise.) In *Sweet Charity*, the fate Bob Fosse wanted for Charity (Shirley MacLaine)—she's dumped by another boyfriend—is played out with much more winning spirit than the ludicrous reconciliation that replaced it.

SUSPICION *(1941)* It's all in Joan Fontaine's head: Her husband, Cary Grant, hasn't really been trying to murder her. That's the predictable conclusion Alfred Hitchcock had to

292

settle for after sneak-peek audiences jeered at his preferred windup: The glass of milk served up by Grant is poisoned, and a pregnant Fontaine buys the farm.

THELMA & LOUISE *(1991)* A test version had outlaw pals Susan Sarandon and Geena Davis speed right off a cliff in their Thunderbird convertible...and drive away unscathed on the ground below. It was a symbolic statement about freedom, said the filmmakers. It was stupid and unrealistic, said audiences, so the heroines are now frozen in a still frame just as their vehicle begins to plummet.

MEET JOHN DOE *(1941)* Frank Capra shot four endings for his tale of a tramp (Gary Cooper) hired by a reporter to say he'll commit public suicide, the better to protest man's inhumanity. *Doe* premiered in different cities with different conclusions; one had Cooper throwing himself off a roof and viewers throwing things at the screen. Capra called back all the prints and filmed yet a fifth finale, wherein Cooper is saved by a squadron of Doe Club believers.

All of which proves one thing: From the beginning, it sure helps to have a good ending. —*Steve Daly*

$99.95; still-frame essay on films about Hollywood, guide to star cameos, five deleted scenes, running audio commentary by director Robert Altman, screenwriter Michael Tolkin, and director of photography Jean Lepine) The overlapping dialogue so characteristic of director Robert Altman continues even after the last scene of his jaundiced, cameo-studded love-hate letter to the movie biz: A videotaped supplement features 20 Hollywood screenwriters holding forth on their town and their craft, with four of them on screen at any one time in four small, inset square blocks; you control which single voice you want to hear from your remote, or you can let their wry harangues blur together in a fittingly discordant chorus.

60 **WINCHESTER '73** *(1950/87, MCA, 2 CLV sides, B&W, not rated, $34.98)* Select the left audio channel for the soundtrack of Anthony Mann's fine, lean Western about a stolen gun. Select the right channel and you can listen to its star, Jimmy Stewart, as he charmingly drawls, stutters, and aw-shuckses his way through vaguely relevant reminiscences.

61 **THE DEVIL AND DANIEL WEBSTER** *(1941/92, Voyager, 2 CLV sides, B&W, not rated, $49.95)* Long available only in an abridged version, director William Dieterle's brooding Faustian fable was reconstructed in 1992 for this edition. While 22 minutes of reinserted scenes look and sound murky (the rest is pristine), they're crucial to illuminating why a none-too-bright New Hampshire farmer (James Craig) would be so easily swayed by old Scratch (Walter Huston).

293

Movie historian Bruce Eder's audio-track commentary turns dry historical background into crackling entertainment, giving *Devil* its due as one of the screen's great fantasies.

62 **A DAY AT THE RACES** *(1937/92, MGM/UA, 2 CLV sides, B&W, not rated, $34.98; reissue trailer)* As riotous a Marx Brothers showcase as its predecessor, *A Night at the Opera*—provided you hit the chapter-skip button to avoid the musical and ballet interludes with quavery vocalist Allan Jones (you actually find yourself longing for Zeppo). You can also thus eliminate a ghastly dark-ies-on-the-farm number, "All God's Chillun Got Rhythm," which culminates with the boys in blackface. No other Marx movie on laser so benefits from a little judicious remote-control editing.

63 **HELP!** *(1965/87, Voyager, 4 CAV sides, not rated, $79.95; trailer, footage of production and premiere)* Whichever Beatles movie you like best, this is the No. 1 disc of a Beatles movie. Why? Psychedelic colors rendered bright as an LSD flash, songs with cleaner digital sound than on the CD, a 300-plus still-frame gallery of witty publicity pics and Beatle-bilia, and a your-voice-here promotional radio interview, with blank spots where deejays could read questions to accompany the Fab Four's canned answers.

64 **KING OF KINGS** *(1961/91, MGM/UA, 3 CLV sides, wide-screen, not rated, $39.98; trailer)* Eschewing abstract invocations of awe to dwell on the bloody realities of political revolt, Nicholas Ray's dynamically visualized life of Christ is the most adult of Hollywood's biblical epics. This disc resurrects Miklós Rósza's score in sweeping stereo, complete with organ-heavy overture, intermission, and exit passages (beware copies mistakenly duplicated without these segments; they say "Extended Play" on the front jacket, which otherwise looks virtually identical to the corrected edition). Collector's note: If you prefer the Gospel according to William Wyler's *Ben-Hur* (1959), don't consider any disc edition except MGM/UA's 35th-anniversary package, with divine sound, wide-screen picture, and a solid making-of documentary.

65 **ONE, TWO, THREE** *(1961/90, MGM/UA/Image, 2 CLV sides, wide-screen, B&W, not rated, $49.95)* It can be harder to find than good beef in the former Soviet Union, but it's worth seeking out the disc version of Billy Wilder's breathless Cold War farce. Tearing around the wide-screen frame like a heat-seeking missile, James Cagney clocks in with what must be a dialogue speed record as a Coca-Cola exec stationed in pre-Wall West Berlin, desperately trying to break a romance between his boss' daughter and an earnest young Communist lad named Otto Piffl.

66 **BLACK NARCISSUS** *(1947/88, Voyager, 2 CLV sides, not rated, $44.95)* Talking as a team on an alternate audio track, *Narcissus* director Michael Powell and his longtime fan Martin Scorsese banter in a way that not only illuminates the picture at hand but also captures the electricity of two kindred artists learning from each other. Powell was married to Scorsese's film editor Thelma Schoonmaker at the time (he died in 1990), and familial feeling is in the air. Ruminating on the *Narcissus* nuns who cling precariously to propriety and sanity in a remote Himalayan convent, Scorsese rants at a speed beyond 78 rpm, often sailing off on inscrutable tangents; Powell spins somewhere short of 33⅓, but his insights are worth the wait.

67 **PATTON** *(1970/93, Fox-Video/Image, 3 CLV sides, wide-screen, partly subtitled, PG, $34.98)* How close did Oscar winner George C. Scott come to capturing the voice and swagger of the real Gen. George Patton? Check out the terrific newsreel footage that follows the movie here—some of which Scott himself reportedly studied—and behold a genius at work. It's a four-star impersonation, always conveying an expressive element above and beyond the mere replication of Patton's tough-guy posturing.

68 **SECRET HONOR** *(1984/92, Voyager, 2 CLV sides, PG, $49.95; twin alternate-audio narration by director Robert Altman and cowriter Donald Freed)* The greatest biopic of the last decade—and nobody saw it. Adapted from a stage play (by Donald Freed and Arnold M. Stone) and shot by Robert Altman as part of a college film class he was teaching, it's an intimate evening at home with a deposed Richard M. Nixon (Philip Baker Hall), who empties his heart and his spleen along with a bottle of Chivas Regal. Inspired writing, act-

ing, and imagery make the ex-President both monstrous and hugely sympathetic, a high-wire trick that seems even more miraculous as you watch, with new eyes, the borderline psychosis evident in the actual Nixon speeches (including the Checkers speech) and campaign ads that close out the disc.

69 **BLADE RUNNER: THE DIRECTOR'S CUT** *(1992/93, Warner, 4 CAV sides, wide-screen, R, $49.98)* With Harrison Ford's original narration removed from the film's soundtrack (it was hastily recorded and mixed in after some disastrous previews), all sorts of sonic detail that got crushed by those dopey, Chandleresque asides can easily be heard, especially in digital disc sound. And the robo-noir flavor the original voice-over dialogue strained so hard to suggest comes across much more simply in the music cues that now play at full volume: Imagine a reedy, lonely-town sax solo on synthesizers and you've got the mood. Other minor fixes (an upbeat epilogue removed, some extra bits of gore back in) barely make a difference; after all, this isn't primarily a story, it's a tone poem.

70 **FOR ALL MANKIND** *(1989/89, Voyager, 4 CAV sides, not rated, $99.95; director's audio commentary, still-frame archive of moon-mission pictures, excerpts from sci-fi space-travel movies)* When U.S. astronauts landed on the moon, the live TV picture was barely discernible. But the images in this documentary, distilled from thousands of hours of NASA film footage to create one composite, 79-minute to-the-moon-and-back journey, look as stunningly vivid as the interstel-

295

lar vistas in *Star Wars*. Voice-over reminiscences by Apollo astronauts mix with an ethereal Brian Eno score on the soundtrack, and at liftoff, the digital-surround disc tracks will make your living room shake like a launch pad.

71 **KOYAANISQATSI: LIFE OUT OF BALANCE** *(1983/89, Image, 1 CAV side plus 1 CLV, not rated, $39.95)* The major drawback to watching Godfrey Reggio's hypnotic global portrait on laserdisc—having to stop to switch to side 2—is more than made up for by the sense of virtual reality you get from laser's superior picture (wow, look at those *sand grains* in that canyon down there!). That feeling you've momentarily become a bat or an eagle or some other acutely sensitive creature, compromised on tape, is what this flick's all about.

FOR ALL MANKIND:
ONE OF THE APOLLO ASTRONAUTS

72 **GUNHED** *(1989, Japanese import on Toho label, in English and Japanese with Japanese subtitles, 2 CLV sides, widescreen, R, approximately $120)* The hottest bad Japanese sci-fi movie in Hollywood. A favorite among fantasy-film directors with disc collections, this weird futuristic spectacle is half in English. The plot thus remains only partly comprehensible—something about routing an army of computer-controlled robots from an abandoned superstructure. Most of it seems a direct steal from James Cameron's 1986 *Aliens*, but that's okay: He appears to have swiped a few *Gunhed* bits right back for *Terminator 2: Judgment Day*.

73 **LA STRADA** *(1954/88, Voyager, 2 CLV sides, B&W, subtitled, not rated, $49.95; selectable English or Italian audio tracks)* As a loutish strongman who misuses his sidekick (Giulietta Masina), Anthony Quinn gives a performance right up there with Brando's beastly-shlub turn in *A Streetcar Named Desire*. Be careful which of the two audio tracks you select: One is "dubbed" into English, yet paradoxically, that's where Quinn actually speaks for himself, his mouth moving in clear sync with his English-language dialogue. Unfortunately, Masina's dubber in this version sounds like Mickey Mouse; whenever she speaks, you'll want to switch to her original, deeper-voiced vocals on the Italian track.

74 **THE LAST EMPEROR (IMPORT VERSION)** *(1987/89, Japanese import, 4 CLV sides, widescreen, in English with Japanese subti-*

tles, not rated, approximately $100)
Slashed by nearly an hour for U.S. theatrical release, Bernardo Bertolucci's
epic ode to Pu Yi, puppet monarch of
China, still managed to clinch Best Editing as one of its nine Oscars. The award
seems a sick joke in light of the director's
3-hour-39-minute cut, showcased in this
import disc (you can get it only by mail
order or in specialty shops). Cohesion
and grace are restored to many truncated
segments, and the disc is far sharper and
more colorful than American laser versions. Caveat: One scene with newsreel
footage of Japanese war atrocities has
been trimmed, for the obvious reason.

75 **CAROUSEL** *(1956/92, Fox-
Video/Image, 3 CLV sides,
wide-screen, not rated,
$69.98)* Rodgers and Hammerstein be-
gan greenlighting film versions of their
Broadway hits just as ultra-wide-screen
spectacles came into Hollywood vogue.
That's why watching a cropped tape
copy of one of their best, *Carousel*, is
like settling for obstructed-view seats:
Half the setting disappears. But in this
letterboxed disc version, you can see the
seamy dockside milieu closing in to
doom star-crossed lovers Billy Bigelow
(Gordon MacRae) and Julie Jordan
(Shirley Jones).

76 **MADONNA: BLOND AMBITION
WORLD TOUR LIVE** *(1990/91,
Pioneer, 2 CLV sides, not
rated, $29.95; chapter stops for each
song)* You'd think a revenue maximizer
like Madonna wouldn't miss an outlet,
but this reedited version of a live HBO
broadcast (there's more polish in the
shot selections) has never been issued
on videocassette. Shot on tape, it's less

MADONNA:
BLOND AMBITION WORLD TOUR LIVE

297

visually detailed than the 35 mm filmed
concert scenes in *Truth or Dare*, made
during the same tour; but with less hy-
peractive cutting, you get a much better
look at the show's inventively lewd
choreography. The steeped-in-bass digital sound is a neighbor's nightmare.

77 **THE TAMING OF THE SHREW**
*(1967/93, Pioneer, 3 CLV
sides, wide-screen, not rat-
ed, $59.95; restored stereo soundtrack,
music-only alternate audio track)* Or,
Who's Afraid of William Shakespeare?
In their rollicking follow-up to *Virginia
Woolf,* Liz Taylor and Richard Burton
lay on the knockabout comedy, ripping
to pieces a good portion of director
Franco Zeffirelli's overstuffed sets. And

in wide-screen, you get to watch both battlers while one or the other is declaiming, instead of only the person who's talking.

78 VIENNA: THE SPIRIT OF THE CITY *(1990/91, Voyager, 2 CAV sides, not rated, $124.95)* Twenty minutes of motion footage and *15,000 still frames* detail what seems like every atom of Vienna's geography, architecture, culture, and history. While a few segments veer into "Sprockets"-style grotesquerie (like the "Orgy and Mystery Theater Group," who make punk rockers look tame), elegance prevails.

79 IT'S A MAD, MAD, MAD, MAD WORLD *(1963/91, MGM/UA, 5 CLV sides, wide-screen, not rated, $49.98; hour-long making-of documentary)* A few scenes are apparently gone forever, but here's a virtually complete, 3-hour-8-minute restored cut of Stanley Kramer's all-star farce, an avalanche of pratfalls, traffic accidents, and hollered insults. When a lull approaches, the disc's copious chapter stops let you skip forward faster than Ethel Merman on a banana peel. And since the Ultra Panavision images were designed to be as broad as the comedy, the fully letterboxed laser picture is the only way to see all the stunts and trashed sets (tape copies labeled "letterboxed" are in fact partially cropped).

80 MONTY PYTHON AND THE HOLY GRAIL *(1975/93, Voyager, 2 CLV sides, wide-screen, PG, $49.95; audio commentary by codirectors Terry Gilliam and Terry Jones, alternate Japanese-dubbed soundtrack, production photos, trailer)* Compared with Columbia TriStar's grimy-looking tape and disc, this spiffed-up Voyager version makes every gag read faster and funnier. A digital soundtrack keeps the Arthurian diction penetrable, and with laser's quick scan-back capability you can even decipher especially thick bits like the "Camelot" song (to wit: "We're Knights of the Round Table/We dance whene'er we're able/ We do routines and chorus scenes/With footwork impec-cable!"). A previously cut, 24-second scene reinserted into the movie has a Castle Anthrax maiden ask into the camera, "Do you think this scene should have been cut?" Now *that's* interactivity.

81 THE THREE CABALLEROS *(1945/88, Disney, 3 CAV sides, animation and live action, G, $36.99)* Crammed with gag-a-millisecond action that even an MTV addict will barely keep up with, this unjustly obscure Disney feature is a hoot to watch and a bigger hoot to take apart shot by shot in CAV slo-mo. It follows Donald Duck on a goodwill tour of Latin America, where to some great tunes he smooches live-action beach beauties à la *Roger Rabbit* and introduces short tales about Latin American culture. High point: a chorus line of phallic, dancing cacti, even more uproariously suggestive when viewed at half speed.

82 AKIRA *(1989/92, Voyager, 5 CAV sides, wide-screen, animated, not rated, $124.95; separate English and Japanese soundtracks, still-frame archive of preparatory sketches, including graphic-novel series that inspired the film)*

EL MARIACHI: SPECIAL COLLECTOR'S EDITION: OSCAR FABILA

Picturing a thug-infested, postapocalyptic Tokyo in staggering architectural detail, *Akira* seems more at home on disc than it was in theaters or on videocassette. That's because the movie, a semicoherent, two-hours-plus fantasia about government agents scrambling to harness a lethal telekinetic force, renders every blown-up body and dynamited superstructure so elaborately that the images simply don't read well in real time; you've got to slow them down to grasp what's happening, and nothing makes that easier than CAV.

83 **THE CLINT EASTWOOD TRILO-GY** *(1964–67/94, MGM/UA, 8 CLV sides, wide-screen, R, $99.98; trailers)* In one handy box, the seminal Sergio Leone spaghetti Westerns—*A Fistful of Dollars*; *For a Few Dollars More*; *The Good, the Bad, and the Ugly*—that made squinty Clint

an international star. The severe letterboxing may leave you a bit squinty, too: It's harder to catch the crucial, occasional tics in Eastwood's unflinching puss when the picture doesn't fill your TV screen. But if the image were cropped to showcase Clint, the inspired gunfight scenes—in which Leone choreographs action through every part of the rectangular Techniscope frame—would be shot to pieces.

84 **EL MARIACHI: SPECIAL COL-LECTOR'S EDITION** *(1993/93, Columbia TriStar, 2 CLV sides, wide-screen, subtitled, R, $49.95; separate Spanish and English-dubbed soundtracks, student short by director)* How did Robert Rodriguez shoot this bloody tale of a fugitive guitarist for $7,000? He tells all in a witty alternate-audio-track commentary that makes this the best in a recent deluge of first-time–director showcase discs (aspiring filmmakers should also check out Voyager's *Boyz N the Hood, Menace II Society,* and *sex, lies, and videotape*). Rodriguez knows that major Hollywood players are laser buffs, and in part, he's networking here. But so what? His résumé makes great entertainment.

85 THE MUSIC MAN *(1962/91, Warner, 3 CLV sides, widescreen, G, $39.98)* When bogus band instructor Harold Hill (Robert Preston) launches into a brassy chorus of "76 Trombones," digital audio tracks bring out the distinct timbre of every instrument. And thanks to a Dolby Surround sound mix as aggressive as one of Hill's con-man pitches, the orchestrations constantly march around to match the widescreen action; when a barbershop quartet ambles along for a serenade, for instance, they seem to stroll from somewhere *waaay* right of your righthand stereo speaker to somewhere far beyond the left one. Minor technical goof: The channels are inexplicably reversed on a few songs on side 2.

86 JASON AND THE ARGONAUTS *(1963/92, Voyager, 1 CLV side plus 3 CAV sides, wide-screen, $99.95, not rated; trailers)* For savoring Ray Harryhausen's animated "stop-motion" creature FX, what could be better than *watching* in stop-motion? The variable play speeds possible with a CAV disc (anywhere from ½ to ⅙₀ normal speed with perfect clarity) give you total joystick control over the scamperings of harpies, hydra heads, and sword-wielding skeletons: *For-*

ward, demon spawn! Backward! Stand still! There's something uniquely expressive in that jerky way they move. The disc features audio commentary by the genteel Harryhausen, as well as a pictures-and-text appendix that lets you study *Jason's* production and the rest of Ray's career in just the manner he forged it: a frame at a time.

87 MYSTERIOUS ISLAND *(1961/92, Pioneer, 4 CAV sides, not rated, $69.95)* Another Harryhausen creaturefest, but the artist actually most honored here is composer Bernard Herrmann. His rousing adventure score (one of four he did with Harryhausen) is presented in a sweeping, exclusive-to-disc stereo mix that thankfully helps drown out some stilted dialogue. An alternate soundtrack contains the music and sound effects only, showcasing how ingeniously Herrmann uses woodwinds to make a giant chicken seem silly and a string section to bring more sting to a monster-wasp attack.

88 GREMLINS 2: THE NEW BATCH *(1990/90, Warner, 2 CLV sides, wide-screen, PG-13, $24.98)* Lighthearted where the first film was mean-spirited, this superior follow-up transplants the fast-breeding beasties to New York City, where they promptly overrun the supermodern skyscraper just built by a Donald Trump–style magnate (John Glover). Tony Randall does some inspired vocalizing as the brainy chief Gremlin, and as elevators and air systems malfunction on more and more levels, the busy soundtrack rises to dazzlingly elaborate heights.

89 **WHO FRAMED ROGER RAB-BIT** *(1988/90, Touch-stone, 4 CAV sides, wide-screen, PG, $39.99)* Thanks to stories in the entertainment press, it's now widely known that two naughty gags evidently got slipped into *Roger* by animators who knew that a couple of risqué frames would never register to the eye during normal projection. But hit the slo-mo button with this CAV disc (practically mandatory for following the frantic action anyway, plus it kills the obnoxious soundtrack) and you can't miss it: On side 1 (around frame 7,320), cigar-chomping Baby Herman rustles a woman's skirt with his middle finger extended, and on side 4 (around 2,111), Jessica Rabbit spins out of a cab collision open-legged, revealing that she's apparently pantieless—and that Sharon Stone's big scene in *Basic Instinct* (1992) wasn't such a taboo-buster after all.

90 **THE WAR OF THE ROSES** *(1989/91, FoxVideo/Image, 2 CLV sides plus 1 CAV side, wide-screen, R, $69.98; trailer)* Not content to have directed the movie, Danny DeVito directed this laser edition, too. He offers a cheerfully bawdy running commentary on an alternate audio track; then, in a filmed segment, he personally introduces a huge, additional supplementary section with storyboards, a complete shooting script, and some deleted scenes it really pained him to lose. Sure it's a vanity project, but DeVito's enthusiasm for filmmaking is so informed and so winning, you've got to admit the guy's got as much talent as he has chutzpah.

91 **THE DAWN OF SOUND** *(1929–30/92, MGM/UA, 7 CLV sides, B&W, not rated, $79.98)* Next to Lina Lamont in *Sing-*

FRANÇOIS DUHAMEL

WAR OF THE ROSES: KATHLEEN TURNER, MICHAEL DOUGLAS

in' in the Rain, there's no more inspired take on Hollywood's lurch into talkies than this 1992 compilation. Three complete features (*Hollywood Revue of 1929*, *The Broadway Melody*, and *Show of Shows*) boast a vast lineup of static camera angles, anxious-looking actor-singers, chunky chorines, and weak variety acts; a selection of excerpts rounds up additional fascinating arcana, including a "barkie" parody, *The Dogway Melody*. For a comparably star-studded spectacle of film folk caught in the headlights, you'd have to watch *The Player*.

92 **THE LIFE AND DEATH OF COLONEL BLIMP** *(1943/88, Voyager, 3 CLV sides, not rated, $69.95)* Butchered to 93 minutes in most U.S. showings (and on cassette), this visually audacious swipe at the English military runs a full 163 minutes here—and looks as sparklingly new as if it were a period piece filmed yesterday. The liner notes explain the fictional Blimp's birth in a British cartoon strip; on the alternate audio track, there's a tag-team analysis by Martin Scorsese and director Michael Powell.

93 **ANIMATION LEGEND WINSOR MCCAY** *(1911–21/93, Lumivision, 4 CAV sides, not rated, $69.95)* It was the *Jurassic Park* of vaudeville: a 1914 cartoon film of one Gertie the Dinosaur, introduced personally by its creator, Winsor McCay, and timed in a way that made the show-off animal appear to be responding to questions and commands. The shock value's gone now, but not the charm in *Gertie* and nine other pioneering shorts collected in this career survey.

94 **MON ONCLE** *(1958/90, Voyager, 2 CLV sides, subtitles, not rated, $49.95)* So you think the U.S. is the first country to develop a serious case of creeping mall malaise? Jacques Tati's lovely comedy demonstrates that the same culture-killing forces were at work in France decades ago. All about a charming little provincial town slowly being torn up and replaced with a sterile, uniformly furnished housing tract, it becomes an expressionistic tale of two cities—the frigid-blue new development, the comfy-brown old village—in this exquisitely colored disc version.

95 **GREAT ARTISTS SERIES: VERMEER & THE GOLDEN AGE OF DUTCH PAINTING** *(1983/91, Pioneer, 2 CAV sides, not rated, $74.95)* The trouble with art-gazing via picture tube is that the average TV set can't remotely convey the sweep of huge canvases. But Vermeer's elegant studies of women in domestic interiors, like almost all the Dutch canvases catalogued here in 755 still pictures and a movie documentary, are typically so small (about 20 by 18 inches) that a 25-inch set barely reduces their dimensions. Each canvas gets an overall shot, then four or five ultra–close-up "detail" frames, revealing subtleties in the brushwork and pigment you'd be hard-pressed to observe even in a museum—just try pressing your nose so close to an original and see how fast the guards come running.

96 **YOJIMBO** *(1961/90, Voyager, 2 CLV sides, wide-screen, subtitled, B&W, not rated, $49.95)* Stand aside, Orson

Welles—this Akira Kurosawa gloss on American Westerns is the true zenith of that movie style called "deep focus," where foreground and background are so equally razor-sharp, they appear to be seen through an artist's rendering hand, not a lens. As Toshiro Mifune's samurai-for-hire sets two warring town factions against each other, a pristine disc transfer exquisitely captures the director's constant visual dynamic between what's near and what's far.

97 SUSPIRIA *(1977/90, Image, 2 CLV sides, wide-screen, not rated, $39.95; trailers)* Set in a ballet school run by witches, Dario Argento's gruesome slasher flick depends mightily on plain old colored lights to sustain the mood. When a new student starts poking around and the hues get superintense, they don't go all fuzzy on this disc the way they do on tape—which, if you're a gorehound, means you can make out the makeup much better.

98 NOTHING SACRED *(1937/93, Lumivision, 2 CLV sides, not rated, $39.95; trailer, Carole Lombard shorts and home movies)* On tape, it's something profane. That's because screenwriter Ben Hecht's riotous screwball tale, charting the rise and fall of a phony terminal patient (Carole Lombard) at the hands of the New York tabloids, is in the public domain. Anybody with a tattered print can slap it onto cassette. But in Lumivision's exclusive Technicolor-print transfer (via Eden Entertainment), '30s Manhattan looks astonishingly vivid. There's no other video program that offers a comparable mix of crack-ling, hard-boiled dialogue and rapturous scenery.

99 GOOD NEWS *(1947/93, MGM/ UA, 2 CLV sides, not rated, $34.98; trailer)* MGM/UA has packaged many of its premier (and some not-so-premier) musicals on disc —including *Easter Parade*, *The Band Wagon*, *Singin' in the Rain*, *Take Me Out to the Ball Game*, *Jupiter's Darling*, and *An American in Paris*—with an irresistible extra: cut production numbers that got pushed out for tone reasons, time reasons, or no good reason at all. They're all surprisingly strong, but the best number is one that got away in *Good News*: pert class-of-'27 coed June Allyson musing that there must be "An Easier Way" to get a boyfriend than being a simpering trollop. The acid Betty Comden–Adolph Green lyrics deflate all that cloying, 23-skiddoo college cheer like a pin in a balloon.

100 WOW! aka the THX Demo Disc *(1990, Lucasfilm, 2 CAV sides, not rated)* Even if you have no interest in the line of pricey, George Lucas–approved THX home-audio equipment it's designed to show off, treat yourself to a screening of this not-for-sale disc at a dealer showroom near you. It's a giddy compilation of thrill scenes from Lucas movies (from the *Star Wars* and *Indiana Jones* trilogies to Lucasfilm FX projects like *Willow*), ingeniously cut together as one extended story and reproduced with staggering fidelity. This doesn't merely beat tape for sound and image; it beats just about any multiplex.

Reviews written by Steve Daly.

303

INDEX

305

307

309

310

311

APPENDIX

Here's a complete list of videos reviewed and graded by
ENTERTAINMENT WEEKLY's critics in issues #1–211.

313

315

Blood Salvage (1990) ....D
Blood Simple (1984) ....A–
Blood Vows: The Story of a Mafia Wife (1987)..........F
Blood Warriors (1993) ....D
Blow Out (1981)..A
Blown Away (1993) ....C–
Blue Angel, The (1930)..A
Blue Collar (1978)...A
Blue Hawaii (1961) ....A+
Blue Planet (Laserdisc) (1990).............................B+
Blue Steel (1990) ....B–
Blue Velvet (1986) ....A
Blues Alive (1993) ....B
Blues by the Book (1993).......................................B+
Blume in Love (1973)...B
Bob Dylan: The 30th Anniversary Concert
   Celebration (1992)..B
Bob Roberts (1992) C
Bobby & the Midnites (1991)....................................C
Bodies, Rest & Motion (1993) ....C–
Bodies, Rest & Motion (Laserdisc) (1993)...............B–
Body Bags (1993)...B–
Body Chemistry (1990)..A–
Body Double (1984)..D
Body Heat (1981)...A–
Body of Evidence (1993) ....D
Body Parts (1991) C
Body Snatcher, The (1945) ....B+
Body Snatchers (1994)..B
Bodyguard, The (1992) ....B–
Boiling Point (1993)..D
Bon Appetit Cooking Videos (4-tape set) (1987)........A
Bon Jovi: Keep the Faith—The Videos (1994)..........D+
Bonanza (1964–65)...C+
Boneyard, The (1990)...B–
Bonfire of the Vanities, The (1991) ....F
Boomerang (1992) ....C–
Bopha! (1993) ....B–
Border Shootout (1990) ....D–
Boris and Natasha: The Movie (1992) ....D–
Born on the Fourth of July (1989)...........................C+
Born to Boogie (1972) ....C+
Born to Ride (1991) ....D+
Born to Run (1993) ....C+
Born Yesterday (1950) ....A
Born Yesterday (1993) ....D
Borrower, The (1989) ....C–
Bound and Gagged: A Love Story (1993) C
Bound by Honor (1993)..B–
Bounty, The (1984)..B–
Bounty Tracker (1993) ....C–
Bowie: The Video Collection (1993).........................B+
Boxer and Death, The (1962) ....B+
Boxing Helena (1993)...C–
Boxing: The Best of the 1980s (1992) ....C–
Boy and His Dog, A (1975)......................................A–
Boyfriend, The (1971) ....B–
Boys of Summer, The (1983) ....A+
Boyz N the Hood (1991)..A–
Brain Damage (1988)...A–
Brain Dead (1990) ....C+
Brain Donors (1992)..D
Brain From Planet Arous, The (1958).......................D

Brain Smasher...A Love Story (1993)......................C–
Brain That Wouldn't Die, The (1963)..........................C+
Bram Stoker's Dracula (1992)...................................B
Branford Marsalis: The Music Tells You (1992) ....B–
Brannigan (1975)...C+
Brazil (1985)..B+
Breakfast Club, The (1985).......................................C
Breakin' (1984)..C–
Breaking In (1989)...B–
Breezy (1973)...C+
Brenda Starr (1992)...F
Bride of Frankenstein, The (1935) ....A
Bride of Re-Animator (1991)...................................C+
Brides of Dracula (Laserdisc) (1960) ....B+
Bridge Across the Abyss: Israel Philharmonic
   Orchestra Welcomes Berliner Philharmoniker,
   A (1992)..A–
Bridge Too Far, A (1977)...B
Brief Encounter (1945)...B+
Brief History of Time, A (1992) ....B+
Bright Lights, Big City (1988) C
Brighton Beach Memoirs (1986) C
Broadcast News (1987) ....A
Broadway Bound (1992) ....B
Broadway Danny Rose (1984)....................................A
Broadway Melody of 1936 (1935)..............................B–
Broken Angel (1988)..D
Broken Blossoms (1919)..A+
Broken Noses (1987)..B
Bronco Billy (1980)...B+
Bronx Tale, A (1993)...B
Bronx War, The (1991) ....D+
Bronze Buckaroo, The (1939) ....C+
Brotherhood, The (1968)...B
Brotherhood of Justice (1986) ....C–
Brother's Keeper (1992) ....A
Bruce Springsteen in Concert: MTV Unplugged
   (1992)..A–
Buck and the Preacher (1972)..................................B+
Buck Clayton All-Stars (1993)..................................B+
Buddy Holly Story, The (1978)..................................B+
Buffy the Vampire Slayer (1992) ....B+
Buford's Beach Bunnies (1993)...............................D+
Bug (1975)..C
Bugsy (1991)...B
Bull Durham (1988)...A+
Bull Riders Only: Best Rides & Best Wrecks
   (1993)..B
Bullseye! (1991) ....C–
Buona Sera, Mrs. Campbell (Laserdisc) (1968)........B–
'Burbs, The (1989) C
Buried Treasures, Vol. 1—Breakthrough
   Directors (1991)...B–
Burns and Allen Christmas (1992) ....B–
Bus Stop (1956)..C
Busby Berkeley Disc, The (Laserdisc) (1992) ....A
Bustin' Loose (1981)..B
Butcher's Wife, The (1991)......................................C–
Cabaret (Laserdisc) (1972)......................................A
Cabin Boy (1994)...D+
Caddyshack (1980)..B
Cadillac Man (1990)...C+
Cafe Romeo (1991) ....D–

317

Dizzy Gillespie and Billy Eckstine: Things to Come (1993)..B
Do the Right Thing (1989)..A
Doc Hollywood (1991)..A–
Doctor, The (1991)..B
Doctor Zhivago (1965)..A–
Does This Mean We're Married? (1992)....................D–
Dog Day Afternoon (1975)..A
Dogfight (1991)..C
Dollar (1938)..B
Dollman (1991)..D+
Doll's House, A (1973)..A–
Dominick and Eugene (1988)..B
Don Daredevil Rides Again (1951)................................C
Don Quixote (1973)..B+
Don't Bother to Knock (1952)..B–
Don't Tell Daddy (1974)..F
Don't Tell Mom the Babysitter's Dead (1991)..........D+
Doors, The (1991)..B
Doors: Light My Fire, The (1991)..................................D
Doors: The Soft Parade, The (1991)............................B+
Doppelganger: The Evil Within (1992)........................C+
Double Edge (1992)..C–
Double Holiday Dose of Hazel, A (1992)....................D
Double Impact (1991)..D
Double Indemnity (1944)..A
Double Threat (1992)..D+
Doubting Thomas (1935)..B
Down and Out in Beverly Hills (1986)........................B+
Down to Earth (1947)..C+
Down to Earth (Laserdisc) (1947)................................C+
Downtown (1989)..D
Dr. Caligari (1989)..A
Dr. Giggles (1992)..D–
Dr. John Teaches New Orleans Piano (1988)..........B+
Dr. No (1963)..A
Dr. Strangelove: Or How I Learned to Stop Worrying and Love the Bomb (1964)....................A
Dracula (1931)..C+
Dracula Rising (1993)..B–
Dracula's Daughter (1936)..A
Dragnet (1987)..C–
Dragon: The Bruce Lee Story (1993)..........................B
Drawing the Line: A Portrait of Keith Haring (1989)..B+
Dream Date (1989)..D
Dream is Alive, The (1991)..B
Dream Machine (1990)..D
Dressed to Kill (1980)..C
Driving Me Crazy (1991)..D
Driving Miss Daisy (1990)..A–
Drop Dead Fred (1991)..F
Drowning by Numbers (1991)......................................A
Drugstore Cowboy (1989)..A–
Dry White Season, A (1989)..B+
Duel (1971)..A
Duellists, The (Laserdisc) (1977)................................C
Dune (1984)..C–
Dune Warriors (1991)..D
Dutch (1991)..D+
Dying Young (1991)..C–
Earth Girls Are Easy (1989)..B
Earth vs. the Spider (1958)..B

Earthquake (1974)..B–
East Coast Flight (1989)..C+
Easy Money (1983)..B
Easy Rider (1969)..B–
Eating (1990)..B–
Eating Raoul (1982)..A–
Edge of Honor (1990)..D+
Edward Scissorhands (1990)..A
Edward II (1992)..A–
Efficiency Expert, The (1992)......................................B
Eiger Sanction, The (1975)..C+
Eight Men Out (1988)..A
El Dorado (1967)..A
El Mariachi (1993)..B–
El Mariachi: Special Collector's Edition (Laserdisc) (1993)..B+
El-Hajj Malik El-Shabazz (1991)................................B+
Electric Horseman, The (1979)....................................B–
Elephant Man, The (1980)..A
Elmer Gantry (1960)..B+
Elmore Leonard's Criminal Records (1993)..............A
Elusive Corporal, The (1962)..C
Elvira Madigan (1967)..B+
Elvis Files, The (1990)..B
Elvis in Hollywood (1993)..B
Elvis—"That's the Way it Is" (Laserdisc) (1970)......B–
Elvis: The Great Performances (1990)........................A–
Emerald Forest, The (1985)..D
Eminent Domain (1991)..C–
Emmylou Harris and the Nash Ramblers at the Ryman (1992)..A
Empire of the Sun (1987)..B+
Empire Strikes Back, The (1980)................................A
En Vogue: Funky Divas (1992)....................................B
Enchanted April (1992)..A–
Encino Man (1992)..C–
Encounter at Raven's Gate (1988)..............................C
End of Innocence, The (1991)......................................D+
Enemies, A Love Story (1990)......................................A+
Enforcer, The (1951)..B+
Equinox (1993)..B–
Erasure: Abba-esque (1992)..C+
Eric Clapton: 24 Nights (1991)....................................B
Eric Clapton: Unplugged (1992)..................................A–
Erik the Viking (1989)..B–
Ernest Goes to Jail (1990)..D
Ernest Scared Stupid (1991)..C–
Erotic Encounters (1993)..C–
Errol Flynn: Portrait of a Swashbuckler (1983)..F
Escape From Sobibor (1987)..B
Eternity (1990)..F
Ethan Frome (1993)..C+
Europa, Europa (1991)..A
Europeans, The (1979)..D+
Eve of Destruction (1991)..C+
Evening With Sammy Davis Jr. and Jerry Lewis, An (1988)..D–
Every Time We Say Goodbye (1986)............................B–
Everybody Sing (1938)..B
Everybody Wins (1990)..F
Everybody's All-American (1988)................................A
Everybody's Fine (1991)..B+

323

325

330

Nutty Professor, The *(1963)* ....B+
O.G. The Original Gangster Video *(1991)* ....B+
O. Henry's Full House *(1952)* C
Object of Beauty, The *(1991)* ....D+
Obsession *(1976)* ....C–
Odd Man Out *(1947)* ....A
Of Mice and Men *(1992)* ....B
Official 1993 NCAA Championship Video:
    March of the Tar Heels, The *(1993)* ....B
Official Video Tour of Hollywood, The *(1990)* ....B
Oh, Heavenly Dog! *(1980)* ....D
Ol' Blue Eyes Is Back *(1991)* ....C+
Old Explorers *(1991)* ....D+
Old Gringo *(1989)* ....D+
Olivier, Olivier *(1993)* C
Omen IV: The Awakening *(1991)* ....C–
On Golden Pond *(1981)* ....C–
On the Night *(1993)* ....B+
On the Road With Jack Kerouac *(1985)* ....B–
On the Town *(1949)* ....A
On Trial: The William Kennedy Smith Case *(1992)* ...D
Once Around *(1991)* ....B
One Against the Wind *(1991)* ....B
One-Eyed Jacks *(1961)* ....C+
One False Move *(1992)* ....A–
One Flew Over the Cuckoo's Nest *(1975)* ....A+
One Good Cop *(1991)* ....C–
One Hand Don't Clap *(1988)* ....C+
One in a Million *(1937)* ....A
One Night in the Tropics *(1940)* ....B–
One Night With Dice *(1989)* ....D+
One Touch of Venus *(1948)* C
Onion Field, The *(1979)* ....A–
Only Angels Have Wings *(1939)* ....A
Only One Night *(1939)* ....B+
Only the Lonely *(1991)* ....D
Operation Dames *(1957)* ....C+
Opportunity Knocks *(1990)* ....C–
Opposite Sex, The *(1993)* ....D+
Oratorio for Prague *(1968)* ....A–
Orchestra Wives *(1942)* ....B
Ordinary People *(1980)* ....A
Original Cast Album: Company (Laserdisc) *(1970)* ..A–
Orlando *(1993)* C
Orpheus Descending *(1990)* ....B+
Oscar *(1991)* ....D+
Oscar's Greatest Moments *(1992)* C
Ossian: American Boy/Tibetan Monk *(1990)* ....B
Osterman Weekend, The *(1983)* ....B–
Othello *(1952)* ....A–
Other People's Money *(1991)* ....B
Other World of Winston Churchill, The *(1964)* ....B+
Otto Dix: The Painter is the Eyes of the World
   (1991) ....A
Out For Justice *(1991)* ....B–
Out of Africa *(1985)* ....A
Out on a Limb (Boxed set) *(1987)* ....D+
Outland *(1981)* ....B+
Outlaw Josey Wales, The *(1976)* ....A–
Outside Chance of Maximilian Glick, The *(1990)* .....B+
Outside: From the Redwoods *(1993)* C
Overexposed *(1990)* ....D
Ox, The *(1992)* ....B

P.M. Dawn: Of the Heart, of the Soul and of the
   Cross *(1992)* ....A–
P.U.N.K. *(1992)* ....A
Pacific Heights *(1990)* ....B–
Package, The *(1989)* ....B–
Padre Padrone *(1977)* ....B
Painted Spider: Rock Climbing in the '90s *(1992)*....A
Pajama Game, The *(1957)* ....B–
Pal Joey *(1957)* ....C+
Pale Blood *(1992)* ....B–
Pale Rider *(1985)* ....B
Palm Beach Story, The *(1942)* ....A–
Pals *(1986)* C
Panama Deception, The *(1992)* ....B
Panic in the Streets *(1950)* ....A
Panther Girl of the Kongo *(1955)* ....B
Papa's Delicate Condition *(1963)* ....C+
Paper Chase, The *(1973)* ....B+
Paper Moon *(1973)* ....B–
Parade *(1973)* ....B+
Paradise *(1991)* C
Paradise, Hawaiian Style *(1966)* C
Parents *(1989)* ....B–
Paris is Burning *(1991)* ....A–
Paris Trout *(1991)* ....B+
Party, The *(1968)* ....B
Passed Away *(1992)* ....C+
Passenger 57 *(1992)* C
Passenger, The *(1975)* ....B+
Passion Fish *(1993)* ....B
Passion Flower *(1986)* C
Past Midnight *(1992)* ....D+
Pastime *(1991)* ....C+
Pat and Mike *(1952)* ....B+
Patriot Games *(1992)* ....C–
Patton *(1970)* ....A
Paul Bowles in Morocco *(1970)* ....B–
Paul McCartney's Get Back *(1991)* ....C+
Paul Simon: Born at the Right Time *(1993)*..............C
Paula Abdul Captivated: The Video Compilation
   '91 *(1991)* ....B–
Pavarotti & Friends *(1993)* ....F
Payday *(1973)* ....A–
Peacemaker *(1990)* C
Pee-wee's Big Adventure *(1985)* ....B+
Peggy Sue Got Married *(1986)* ....B+
Pelican Brief, The *(1993)* ....C–
Penn & Teller Get Killed *(1989)* ....D+
Penn & Teller Get Killed (Laserdisc) *(1989)* ....D+
People Under the Stairs, The *(1991)* ....B
Peppermint Soda *(1977)* ....B+
Perfect Bread: How to Conquer Bread Baking
   (1990) ....A
Perfect Weapon, The *(1991)* ....B
Perfect World, A *(1993)* ....C–
Performance *(1970)* ....B
Perry Mason Returns *(1985)* ....B+
Personal Best *(1982)* C
Personal Services *(1987)* ....D
Personals *(1990)* ....D
Pet Sematary Two *(1992)* ....D
Peter Gabriel: POV *(1991)* ....B
Peter Pan *(1953)* ....B–

333

Seems Like Old Times (1980) ....B−
Semi-Tough (1977) ....B+
Separate But Equal (1991) ....B+
Separate Tables (1958) ....B+
September 30, 1955 (1978) ....D−
Sepultura: Under Siege (Live in Barcelona) (1992) .B
Sergeant York (1941) ....B+
Seven Little Foys, The (1955) ....B+
Seven Samurai, The (1954) ....A+
Seven Year Itch, The (1955) ....C−
Seventh Veil, The (1945) ....B+
Sex, Drugs, Rock & Roll (1991) ....B+
Sex & Justice: The Highlights of the Anita Hill/
   Clarence Thomas Hearings (1993) ....B
sex, lies, and videotape (1989) ....B
Sexual Response (1992) ....C+
Sexy Lingerie V (1993) ....D
Sexy M.F. (1992) ....C−
Shadow of the Wolf (1993) ....D+
Shadowlands (1994) ....B−
Shadows and Fog (1992) ....C+
Shaft (1971) ....B+
Shag (1989) ....C+
Shakes the Clown (1992) ....D−
Shakespeare Wallah (1965) ....C+
Shame (1968) ....A+
Shampoo (Laserdisc) (1975) ....B−
Shanghai Express (1932) ....A+
Shattered (1991) ....B
She Done Him Wrong (1933) ....B+
She-Devil (1989) C
Sheltering Sky, The (1990) ....B+
Shindig! Presents Frat Party (1991) ....A
Shindig! Presents Jackie Wilson (1991) ....A
Shining, The (1980) C
Shining, The (Laserdisc) (1980) ....B−
Shining Through (1992) ....B−
Ship of Fools (1965) ....C+
Shirley Horn Sings and Plays Here's to Life
   (1992) ....A−
Shirley Valentine (1989) ....A
Shock to the System, A (1990) ....A
Shock Treatment (1981) ....D+
Shocker (1989) C
Shoot the Moon (1982) ....A
Shoot the Piano Player (1960) ....A
Shooting Elizabeth (1992) ....C−
Shooting Party, The (1977) ....B−
Shooting Stars of the NCAA (1993) ....B
Shooting, The (1967) ....A−
Shootist, The (1976) ....A+
Shop on Main Street, The (1965) ....B+
Short Cuts (1993) ....A
Shot in the Dark, A (1964) ....A
Show Boat (Laserdisc) (1951) ....B−
Show of Force, A (1990) ....D+
Shrimp on the Barbie, The (1990) ....C−
Sibling Rivalry (1990) ....D
Sidekicks (1993) ....B
Silence of the Lambs, The (1991) ....B+
Silent Night, Deadly Night 5: The Toy Maker
   (1991) C
Silent Victim (1992) ....C−

Silk Road Collection, The (1991) ....A+
Silk 2 (1990) ....D
Silver Streak (1976) ....B+
Silverado (1985) ....B+
Simple Justice (1990) ....F
Simple Men (1992) ....B−
Simple Story, A (1979) C
Simply Mad About the Mouse (1991) .....B−
Simpson's Christmas Special, The (1989) ...B
Sin of Madelon Claudet, The (1931) ....B+
Since You Went Away (1944) ....B−
Singin' in the Rain (1952) ....A
Singin' in the Rain (Laserdisc) (1952)
   CAV version ....A+
   CLV version ....A−
Singing Nun, The (1966) ....D+
Single White Female (1992) ....B
Singles (1992) ....B
Sins of Desire (1992) ....F
Sister Act (1992) C
Sister Act 2 (1993) ....B−
Sisters (1973) ....B
Sisters in the Name of Rap (1992) ....A−
Sixteen Candles (1984) ....A−
Ski Patrol (1990) ....D
Skid Row Roadkill (1993) ....C−
Slacker (1991) ....B+
Slammin' Rap Video Magazine, Vol. 3 (1991) ....D
Slaughter in San Francisco (1973) ....D+
Sleeping With the Enemy (1991) ....D
Sleepless in Seattle (1993) ....B+
Sliver (1993) ....D
Slumber Party Massacre 3 (1990) ....D
Small Sacrifices (1990) ....C−
Smile (1975) ....B
Smithereens 10, The (1990) ....A−
Smiths: The Complete Picture, The (1992) C
Smithsonian's Great Battles of the Civil War,
   Vols. I−III (1993) ....A
Smokescreen (1988) ....B
Snapper, The (1994) ....B+
Sneakers (1992) ....B
Sniper (1993) ....B
Snow Kill (1990) ....C−
Snow White and the Seven Dwarfs (1937) ....A
So I Married an Axe Murderer (1993) .....C−
Soapdish (1991) ....C−
Solar Crisis (1989) ....B
Soldier's Story, A (1984) ....A−
Some Girls (1989) ....A−
Some Kind of Wonderful (1987) ....B
Some Like It Hot (1959) ....A+
Somebody Has to Shoot the Picture (1990) ....B+
Someone to Love (1987) ....A
Something Wild (1986) ....B+
Sometimes They Come Back (1991) C
Sommersby (1993) ....B+
Son of Kong, The (1933) C
Son of Paleface (1952) ....B
Son of the Pink Panther (1993) ....D
Son-In-Law (1993) ....F
Song Without End (1960) C
Songs From the Life of Leonard Cohen (1988) ....B+

336

340

VIDEO DISTRIBUTORS

A listing of companies willing to sell or rent titles contained in this book
that may not be available at your local video store.

A & E 800 423-1212
A*Vision 212 275-2900
Academy 800 972-0001
Atlas 800 999-0212
Cabin Fever 203 863-5200
Central Park Media 212 977-7456
Central Picture 800 359-3276
Cinevista 212 947-4373
Columbia TriStar 818 972-8821
Connoisseur Video Collection 800 345-6278
Direct Cinema 800 525-0000
ESPN 800 662-3776
Facets Video 800 331-6197
Flower 800 572-7618
Fox Lorber Home Video 800 229-9994
FoxVideo 800 800-2369
Fusion 800 338-7710
Home Vision Cinema 800 826-3456
Ignatius Press 800 635-1531
In the Black 800 433-8096
Ingram 800 937-8100
Interama 212 977-4830
International Historic Films 312 927-2900
International Mountain Equipment 603 356-6316
Kino on Video 800 562-3330
Kultur 800 458-5887
LandyVision .... P.O. Box 836,
                                                                  Woodstock, NY 12498
LIVE Home Video 800 326-1977
Malibu 800 235-2153
MCA/Universal Home Video 818 777-4300
Movies Unlimited 800 523-0823
MPI Home Video 800 323-0442
Music Video Distributors 800 888-0486
Mystic Fire Video 800 292-9001
New Film 800 462-2306
New Yorker Video 800 447-0196
Nostalgia Family Video 800 784-3362
Pacific Arts 310 820-0991
Paramount Home Video 213 956-5000
PBS Video 800 344-3337
Public Media, Inc. 800 826-3456
Questar 800 633-5633
Rhino Home Video 800 432-0020
Sinister Cinema 503 773-6860
Subtle 800 522-3688
Tapeworm 800 367-8437
Time-Life 800 621-7026
Turner Home Entertainment 404 827-5171
Video Dimensions 212 929-6135
Video Project 800 475-2638
Video Yesteryear 800 243-0987
Voyager Company 800 446-2001
White Star 800 458-5887